THE BIOGRAPHY OF
LEEDS UNITED

THE BIOGRAPHY OF LEEDS UNITED

BY ROB BAGCHI

VSP

First published by Vision Sports Publishing in 2020

Vision Sports Publishing
19–23 High Street
Kingston upon Thames
Surrey
KT1 1LL

www.visionsp.co.uk

ISBN: 9781909534841

Editor: Ed Davis
Editorial consultant: Jim Drewett
Photography: Varley Picture Agency
Additional photography: George Wood Photography
Design and typesetting: Our Kid Design

A CIP Catalogue record for this book is available from the British Library

Printed and bound in the UK by CPI Group

CONTENTS

ACKNOWLEDGEMENTS

Without the kindness and contributions of so many people this book would not have been finished in 10 years rather than the three it has taken in its various guises. I would like to thank Toby Trotman, Jim Drewett, Ed Davis and Neal Cobourne at Vision Sports Publishing for their patience with me and Leeds United. David Luxton has been a firm friend for 30 years as well as the most sympathetic and enterprising of agents. I thank him for all his advice and support.

I owe a great debt to my brother, Andrew Bagchi, and the co-author of *The Unforgiven*, Paul Rogerson, for their forthright and shrewd thoughts during more than 40 years of conversation about Leeds United and their company on countless trips to watch them play. This book has been shaped by those experiences. Rob Smyth, Scott Murray and Paul Doyle have also been a constant source of encouragement and sound judgment.

Thanks to John Giles, Eddie Gray, Scott Sellars, Gordon Strachan, David O'Leary and Gary Kelly, and to Paul Lennon for his generosity and for his assistance in setting up a memorable day in Drogheda, and Declan Wheldon and Ann Tracey for their help and hospitality. Also a big thank you to Simon Moss at Leeds United for his help at a very busy time. Thanks, too, to my colleagues on the *Telegraph* sports desk, past and present.

My dad and Sidney Brooke are no longer with us but both were instrumental in fostering a love of sport and facilitating a lifetime of match-going adventures. I would also like to record my gratitude to my mum and sister, Angela and Tara Bagchi, for their nonstop support.

Lastly, and most importantly, to Alison Kirby, Eden and Casper Bagchi who have put up with me and this project for far longer than anyone bargained. I could not have started, never mind finished, without you. Thank you for all the love and belief. We, and they, got there in the end.

HEADSTART FOR HAPPINESS

We have seen Marcelo Bielsa on his haunches. We have watched him nattering to himself as he takes precisely 13 paces across his technical area. We have heard him begin every answer with a stopgap 'Bueno' before knitting his brow. We have never seen him like this. He is lurking discreetly at the edge of the back row on the podium. He is wearing a white Leeds United shirt, like his players, back-to-front. It is stretched over his ubiquitous tracksuit with 'champions' and the number 20 emblazoned on the front. He has taken off his glasses, conscious, no doubt, of the champagne shower about to douse him. Immediately it makes him look younger. Or is it the pure joy? Despite the urging of his players he will not join the front rank. Liam Cooper, the captain, is ready. He counts to co-ordinate what is going to happen next. They are going to milk this. Of course they are. Wouldn't you?

The last time this trophy was awarded at this ground, it was not draped in ribbons and there were 32,673 supporters present. Twenty-eight years on there are just a handful of players, staff and their families to watch. They have played nine games in 31 days behind closed doors, the only accompaniment the yelps and guttural clamouring of their sporting director, Victor Orta. Outside there is a racket, thousands of fans on Lowfields Road, drawn to the statue of Billy Bremner, Leeds' own eternal flame. Inside almost all have their cameras raised waiting for the moment. One of the men on the rostrum, Gaetano Berardi, is on crutches. Another, Kalvin Phillips, has a brace on his right leg. Neither is going to let pain and caution restrain him. It has taken them 23 months and a lifetime to get here.

Cooper begs for silence. Fat chance! He bends his knees. The players follow him and their hubbub crescendos. At last he raises the Victorian silver cup, only the third Leeds United captain to do so, though it has been relegated since then, like them. Each player takes a turn. Gjanni Alioski could do anything with it but merely gives it a kiss and brandishes it. Patrick Bamford has a go then retreats to have a word with his manager.

Bielsa shakes his head. Fourteen months before, 30 yards from here, he had sounded broken. "We had 20 minutes of disorder," he said. "I could not find a solution." He was the man who always found a solution. And now he had.

Bamford will not be discouraged and enlists the help of Phillips. Bielsa allows himself to be persuaded and is shepherded through his squad. The trophy is passed to him and he lifts it with the look of a man amused to find himself surprised by his own actions. He is beaming. It is only for a moment. They are dressed in white and have been for almost 60 years. But the ribbons are blue and yellow. They are United but these are the colours of the city and City, another club, another time. What are they doing there?

We are the resurrection and the life. For United to be born, City had to die. Professional football in Leeds scrabbled from the grave to the cradle in 17 days during October 1919, a month of funeral shrouds and christening robes. The manner of Leeds City's demise – expelled from the Football League by a joint Football Association/League commission for illegal wartime payments to players – is a complex tale involving two attempts at extortion, a feeble, blustering cover-up and the Lord Mayor busking a doomed appeal for clemency.

The details are both excruciating and ridiculous, as we shall see, but its significance is ambiguous. Our past, to corrupt LP Hartley, is a foreign club and its relevance to us is nominal. Had City survived, they would not be United and while most of us would have been on their side, we would not have been forged by the same experiences. We can speculate that City's ingenious manager, Herbert Chapman, might have established the club as the sultans of the Twenties. Perhaps they, and not Huddersfield Town, would have been his greatest triumph. And having done so, City – not quite so provincial as Town – might have persuaded him that he could have founded a dynasty on the planes of Beeston Hill, this forgotten Islington of the north. Would he have rebuffed the seduction of London to build his marble halls at Elland Road instead of Highbury? Arsenal's grandeur and Chapman's brilliance stimulate such wistful thinking. In that parallel universe we would now be toasting City's 116th anniversary, consecrating Edwardian roots and commemorating Leeds' navy and gold immortals' days of splendour. Household gods would have waxed moustaches rather than resembling hastily demobbed publicans in an episode of *Peaky Blinders*. Picture this: our world would be blue with gilded chevrons. But they and we never had the chance.

Leeds United gained more than a syllable from the dissolution of City. They acquired an identity distinct from the straightforward civic association of their location. The city of Leeds has weathered a turbulent relationship with its clubs and vice versa, sometimes white hot, often Ice Station Zebra. Yes, some of its sons, notably Len Browning, Paul Madeley, David Harvey, Terry Connor, David Batty and Kalvin Phillips, have served their hometown team nobly, but the club itself is a confederation representing all those who support it and not just the lump of earth on which it stands. There is no trace of everything we associate historically with the heart of Leeds in the last century in the make-up of United today: the cloth trade, the owls, the glum town hall lions, its mercantile golden age, 'for King and the law', the soot-blackened relics of the gothic revival, the glazed brick of the Victorian ale palaces and the bankruptcy of the grand, modernising architectural project. Only one sentiment lives on from 1919 and it has had a defining impact on United's nature. Leeds City Football Club did not simply die. It was not a casualty of neglect or apathy. Nor was it killed in any orthodox way, a victim of a swindler or a delinquent or a psychopath. It was executed – put to death by official decree.

The course to the gallows was set during a hearing at Manchester's Grand Hotel. The lever was pulled 163 miles away in Bloomsbury's Russell Hotel by men in drab hats and sombre, heavy flannel suits. It could be argued that this fertilized grievances about injustice from the beginning and, more whimsically, like Maximus Decimus Meridius played by Leeds fan Russell Crowe, a ravenous appetite for vengeance in this life or the next. Add hardened perceptions of maltreatment to that origin story – from referees like Ken Burns, Ray Tinkler, Christos Michas, Michel Kitabdjian and Ryszard Wojcik or administrators such as Charles Clegg, Alan Hardaker, Denis Follows, Ted Croker, Lord Mawhinney and Shaun Harvey – and one can construct the narrative of a 'Damned United' pretty plausibly. But this sense of self is not without nuance. Even the cynics temper suspicions with acknowledgments of the culpability of chairmen, directors and managers. Conspiracy theories beguile because they provide deceptively simple solutions. Once tested, though, their advocates require true faith and convoluted reasoning. Whiteboards, press clippings, drawing pins and ribbon woven like a clutter of spiders' webs must be employed to give the illusion of order to random events.

Much of the damage that has hobbled United over the past 101 years has been self-inflicted. Precariously funded for almost its entire history, Leeds have never had the luxury of 'fuck you' wealth. During the decade from 1965-75 when they had the best team in England, attendances beeped up and down like waves on a hospital vital signs monitor. Money invested in the club has been recouped, 'benefactors' have left Elland Road richer men, scores of creditors have been stiffed and we are granted a coherent understanding of the finances, usually opaque, only in the final throes of an existential crisis.

Scepticism towards authority thrives in the many yet mistrust extends beyond the men in blazers, the governing class in Lytham St Annes, Preston, Russell Square, Lancaster Gate, Soho Square, Wembley, Bern and Nyon. It exists alongside wariness about the behaviour, competence and intentions of some owners and their associates. Leeds have fans who sing 'The Football League's corrupt' and 'Sky TV is fucking shit' but they also have a rich, crudely inventive back catalogue of condemnatory verses with targets much closer to home. There were anthems chastising Peter Ridsdale's ruinous profligacy, calls to arms to run Kenneth William Bates out of town, requests for the garrulous, desperate-to-please, Cornish, schoolboy owl enthusiast David Haigh to stop prevaricating and prove his employers had the money they claimed they had, plus an entire opera's worth of songs of bemusement and resentment about the impulsive way Massimo Cellino was running the club.

For much of the past 17 years where once we had spoken about history and tradition, goals, formations, the potential for fun or wallowed in misery, we practised eternal vigilance, attempting to divine the meaning of official statements, some of them even crafted by Max Clifford, put on the payroll by Ridsdale. We had to teach ourselves the rudiments of accountancy to decipher the books, turn sleuth to piece together offshore ownership arrangements and liabilities, delve into Italian criminal and civil litigation, trawl Gulf-based financial newswires searching for clues and scour Amnesty International reports.

Throughout, while the club's fortunes have been hostage to the whims of the fanciful, sulphurous, vapid or volatile regimes that stretched between the Caspian purchase in 1996 and Cellino's final farewell in 2017, the saving grace has been the fans. They, especially the large, rowdy away support, have kept the flame burning, mounting the barricades of resistance, asserting the club's exceptionalism and rousing its spirit. In practical terms many have become activists in the supporters' trust and community benefit society. They have built an institutional framework to save Leeds from the need for saviours when the day comes, while also rallying to help food banks, raise money for hospices and hospitals, work truly worthy of the name 'United'.

What characterises Leeds, then, is not paranoia or victimhood but dissent. It is a status that can be described as 'in opposition' to the establishment, the board, sometimes the whole lousy world and part of it stems from the reasons for the club's existence as well as its experiences. Not everyone subscribes to it and there have been several outbreaks of civil war where some have aligned themselves with the current messiah, demanding deference and gratitude from the rest, that they should fawn, know their place and let the owners (and betters) go about their business as they please. It's an *Upstairs Downstairs* view of the game where those who sold their loyalty, converting it from the institution to the individual, formed a 'Twittorian Guard' of eunuchs. They were bought by fatuous snippets of supposed insider knowledge and the laughable belief that they were now 'in the know'. Mercifully, though, the supporters' code is not scripted by Julian Fellowes. Bowing and scraping is his game, not ours.

Football clubs are genuine coalitions and the blessed peacemakers, who only ever want to watch the game, have been the chief part of the club's makeup. They remain far more prominent than the rebels and that routed, servile sect. The sentiments articulated by *Marching On Together* have been made more explicit in *All Leeds Aren't We?* That song celebrates the emotional ties allegiance cements and has also been used as an injunction to stifle discord, the unifying, banal adhesive that emphasises that while we might diverge over means, we are united by the cause. And it is that cause that is the theme of this biography, the story not only of who we are but why we are this way.

For too long the 'ups and downs' memorialised by Barry Mason and Les Reed in *Leeds, Leeds, Leeds* were cockeyed and the disappointments were dominant. While it would be fair to say that United have been shaped more by the reverses, the highs have been magnificent and not just by contrast, not only as evidence of where we could or should now be. Leeds have been privileged to cheer on scores of players of substantial class from Tom Jennings to Wilf Copping, John Charles, Bobby Collins, Billy Bremner and his 'Glory Years' comrades, Tony Currie, John Sheridan, the Strachan-Batty-McAllister-Speed axis, Tony Yeboah, O'Leary's brash kids, Luciano Becchio, Pablo Hernández, and the dozens of young players – from James Milner to Lewis Cook – whose best years were spent delighting others long after the money the club traded them for had been absorbed by basic subsistence.

Some have captured the imagination more fleetingly because their intrepid approach and obvious quality suggested that, despite our scepticism, we too were entitled to an occasional luxury. Skill is most prized in these parts when it is accompanied by grit and resilience – too blind to Viduka's talent, too besotted by Smith's. Yet sometimes a dandy – Duncan McKenzie, Frank Worthington, Eric Cantona, an adornment not a fulcrum at Elland Road –

can pierce hardboiled hearts for a while. Self-indulgence or fannying about are never tolerated but their swank and infectious joyfulness momentarily brightened lives. Others have embodied the way the club's fans feel about it, playing with the kind of gallus, emotional investment, dauntless obstinacy and intense dedication they would hope themselves to display if the call came: Vinnie Jones for a year, Ian Baird throughout a couple of spells and, most recently, Andy Hughes and Gaetano Berardi.

The club has always enjoyed a cachet in the game unequal to its achievements. Attracting a coach of Marcelo Bielsa's stature even in the Championship was unique only in that it ended a sequence when successive regimes took a punt on alchemy over science. From 2003-2018 they appointed a series of broadly unsuitable candidates, all of whom seemed designed to make us submit to our reduced circumstances. Yet Leeds had been a moribund Second Division club in 1948 when it attracted Major Frank Buckley, one of the most famous, charismatic and radical managers in the game. Raich Carter and Don Revie did not match the major's coaching pedigree when they were appointed but their prestige as two of the finest players in our nation's history underscored United's drawing power. Brian Clough, Jock Stein, George Graham and Terry Venables are in their trade's hall of fame and all were enticed by the club and its prospects. Howard Wilkinson left his boyhood club in the division above to move to Leeds from Sheffield Wednesday. It has always been viewed as a project – a construction venture before it became an endless cycle of rebuilding schemes.

Everyone recognises United's inherent, exploitable assets. Leeds is at the centre of the third most populous urban sprawl in the country and is its biggest one-club town. Given those blessings it would be fair to argue that its history has been a study in relative failure. It has been punctuated by the vibrancy of Revie's last 11 seasons, Wilkinson's first three, the same for O'Leary and two of curative, substantial progress under Bielsa, while six months of defiance under Dennis Wise, Simon Grayson's second and third years plus twitches on the thread from Garry Monk and Thomas Christiansen have kept despair at bay.

In spite of those natural advantages, it's a club that had to sell Elland Road twice in 20 years to pay off a portion of the debts which threatened to consume it, one that still rents its training compound. Leeds were persistently overlooked as oligarchs, sovereign wealth funds, Oriental plutocrats and American tycoons swallowed much of the English professional game, buying up teams with a fraction of United's' past success, potential and baggage. The scale and complexity of the liabilities once spooked suitors.

We have lost decades to those without the wherewithal to stake the risk but who hung in, hoping for a fluke because they coveted the rewards 'getting it right once and for all' would yield. 'When it clicks' has been on every shareholder's lips and could have stood in as the club's motto on the days when 'we're going to see you win' required a generous quantity of LSD.

'When it clicks' serves also as an explanation of the club's enduring appeal. We have a go. In four attempts at the European Cup, Leeds have made the semi-finals twice and the final once, not a Nottingham Forest-style hit rate but none too shabby. The year after promotion in 1964 Leeds went to the wire: runners-up in the First Division on goal average and the FA Cup only after extra-time. A quarter of a century later, Wilkinson won Division Two, finished fourth and then won the last Football League championship in successive seasons before O'Leary managed fourth, third and fourth and reached two European semis.

As the song says, we've had our ups and downs and both have chiselled the club's character. Leeds is the club of Charles and World Cup-winner Jack Charlton, of 12 names tripping off everyone's tongue, the Southampton showboating olés, 'Clarke 1-0!' in the Centenary Cup Final, 1-6 at Hillsborough and beating Manchester United at Old Trafford from the depths of League One.

Yet it is also the team that dropped and sold Denis Irwin and replaced him with Brian Caswell, of World Cup-winner Roque Junior, the club without an FA Cup victory for 10 consecutive seasons, sides who froze into embarrassing torpor in two play-off finals. We are the one that lost to Histon in a Fenland torrent, that embraced 'here today, gone tomorrow' like a rat-arsed buffoon in a casino, that recruited more than a hundred loan players in 13 seasons, and Cellino's 'Sicknote Six'.

These extremes of experience define Leeds as a hybrid of erstwhile nobodies, Unlucky Alf and 'the greatest in the land'. Wilkinson thought the club 'a Rolls-Royce in a breaker's yard' when he took over and merely eight years after his tireless renovation work ended, it was back with the knacker. Brass comes and goes, success and crises, too. This is United's core value: a volatile club in a volatile world. When opposition fans ask 'who are you?' the answer comes back 'We are Leeds'. This is the story of what that means.

.

1

DISSOLUTION
DISHONOURS

Among the founding fathers of Leeds United, Charlie Copeland and George Cripps rarely merit a mention but without their vital if embittered contributions, Leeds City would likely have survived. The club had scraped along for 10 seasons in the Second Division from their election in 1905 until the suspension of the Football League in the spring of 1915, stricken by financial paralysis and the rival attractions of the Northern Union's Hunslet, who won All Four Cups in 1908, and Leeds RLFC, Challenge Cup winners in 1910.

City owed their life to Norris Hepworth, the son of Joseph, founder of the made-to-measure and ready-made 'world's clothiers', the country's largest men's tailoring manufacturer and retailer. Norris was the club's first chairman and its principal benefactor through multiple flirtations with bankruptcy after annual four-figure losses. As managing director and heir to his father's company, he had the wealth to turn the bank manager's eyes pragmatically colour blind to the red ink bleeding through City's books. The club's ownership structure was as a conventional limited liability company with Hepworth as the de facto underwriter, although he repeatedly tried to recapitalise it through share subscriptions and rights issues, all of which foundered once the ingratiating, honeyed pledges that greeted them had evaporated.

On his death in Headingley in February 1914 at the age of 56, City were about to complete their second year in receivership. Hepworth, whose investment stood at around £18,000 including the deeds to Elland Road, had been willing to wipe out the club's debts to him and give it the ground if £13,000 could be raised in debentures to pay off the overdraft and outstanding mortgage. Once his offer had failed to entice sufficient backers at £1 a share, he appointed the insolvency accountant Tom Coombs as receiver but continued to act as the club's obliging patron. He paid for the recruitment of Herbert Chapman, who came from Northampton Town and successfully lobbied for City's re-election when they finished second-bottom of Division Two in 1912, and for the signings who would push Chapman's side to sixth in 1913 and fourth, merely two points off promotion, a year later.

Coombs' title as 'official liquidator' was far more foreboding than his actions proved to be, though in 1915 he did entertain an approach from the Leeds Cricket, Football and Athletic club, owners of Headingley and Leeds RLFC, which envisaged consuming City, abandoning Elland Road for north-west Leeds and forsaking their code for association football. Joseph Connor, president of the West Riding FA, objected on behalf of the people of south Leeds, citing the loyalty of the communities of Beeston, Holbeck, Hunslet and Morley, and made a modest counter-offer that was accepted although it did nothing to address the chronically under-resourced balance sheet and committed only to a short leasehold on the ground. It had always been a hand-to-mouth existence, but the hand and its contents were forever shrinking, like trying to feed a dreadnought's boilers from a hearth scuttle.

City prospered in wartime football, using guest players of the calibre of Aston Villa's Clem Stephenson and Tottenham's Fanny Walden over four seasons to win the Midland Section twice. But crowds were understandably down with so many men away on service, and in 1916 Chapman was seconded to a senior management position at the munitions factory at Barnbow to the east of the city. Connor, the chairman, squabbled with Chapman's deputy and chosen locum, George Cripps, saying that the acting secretary-manager's accounts were so muddled that the directors discussed winding the club up in 1917, fearful of being wiped out by a gaping hole in the books, suspecting incompetence rather than fraud.

They were persuaded to carry on by the Football League president, John McKenna, who would co-star in the role of lord high executioner two years later, while Connor brought in a bookkeeper to straighten out the administrative shambles. Chapman returned to Elland Road at the end of the war in which two of City's most recent captains, Evelyn Lintott and Jimmy Speirs, had been killed in action – Lieutenant Lintott of the Leeds Pals on the first day of the Battle of the Somme, and Sergeant Speirs, of the Queen's Own Cameron Highlanders, at Passchendaele.

Cripps threatened to sue the club for wrongful dismissal when forced out in December 1918 unless they paid him £400. He had taken possession of club documents showing illicit payments to players above legitimate but ill-defined 'token wages' and genuine expenses during the war and lodged them with his solicitor, James Bromley. City were either threatened or cautioned by Bromley that the 'evidence' would be the ace up his sleeve in any court case and he advised them to settle.

It remains unclear whether this was explicit blackmail or if the legal leverage was only implied but the club took it seriously enough to arbitrate a deal, beating Cripps and Bromley down to £55 to sign a confidentiality covenant and hand over the chequebooks, letters and club accounts. Little wonder, then, that the reserve right-back Charlie Copeland, one of the many Teessiders who punctuate this tale, when demobbed and offered only a 16 per cent raise on his 1914 basic pay to £3 10s for the 1919-20 season instead of the £6 maximum he was certain he had been promised, turned to Bromley to weaponise his hand in negotiations. Having already forked out once to hush up the extra payments, City granted Copeland a free transfer, calling his bluff because they now had Bromley's word and Cripps' cache. Copeland went to Second Division Coventry and from there blew the whistle, informing the FA and the Football League by letter that the club had paid him for his guest appearances. Men may have noble intentions to make significant contributions to the notion of fair play, but there are few motivations in life more compelling than spiting an ungrateful boss.

Having received notification from Copeland, the two governing bodies began an inquiry that called City to the Grand in Manchester's Piccadilly to answer the charges, six games into their Division Two campaign. Leeds were represented by their solicitor, Alderman William Clarke, into whose care Cripps' documents had been placed. Naturally enough the joint commission demanded to inspect the files from 1916-18 to determine whether there had been any misconduct. Clarke refused to hand them over, claiming he was unable to do so, and the meeting concluded with an ultimatum that they should be produced in 10 days or face the consequences. The deadline passed without Clarke yielding to the decree and the League ordered the postponement of City's match against South Shields pending a final tribunal.

In 1912 Leeds had been fined £125 for making a miscalculation with three of their players' contracts that paid them a full year's wages instead of a season's and hence breached the maximum sum allowed. One can only presume that with such a recent transgression on their record Clarke felt, as a second offence, the papers were so incriminating that it was better to bluster. He must have calculated that the absence of evidence would acquit the club, yet quite the opposite happened. At the follow-up hearing at the Russell Hotel on 13 October 1919, nine days after a 4-2 victory over Wolves at Molineux, it was the absence of evidence – the wilful failure to produce the accounts – that convicted and condemned City, a case considered proven by omission. The club was hung for the cover-up more than the crime. "The books were never placed on the table," wrote the

FA Secretary, Sir Frederick Wall. "They were not obtained. The inference was that Leeds City had in a broad sense carried on as though no embargo had been placed on their action. The FA decided to suspend the club, the directors and the officials for ever."

The fate of the papers and Clarke's subsidiary motives remain a mystery. Was he trying to protect the players and City's directors? Had Bromley diddled him and surrendered only part of their spoils or did Cripps retain some veto over their disclosure? Clarke, later Sir William, City of Leeds coroner and president of the Leeds Conservative Association, never revealed his reasoning. His council colleague, Alderman Joseph Henry, Lord Mayor of Leeds, accompanied him to the Russell and the 73-year-old Liberal, while offering no explanation for the club's noncompliance, begged for City to be spared and for him to be put in charge as a white knight. The commission turned him down, expelled Leeds City from the Football League, elected Port Vale in their place and gave them the 10 points City had accrued from 10 matches. Connor and three of his fellow board members were banned *sine die* from involvement in football, which included attending matches, while Chapman and Cripps were also banished from the game. Chapman's second appeal, built on the argument that had been unsuccessful in 1919, that he had been only a consultant to City from 1915-18 and was engaged in war work when the payments were made, truncated his suspension from life to 17 months and he joined Huddersfield Town, first as assistant manager, in February 1921.

The mayor, wearing a lacerated look, blamed the League rather than the commission, saying that soundings he had taken at a meeting in Sheffield the previous week suggested that it was sympathetic to the club's plight and could be minded to punish those in charge rather than the Leeds public. He had, therefore, persuaded the syndicate of owners to relinquish control to an associate, WH Platts, who settled their outstanding loans and took sole control of Leeds City and the Elland Road lease. But the impression he was given in Sheffield was disabused in London and on his return home he revealed: "The chairman had been fully informed by someone of many of the doings of the Leeds City management of which I was totally ignorant. I was also very much handicapped by several local people sending letters to members of the League of which no copy had been sent to me." There was no appetite to pursue the identity of the informants and any insinuations of betrayal by specific individuals were dispatched as swiftly as the club itself. The inference, given the iniquity of the maximum wage, widescale duplicity of supposedly amateur players and the almost universal practice of Eric Idle-style, 'nudge-nudge-wink-wink' payments to working men, was unavoidable. This was a custom, in the truest sense, more honoured in the breach than the observance and so a resentment that Leeds were the most convenient scapegoat lingered.

The third and final act of Leeds City's elimination trilogy also took place at a luxury hotel. Tried at the Grand, executed at the Russell, all that was left was the scavenging. Invitations were sent to the vultures to meet at the Hotel Metropole on King Street in Leeds, just four days after City were slung out of the League. On that Friday afternoon, the League auctioned the players off, taking 'sealed tenders' from representatives of more than 30 clubs for 15 of them – and forcing each to sign for the highest bidder. Billy McLeod, City's record scorer, went to Notts County for the top price of £1,000 even though he wanted to go to Stoke. "As the sub-committee indirectly pointed out," noted the *Sheffield Star*'s 'Free Lance', "they had secured the player a post, and if he didn't take it, well... McLeod went to Notts County, for he could not do otherwise."

The carrion, otherwise known as the Leeds City squad, were paid their wages for the preceding week out of the proceeds and the balance was stashed to settle other debts. No better symbol exists of the indentured relationship of professional footballers from 1888 until Eastham v Newcastle United in 1964, which reformed the retain-and-transfer manacles. Unhappily no photographer was allowed in to capture the moment when redundant players from a defunct club were passed pound notes, half-crowns and tanners across a committee table and then peddled on as chattels.

And with that cursory clearance sale, Leeds City were done, wiped out. At that point the stories of Leeds' two football clubs should have diverged and they did, save for a period from June 2008 when Leeds United Football Club Limited changed its name by special resolution to Leeds City Holdings Limited. The owner, Forward Sport Fund, incorporated in the Cayman Islands and administered from Geneva, remained the same, as did the directors, principally Kenneth William Bates, who maintained that he never knew the identity of the individuals behind the company that had invested all its trust in him.

Leeds United Football Club Limited, the company that held the share in the Football League and its membership of the Football Association, became a wholly owned subsidiary of Leeds City Holdings. It was a loaded choice for the name and a few sceptics suspected mischief in the hat-tip to the derelict past. After all the chairman had recently taken the club into administration only for the largest creditors, based in the British Virgin Islands and Nevis, West Indies, to refuse all offers except for one that kept Bates in charge. It may have been coincidence rather than a grab at first dibs on the name for a phoenix club. But at a time when its golden share in the Football League had been jeopardised, unsecured creditors paid 4p in the pound and Leeds hobbled by a 15-point deduction, it was hardly the most reassuring spirit to summon up. Perhaps it was a joke, like many of Bates', chiefly enjoyed by himself. To those with an eye on the past though, it was an uncomfortable reminder of the worst that can happen when somebody is prepared to threaten the club's very existence if they do not get their own way.

2

SOMETHING OLD, SOMETHING NEW, SOMETHING BORROWED, SOMETHING BLUE

On the evening before Leeds City were pillaged at the Metropole, Dame Nellie Melba appeared in concert at Leeds Town Hall. She was 58 and, according to the *Yorkshire Evening Post*, "it would not be true to say she was at her best. Her top notes are not what they were". Yet she still included Tosti's soaring Goodbye in her repertoire, climbing towards the pitiful climax: "Goodbye, forever! Goodbye, forever! Goodbye! Goodbye! Goodbye!" It could have been a moment of supreme poignancy to end a distressing week for the city but merely 24 hours later in the hall of Salem's Chapel on Hunslet Lane, 1,000 Leeds City season ticket holders and supporters gathered in the Congregational church for a secular revival meeting.

Alfred Masser, a 43-year-old Liberal city councillor for the north-west ward, had been present at the Griffin Hotel in 1905 at the moment of Leeds City's birth. He had been one of the original shareholders of the club, spent a spell as vice-chairman and stood down from the board at the beginning of the war. Masser practised law from Park Square East and reckoned he clocked up 2,000 court appearances a year. Even so he managed to fit in a bewildering array of sporting engagements: he was founder and honorary secretary of the Yorkshire Automobile Club and had been one of the saviours and 'A team' captain of Headingley Football Club after the secession of the 12 Yorkshire Northern Union teams in 1895 threatened the existence of the 15-man code in the county. He captained Leeds Springfield Cricket Club and stayed on as secretary and then president, annually visited Arosa in Switzerland to indulge his passion for winter sports, particularly curling, and – in four decades on the Parks Committee – was the implacable campaigner for the cause of municipal golf in the city, a goal he achieved with the opening of the public course at Temple Newsam in 1923, designed by Alister MacKenzie, no less.

It is exhausting to chronicle the details of such an active life, never mind live them. But when Masser died at home in Roundhay in 1950 after a 40-year stint on the council, the last 24 as an alderman, higher up his obituary than all those years of diligent duty was what came out of that gathering at Salem Hall, the founding of Leeds United Football Club. As the city's most influential friend of sport, the inveterate committee man and advocate was the most appropriate person to preside over the meeting. He began by entreating everyone to think only of the future, saying it would be foolish to dwell on the past and apportion blame. Like many effective politicians, he almost immediately contradicted himself with a crowd-pleasing flourish, saying what had been done to Leeds City "was rather like hanging a lad for stealing his first apple". Overlooking for a moment the weeks of obstruction, he burnished the feelings of maltreatment to unite his audience, hoping, one suspects given his history with the perennially cash-strapped City, to consolidate their commitment, emotionally and financially, to the fresh enterprise.

Masser revealed that he had spoken to Football Association officials at the Metropole auction along with the mayor and had received "a little hope" that a new club's two-year probationary period before it was eligible to apply for election to the Football League could be slashed. "Four of the most prominent members of the FA," he said, "gave an expression of opinion that Leeds ought to have a representative Association club." He set out the boulder-strewn path that lay ahead of them and asked who was with him as "unless I have you behind me, I finish". The volume of applause encouraged him and he concluded his rally with a rousing call to arms which placed practical reason as well as hope on their side. "Are supporters ready to make another start?" he asked before pointing to the sunlit uplands. "If somebody went to the Football Association at the proper time, with a proper team and organisation, the view is that Leeds is such an important centre that it deserves full recognition. If the 'powers that be' refused to entertain our application, they would be cutting off their noses to spite their faces."

From the floor, a Mr Smart proposed a resolution that a professional football club be formed in Leeds, seconded by a Mr Leggatt, which was carried unanimously. A committee was elected, the motion to establish a limited liability company to fund administrative costs until a share issue could be launched went through on the nod and the meeting adjourned for two weeks. Like a baby with unprepared parents, the new club came into the world nameless, but that decision could wait – what mattered most was that on the evening of Friday, 17 October 1919 at Salem Hall, Leeds United were conceived and, with the mass cry of "Aye", born within 90 minutes.

Over the next few days the committee met under the chairmanship of Joe Henry, the son of the mayor. Masser, who would have been the obvious choice for the role, had asked to be exempt from the board to concentrate on seducing further allies within the game and lobbying the FA and the League. The committee appointed joint secretaries, proposed one of their number, Dick Ray – a 43-year-old former Leeds City left-back recently demobbed from the Royal Army Service Corps – as team manager, and registered with the West Riding Football Association as 'Leeds United Association Football Club'. Of the viable options – 'Leeds Albion', 'Leeds Athletic', 'Leeds Rangers', 'Leeds Rovers', 'Leeds Wanderers' etc – only United was seriously entertained and adopted, presumably, because there was no better way to present a common front than stating it explicitly in the name.

By the time of the next meeting on 29 October, the committee had paid out of their own pockets to place recruitment advertisements in the local papers as well as the national sporting press for players, formed a selection sub-committee to assess the 100 or so respondents and were negotiating with Mr WH Platts, the last surviving and only exonerated Leeds City official, about a lease on Elland Road. Platts, an accountant who had paid out £4,000 at the mayor's behest to try to save City between their trial and sentence, had just instructed more orthodox auctioneers to dispose of the effects of the club – "shower baths, billiard tables, jerseys, shirts, vests, knickers, spare goalposts, football, nets, boots etc" – and in the past few days had accepted Yorkshire Amateur FC as his new tenants. The Ammers, a year older than Leeds United, generously offered the professional club precedence over the ground. Back at Salem Hall, Joe Henry was able to announce that in the 12 days since they had first met, the club now had a broad pool of possible players, were closing in on a deal for a home and, crucially, membership of the Midland League, to which they had been invited in Leeds City Reserves' stead. Only an idea on the Friday, by a week on Wednesday Leeds United had a name, a place, personnel and competitive fixtures.

The chairman's father, Joseph Henry, the lord mayor, wandered over old ground and new. He asked City supporters not to hold grudges against the directors of that club and instead turn their eyes and hearts to United, but all that spiel about accepting their lot notwithstanding, Henry could not resist refighting the propaganda battle over his defeat. "They had only broken the commandment that said, 'Thou shall not be found out'," he argued. "If everybody with a connection with football were excommunicated for particular wrongs they had done, they would be like a long worm cut into little bits; they would all be wriggling." He ended with a call for the public of Leeds to show the authorities in London and Sheffield (the Victorian hotbed of the game and capital of Yorkshire football) "that there was no lack of Association vitality left in Leeds". It was unreported whether he was wearing his chain of office when making his nakedly anti-establishment pitch.

Masser was more sharply focused on the next steps but no less rousing. Both had spent decades canvassing, debating and stirring a crowd into action and knew precisely the location of an audience's political erogenous zones and how to tickle them. He summarised the progress the committee had made and then told the audience what he had been up to. "Without venturing too far into the region of prophecy," he said, "given the possession of ground and fairly successful team I believe the club would be successful in applying for re-admission to the Second Division of the English League at the beginning of next season." And why did he think that a 12-day-old club could achieve something he feared would take at least twice as long when he last addressed them? "I am assured from inquiries made that English League clubs as a whole were heartily sorry to part with Leeds City and would be only too glad to renew acquaintance with their successors at the earliest opportunity."

Ringing applause greeted his good news. If he was right, and they had no reason to doubt him, the city's exile from the professional game would last only 10 months. It was in the League and FA's interest to be seen to have done the right thing for decorum's sake but neither was interested in a draconian exclusion order injurious to their clubs. Leeds City had never commanded enormous crowds but in their last two pre-war seasons they had been in the top four highest in their division and since regulations had been changed after the war to give away teams 20 per cent of net gate receipts, a Leeds club would significantly benefit Second Division owners. The apocalypse was now merely a hiatus.

With 'to be or not to be?' answered resoundingly in the affirmative in less than a fortnight of constructive endeavour, next came the rub. So far the spadework had been funded by contributions from individual members of the committee but Masser now sketched out how they proposed to put the club on a proper financial footing. He reminded the hall that they had elected the committee and that deliberations had been undertaken in their name and with the club's best interest as the sole motive. Consequently, he reported, they had decided that the club should be floated with a nominal share capital of about £25,000, of which £10,000 should be fully paid up at a pound per share. "What was needed," he continued, "was that all supporters should subscribe in order to establish the new club on a thoroughly democratic basis."

Here, right from the beginning, was a vision of co-operative ownership and supporter participation that promised to preserve United from the need for a saviour. Having seen one club struggle, collapse and plunge into receivership when its benefactor lost heart before being 'rescued' into the purgatory of a pauper's subsistence, Masser and the committee devised a model that was designed to be robust. Yes, the club would at least have to break even on trading – as City had eventually managed in their final season – because small, possibly first- and/or only-time investors would need to be confident that they would be immune from cash calls and the dilution of their stakes should, for example, another 15,000 shares have to be issued to raise funds. It was a bright and radical proposal founded on Edwardian Liberal ideas about diffusing ownership as one step on the road to a more just society. Sadly, however, from an audience of 1,000, pledges were taken totalling merely £400 or six per cent of the required amount. Now, before we rush to judgment about fine words and their worthless effect on parsnips or Yorkshiremen and their brass, it is important to remember that they were not yet a year on from Armistice Day, the average weekly pay for a skilled worker was a little shy of £5 and access to personal credit, in what we would consider its orthodox forms, was restrictive.

Even so, Leeds was a city of immense industrial and mercantile pride. It was the place where Marks & Spencer was founded and from where Hepworth & Co and Montague Burton would vie for international supremacy in the mass production of tailoring for much of the first half of the century. Yorkshire Bank and The Leeds Permanent held millions on deposit and invested the savings of the populace, while Hunslet was home to the steam engine foundries and works of Kitson and Co, J&H McLaren and John Fowler and Co. Waterloo Main, in the south-east of the city, and the collieries ringing Allerton, Methley and Rothwell were vibrant concerns still in private ownership, while the city centre itself housed Schofield's department store and thriving retailers in the ornate Victorian arcades and the streets surrounding them. It was a city of churches and synagogues, the covered market and baroque pubs, the smell of unyielding furnace smoke and, drifting over the Aire, hops from the brewery of Joshua Tetley & Son. And all it could come up with was £400. In 1919 the dream of expansive shareholder activism was stillborn.

In fairness, although the first indications from the subscription drive were depressingly inauspicious, we cannot be certain that the club would have ultimately fallen so far short of the prospectus because within a week came an extraordinary intervention from the foothills of the Pennines. The United committee's public work was spent on trials, an agreement to sub-let Elland Road on alternate Saturdays and a positive response to the formal invitation to join the Midland League. But, out of the spotlight, the *Yorkshire Evening Post* had observed "mysterious comings and goings" and "portentous committee meetings" which it eventually revealed while fleshing out the sensational story of "an unexpected development" first broken by the *Yorkshire Post* on 6 November. The directors of Second Division Huddersfield Town, it reported, had been in discussions to transfer the club "lock, stock and barrel" to Elland Road within the month. The question of whether this club would become Leeds United or a separate club with another name – Carpetbaggers City, perhaps – was left ambiguous initially but as soon as the notion was floated the implication was glaring; Town would either possess the new club or kill it stone dead.

The attraction for the majority shareholders of Huddersfield Town was obvious. On Saturday, 1 November for their 3-0 victory over Fulham at Leeds Road, the official attendance of 2,500 was 4,000 worse than the next lowest in the division and had produced gate receipts – not counting the season tickets paid up in August – of £90 in a stadium built to hold 50,000. Three miles to the west, at Fartown in the Northern Union, Huddersfield had beaten Hull 33-8 in the second round of the Yorkshire Cup in front of 22,000 spectators, who brought in £1,600. The stark contrast provided that afternoon underlined more than ever that Huddersfield, the birthplace of the game, was a rugby town. Such a feeble attendance for the football club was an anomaly but in their six Football League seasons they had scraped above an average of 7,000 only in their debut campaign, while Herbert Chapman's Leeds City had managed 15,845 at Elland Road in 1913-14. Thus the reasoning behind this new move was simple: Huddersfield Town's owners coveted Leeds' crowds as the missing ingredient which could stimulate a fresh start into a flying one.

Hilton and Stoner Crowther, two of five wealthy brothers, were third-generation mill owners and their businesses in the Colne Valley were among the largest woollen cloth manufacturers and exporters in the world. They were philanthropists, patrons of the arts and Freemasons, while Stoner was also a crack amateur golfer who would defeat Tommy Armour by a stroke to win the Golf Illustrated Gold Vase at St George's Hill in 1920. Their investment in their hometown club amounted to £40,000 plus

£18,000 held in debentures. Hilton, the Town chairman, had approached WH Platts, Elland Road's leaseholder, on the Monday following the sparsely supported, final-straw match against Fulham. He had put him in touch with the Leeds United committee and discussions between the three parties evolved in the 72 hours before they went public from tentative introductions to the spectre of a shotgun marriage. Platts broke cover first, pushing himself forward to herald the second new dawn of a convoluted and bewildering month. The new proposal, he said, was to amalgamate and "subject to the consent of the Association and the League… [which] I think will be given, you will be seeing an English League club at Elland Road playing either in the name of Leeds United, or of Leeds Trinity, which would carry with it the significance of three clubs in one – Huddersfield Town, Leeds United and Leeds City".

Platts saved the element of coercion for the end, a rancid olive in the sparkling cocktail. "Whatever Leeds United might do," he said, "the ground at Elland Road would now go to the Huddersfield Town directors if they want it. The certainty of Second League football at Elland Road, even from an imported club, in the immediate future would make an irresistible appeal to the Leeds public and would be far preferable to the toilsome, uphill journey Leeds United would have to encounter in qualifying for the Second Division." He reported that the mayor had been consulted and he, naturally enticed by the offer of a bypass that would return a League club to the city before his term of office was out, rather than going the long way round, had called another meeting of the club's supporters to be held at the YMCA on Albion Street the following evening.

Giving the people of Leeds League football in this way was not a zero-sum transaction: it left the Huddersfield football-loving public comprehensively disenfranchised. Proponents of the switch pointed to precedent – Millwall's move from the Isle of Dogs to New Cross, Crystal Palace's from Sydenham to Herne Hill and on to Selhurst, Port Vale from Burslem to Hanley and, of course, Woolwich Arsenal from Plumstead to Highbury. It stood to reason, therefore, that "geographical objections", according to the *Evening Post*'s conclusion, "cannot therefore be held to operate adversely in the present instance". It is an argument of impeccable logic but stretches the point beyond credulity. It is one thing for clubs to shift across a city, even a metropolis, quite another to desert one town for another. The distances involved were not broadly dissimilar to the flight from Woolwich but the principle of relocating a club en bloc between distinct communities had not necessarily been established by Arsenal's flit across the water. Still, Crowther, Platts and Henry Snr were confident of official approval and assembled the next night to sell their budding Exodus FC scheme to the supporters of the defunct and newborn Leeds clubs.

The Lord Mayor took the chair and moved that Leeds United and Huddersfield Town should formally merge. It was, he said "the readiest way of getting back into the League". His son, in his role as chairman of Leeds United's management committee, then answered his father's sole stated doubts – that building up the new club should take priority over reimbursing the debenture holders. Henry Jnr confirmed that "our Huddersfield friends" had made those assurances. Town, he said, would be transferred in its entirety – players and staff, assets and liabilities – along with Hilton Crowther's dedicated pledge of financial support. Five directors would be appointed from Huddersfield and four from United to run the club, with the covenant that they would hand the whole concern over to the Leeds quartet once the Huddersfield directors' loans had been recouped. But repayment, he stressed, was not an immediate concern.

Platts spoke next, making Crowther's pitch for him, calling it a "magnificent offer" and revealing that the twill tycoon's largesse, shaped by his sportsmanship, would pare the new company's debts to a sustainable level. Finally, Crowther rose reluctantly. "I want to help you and I want you to help me," he said, before elaborating on his belief that if the Football League Management Committee meeting the following week went their way, the yet unnamed new club, 'Leeds X', would take on Coventry City at Elland Road on Saturday, 15 November. And why did he think the League would be sympathetic to his request? Pure self-interest.

"It is really useless to compel [us] to remain at Huddersfield," he said. "It is a tax on all the Second Division clubs for their gates are the worst in the League." His motivations were twofold, he concluded: "To help the Leeds people and to show those in Huddersfield that Leeds could get the team into the First Division." It is revealing to note this rapid detachment – "their gates", not "our", and the longing for vindication – and their possible ramifications down the line. If anyone stopped to think, they remained silent, content to be the beneficiaries of a sovereign's grace. The motion was passed unanimously, the amalgamation approved and Crowther was given a rousing rendition of For He's a Jolly Good Fellow. In three weeks Leeds had spun the compass from dead club to phoenix club to franchise club.

"And so say all of us" was not a positive endorsement of the Crowthers' ambitions that could be heard 20 miles away in Huddersfield where another gathering of supporters congregated on Sunday in protest. At Saturday's reserve match, shouts of "Who's been twisting us?" and the grimly sarcastic "C'mon Leeds!" had articulated the fury. The knowledge that the League was due to evaluate the project within 72 hours should have impressed discretion upon the president, John McKenna, but the former Liverpool chairman was an impulsive and obliging rent-a-quote once the bashful formalities had been observed. "I know so very little about the official facts," he conceded, "that it is rather difficult to say anything. In fact, I would rather not. But I am sure everyone knows that Huddersfield people have shown they do not want 'Soccer' football." Not only was it prejudicial it was plain wrong, albeit on the Big Yellow Taxi principle that "you don't know what you've got 'til it's gone". At Leeds Road, 3,000 Huddersfield fans answered the call on the afternoon following Town's victory at Highfield Road, and agreed to unite in opposition to enforced relocation. Some of the original founders of the club, dissenting directors, former players and the chief constable put forward a plan to pay off the debentures, received promises of £3,000 in share subscriptions and empowered a delegation to take the first steps to save Town by pressing the League to stay the Crowthers' request. At Manchester's Grand Hotel on 11 November, the League management committee convened. The significance of the day could not have escaped them.

Indeed they did manage to broker a truce of sorts after hearing out the deputations from Leeds and Huddersfield. Arthur Fairclough, the Town secretary-manager who had led Barnsley to the FA Cup in 1912, actually appeared for Leeds, having defected from the Huddersfield cause but not his de facto employer. He, along with Hilton Crowther and Masser, briefed reporters that all had gone well and intimated the board was likely to rule in their favour. That was, however, before Huddersfield went in and argued that there had been a lack of notice, abuses of process – not all shareholders had been consulted – and that their townspeople deserved an opportunity to prove how much they prized the club. After half an hour's deliberations, the committee settled on a compromise: Huddersfield had a month to find the £28,000 (approximately £1.5 million in 2019) required to purchase the Crowthers' interests in the ground, shares and loans, a discount of 50 per cent on their total investment, or the club would be removed to Leeds with the unequivocal blessing of the League and Town's 'pro-remain' directors.

The Huddersfield intrusion, however welcome, had necessitated the postponement of Leeds United's debut in the Midland League scheduled for 8 November but with the moratorium on the move in place, it was decided that United should go ahead and play their first match. Despite three inches of snow on the morning of Saturday, 15 November, and weather so severe the *Yorkshire Post* was reporting a "city-wide run on galoshes", United, managed by Dick Ray and playing in blue-and-white-striped shirts – in a nod to the jerseys they envisaged wearing in a few weeks – dark shorts and socks, took on Yorkshire Amateurs at Elland Road in a friendly and beat them 5-2. Thomas Heslop from Middlesbrough – that place again – scored United's first-ever goal. The following week the scratch side opened their Midland League campaign in a goalless draw with Barnsley Reserves, attracting a crowd of 4,025 to Elland Road, a little more than half the number who turned up to Leeds Road for Huddersfield's victory over Bristol City. However, if anyone involved in the fight to save Town thought that doubling their normal attendance put them in the clear, Crowther had a cure for their complacency.

When the management committee reconvened, this time in London, Huddersfield divulged that they had banked £8,000 in pledges from about 2,000 donations received at fundraising events. Hilton Crowther and Fairclough, the latter still engaged as Huddersfield's manager while working for the club's removal to Leeds, urged the League to honour its undertaking forthwith. But Crowther, who had made the tactical error of resigning from the Huddersfield board, had no legal standing before the committee and the club's directors successfully argued that it was their prerogative not a mere debenture holder's to request the club's transfer. Since they were unwilling to do so, the committee had no case to hear and therefore granted Huddersfield another three weeks to come up with the outstanding £17,000 to get him off their backs.

It was at this point that Leeds United made a critical decision and committed themselves wholeheartedly to the Midland League. Although they had played their first match in the competition the previous month, they had been censured for subsequently postponing some fixtures in the imminent expectation, in the pejorative words of one letter writer to the *Evening Post*, "of the Town club wreck being towed to the Leeds dry dock". As part of this twin strategy the club got on with the task of proving itself a viable venture independent of Huddersfield and let Crowther pursue his increasingly tortuous quick fix. The next implement he reached for was a legal sledgehammer. Six days before Christmas a writ was issued in the name of his brother, Stoner, demanding £10,137,18s 6d as payment of a promissory note issued in 1913 and that the trustees of the debenture – including Sir Charles Sykes, MP for the Huddersfield constituency – thereby gave notice that they intended to enter and take possession of the club's premises. Eviction would have given Leeds the upper hand. The collapse of the National Liberals, his party, might have had more to do with it but Sykes' participation in these proceedings cannot have been unconnected with the loss of his seat by 650 votes at the 1922 general election.

Fishier still, was Fairclough's role in this. As secretary-manager of Huddersfield Town, he was the man upon whom the writ was served. He delivered the notice to the board, offered his resignation on the spot, announced that he had been appointed as the receiver on behalf of the Crowthers and would therefore now press on with winding the club up. He was swifter than Tommy Cooper at switching hats. Although the Crowthers' 'armageddon ploy' broadened the threat from the club's location to its very existence, the Huddersfield directors refused to cave. And now, vitally, by issuing a writ, the Leeds camp enabled Huddersfield to trammel the case in the High Court. Now they could legally object and exercise their rights to adjournments for the production of evidence for their defence and counterclaims. Intended as a death warrant, it turned out to be Huddersfield's lifeline.

For the next four months the future of Town remained in limbo. The management committee sat again in January 1920, reaffirmed that permission for the transfer to Leeds to go ahead was dependent on the court determining the Crowthers were legally entitled to proceed and decided to call a special meeting at the George Hotel in Huddersfield to discuss it further. It was there that they heard from the president of the Discharged Soldiers' Association, IH Jones. "It would be a direct violation of that justice and right and the protection of the weak for which we have fought," he said. "Huddersfield's ex-servicemen appeal to you today to do your duty to them, as they did their duty in the trenches in safeguarding these very interests which today are attempting to deprive them of their sport." This perfectly pitched emotive appeal ought to have converted the room to the cause of clemency, but the committeemen simply restated their view, with relief, that the writ absolved them from having to make a verdict and placed it in the hands of the judiciary.

Away from all these private rooms in public places and arguments in a judge's chambers, something far more critical was happening in a realm that should have been central to proceedings but had become marginalised. In short, Huddersfield concentrated on the football. From the day that Fairclough resigned as secretary-manager of Huddersfield Town with the club fifth in the Second Division until the end of the season, they lost only two more games, one of which was the FA Cup Final. Their run, despite having sold the England centre-forward Jack Cock to Chelsea for a record fee at the end of October, earned them promotion as runners-up behind Tottenham and rising home gates through the spring which demonstrated emphatically the town's support. The story of what happened to Huddersfield Town hereon is theirs to tell but as far as Leeds were concerned the Crowther brothers agreed a resolution. Buoyed by the climb up the table and the Cup run, three local cloth merchants augmented the amount already raised to £17,500 in April 1920, a sum accepted by Stoner Crowther as well as 12,500 new shares which confirmed his controlling interest in lieu of the other £7,500. The belated settlement now obliged Hilton, who had found the low road blocked when he erred with a hasty, imperious lawsuit, to be true to his word and take Leeds on the high road back to the Football League.

While Leeds United caught up with their Midland League fixture backlog (having had to start the season three months after the other clubs) and the Town case was entangled in court, the club's committee appointed Fairclough as secretary-manager and dispatched him on a mission to charm Football League members. The bottom two in the Second Division at the end of the season would have to face re-election and United now focused on honing their candidacy to win one of the places. The pitch was made persuasive by the city's natural advantages – a population in the district approaching one million, a place reachable directly by all five main railways and Hilton Crowther's wealth and success in negotiations to purchase Elland Road. The difference between Leeds City's crowds at the start of the season and those of Grimsby Town and Lincoln City at the foot of the table – 4,000 fewer – was also specified, reiterating once more the economic benefit for member clubs. Once the Huddersfield Town transfer had been abandoned in April, Crowther agreed to loan United a sum of about £35,000, repayable on promotion to the First Division. Their Midland League campaign had broken even, the limited company that had not been incorporated when it was first proposed in October was now set up and £10,000 of the £25,000 capital was again offered for subscription. At the end of May, Crowther, Masser, Fairclough and two other directors, Kaye Aspinall and Mark Barker, embarked for London and spent the weekend before the League's AGM touring the Bloomsbury and Holborn hotels canvassing support.

On the last day of the month at the meeting at the Connaught Rooms on Great Queen Street, Fairclough told League clubs that Crowther's support had given Leeds United a working capital that few, if any, had enjoyed for a launch season and that they were already working on plans to extend Elland Road's capacity to 60,000, a programme they would enact as soon as they had built a competitive team. When the votes were counted Leeds United came top with 31, Cardiff City next with 23, which shoved Grimsby (20) and Lincoln (seven) out of the League (though Grimsby were enlisted in the new Third Division which started the following season). Crowther ceded the moment of triumph to Masser, who addressed the city's newspapers with a strange homily that touched on repentance and catharsis. "I hope one day to find the name of Leeds inscribed indelibly on the rolls of the FA as the city which passed through fire, was cleansed and was given again a fair and sporting chance to rehabilitate itself amongst its fellows." Given his strenuous year and sincere civic pride, we can excuse him his hammy tone.

Free of Leeds City, free of Huddersfield Town, on 31 May 1920, Leeds United at last had an identity of their own. From this moment on they could finally be themselves.

3

HOUSE ON THE ROCK

For some of us it will always be Sprake, Reaney, Cooper, Bremner, Charlton, Hunter, Lorimer, Clarke, Jones, Giles, Gray, even if we know that omitting Madeley is a crime Don Revie was loath to commit. For others, the line-up embedded in their frontal cortex like a mantra will begin Wood, Dunn, Hair... or Lukic, Sterland, Dorigo... or Martyn, Kelly, Harte... or, for those thankful for light at the end of the darkest tunnel, Ankergren, Crowe, Hughes... or, one day soon, Meslier, Ayling, Dallas...

Each generation should be blessed to find its own resonant sequence of names to reel off by rote. Football fans can use them as a kind of consoling ritual even as age or something worse makes Swiss cheese of our memories. No one, though, would find Down, Duffield, Tillotson, Musgrove, Baker, Walton, Mason, Goldthorpe, Thompson, Lyon, Best readily tripping off the tongue. Yet it was these 11 men, two of whom were 19, one 17 and Jimmy Walton only 16, that Arthur Fairclough sent out in blue-and-white-striped shirts at the Old Recreation Ground to play Port Vale in Leeds United's inaugural league match on 28 August 1920. The opponent, coincidentally we have to believe, were the same club who had replaced Leeds City the previous season and taken their points. They took the points this time around, too, but in the customary fashion with a 2-0 victory. It proved the first and last time that starting XI, in both senses, ever played together.

In 2001 the England cricket team decided to follow Australia's lead and inscribe a number on their shirts to denote their place in Test history. Ryan Sidebottom, who made his debut against Pakistan at Lord's that year, was assigned 604 but the initiation of this new tradition entailed retrospectively working out where everyone else stood in the lineage. Going all the way back to the first Test in Melbourne in March 1877, it emerged, purely on alphabetical order, that Tom Armitage, the Yorkshire seam and occasional lob bowler, was No.1, England's original Test cricketer. But he isn't the sole pioneer in his family: his grandson, Len Armitage, a 20-year-old utility player signed from The Wednesday, scored Leeds United's first-ever league goal as a stand-in centre-forward in their home debut, a midweek 2-1 defeat by South Shields watched by a crowd of 16,958 on a summer's evening at Elland Road. It was the equaliser, lashed in from outside the box, but United could not hang on for a point. Jim Baker, the captain and centre-half, a position which put him in front of the full-backs because the old offside law required three opponents rather than two to play a ball-receiver onside, did very well, recalling his finest days at Huddersfield, but the defenders behind him were overwhelmed by the Sand Dancers' wingers.

Baker, we are told, swiftly acquired the nickname 'T'owd war hoss' for his commanding, dignified and tireless displays at the heart of midfield. It seems suitably appropriate for the time and convincingly affectionate. Even so one wonders whether it was more an occasional, newspaper label than one universally applied by team-mates and supporters during his three-year run of 149 successive appearances for United. It is one of those that sounds contrived and too much of a mouthful to be employed instinctively. Did anyone normal, for example, ever really refer to Gheorghe Hagi as 'The Maradona of the Carpathians' apart from journalists? Nonetheless it did probably serve Baker well in his post-retirement career as the landlord of the Smyth's Arms on Gelderd Road, a stone's throw from the ground.

After taking their opening two steps tentatively as if progressing by increments – initial game followed by opening goal – Baker's United completed the trilogy with their first League victory at the third attempt, when Jerry Best and Matt Ellison with two scored in a gale to beat Port Vale 3-1 in the return. Fixtures for the first few seasons of United's life in the Second Division were generally played in pairs against the same opponents, home and away. It is telling that in 1920-21 Leeds improved their fortunes in the second round on 14 occasions, most of them coming at home. Of course it reveals a team that was more comfortable at Elland Road but it also shows one that was better against more familiar opposition. United were often inadequate when they had to play off the cuff, not so good at problem solving quickly for themselves and working out a way to win. After a sighter, however, and Fairclough's analysis of what he had seen, they usually turned it round in seven days. It is not so surprising when we consider these players had been flung together in a few short weeks from sides as disparate as Castleford Town, West Stanley, Durham City and Frickley Colliery as well as Hull City, Huddersfield Town and Bradford City. Fairclough is often feted as the recruitment maestro but he also deserves credit for how his autopsies of defeat were followed by revival. If only some logic had been applied, he could have scouted the opposition himself before they played Leeds and left all matchday duties to his assistant, Dick Ray.

United finished in 14th, rising as high as eighth halfway through December after a run of three wins followed by slumps in midwinter and late spring. Victory over Leicester City in September had left the visitors grumbling about Leeds' 'kick and rush' methods on their 'sliddery pitch' but it was a forgivable approach given they were still essentially trialling and sifting players in matches. Of the 27 used in 42 league games, 10 of them mustered fewer than seven first-team appearances in their entire spells with the club and were thanked for their service and discharged by the season's end.

The previous summer's work on rebuilding the terracing in the stand abutting Elland Road and improving the embankment opposite to increase capacity to 40,000 was not properly exploited, the closest was the 25,000 crowd Leeds reported for the Christmas Day goalless draw with Fulham. The Football League only began recording attendances in 1925 and figures before that date come from estimates printed in *The Football Field*, *Athletic News* or local papers but the club did not correct regular mentions of receipts comprising more than £1,000 or totals suggesting an average somewhere between 15,000 and 16,300, which is admirable when the national unemployment rate by May 1921 was 23.4 per cent. Few if any Leeds players, many of whom had been scouted in the North Eastern League or Northern Football Alliance, would have been engaged on the £9 weekly maximum wage so it would seem safe to assume that the club was at least breaking even as City were with their lesser crowds right before the end. As fans came to learn, however, only a dimwit would take anything for granted about the healthy state of Leeds United's finances.

When Fairclough, 'the master teambuilder', had sided with Crowther and moved to Leeds, he estimated the ambition of First Division football would need three seasons' preparatory work. Wildly ahead of schedule he led them to the top of the Second Division for the first time in the middle of September 1921 after a seven-game unbeaten start propelled them above Barnsley. United's summer signings, Fred Whalley from Grimsby, Bill Poyntz from Llanelli, Harry Sherwin, the Sunderland wing-half who had been stationed in the West Riding during the war and made scores of appearances for City, and Southampton's Jim Moore, a Fairclough favourite who played for his FA Cup-winning Barnsley side in 1912, all featured regularly. Whalley, the first-choice goalkeeper for a couple of years, was the most charismatic and remembered long after for his willingness to natter with the crowd behind his goal and share his sweets. In August 1921 he was summonsed for deserting his wife, who was awarded maintenance of 35s a week after disclosing to the magistrate that he had told her to pack her bags, go back to Preston and "if you come back again I will take your life". Either few fans read the court report or most did not care because it did not affect his popularity nor prove an impediment to his post-retirement career as a police officer.

More pertinently, it revealed he was on £5 10s a week plus £2 for a win and £1 for a draw. As one of only a handful of players with league experience on joining Leeds in those opening seasons, Whalley's contract shows Fairclough's prudence with the playing budget. The UK economy was in a parlous state after the brief post-war boom. Stagnant growth and masochistically tight monetary policy in pursuit of a return to the gold standard fostered deflation and persistently high unemployment. As a consequence, Elland Road crowds ticked down to an average of about 13,500 and a 12-match string from the middle of November that contained merely one win and a three-month span from Bonfire Night without a home victory, pushed them as low as 5,000 for the snow-swept visits of Bury and Leicester City in February 1922. Jack Swann, signed from Huddersfield Town in November, and the promotion of Ernie Hart from the reserves to play at centre-half and thus nudge Baker over to left-half, reinvigorated the side in the final 12 weeks and they finished in eighth, seven points better off than their debut campaign.

They ended up a place higher in 1922-23, the year Hart turned 21 and played in all but one of the league matches. His presence and the work of Baker and Sherwin either side of him helped Whalley to 19 clean sheets but the failure to rattle in goals in morale-boosting or match-turning quantities – they could not break 50 in 42 games for the third season in succession – continued to hobble their promotion chances. They were only four points behind the runners-up and they paid the price for their sterility in six 0-0 draws and half a dozen 0-1 defeats. Percy Whipp, a £750 signing from Sunderland in November, scored a hat-trick from inside-right on debut against West Ham and managed 15 in the league by May. The Glaswegian had an elusive quality shared by the best in his position, a predatory sharpness when pushing high up the pitch. His vision and passing earned him the sobriquet 'The Arch General', it is said, a title so meaningless it can only be authentic even if it can plausibly have been used only in the sense of "There he is, the Arch General" rather than an insistent, vociferous cry of "C'mon the Arch General" let alone "Shift your bloody arse, the Arch General".

Whipp exerted his creative influence more forcefully in 1923-24 alongside Joe Richmond, signed from Shildon, at centre-forward and Swann, now at inside-left. Between them they scored 44 goals, one more than the whole squad the year before, and were well-served by Joe Harris, the nimble 32-year-old outside-left. Moreover, the robust tackling of Sherwin, Hart and Baker muzzled the bite of opponents in return. It was a peculiarly spasmodic season of spurts and ruts: United won one of their first six games then went 11 matches unbeaten, a run which included seven consecutive victories; in five games from 1 December to Christmas Day they lost three and drew two, won six on the spin from late January to early March then drew four in a row up to Good Friday and lost on Easter Saturday. They went top in late October, fell back in the build-up to Christmas, regained first place at the end of February and clung on in spite of the jitters to go up as champions. A home victory over Stockport County on Easter Monday ensured promotion and beating Nelson the following Saturday, also at Elland Road, confirmed the title.

Only 22,500 people were at the Stockport game on a Bank Holiday and 20,000 for the Nelson game and the chance to acclaim the first club in the city's history to win anything. It is perfectly reasonable for only 8,000 to be able to go to a rare winter midweek afternoon game, a 2-1 win against South Shields, but just 12,000 turned up on Boxing Day to watch the 5-0 larruping of Oldham. Economic hardship notwithstanding, Leeds people could never be accused of pot-hunting and glory-seeking when it came to United in those fledgling days. Barely two miles from the statue of the Black Prince in City Square, glory of a kind was right there at Elland Road, and not many could be bothered to witness it. Indeed four Second Division clubs who achieved nothing that season and could not claim to come from affluent places more protected from recession – Manchester United, Leicester City, Clapton Orient and Fulham – all had bigger crowds as did Millwall from the tier below. Down the road Huddersfield were closing in on No.1 in an eventual hat-trick of First Division titles but their allure and drain on Leeds' attendances was not something the club counted as significant. They did not require a survey to find out what was keeping people away – it was there in the letters pages of the three local papers. In essence it was the perennial problem: ticket prices.

In his diary for 1997, the great Armley-born dramatist Alan Bennett cites an old verb when confronted by a discrepancy between something's price and its worth. "There's a Yorkshire dialect word that covers this feeling more succinctly than any phrase in standard English," he writes. "When you can afford something but don't like to see the money go in that particular way you say: 'I can't thoil to pay it.'" In 1924, even when United were en route to a maiden promotion for a Leeds club, too many people could not thoil to pay the price to watch it happen.

The issue had its roots in the summer of 1920 after election to the Second Division. When Hilton Crowther abandoned the Huddersfield gambit, Alf Masser had rekindled the share issue and told the supporters' club at various points over the spring that they had received around £3,500 in pledges towards their goal of £10,000, that Crowther and William Platts had each subscribed to a 10 per cent stake of £1,000 and then by June that "the appeal for share capital from the rank and file had realised £10,000 of big money". It's all somewhat opaque, as was normal with limited liability companies, but these things we do know: the club did attract far more money from supporters once Crowther was on board than the £400 promised at the first fundraiser, his status and resources acting as an assurance that it was unlikely to run out of money; systematic door-to-door efforts to canvas investments of £1 a share were deemed a success, particularly in Holbeck; share certificates were issued signed by Fairclough and Crowther in 1920 and, by 1923, a shareholders' association was formed in direct response to Masser's haughtiness at the annual general meeting and because the directors delegated to represent those with smaller stakes – Kaye Aspinall and Mark Barker – had sided with the board.

What we do not know is precisely who owned what portion of the share capital, which Masser said at the 1923 AGM amounted to £9,668. When the West Stand was consumed by fire in 1956, the club's records and archive were incinerated and ever since trying to work out the exact distribution of shares and scale of debts has been a gallingly speculative exercise by virtue of Masser's contradictory statements. He said in May 1920 that the League Management Committee had told him squarely "we want no more one-man clubs" and that "a democratic effort is required to put the club on its feet". In 1922 Sir Berkeley Moynihan, surgeon at Leeds General Infirmary and professor of clinical surgery at the University of Leeds, and Colonel Harold Tetley of the brewing family joined the board. Moynihan found himself too busy to spare the time and resigned after serving only a few months but as late as 1980 his son, Lord Moynihan, father of the Conservative politician and appropriately nicknamed 'miniature for sport' Colin Moynihan, was registered as still possessing 50 shares while Allied Breweries, which had acquired Tetley's, owned 1,450. If the shareholding was as broad as Masser suggested and deeper pockets bought more clout, we can be certain there were only a couple of actively dissenting smaller shareholders among the 900 said to be on the register and it was fundamentally run as a "one-man club" for the first four years. Debt is power and the so far benign bank of Crowther was Leeds United's driving force.

At first the club restricted season tickets to shareholders, treating a perfectly commonplace transaction as a privilege. There was no right to buy, they were held to be a perk and those with a minimum stake of £5 were given a ground ticket worth £1 10s, those with £10 or more in the company received a 'pavilion' ticket – a seat in other words – worth £3 3s. Everyone else had to pay on the gate, 1s or 2s behind the goal, 3s 6d to stand on halfway and 5s 9d for a seat. All prices were inclusive of the hefty entertainment tax and the price bands outraged complainants. When United relented two years later and offered 3,000 season tickets for general sale at £2 and £4 3s, the ship of goodwill had sailed and there were only 382 inquiries so the club refused to sell any. When it was put to Masser that the standing charges were too high and the reason for stagnant gates in 1923, he replied that he and his fellow directors "had just cause for complaint at the lack of patronage received from the public of Leeds". Crowther chipped in here too, noting "the fact the Leeds public had only put £9,000 into the club reflected a certain amount of apathy". It is said that Yorkshire people treasure blunt speaking, but you do not have to have read sales guru Dale Carnegie to know the self-satisfaction when saying something tactlessly does not immunise anyone against umbrage when they are on the receiving end. Masser's refusal to circulate copies of the balance sheet at that AGM, inviting those who wanted to inspect next year's accounts to exercise their right to read them at the company's registered office in the week preceding the meeting, inspired the formation of a shareholders' association but his contemptuous tone throughout which reflected his exasperation would not have helped.

It was there, at Salem Hall in September 1923, that Masser revealed the extent of Leeds United's indebtedness to Crowther in the first of a constantly fluctuating series of apparently factual statements. The club's accountant, Norman Vine, announced a net loss for the year's trading of £833 (down from £1,333 in 1922 and £2,100 in 1921), figures that Masser blamed on the attendance figures. But at the club's initiative, they would improve imminently, he said, because the board had successfully lobbied the council (of which, of course, he was a prominent member) to construct Lowfields Road to link Elland Road with Gelderd Road. This new thoroughfare would take charabancs to and fro, and ease congestion for trams bound for Swinegate after the final whistle. In addition, he said, the club was engaged in talks with the London and North Eastern Railway to build a station at the top of Elland Road on the express line to Doncaster. This scheme has been proposed multiple times over the century but remains a pipe dream. After three completed seasons, the meeting was informed, the club owed Crowther the sum of £19,826 on which no interest had been levied and they had not yet paid a penny in rent to him for Elland Road. "When you realise the considerable amount of money which he had put into the cub without receiving anything by way of return you must feel that we are extremely fortunate to have such a sportsman at our back," said Masser. "In the near future we hope to be able to relieve Mr Crowther of some of his financial responsibilities in respect of the club." That day drew ever nearer because he had said as early as 1920 that promotion would be the trigger to claw some of his outlay back. "I shall then have completed my mission and [shall] finish with Leeds," he had warned.

But what had his loans been spent on? Budgeting for gates of 16,000 had left deficits for the first three seasons totalling just shy of £4,300, 7 per cent of trading income. Some of it, therefore, had been used to offset the overdraft. The rest, contrary to the unambiguous vow to build a team first, had been spent on the stadium and land on the city side of the ground. Fifty steps of terracing had been constructed by 1921 on the cinder banking behind the north goal. That stand was intended to triple in size to 150 rows and become the Spion Kop. The terrace on Elland Road, behind the south goal, had been extended to 36 steps, refitted with a retaining wall up against the public highway and covered by the distinctive 'Belfast' barrel roof. Supporters soon started calling it 'the Scratching Shed'. The paddock terraces on the west side also gained a roof to match the one over the seats, giving it a distinctive double-barrel effect and work on a ferro-concrete wall to enclose the pitch and replace the old palings had improved the sightlines and given it a clean, modern look. In Field of Dreams, a disembodied voice persuades an Iowan farmer to carve out a baseball diamond in his cornfield with the words "if you build it, he will come". And when he does Shoeless Joe Jackson, or at least his spectre, duly appears. Frustratingly, Crowther's labours did not have the same seductiveness for the people of Leeds.

United were in third place in January 1924 with games in hand over the two teams above them when Crowther made his first move to extricate himself and some of his money. While it is true that he had always said he would step back on promotion, his timing was premature and developments the following month in London played their part. In February Mrs Maud Crowther, taking advantage of the Matrimonial Causes Act of 1923, was granted a decree nisi with costs on grounds of Hilton's adultery. Her counsel, the splendidly named Mr Talbot Ponsonby, told the divorce court that her marriage had been a happy one for 12 years until 1917 but she had suspicions "as to her husband's association with other women – in consequence there were frequent quarrels". They had moved into separate bedrooms in 1918 and different houses in 1920. Hearing that Mr Crowther was a frequent guest at the Cranbourn Hotel on Shaftesbury Avenue in London, she had had him watched and discovered, by interviewing the porter, that he had signed in with a "lady who was not the petitioner" as Mr and Mrs J Hilton Crowther, occupied a bedroom together for the night and left the next morning. The identity of the co-respondent was not revealed and the settlement was undisclosed. But it was reported that when his second marriage to the revue actress, pantomime principal boy and singer Mona Vivian ended in the next decade, it cost him the equivalent of £1 million. He spent a great deal of his time after his wedding to Vivian in 1927 travelling around in a motor caravan from theatrical engagement to engagement with her and spent months abroad convalescing from a bout of typhoid. It was a lifestyle incompatible with running and funding Leeds United, never mind playing an active role in the selection committee.

The board had envisaged that Crowther would be reimbursed in the usual fashion – by an individual or group taking a stake which would allow him to recover part of his investment. It had kept three directors' places vacant for that very purpose but none were forthcoming. In January 1924, the smaller shareholders attempted to fill the breach. Kaye Aspinall, supposedly their man on the board, told the first meeting of the new body's executive that Crowther had spent £28,000 on ground improvements, £10,000 on the freehold of Elland Road and further sums on general expenditure that inflated his exposure beyond £40,000. He urged them to make an appointment with the chairman to discover what he would accept to relinquish his stake. They agreed to seize "time by the forelock" and try to pre-empt the "bombshell" and "catastrophe" of him abruptly making a cash call on them at the end of the season. In February they called a public meeting at Salem Hall to report back on their discussions and plans. Old Ebor, the byline used by the *Yorkshire Post*'s doyen of cricket writers and famous sports correspondent AW Pullin, had argued: "It must be patent to any thinking sportsman that Mr Hilton Crowther has done all for association football in Leeds that any man could do and very much more than Leeds people had any right to expect him to do. The plain duty of all who wish association football to flourish in Leeds is to support the team to bring the gates up to such dimensions as will justify [him] in believing his generous outlay has not been in vain." But the attendance for the Coventry match after his appeal, 11,329, was the worst for a Saturday kick-off all season.

An alternative approach was necessary and advanced by the shareholders and supporters' club after talks with Crowther who had told them he wanted half his money back, making a gift of the other £20,000. A Trust Fund was proposed and a roll call of council worthies, businessmen and solicitors announced as trustees or vice-presidents. The chairman of the ordinary shareholders, J Stonehouse, said "he had every confidence now that Leeds United were doing so well that the rank and file of the club would play their part in subscribing their pounds and five pounds to the fund". As ever he called on the business people and "wealthy sportsmen of the city" (an enviable position in any age) to do the rest. What made it unique compared with all the drives of the past was that voting shares in the trust cost a pound and that coupon books with vouchers for a shilling so that they could be bought on tick had already been issued for volunteers to sell at matches, in the workplace and by knocking on doors. If they could not raise the £20,000 within six months, 50 per cent by subscription, 50 from business and sportsmen doing their "duty", the meeting concluded gruffly, "it would be a disgrace to the city".

During that season United had made it into the third round proper of the FA Cup for the first time in Leeds' history (back then this meant the last 16) and a fan's blue and white umbrella, conspicuous in a tortoise formation of black on the terraces, was adopted as a symbol of the run by the newspapers. The Trust Fund also took it up and began selling the shilling coupons "under the umbrella" outside Elland Road in March. Crowther, it was noted, was "in hearty agreement with the movement" but the tenor of the appeal fed to the press was so preachy and patronising it beggars belief. "The system has been devised in order that the working-man follower may be able to do his bit for the club in a convenient way, and that he may also be made to realise that it really is up to him to display a little more enthusiasm and responsibility than hitherto." When put like that – "made to realise" indeed! – how could anyone resist emptying their pockets to repay the millionaire? They raised £100 in the first week. At the end of the victory over Nelson which won United the Second Division championship, the Trust Fund held another mass meeting in the West Stand where Stonehouse proposed a vote of thanks to Crowther, said the sum he had put into the club was actually £50,000 and asked for 10,000 working men to cough up a pound each. They had asked for £10,000 from supporters in the middle of February and 11 weeks later, with First Division football assured, they were still £10,000 short. Something had to give.

At the end of the season, after an away defeat by Nelson at Seedhill, Crowther stood down as chairman and formally requested that he be "relieved of the heavy financial responsibility which I have carried". An official statement supplied by the club to the *Evening Post* on 27 June stated that Crowther had advanced a sum which, with 5 per cent interest now applied, exceeded £50,000 plus a £15,000 holding in the share capital of the company. "Subject to the immediate success of a scheme which is about to be put forward," it continued, "Mr Crowther has agreed to accept a sum of £45,000 in full discharge of the club's indebtedness to him. This is to be paid by £30,000 in cash within two months, the balance to be secured by second debentures to be repaid out of future profits if and when made." Finally, stripped of deferential vagueness, a figure we can trust.

The two-month deadline for the first tranche to be paid, £30,000 in cash (about £1.8m in 2019 using the composite price index), fell on 26 August, four days before Leeds United were scheduled to host Sunderland in the city's first-ever Division One game. Crowther may have been the club's 'fairy godfather' according to one director but he also seemed to be suffering from a Moses complex: just as he caught sight of the Promised Land – with Huddersfield Town in 1920 and Leeds United four years later – he gave up the ghost. United had little time to spare to prevent their greatest opportunity being strangled at birth. Once more they were flirting with destitution and even the remote possibility of extinction if Crowther's patience expired and he foreclosed. Having come so far under one man and his plan, they urgently needed replacements for both.

4

—

LEND US A FIVER

Leeds United's promoted players, feted modestly as Second Division champions in a motorcade up Park Row on their Saturday evening return from Nelson, were treated to a tour of the Netherlands to celebrate their triumph. They played four matches in a fortnight, taking on the Dutch Olympic team, Ajax, Den Haag and Bolton Wanderers, sending back cheery dispatches from a trip to the tulip bulbfields, "a night that will never be forgotten by all the boys". As the windmills kept on turning in Amsterdam, back home Hilton Crowther's heart kept on yearning for a plausible exit strategy. Sixteen years after putting his first penny into the game, one of the two clubs he had helped to found and fund, Huddersfield Town, were champions of England and the other had made it a unique double for the broad acres of the supposedly soccer-resistant West Riding north of Sheffield.

As a financier, Crowther had a flair for creating a sound infrastructure, exerting influence on the city's officials and politicians and ground development. Building a successful football club is punishingly difficult but even for the extraordinarily wealthy prepared to take a savage haircut for purely philanthropic motives, disposing of one is trickier still. He had made himself a figure of hate in his home town in 1919 with the botched attempt to take the club out of Huddersfield rather than himself out of the club and had needed new money and a brother, as co-benefactor, to save his face. In theory, then, disentangling himself from Leeds United should have been simpler because it was a far more conventional exchange – assets (including debts) for a settlement on his investment. But having mortgaged United's debt to him to pay off his wife, his need, and those of his creditors, were pressing. Long before crowdfunding got its name, the Leeds board considered their options, patted their own pockets and shrugged, then sent the cap round again.

The latest recruit to the board, Major Albert Braithwaite, who was 29 years old when he took up the invitation and bought some shares, was elected chairman in Crowther's stead in June 1924. His father, also Albert, was an affluent businessman with interests in property, farming, sand, gravel and earthenware as well as a Conservative city councillor who had served a term as Lord Mayor in 1920-21. The younger Albert had enjoyed the classic Edwardian education for a member of the second generation of a newly prosperous family in the city – Woodhouse Grove, Leeds Grammar and Leeds University – before enlisting at the outbreak of war. His gallant service, at first with the Leeds Rifles, was rewarded with a commission and promotion, an MC and DSO. He returned to the city in the early Twenties after a spell with the British Military Mission to the United States where he met his wife. An ardent anti-socialist, he stood on the Conservative & Unionist ticket in Rothwell constituency at the 1922 general election, making a series of visceral speeches denouncing the Labour manifesto, yet despite the considerable advantage of facing no candidate from either of the Liberal factions and harvesting their voters, Braithwaite could not prevent the Labour incumbent from doubling his majority. A year later he stood in Pontefract and again came second to a Labour opponent who, this time, tripled his majority but came closer in the third general election in 23 months in October 1924 in Elland, losing to Labour by 488 votes. He would eventually find a safe haven in the north-east of the county, winning the rural Buckrose seat that took in Bridlington in a by-election in 1926, but when he took his place in the Leeds United boardroom, his primary income came from property and family businesses and his main non-political preoccupations were the troops with whom he had served.

This very establishment bright young thing made his first public proposal in June thanking Crowther for his generosity and, for the third occasion in five years, reminding the Leeds public that the club's future was in their hands. The twist this time was not framing it as a begging bowl appeal, nor a call to duty to buy shares of nominal value to prove their loyalty, 'owt' for essentially 'nowt'. Braithwaite cleverly sold it as an opportunity. They would pay Crowther off by raising £35,000 in mortgage debentures, which would be backed by a charge on the freehold, stands and entire assets of the company including the squad. It would take the form of £5 bearer bonds – an instrument notoriously guaranteeing anonymity – with the usual coupons attached to allow 'the bearer' to redeem the interest. Braithwaite said the club was willing to offer a return of 7.5 per cent per annum and would sell £5 debentures to cash buyers for £4 18s (a two per cent discount) but "the working man" (him again) could put 10s down followed by nine monthly payments of the same amount. Once fully paid up, each £5 bond would entitle the bearer to five voting shares, reviving the original idea of a democratically run club.

Braithwaite's conception and promotion of this financial device as the answer to United's problems won the approval of his predecessor. Tellingly, although we do not know how he did it because the minutes of the board meeting were cremated when the offices, dressing rooms and biggest stand were gutted by fire 30 years later, the new chairman proved persuasive in his request to be given longer than Crowther's two months for his scheme to mature. We can assume they were kindred spirits in terms of background and tastes – both were sons of rich men and had added to what had been passed down to them, they were well-travelled, patrons of numerous charities, familiar with a way of doing things, in or out of the lodge, and pillars of Leeds society. Braithwaite's connections and national political aspirations enveloped him in respectability to someone of his breed, something more substantial than the lawyers, accountants and council worthies who had been Crowther's allies before. Braithwaite's father was an alderman but he and Crowther, though devoted to the region, had wider horizons. Both saw themselves as being in business, a cut above the others who were very much in professions or trade.

In July, Braithwaite wrote a letter to the shareholders' association with more details, outlining a plan to issue 15,000 new shares as well as the debenture and to create a sinking fund of 2 per cent of the money raised to pay out the interest on the bearer bonds. The pre-eminent stadium architect Archibald Leitch had been engaged to value the ground and his estimate would form the lion's share of the assets in the scheme. The extra £15,000, he said, would be needed by the club to "pay its way" and strengthen the team. He would publish the prospectus in August and said that his ambition was to unify city and club by attracting and enfranchising "not less than 10,000 shareholders". Braithwaite addressed them in person the following month back at Salem Hall. Between the two meetings, in anticipation of the club turning a profit for the first time (though not announced until the filing date in October), Arthur Fairclough signed 10 players for the Division One campaign, merely a couple of whom played more than a dozen games. For example he recruited Cud Robson, an outside-right, from Cockfield Albion of the Northern Alliance, who did well for a while, and Jock Thom from Workington for a highest-priced £430, who did not. His knack for spotting players had not deserted him but those kinds of fees made dredging up dross an unavoidable hazard of sifting a diamond. Such was the high standard at the top end of the semi-professional game, particularly in the north-east and the junior teams in the west of Scotland, it was by no means uncommon to pitch new signings from those clubs straight into top-flight football. It was a policy at such frugal cost which was defined only by its successes and those who left after a year in the stiffs – in an era before clubs ran their own youth teams – had fulfilled their function: reserve teams needed populating as well. Still, one man's loosening of the purse strings is another's shoestring budget when buying in bulk.

As they went through their practice schedule of warm-up games at Elland Road and before the fans could assuage the nagging uncertainty caused by the precarious financial situation by watching them play, the city at large waited for Braithwaite to put some flesh on the bones. As a soldier he had enjoyed marching anthems and told his Salem Hall audience that he had commissioned a "war song" and new blue and white outfits for the Elland Road band to wear when they played it. The tune, if ever completed, has sadly been lost but Noel Coward's song from that year, *There's Life In The Old Girl Yet*, would have fitted the bill.

The chairman had spent a month finessing the offer and had devised an attractive incentive but first he had to lecture them in the old Tory patrician manner, which echoed some of his stump speeches about malingering and trade unions stifling entrepreneurial initiative. "Until it is properly stirred up," he said, "Leeds is the most lackadaisical place in the world and would let anybody else do its job. But with sound backing and enthusiastic workers I have no doubt about the success of our effort." It was emblematic of a political view that nothing was wrong with the world that could not be righted by painting on a smile and rolling up one's sleeves. Even with 90 years of overwhelming evidence to contradict it, such bollocks thrives today.

He had come up with two slogans, he said, "support your sport" and "lend us a fiver". They had all heard the first one before but the second struck a perfectly practical tone because it was a deal, not a gift. And now he explained how they would be paid back. Gross gate receipts of £25,000 had been taken in their promotion season and, fancifully forecasting a crowd of 50,000 for the first game of the 1924-25 season against Sunderland at Elland Road, he said they could comfortably expect at least £40,000 by May. Ten per cent of that would be put into the sink fund to pay £2,000 in interest each year and £2,000 to put aside for the redemption of the bonds at par, entitlement to which would be drawn by lot. He did not mention it but visiting clubs' share of the takings would be more than offset when Leeds played away in the First Division against clubs with bigger average crowds. It did mean that if they did not stay up, the income stream to his fund would dwindle to a trickle. The inherent risk of insolvency was not raised by the floor either. To do so, presumably, would have seemed defeatist. The leaders of the Conservative, Labour and Liberal parties in

Leeds were named as trustees and finally, to great applause, he declared that if they could raise £30,000 he would purchase the remaining £5,000 himself, stating that "nothing would please me better than to be made to pay". There was only one objection from a man who protested that as a £5 shareholder the debentures were prejudiced against his claims on dividends. After "shouting abusive remarks at Mr Crowther" he was ejected and the motion approved. The prospectus, it was agreed, would appear in the programme for the Sunderland match which, for once, would be handed out free as a marketing ploy and mark the launch.

The pre-1945 convention of opening the season on the last Saturday in August gave cricket adequate time to breathe but the 17-week break also afforded time for one last meeting before Leeds United could get the ball out in earnest. The subject, of course, was the club's future but even anxiety can only be sustained for so long before it dissolves into an everyday concern and fatigue. On the eve of the Sunderland match Braithwaite seized the moment to make one more push. Addressing the shareholders once more, he won their support to change the club's articles of association, which would allow the debenture to proceed. Crowther had spent £26,000 on improving Elland Road, he said, and Leitch's report, which he read out, had listed it as a tangible asset worth £45,000, more than enough on its own to cover the bond. The implications of what they would have to do to realise it – liquidate it by selling to a new tenant or finding buyers for the stands and a property developer for the land – were not addressed. The sole protest came from another original £5 shareholder and Braithwaite defused it by ignoring his reasons and offering to buy him out instead. When he refused to sell, the meeting treated him as if this had undermined his argument, applauded the chairman for playing the man rather than the ball and rallied behind Braithwaite. It concluded with a vote of thanks to Crowther, anointing him not just United's best pal but the greatest the sport in the city had ever known. In only three months Braithwaite had plotted a way out for him with honour and some of his money intact. They reconvened at Elland Road on the Saturday, ready "to give the scheme a good send-off". A club seemingly in harmony gratefully turned its eyes to the team.

Arthur Fairclough and his two members of staff – Bill Norman, who had rejoined his former Barnsley mentor from Blackpool in 1923 when Dick Ray went to Doncaster Rovers, and Allan Ure – picked none of their new signings and three survivors from their first-ever Football League match in the XI to take on Sunderland. Even though it was Wakes Week in the wool towns, which affected the entire cloth trade in the city, Elland Road's record crowd of 33,722 – 2,500 more than their previous high – was a chastening disappointment after Braithwaite's prediction of 50,000. But what they lacked in numbers they made up for in volume. The established half-back line of Harry Sherwin, Ernie Hart and Jim Baker had been first-choice for three years while Percy Whipp, Joe Richmond and Jack Swann had proved themselves the best central attacking three in the Second Division. They should have been the foundations of a decent side but age was catching up with Sherwin and the stalwart captain Baker, while Richmond's inexperience at centre-forward was unmistakeable. The *Yorkshire Post* had previewed the "epoch-making event" with boundless optimism in spite of Sunderland fielding internationals in each department and players of the calibre of Billy Clunas, Charlie Buchan and Warney Cresswell: "Considering how [they] romped away with the Second Division last season there cannot be a great deal of difference in class between them and their opponents... It would be fitting, and not at all contrary to precedent, if they were to make an equally brilliant start to their new career." And in their own way, they did. Sunderland had been third in 1923-24 and runners-up the season before but Leeds, as they have always done at their best, bared their teeth and tore into their opponents from the first blast of the referee's whistle.

Along the facing of the roof of the Scratching Shed ran a white hoarding a hundred yards in length with 'Support Your Sport – Lend Us A Fiver!' emblazoned in royal blue letters, emphasising the inception of two campaigns on and off the pitch. The reports in the city's papers were measured in the traditional style, describing a grand day out with typical detachment. The football beat back then was a small part of a journalist's general duties and some of the writing reads like everything else in the Post that day – dry as dust. We have to turn to *Athletic News* for a more authentic flavour. Beneath the headline 'Shock Tactics', Ivan Sharpe tells us, "For half an hour we might have been at Wembley with the magic FA Cup on view and prompting the players to frantic exertions. Sunderland struck a whirlwind. Leeds bore down upon their goal in a series of spare-nothing assaults. Their enthusiasm was wild and almost terrifying, coming so soon after the placid progress of cricket. We must prepare for the ear-piercing explosions of the football crowd but this record company raised at every expectation of a thrill – at Sunderland's end – the clamour normally associated with a goal."

Sharpe wrote that the crowd's intensity that day was the same he had witnessed at Doncaster, when the hooves of the leaders thundered up the straight, and reached twin peaks when Swann scored from an offside position and followed it on 30 minutes by heading in Joe Harris' corner to put United 1-0 up. Before the goal Albert McInroy, the Sunderland keeper who would move to Leeds a decade later, had thwarted several menacing attacks with "the power of anticipation and the safety of his clutching hand". In Elland Road's euphoria at scoring, and a cheer for Swann worthy of a St Leger winner, Sunderland hit back swiftly by outwitting Bert Duffield and Sherwin down the right and Jock Paterson turned in Billy Ellis' crisp centre. "The richly earned reward of much unusually hard labour had vanished within a minute," wrote Sharpe. Leeds tired in the second half, survived a scare when a probably legitimate Sunderland winner was ruled out for offside and Sharpe concluded by praising the hard-tackling of the half-back trio and the strategy of direct attacking, of taking the shortest route to goal. The illusion of 'burn out' plagues us still but here we have a bona fide example of a promoted team blitzing the opposition before fading away. It had been a raucously promising start. Now Fairclough and his trainer Allan Ure had to find a way to sustain such an urgent tempo if they had any chance of shocking the rest of the division.

That night at the Town Hall, Braithwaite presided over the official launch of the debenture and Kaye Aspinall, the director standing in for Crowther, accepted the honour of awarding the players their Second Division championship-winning medals at a cheerful civic ceremony. The supporters' club made gifts of a gold watch to each player and the directors made similar presents to Fairclough and his staff. "Now that at long last the city has secured First Division football," said Braithwaite, "it should not be necessary to urge upon the people, and more particularly the tradespeople, the desirability of leaving nothing undone to keep it." He was received warmly and the day's performance had obviously had a positive impact, as a Mr Clarke acknowledged when he moved his vote of thanks. "Leeds have already demonstrated their fitness for First Division football," he said. "They did not play second fiddle even to so formidable a combination as Sunderland." When the happy gathering broke up, all seemed set fair – the team could hold its own and the club's grand plan to get the orangutan of debt off its back had won the universal backing of all its vested interests.

United stumbled after their encouraging start, losing at Notts County and going down 3-0 at Cardiff City where 'the whirlwind' of the previous week was viewed by a different reporter as characterising "determination rather than finesse" from a side that was nothing more than "a well-balanced team of zealous workers". Only 20,000 turned up at Elland Road to watch their first win of the season, a 4-0 trouncing of Preston, who would go down that year, which brought 2,000 more to the ground for a 1-0 victory over Everton in their next home fixture. It was an autumn of spurts and slides, three wins on the trot when Whipp and Swann capitalised on the strength of the half-backs, followed by a run of seven games without a win in early winter that built up to a 6-1 rogering by Arsenal that left them in 17th. Bury, who had come up with them in second place, by contrast, were five points ahead in 12th and had won at Highbury. The turbulence was mirrored at the turnstiles. A new record 41,800 came for the visit of the champions Huddersfield in Herbert Chapman's competitive return to the ground when Swann's rasping shot held them to a 1-1 draw. Such was the crowd surge when the ball went in that one journalist complained his hat had been squashed down over his ears in the melee and ruined. Yet only 17,000 were present when they beat West Ham and, to universal relief, all hats present survived unmolested.

Footage of fans waving their caps as the players ran out to play Newcastle in November was captured by the newsreel cameras for a silent report about the 'Lend Us A Fiver' campaign. In two of three captions, obviously briefed by Braithwaite, it raised the stakes. "Though drawing huge gates the team may be sold if help is not forthcoming," read the first one, glossing over the shortfalls from pre-season estimates, then "these players are valued at £25,000", straight after a team shot staged on the pitch. Both were misleading and probably unnecessary but publicity is the oxygen of fundraising and any means of spreading the message was embraced. In truth the scheme was going well. By late November, one anonymous official said the club had to "guard against undue optimism" when he revealed that the sum of £20,000 had been reached. In one day of shop-to-shop canvassing in the city centre, volunteers had taken cheques for £250 and £200 and the *Leeds Mercury* reported: "At the offices in the Corn Exchange a miner placed 40 £1 notes on the counter and said, 'I want eight shares, lad.' Not content with that, he took two more shares, for which he will pay at the rate of 10s a month. A woman took two shares and paid £6 10s of the £10 in gold."

The club continued to pay to advertise the prospectus in the *Evening Post* throughout the winter, having failed to hit Crowther's December 31 deadline to pay off the £35,000 divorce mortgage guaranteed by Leeds' debt. The team managed its first win for eight weeks on Christmas Day when Whipp scored a hat-trick at home as they hammered Aston Villa 6-0. The visitors, however, carried a lame passenger on the right wing for 85 minutes and with 11 fit men won 2-1 in the return on Boxing Day. Sadly, the initial thumping victory was merely a welcome festive fillip and not a revival – United won only one more game in their next 13, the double over Preston. They were spared humiliation by their defensive resilience, but going scoreless in six of those matches exposed their shortcomings.

The half-backs and inside-forwards were not creating enough chances and the centre-forward was not clinical enough to convert the few that came his way from the wings. As we have seen, the average match-going United fan, for whom it is a choice rather than a compulsion, will not stomach tripe for long. There has always been a plentiful supply of that at far more competitive prices in the covered market. Understandably, then, Elland Road attendances in early 1925 were stuck fast under 20,000. They still flew the Second Division championship flag above the stand and were seven points ahead of Forest in 21st place. There was no panic but stagnation can be a poisonous blight on an ambitious club. United needed a shot in the arm and while the supporters provided the adrenaline, Braithwaite was at last ready to flick a vein and insert the hypodermic.

In early March he called a meeting of the debenture holders at Salem Hall and told them that the sum of £33,066 had been received and the bonds issued, £715 had been promised but not paid and would be chased while £1,218 was outstanding from those who had chosen to pay by instalment. Not only had they raised the money but they also had paid off a mortgage of £1,544 on land surrounding Elland Road from ordinary trading, and in addition to writing a £35,000 cheque to clear their debt to Crowther, had been able to give him £2,000 more against his charge on the profits. Braithwaite revealed that 1,330 people had come forward to buy bonds and he thanked them all, particularly those involved in the licensed trade and the markets. "It is with pride," he said, "that I can report that the Leeds United club and the whole of the property at Elland Road, free from mortgage and unencumbered, is now an asset of the Leeds public. Whatever money you have put into this debenture issue, whether it is £5 or £1,000 you will have in two years a security that will be well above par and there is no doubt at all that the club will be able to pay both interest on debenture bonds and provide a very considerable sum for the redemption of these debentures."

He announced the appointment of new directors and closed by thanking Crowther for his gift of £20,000 and for "handing over to the Leeds public a First Division football club". He said he hoped he would stay on the board for years to come and presented him with an album of photographs of his time as chairman, which had been signed by the players. Crowther, a man of few words, thanked the room and said: "The five years I have spent in Leeds have been among the happiest five years I have had." And with that he gradually began to recede from prominence. Though he continued to be a director for the next 32 years until his death at home in Blackpool at the age of 77, Crowther had done his bit and focused his charitable impulses on less troublesome causes.

Election to the Football League or promotion to the First Division ought to mark the points when Leeds United came of age. Yet March 1925 is a more appropriate moment because it was then that the club stopped being a one-man band and a financial hostage to his favours. 'At last,' one is tempted to sigh, 'are we done with the money?' Regrettably not, but at least for the next 55 years it becomes an undercurrent, throwing up the odd tsunami that threatens to engulf all rather than the exhausting and constant angst that began and all but finished the club's century. The success of the bond scheme was Leeds United's rope to the shore. Now the club was secure they were free to turn their attention to the team.

After years of bargain-hunting, following the meeting Fairclough spent "a considerable sum in excess of £2,000", according to the *Leeds Mercury*, for the Raith Rovers centre-forward Tom Jennings, £1,500 on Chesterfield's wing-half Willis Edwards and £2,000 on the nose for Russell Wainscoat, the Middlesbrough inside-forward. The secretary-manager had always operated at the 'hit-and-miss' level during his time at Elland Road but armed with significant funds he struck gold: Jennings became the first United player to score a hundred league goals, Edwards their first England international and Wainscoat bagged 93 goals in six seasons and also earned an England cap. Not bad for a week's work. The gate leapt by 10,000 for Jennings' debut and when all three started together for the first time, Leeds beat Liverpool, who were 13 places ahead of them in sixth, 4-1. They managed three more victories from their last seven games and ended their maiden Division One season in 18th.

Jennings had scored 61 goals in three seasons for Raith and he quickly established himself as United's most charismatic and effective player, Elland Road's first proper darling. Contemporaries talk of a "nippy" striker who "knits his wings exceedingly well". He was one of the Rovers players who was shipwrecked off the coast of Galicia in 1924 en route to a tournament in the Canary Islands and made light of the alarming incident with a comment that would endear him to his new public, too, claiming that before jumping into the lifeboat "being good Scotsmen" they had gone below deck to grab their money. Jennings was lithe and smart and fully exploited the change in the offside law that was enacted in the summer of 1925, reducing the number of players between the attacker and the goal required from three to two. Mayhem proliferated throughout the First Division where two-man defences were left horribly vulnerable by centre-halves who maintained parallel lines with the right- and left-halves and were slow to drop back and help their seriously overloaded full-backs. At the most extreme example, Burnley, there were 193 goals in their 42 matches – 85 for, 108 against – contrasting with a combined total of 121 from the previous season. Nothing quite so dramatic for Leeds, who managed 64 goals, up 18 from the year before, and conceded 76, 17 worse off. Jennings scored 26 of them in another worrying campaign of short positive bursts and longer troughs. For all their outlay, and Edwards' form earning him a call-up to play against Wales at the age of only 22, United improved by a mere two points and came perturbingly close to relegation. John Armand, an Anglo-Indian inside-forward, inevitably nicknamed 'Snowy' for obvious if primitive reasons, chipped in with nine goals in Wainscoat's absence through injury but Hart, the No.5, and the entire team did not adjust quickly to the new law and the defence was overrun 4-0 by Huddersfield, 4-3 by Manchester City, 6-3 by Burnley, 4-1 at Arsenal and 4-2 by West Ham. Such were the toils that losing 2-1 at Maine Road in their penultimate game put them in serious jeopardy of the drop.

In 20th place and above Burnley on goal average with City one spot higher, United took on Tottenham at home. Cicero's well-worn adage of "where there's life, there's hope" did not seem to apply that day as only 16,158 turned up to roar them on in an Elland Road monsoon. In mitigation, as well as the weather, Saturday, 1 May 1926 was also the day the TUC called for a general strike to defend the miners and announced it would start on Monday. *Athletic News*' Rufus discerned widespread "palpitations" in the stands and on the field. He was not impressed by United, "candidly not of the First Division standard" but they prevailed all the same, bludgeoning their way to a 4-1 victory with Jennings scoring twice in the second half and Whipp bundling the ball over the line with his torso. Manchester City's 3-2 defeat at Newcastle, a match where the curse of 'typical City' was born after they missed a life-saver penalty, sent them down instead.

Although Leeds were safe, Rufus' keynote was cautionary. United's forward line, he wrote in tribute to Jennings, comprised "one player and four nondescripts" but he contradicted his disdain by singling out the Scottish full-backs, Jimmy Allan and Bill Menzies, the half-back Tom Townsley, a December signing from Falkirk, and Edwards for praise. Add in Jennings, Ernie Hart and the injured Wainscoat and it gave them more than half a team that should have been good enough. Fairclough was counselled to change tack, tighten up and find better wingers. After two close shaves, the razor's edge was getting too close to the throat for comfort.

5

THE DEMON MARKSMAN

Four days after the victory over Tottenham had confirmed First Division football for a third season, the chairman, Major Albert Braithwaite, was elected to parliament in the Buckrose by-election. He had fought a vigorous campaign under the Conservative and Unionist slogan 'Keep the Reds Out' and toured the constituency with a party from Leeds that included his parents. His friend Sir Charles Wilson also accompanied them. To Tories he was, 'Good Old Charlie', simultaneously the member for Leeds Central and leader of the council, a United debenture trustee and a man who modestly professed "I am Leeds" when introducing himself to a friendly audience. In his hometown and surrounding coalfields the Emergency Powers Act had enabled the government to put troops on the streets to ensure supplies of food and fuel during the General Strike. But up in the Wolds, Braithwaite charmed the landladies of 'Brid', assured 'the fisherfolk' of Filey that he would be their champion, and rode with the gentry and their foxhounds. In spite of an outbreak of foot and mouth disease in the county, he held one rally in a large farmhouse kitchen, standing on the stone flags to address agricultural workers in front of a roaring fire while curtained by curing hams dangling on strings from the ceiling above him. Throughout he stressed his practicality and that of his party "led by businessmen and not theorists", claiming that socialism meant "the speed of the nation would be the speed of the slowest worker in the land" which would force "the country to go down in just the same way Russia had done". It was effective enough to earn him victory, albeit on a reduced majority, and he held the seat until the Conservatives were swept away in 1945. One of his bolder electoral pledges took him to Hull's Paragon Station to fulfill his promise to help break the strike by driving a locomotive on the Hull-to-Scarborough line but on the day he reported for duty the TUC called off its action and left the miners to stand alone.

While United's chairman may have been denied his engine-driver fantasy, Braithwaite's time during the summer was absorbed by constituency and parliamentary business as well as running his other companies. The United board had been swollen to 10 members in the wake of the debenture.

Ernest Pullan, scion of the Beeston building firm which had built up the Spion Kop banking with its waste, was joined by Rowland Winn, a friend of Henry Ford, who combined ownership of a successful car dealership on Woodhouse Lane with chairmanship of the council's Highways Committee. That conflict of interest, which seems astounding today, was compounded by the free rein he was also given to argue publicly for the banishment of trams from the city centre to create more room on the roads for the motor vehicles he sold. Eric Clarke, a solicitor and alderman of the city, essentially replaced Alf Masser, who stood down in November, and the leading lights of the Shareholders' Association took their seats alongside Hilton Crowther and the rest of the originals. It was these men, after 18th- and 19th-place First Division finishes, who declared themselves quietly optimistic before the season began. Arthur Fairclough disposed of seven reserves, including the former captain Jim Baker, and bought no one into his first-team squad, hanging his hat on an injury-free season for his major players. Kaye Aspinall, the wine and spirits merchant, owner of the Lyceum Picture House and chairman of Betty's Cafes, increasingly became the board's spokesman when Braithwaite was otherwise engaged. It fell to him to blame their past struggles on "over-anxiety" and said the board "deserved sympathy not blame". The policy, he said, had been "building up a team so we can be ranked with Huddersfield and among the best" and he was confident that day was now imminent.

Having made gradual progress with the Crowther stabilisers on, Leeds had a foothold of sorts in the First Division, financially free at last with a team including Willis Edwards, an England wing-half, a much-coveted 'centre' in Tom Townsley, 'master craftsman' Russell Wainscoat at inside-left and Tom Jennings, a prolific striker with sadistic shooting power and an uncontainable, pogo-stick jump. So what is the quintessential Leeds United thing to do when the game's afoot and the time is ripe to push on? Of course, they got themselves relegated.

Aspinall sneaked an interesting nugget out on the publication of the annual accounts in November which showed a loss for the previous season of £4,103. When asked whether it had affected United's ability to strengthen the team, he revealed that the three players bought to save them from relegation in 1924-25, Willis, Wainscoat and Jennings, had cost a combined total of £9,568. Only Jennings' transfer fee had hitherto been undisclosed and if we subtract the £3,500 they had registered paying for the other two, and account for small add-ons it suggests a sum that might have challenged the British record of £5,500 Sunderland had given for Warney Cresswell in 1922. Whatever the cost, he was worth every penny and his feats in his second full season at Elland Road deserve greater recognition than to be remembered as the one solace of a grim slide.

It took him a while to get going – he scored his first goal in the third match a 2-2 draw at Old Trafford, a game between teams described ominously by our old friend Rufus as "two Uniteds of no distinction". After a 5-2 hammering by the FA Cup-winners Bolton at Elland Road on opening day and a frustratingly drab 0-0 away draw with Cardiff, it was an improvement of sorts but their squandering of a 2-0 lead was the stark harbinger for a winter of disintegration. Victory came at last in their fifth game, the first of four successive home wins that pushed them up from 20th to seventh. In the third of them, the 4-1 drubbing of Arsenal, Jennings scored a hat-trick, each of them the result of rasping shots and the more direct passing of Townsley through the middle to compensate for the enduring weakness of wingers who, in the vernacular of the game, couldn't knock the skin off a rice pudding let alone tear the arse off a Bluto-sized full-back. The match-ball on Jennings' mantelpiece was joined by two more from the next two games – he bagged four goals in a 4-2 defeat of Liverpool at Anfield and four again in the 4-1 thrashing of Blackburn Rovers to turbo-charge a run of scoring in seven consecutive matches that began with 13 in four games. A fourth hat-trick against Bury in mid-November ended his remarkable streak with 19 from nine. As a bonus, this spree bequeathed Leeds a decent player's nickname at last when Jennings, courtesy of the *Athletic News*, mutated into 'The Demon Marksman'. The *Yorkshire Evening Post* opted less resoundingly for 'Prince of Good Fellows'. Against Liverpool he was praised for his thunderbolt shooting and opportunism. When he caught the old Thompson laced-ball cleanly he had enough power to bruise the casing and strain the iron stays that pinned the nets down. He had a touch of that gallus common to all the best Scots and gorged on balls struck over the top or straight through the middle that allowed him to terrorise half-backs and catch keepers unprepared with pot shots.

However it is hard to contend that Jennings' glut of goals were anything more than camouflage for an unbalanced team. Willis Edwards had established himself as England's regular right-half, assuring his place with doughty box-to-box stamina, sturdiness in the air and crisp tackling, a player of poise and precision whose passing was admired by his greatest contemporaries such as Charlie Buchan and Eddie Hapgood. 'Towering' Townsley, too, was highly praised for his ability to loft accurate passes upfield for Jennings in addition to his diligent defensive work but Hart managed only eight games all season, while Wainscoat, who had briefly been put on the transfer list by Fairclough at one point, missed three months with injury. The fallibility of the full-backs, weakness out wide and long-standing holes at inside-right and left-half were not addressed in time.

It all caught up with United in the autumn when they lost three successive matches including a 4-1 home defeat by champions Huddersfield. In that game they had maintained a 1-0 lead given to them by Jennings' goal until the 78th minute before crumbling. On 18 December they beat Wednesday 4-1 at Elland Road when Edwards scored the only goal he would contribute in his first nine seasons at Leeds United, a sub-Batty return from the man in the No.4 shirt. After two defeats the win was portrayed as a corner turner, but then they lost five on the bounce, which kicked them all the way down from 11th to 19th, and they could not rise from the canvas. The winless run stretched on and on to 14 games and a 2-1 March away defeat by Everton, who had been in the bottom two, consigned United to 21st and two points from safety. They had tried to recalibrate by signing the Scotland inside-right Jock White from Hearts for £5,700, a forward as prolific as Jennings, who had been the Jambos' top scorer in each of the past five seasons. He chipped in with two goals and made a couple more with his incisive throughballs for the centre-forward but would only show his true quality the following season.

As for United's relegation rivals, Dixie Dean's absence with injury at the start of August had hit Everton hard and they lost seven and drew one of their opening eight League games without him. Although they had gradually clawed their way back to proximity with the clubs in and out of 20th place over the winter when Dean shook off the rust, by contrast with Leeds, Everton's board put their thumb on the scales in the usual way, spending £20,000 on 10 players in February and March, the five most expensive of whom, Warney Cresswell, Jerry Kelly, Ted Taylor, Dick Forshaw and Tony Weldon, went straight into the first team and were in the side that did for Leeds at Goodison Park. Taylor, a former England keeper, Cresswell, an England right-back, plus the others, a right-half and two inside forwards, represented a serious transfusion of fresh blood, an expensive expression of intent. All five, incidentally, also picked up league championship medals the next season.

In lieu of the chequebook, the United board offered a consoling arm. Fairclough said after the defeat by Everton that the directors "had decided to make the best of things with their present team. We have abundant faith in them and believe we will yet avoid relegation. The play of the team recently has been of such a character that no great improvement could be guaranteed by the securing of one or even two new men. At times the team moves so well together as to give every hope of success, yet a little later in the same match the whole side seems to fall to pieces. Confidence and encouragement are the two principal requirements of the team at the moment". Coincidentally they were the two cheapest as well but on this occasion the directors command some sympathy. How can you budget with any accuracy when gates oscillate wildly? Yorkshire derbies and feast day games were well attended – 48,590 on 27 December for the visit of Newcastle United, 36,364 for Huddersfield in March during that barren spell but merely 16,816 for a Saturday match against Manchester United and 13,776 on a Wednesday for Liverpool. Paying £785 for the left-winger Tom Mitchell from Newcastle's reserves and that large fee for White was about as much as they could afford.

After Everton, United had 10 games to save themselves yet the defence kept capsizing them. Using the centre-half Townsley as Jennings' schemer was well-rewarded in the goals-for list. It also left them conceding 88, evidence that Fairclough, who had begun his managerial career at Oakwell in 1898, was too slow to adapt to the offside law changes that left his team's goal hopelessly exposed. Their first league win of 1927 did not arrive until 2 April, 3-1 over bottom side West Brom the week after a 6-2 gubbing at Roker Park. Back-to-back defeats when only victories would do allowed Everton to pull away, Leeds never got close enough to make them quiver and were relegated with two games to spare when they went down 4-1 at White Hart Lane on St George's Day, one of 18 away defeats in 21 matches. The *Yorkshire Post* called them "Victims of bad luck" in the headline of the match report but it was too kind. They had half a fine side who always put up a good fight but they had become increasingly incapable of covering for the positional indiscipline, timidity and chronic inconsistency of the rest. In Athletic News on Monday morning, the following item appeared at the back of the book, nine pages on from the report: "Leeds United invite applications for the position of secretary-manager. Only men of experience need apply with full particulars to the Chairman." Arthur Fairclough, 'the man in the bowler hat', the football insider at the spearhead of the charm offensive whose popularity in the game had delivered election to the Football League and United's secretary-manager for seven seasons, had fallen on his sword.

Fairclough's discontent had been brewing for some time. Profiles of him typically mentioned his Pickwickan girth constrained by an inflated tract of waistcoat, the hat and ready smile, but the latter had been missing for most of the season. He first tendered his resignation after the 4-2 defeat at Bury in early April, an offer that was neither accepted nor rejected. He was told to wait for Braithwaite's return and a full board meeting. In that hiatus Leeds won one and lost three matches, relegation was confirmed and the classified ad was placed. He left saying he had "not been comfortable and not seen eye-to-eye with the directors" for a while. The exact nature of these disagreements is difficult to identify but probably his desire to sell Wainscoat, an initiative from which Leeds later rowed back, the continuing influence of the selection committee which led to rotation rather than replacement in the problem positions, and the transfer budget played a part. At the age of 54 Fairclough had already earned a Football League long service medal but with the exception of one last year at Barnsley at the end of the decade, his days in team management were done.

Five men were shortlisted for the vacancy and were interviewed in June: Jimmy Seed, the Tottenham and England inside-forward, John Chapman, the former Manchester United manager who had been suspended for the 1926-27 season by the FA for mysteriously and still unspecified 'improper conduct', Harry Parkes, the Chesterfield manager who had nurtured and mentored Willis Edwards, Percy Smith, secretary-manager of Nelson, and Dick Ray, Fairclough's former assistant whose highest position in the Third Division North with Doncaster Rovers in four seasons at Belle Vue was eighth. Aged 32, Seed would have been the most intriguing candidate but would have cost a fee to be installed as player-manager. When Leeds chose someone else Aldershot appointed him as their manager but Tottenham refused to release him from his contract without recompense and instead sold him to The Wednesday as a player. Spurs went down without him and he captained Wednesday to the title in 1929 and 1930. In management he took Charlton Athletic from the Third to First Division and won the FA Cup with them in 1947 but he was lost to Leeds for want of a nail (and some foresight). They instead went for Dick Ray, the man they knew best, the 51-year-old former Leeds City full-back and United's team manager in their first Midland League games, a sound if not spectacular appointment.

Ray had been born and grew up in the Potteries and retained a Staffordshire stubbornness and terseness of expression more common to the Leeds native than the talkative Fairclough's Barnsley affability. He used his contacts at Doncaster to make his first and only significant pre-season signing, bringing in Charlie Keetley, younger brother of two of his Rovers players, a 21-year-old from the Rolls-Royce factory who had scored 80 goals in a season for Alvaston and Boulton in the Derby and District League. United did not need him until the new year when he made a formidable contribution after Tom Jennings succumbed to a bout of blood poisoning that would blight the rest of his career.

Leeds got off to a blistering start, at least in terms of goals, and it was emblematic that of the 14 they scored in their first five games, Jennings claimed only four. Ray had stuck with the same team that finished the relegation season, the "boys of the old brigade" as the *Leeds Mercury* put it, and out wide Bobby Turnbull and Billy Mitchell, who had flailed about in the First Division, benefited from the team's new tactics, encouraging wing-halves to hit more diagonal balls down the outside instead of hoisting them up to Jennings. Russell Wainscoat and Jock White diligently linked midfield to the wide men and fed off the centre-forward, their touch allowing them to thrive in the broader inside channels left by Division Two defenders. Ernie Hart's return to form and fitness inspired Ray to reinstate him at centre-half and move his captain, Tom Townsley, to right-back, and when George Reed, signed from Altofts in 1924 made the left-half position his own, all the main flaws in Fairclough's side had been addressed. Consistency of selection meant that 10 players featured on 30 or more games and five in 40 plus, a luxury denied Ray's predecessor. At the end of the annual pre-season dinner at the Griffin Hotel, Major Braithwaite told the players the club "was satisfied they had some of the finest players in the country and wanted to forget forever the performances of last season". It took them three weeks to erase the stain. As early as September the *Mercury* was praising the "tenacious as a ferret Edwards", the "*esprit de corps*" and concluding that "Leeds are a united team nowadays is beyond dispute".

There were some sensational victories in the autumn – 4-0 over Forest, 5-0 at Swansea, 6-2 when Reading visited – but it wasn't until December that United properly clicked and a run of seven successive wins, starting with the 5-0 evisceration of Chelsea who were top and seven points ahead of Leeds at kick-off, propelled them into contention for the title. Frustratingly, they continued to be plagued by embarrassingly poor gates during that sequence – 12,889 for Stoke City on Christmas Eve and 12,752 on New Year's Eve when South Shields came.

Ray then showed his mettle during a wobble in February that began with a 3-1 defeat at Hull when he dropped Jimmy Potts, the popular goalkeeper who had played 84 matches in succession, for chucking two in at Boothferry Park. His back-up, Bill Johnson, fared little better although another reserve, Keetley, who had fired in six goals in four starts as Jennings' winter deputy, flourished in the spring when illness ruled the Scot out for months with 11 games left. The centre-forward was not as clinical as Jennings and was prone, according to his critics, to hitting rising shots so hard that they frequently cleared the bar. For the first season, though, enough chances were being created by the wingers for a Leeds striker to shine regardless of the mediocre conversion rate one would expect of such an inexperienced player and he claimed 12 goals in a promotion-clinching unbeaten charge of eight wins in nine games. In the last of them, at Chelsea, Keetley's double in a 3-2 victory sent them up with two matches to spare in front of a crowd of nigh on 50,000. United had taken a 3-0 lead when Keetley grabbed his second with a fierce strike before injuries to both wingers left them overwhelmed and Chelsea, who needed to win, rallied. Potts, happily reinstated, pulled off three saves Athletic News describes as "miraculous" to close out the game.

By the season's end Keetley had 18 goals to match Wainscoat's tally while White and Jennings had 21 apiece in United's total of 98, 29 more than their previous peak and a figure unmatched 91 years on.

Ray and his team were met at Wellington Station on their return from Stamford Bridge to the city on Saturday night by the Lord Mayor and a large party of well-wishers who clustered round them and drummed their backs in appreciation. They missed out on the title by losing their final two matches, but it did not dampen enthusiasm for the civic reception on the evening they came back from defeat at Stoke. Thousands lined the charabanc's route through the city and scores were locked out of the packed 'smoking concert' held in their honour by the supporters' club. George Ratcliffe, the mayor, said in his 40 years as a fan of the game, he was sure "in the past three months Leeds United were playing the finest football he had ever seen" and Braithwaite added that he was "probably the proudest man in England right now". Going straight back up is always the best remedy.

Guilty of getting ahead of themselves all too frequently in the past, the board gave Ray the attainable target of winning more games than he lost on their return to Division One and he fell short of accomplishing it by one. United won 16 matches and finished in a highest-ever position of 13th. It was a curious season which they began carrying a £6,000 deficit from the year in the Second Division when they had maintained their squad and turned down a £6,000 bid from Sheffield United for Jock White. Their style in winning promotion would probably have precluded significant player purchases anyway and the policy brought an immediate if temporary boom. They were fourth at Christmas, having won their first seven home games and also beaten champions Everton at Goodison Park. Hart and Wainscoat won their first England caps but for all the class and early season goals, putting four past Villa, Manchester City and West Ham and three into the net against Bury, Manchester United, Portsmouth and Cardiff in their first

11 games at Elland Road, leaving aside the usual pre-season guff about a city proud of its club, gates leapt above 30,000 merely twice. Jennings managed only 17 games and Keetley again stepped up, top-scoring with 20 in 28 matches including two hat-tricks in the second-half of the season when the whirlwind attacking strategy had all but petered out.

Leeds had fallen only one place to fifth by 9 February when they played West Ham at Upton Park with reserve keeper James Wilson in goal, a Ray signing from Rothwell Amateurs. The poor chap, playing his third and last game for the club, was made the scapegoat after a 2-2 draw at half-time on a treacherously icy pitch was transformed by the Hammers' England centre-forward Vic Watson, who completed a double hat-trick in an 8-2 defeat. The press blamed Turnbull, the Leeds winger, for self-indulgence on the ball and not being content to beat just one man. The half-backs, including Hart and Edwards, did not escape censure either for roaming too far forward. But it was Wilson who paid the price.

Leeds' rise in Ray's first season had been earmarked by a string of winning runs and their consolidation during his second on their return to the First Division by a fast start. In his third season, United's last of their first decade, they combined the two, winning seven straight in September and October to take them to the top for the first time in their history on 28 September, a spot they occupied for six weeks, not a bad way to commemorate the 10th anniversary of the dissolution of Leeds City. Dave Mangnall, a 24-year-old Wigan miner, score 10 goals in a single reserve game in September and was given his debut when both Jennings and Keetley were injured the following month. He pitched in with six goals in nine games but never featured again. Another September debutant Jack Milburn, on the other hand, became the darling of the Elland Road crowd, a tough combative full-back with cannon-footed clearances who could play on either side and would be a regular for 10 years.

It was not such a two-faced season as the one that preceded it – United did lose five in succession in November but recaptured their verve in fits and starts when 1929 turned into the Thirties. They ended the campaign with four home victories to cement fifth spot, a record high that would last for 36 years. And yet there were the usual disappointments: the gate for a 2-2 draw with Sheffield United was 7,569, while the day a Keetley hat-trick helped them do the double over the reigning and future champions, Sheffield Wednesday – albeit, appropriately, on a Wednesday afternoon in April – saw 3,950 fans brave the rain and gloom, and a mere 10,596 clicked through the turnstiles for the 'Roses' match against Manchester United on a Saturday, their last at home in Leeds' finest season to date. Still, the club turned a profit of almost £5,400 and announced when the accounts were published that in five years they had paid off £7,000 of the £35,000 taken up in debentures. Because of their obviously encouraging trajectory and Ray's aversion to buying ready-made and established talent, the board was hopeful of persuading the outstanding bondholders to convert the balance into ordinary shares. The directors spoke of their pleasure that they had not wasted money on signing players, unlike relegated Everton and Burnley, and congratulated themselves and Ray on their prudence. Isn't hubris a bugger? Leeds United had finally made it to calm waters and a new decade. Cue the next storm.

6

POLISH WITHOUT PUSH

Leeds is fortunate to have two eminently wise and engaging observers of working-class life in the city during the Thirties and Forties. Alan Bennett grew up in Armley to the north-west of Elland Road, while Keith Waterhouse was born just to the east but moved further out as an infant to the Halton Moor Estate, where he set his first novel, *There Is A Happy Land*. Neither, sadly, had much time for sport but their great contemporary Peter O'Toole did, his Hunslet boyhood and bookie father nurturing a lifelong love for rugby, cricket and the turf. United were absent from his passions, depriving us of the spectacle of our finest actor joining another celebrated Jimmy Porter, Kenneth Haigh, as a regular in the VIP seats in the Sixties, welcome in the exclusive, carpeted innards of the West Stand among the camelhair-coat 'quality'.

It is O'Toole who best captures the communities around the club in those decades though typically, in his flamboyant and impressionistic memoir Loitering With Intent, he marries Hunslet to Holbeck to create 'Hunsbeck', a childhood playground of grazed knees, racing tricycles and diphtheria. "These brick rabbit hutches," he writes, "had been studded up, squat and meagre, back to back, row upon row along criss-crossing cobblestoned miles of nasty, sunless streets. These shelters and dormitories had been squashed between and around and up and down their places of work. Factories which had manufactured iron goods, steel goods, wooden goods, lead goods, rubber goods; engine-makers, string-makers, paper-makers, nail-makers; cotton mills, wool mills, saw mills; freight yards, gas works, coal mines, slagheaps, potteries, warehouses and tall, tall, thick brick chimneys."

This is the ground on which Leeds United stood in 1930, before the slum clearances and corporation housing schemes transformed the landscape. For all the squalor and choking black smoke, the diversity of the economy inoculated the city from the worst of the Great Depression and the clothing industry, the largest employer, did not merely survive, it prospered. When Labour finally won control of the council in 1933, it gradually began to take on more responsibilities and workers, commissioning construction firms to build the city of the future with thousands of houses and flats to increase the municipal stock, expand the university and undertake other public works to reshape the civic heart of Leeds. Exploiting its geography the city also thrived as a distribution centre for the north of England, via rail and road, and developed its expertise in the printing business to expand from newspapers and theatre bills to text and exercise books and even, famously, playing cards and board games, including the British licence for Monopoly, at Waddington's in Thwaite Gate.

Leeds United's fifth-place finish in 1929-30 should have empowered them to capitalise on the progress they had made and kick on to establish themselves as serious contenders. They had a young team, a secretary-manager with an astute eye for semi-pro players who had the skills and character to make it in the First Division, a broad and productive scouting network and a stadium that was, perhaps for the only time, up to date if not exactly state of the art. English football in the interwar years was not a closed shop at the elite level. West Bromwich, Burnley and Manchester City were all champions for the first time as well as Huddersfield and Arsenal, who built on winning maiden titles to become the league's dominant team for five and eight of those years respectively. In addition Huddersfield, Bolton, Cardiff, Arsenal, Sunderland and Portsmouth were all first-time FA Cup winners during those 20 seasons. It should not have been beyond the wit of Leeds United to match their achievements. Instead it was a decade of missed opportunity, shortfall of ambition and failure to fulfil promise, all bound up with the seemingly fixed half-heartedness of the fanbase. The extreme financial hardship suffered by the north-east, north-west, South Wales and Yorkshire coalfields during the Thirties, when unemployment on Tyneside and Wearside was pushed as high as 70 per cent, did not buffet Leeds' mixed economy of industrial, retail, service and export sectors with such devastation. Yet the drop-off in gates at Elland Road was more severe than at St James' Park, Roker Park, Hillsborough and Maine Road, and much slower to recover. The take it or leave it vacillations of the Leeds public towards its football team were ingrained and only winning something would change that. The debate about whether support or success was the chicken or the egg in all this would confound the board for most of the century.

Take the first full season of the decade, for example. In August they blooded the 21-year-old Wilf Copping at left-half in the opening game against Portsmouth and he established himself so swiftly that George Reed never got another look-in when he recovered from injury. Copping would not be picked for his country until 1933 and for a season Leeds enjoyed an all-England half-back line of Willis Edwards, Ernie Hart and Copping, but it did not need a velvet and gold braid, tasselled cap or winning the fancy of a master butcher on the national selection committee to confirm their excellence. The Earl of Harewood, who would serve as United's club president for half its life, from 1961-2011, first went to a match at Elland Road at Christmas 1932 as the eight-year-old Viscount Lascelles for a 0-0 draw with the champions Arsenal. "It had Alex James and Cliff Bastin on one side," he remembered, "and Willis Edwards, Wilf Copping and Ernie Hart on the other. Since then, at least partly as a direct result, any Saturday during the season when I don't watch football seems to me a day that has got unaccountably out of step."

Copping had joined Leeds from Middlecliffe and Darfield Rovers in March 1930, a team based in the shadow of the Houghton Main pithead in the Dearne Valley to the east of Barnsley. As a boy he had wanted to be a jockey but went down the mines at 14 and stayed there when he was not taken on by his boyhood club after a trial at Oakwell in 1929. It was said by his team-mate Ted Drake at Arsenal that in the long break between seasons when Copping was on summer wages, he sometimes still put in a shift at the pit because he was embarrassed by "how cushy a life London footballers had". In similar vein, in 1990 David Batty spent part of the off-season following promotion accompanying his father's crew on their bin round, "days of back-breaking work" carried out surreptitiously, like Copping, to stop the hazards from giving his manager a heart attack. "I got a genuine sense of satisfaction out of the experience," Batty wrote, "probably the first and last top-class professional footballer to combine his sporting role with that of corporation bin man." When Copping moved to Highbury in 1934, he revived union membership at the club, overturning years of Herbert Chapman's disregard for the Professional Footballers' Association. It is a measure of both men that they never forgot where they came from. Copping, in particular, aged only 17 but three years a collier at the time he was called out on strike in 1926, clearly appreciated the value of solidarity.

Although Copping played more games for Leeds United in two spells than he did in five seasons at Highbury, Arsenal's trophies and glamour have given them proprietorship of his memory. Newspaper convention deprived professionals of their first names in reports, they were deemed unworthy of interview, the few contemporary quotations tended to appear fleetingly in the local press and the players' modesty generally rendered them banal. His character was plain to see in his performance but any embellishments we owe mainly to Arsenal. At Leeds his habit of not shaving three days before a game was well-known, one of his many superstitions that came with the bonus of giving him an air of intimidating, blue-chinned barbarity. "He felt it made him look mean and hard," wrote Sir Stanley Matthews. "It did and he was." His wonky, flattened nose, splintered on several occasions, added to the terrifying aspect and Bob Wall, Chapman's personal secretary and later Arsenal's club secretary, noted his "satanic appearance". Any team-mate who made the mistake of disrupting his concentration by talking to him in the dressing room, was verbally and physically threatened. He had two maxims – "the first person in a tackle never gets hurt" and "get stuck in" which summed up his approach. He was bone-jarringly uncompromising in the challenge, worthy of the nickname 'Iron Man' which was later exhumed for his true heir in the No.6 shirt, Norman Hunter, with one difference. While Norman often struck his prey from the side or less frequently from behind, Copping more usually stopped them head on, using the full weight of his body to pole-axe opponents, his left leg braced for bowel-withering impact. Like Hunter, he was more than a guided missile. A fine defensive header of the ball, he was equally as good at giving a pass as winning possession and was 'boy stood on the burning deck' brave. Although he was never cautioned, his reputation as a player who was 'hard but fair' was more the product of team-mates who benefited from his toughness and the hard-nosed culture of the game back then than a just appraisal. Bill Shankly thought him an assassin who deliberately did him in an England v Scotland match at Wembley, Matthews remembered him hitting the Italy captain Luis Monti so hard during 'The Battle of Highbury' in 1934 that "he went up like a rocket and came down like a bag of hammers" while the journalist Ken Jones, a former winger with Southend United and Swansea Town and subsequently the chief sports writer of the *Sunday Mirror* and *Independent*, recalled the advice given to him by Copping, his coach at Roots Hall: "There's no sense in raising tha' hands on the field," he preached. "Tha' can do more damage with tha' feet."

In normal circumstances, augmenting a team that had stormed to fifth the previous season with such a singularly abrasive and effective half-back ought to have galvanised United's chances, even though he was understandably green. Instead they got off to a poor start, tricked everyone by scoring seven goals twice in the autumn in victories over Blackpool and Middlesbrough, but could not rise above 13th place and suffered long winless streaks in October, November, January and February. Their short passing game and lack of pace, a strategy of using inside forwards, who were plainly not up to it, as the creative impetus, was found wanting on waterlogged pitches with swollen, saturated, heavy footballs when looking for longer passes. Belting over crosses from the wings would have suited conditions better. In October a letter writer to the *Yorkshire Evening Post* after a 4-0 defeat at Filbert Street identified Leeds' best line-up as follows: Potts; a New Man, Milburn; Edwards, Hart, Reed; a New Man, a New Man, Jennings, Wainscoat and a New Man. In fact Jennings was almost finished, making eight appearances and scoring four goals as Dick Ray stuck with the more robust Charlie Keetley and the likelihood of the manager signing one 'New Man' who could go straight into the first team, let alone five, was remote. Whenever he was asked why that was, he reiterated his faith in his players and emphasised that they were young and would improve. He would always prefer paying £50 to Usworth Colliery for Billy Furness or signing Tom Cochrane from St Peter's Albion and bringing them through the reserves than buying an international.

On 30 December the club held its AGM and announced a profit of £5,400 after setting aside the sum to pay the return on the debentures and said the board intended to pay a dividend to ordinary shareholders of 5 per cent for the first time in 10 years. United were 15th in the table but the director, Ernest Pullan, recorded his contentment with the season so far and ruled out strengthening the team regardless of Ray's prejudices. "The club is training young players very well indeed," he said. "When the question arises about getting a player from another club, apart from having to pay anything from £5,000 to £10,000, there is often some reason why he was leaving, and that might well be a reason why he should not come to Leeds. Also he might take the place of a player who has been trained for three years by Mr Ray." Pullan omitted a couple of issues from his analysis, notably if the player were better than the man he would replace, then surely that is the whole point of the transfer. More pertinently he, a recipient of the dividend, bypassed the salient matter that United in their best-ever season had turned a profit only by selling Jock White back to Hearts for about £3,000 and the reserve centre-forward Dave Mangnall for around £4,000 to Huddersfield Town, for whom he scored 61 First Division goals in 79 appearances. It is always easier for directors to pat themselves on the back for thrift than kick themselves up the arse for complacency.

Leeds slid into the bottom two in mid-February and could not recover, managing four wins in the 12 games they had to save themselves. Even so their 3-1 victory over Derby County on the final day would have been good enough had Blackpool lost at Manchester City. They were 2-1 down with 10 minutes to play and the 11,190 souls at Elland Road spent the second-half rubber-necking between the pitch and the manual scoreboard until the attendant extinguished all hope by replacing the '1' after Blackpool with a '2' shortly before the death.

Gates had been poor all season, 6,500 down on the previous season's average, and while the afternoon Wednesday figures were excusably low, 7,595 on a December Saturday for Bolton at home was a humiliation. Yet on 10 January 1931, for the visit of Huddersfield in a third-round FA Cup tie, Elland Road's attendance breached 41,000. A fortnight later more than 40,000 again turned up to watch Leeds thrash Newcastle 4-1 and set up a fifth-round tie against Exeter City of the Third Division South. There could be little doubt about the relative attractiveness of the two competitions and Leeds supporters' yearning for a trip to Wembley. United's record in the FA Cup, however, with a couple of exceptions, continued to be farcically bad until Don Revie's side hit its straps and has remained so for most of the 45 years since. Needless to add, then, that Exeter massacred them on St Valentine's Day, 3-1 at St James Park. "The blunt truth," wrote the Leeds *Mercury*'s Herbert Campbell, "is United had shed their fighting armour. As a team they were completely lacking in wilfulness, in determination. A team of polish without push, a team of make-believe, a team of sham." It was an unimprovable epitaph for their season.

Braithwaite stood down as chairman that summer in acknowledgment that his long and frequent absences on parliamentary and personal business were unsustainable. He was replaced by Eric Clarke, the chairman of the finance committee, a solicitor and Conservative city councillor for the north ward. He was the son of the late city coroner, Sir William Clarke who, you might remember, was the Leeds City club solicitor who refused to hand over the club's books to the Football League and FA back in 1919, a stance that led directly to their expulsion. In their small world, where the law, commerce, the council, trade and public service were all intertwined and Liberals and Tories were too polite to let their differences divide them socially, it tainted neither.

Alderman Clarke's two seasons in the chair replicated the two succeeding the last relegation. The United side, assembled at virtually no cost and with money banked by the sales of Jennings (after 112 goals in 167 games), Reed, Turnbull, Townsley, Wainscoat and Mitchell, went back up at the first attempt and enjoyed a relatively worry-free return to Division One. Attendances were up slightly from an average of 13,400 to 14,100 but Clarke articulated complaints about their behaviour to go with habitual ones about their size. Just as four years previously, a string of victories was the engine of promotion, this time nine, one of the few positive pre-Revie records that still stands. It began at the end of September but at the start of the month, back-to-back defeats by Barnsley and Millwall and the Elland Road crowd's reaction to them, launched Clarke aboard his high horse. "The supporters are a great deal to blame for the home defeats inflicted on United," he told the Armley branch of the supporters' club. "The young players who constitute the Leeds United forward line were not trained temperamentally for the disgraceful barracking to which they were subjected. When playing away in front of an impartial crowd, they were allowed to play their own game, with the result that they have gained seven out of a possible eight points from away games. The way to instil confidence into young players is to encourage, and not to hiss and jeer and boo when they make mistakes." Much of it was incontestable apart from the oddball view that away crowds were somehow 'impartial' but he must have know that losing their opening two home games was always going to exasperate supporters.

In any case United were not so delicate thereafter and they overcame a wobble in the spring when Edwards was out injured to clinch the runners-up spot, two points ahead of Stoke by virtue of a 4-3 victory at the Victoria Ground, Keetley's 23 goals and a defence with Copping and Jack Milburn to the fore which cut the number conceded from 81 in the top flight to 54 in Division Two. For all that, only the visit of Bradford Park Avenue on Boxing Day brought more than 20,000 into Elland Road, a deficiency that taxed the board throughout the good run. Not reducing prices to account for relegation was one conspicuous reason while a letter writer to the *Yorkshire Evening Post* proposed another. "To my mind the Leeds United ground is on the wrong side of the river for any hopes of better gates," wrote 'Lover of Sport and Fresh Air'. "After a week's work, it requires a strong will and enthusiasm to go down Holbeck way when there is hardly a green leaf or blade of grass to be seen. Even as you stand in the ground, you seem to be weighted down by the heavy atmosphere. And when it is wet, dull, or nasty, well, it is quite enough to make anyone stop at home. What a pity the ground could not be moved to Roundhay, Headingley or Chapeltown where it would be a pleasant ride or walk, even if your team does disappoint." A whole club, then, damned from day one by being born on the wrong side of the tracks.

Arthur Hydes, a Barnsley-born former confectioner, emerged as a first-team regular on United's return to the First Division and scored 16 goals to compensate for Keetley's long spells out with injury. George Milburn joined his elder brother in defence and both played every game. United essentially earned some security with a 13-match unbeaten run after opening the season with two defeats, and average attendances – boosted by a remarkable record 56,796 for the visit of the champions, Arsenal, on 27 December, the first game Lord Harewood attended – allowed the club to turn a profit of £1,226 against a loss of £3,500 for the years spent in Division Two. Again, though, outlay on transfers was down in three figures, £145, while £2,000 was brought in from the sale of reserve centre-half Bob Danskin.

Ray's shrewdness kept all the balls in the air without burdening the board and while his taste put him on the path of sound recruitment and disposal as a way to finance the operation, it also characterised Leeds as a selling club. In the summer of 1934 when Arsenal came calling with £8,000 for their best player, 24-year-old Wilf Copping on the verge of his prime years, there was never any doubt that Leeds would sell. He had caught Herbert Chapman's eye during the 1933-34 season when Leeds followed their eighth-place finish the year before with ninth. Edwards endured a string of ailments from muscle injuries to scarlet fever and managed only 15 matches, which put more responsibility on Copping to distribute the ball as well as snatching it back. Chapman died in harness in January 1934, not even a fortnight after another Christmas double-header against Leeds, so it was left to his successor, George Allison, to fulfil his wishes and purchase the left-half in the summer.

In October 1934, the board explained why their hands were tied when it came to selling players. Under the terms of the debenture, they had been paying out 7.5 per cent interest on each bond, a return agreed 10 years earlier, when bank rate had been 5 per cent. Now the lending rate had fallen to 2 per cent, and Elland Road attendances were an average 7,300 smaller than the 1924-25 season, their inaugural top-flight campaign, meeting their promises was bleeding the club dry. In another 10 years the bonds would mature and Leeds needed the ring-fenced portion of the gate receipts to redeem them rather than servicing the interest or they would be back to where they started and have to borrow a similar sum to pay off their lenders all over again. The board proposed a reduction in the rate, appealing to the fair play of the bondholders whose investment had been a cash-generating machine for a decade. Alf Masser, back on the board and in the chair following Alderman Clarke's resignation after two seasons, called a meeting of the debenture-holders at the Griffin Hotel to ask them to take 5 per cent for the final 10 years, still a rate any bank or building society would refuse to imitate. The trustees recommended acceptance and the motion was carried on a show of hands.

In April 1934 Leeds had beaten Leicester 8-0 at Elland Road but without Copping they were drubbed 8-1 by Stoke City in the second game of the new season. In November Ray finally relented to 'the grousers' and paid Sunderland £6,000 for the 33-year-old Scotland centre-half Jock McDougall who quickly succumbed to Sod's Law, managed five games before injury struck and ended his season. The raw-boned Hydes scored 22 goals and Bill Furness 16 but United could not climb higher than 12th. They let in 92 goals and the cause of it was self-evident – their best defender was now playing for Arsenal and England. A 3-1 victory over Portsmouth on 2 March, which helped Leeds up to 14th, was the unlikely prompt for Ray to offer his resignation after eight years in charge. He had brought in a profit of about £22,000 in transfers to subsidise the club he had strived so hard to found and made internationals of Copping, Wainscoat and Harry Duggan, while Bert Sproston, signed from Sandbach, and Eric Stephenson, who joined the club initially on amateur forms after being spotted by Ray playing for Harrogate, would go on to play for England after he had left. 'Midas' barely does him justice and he faced no blame for tiring of it. The administrative duties of a secretary-manager alone were exhausting but Ray had also insisted on standing down the selection committee and picking the team on his own as well as travelling thousands of miles each season in pursuit of prospective players. Ernest Pullan, the director and former referee, took on the caretaker role while applications were sought for a full-time replacement.

There was one more fundamental change that season, too, when United finally got the Huddersfield out of Leeds a month into the season by upgrading the new change strip of blue and old gold halves, contrasting sleeves, white 'knickerbockers' and blue and gold stockings, into their default kit. Getting rid of the alien blue and white stripes had been a staple subject in the letters pages of the *Evening Post* for years and the decision was an easy win at a time of stagnation on and off the field. The azure and gold were taken from the city's coat of arms and had been represented on Leeds City's jerseys. In their 15th season, United overcame their inhibitions and Hilton Crowther's preferences and at last stamped the city of Leeds' identity all over themselves.

Dick Ray had captained City and United turned to a First World War-time alumnus of the defunct club, the former Newcastle United full-back Billy Hampson, who had just started work for the Northumberland Schools Association, to replace him. Pullan and his fellow board members had kept Leeds clear of relegation with four wins and four draws while he minded the shop for 12 games, though a 7-1 monstering at Stamford Bridge stuck in the throat for years. Hampson was a stereotypically wry Geordie, chosen from more than a hundred applicants. His players spoke affectionately of his kindness and composure, a man who trusted and defended them. He stayed for 12 years and kept them up, once by the seat of his pants, in the four seasons leading up to the war, an achievement which belied earlier financial strife with Carlisle and Ashington that left him constrained by cost-cutting. Attempts to transplant a spine with experience into the Ray team he inherited left them with lumbago until he, too, followed his predecessor's financial model and used the club as a talent farm and finishing school to support its existence. Looking back, Hampson's tenure in many ways seems like lost years, diminished into meaninglessness by the war but as ever with Leeds they were years of constant financial anxiety, flip-flopping crowds, conflict with the board, the fanbase and the League. Hampson would need every ounce of resilience to navigate them.

7

—

INTO THE ABYSS

In the summer of 2014, Leeds United's new head coach, Dave Hockaday, a preposterous appointment who has lately enjoyed some sympathy rather than the dishonour, say, Steve Evans commands, ordered his squad to wade into the Rienza in lieu of an ice bath after their exertions at the club's training camp in the Dolomites. The photographs were published almost before the players had emerged from the river and the story written up to ridicule Massimo Cellino's cheapness and Hockaday's pound-shop, boot-camp bullshit. Yet in 1935, Billy Hampson had done much the same. Having won the FA Cup Final as Newcastle United's right-back at the age of 41 in 1924, Leeds' third manager was a staunch proponent of swimming's benefits for suppleness and incorporated it into United's pre-season programme alongside the country walks, golf tournaments and fitness work. In August, en route to play an inter-squad cricket match – 'Marrieds' vs 'Unmarrieds' at Boston Spa CC – he even stopped the charabanc at Collingham, 10 miles north of the city, and ordered everyone into the Wharfe to bathe. No one would have thought to mock them. It was emblematic of a relaxed approach that charmed his players.

Hampson may have been 52 but had stopped playing League football merely five years earlier and was much closer in temperament and outlook to the men in his charge than his two predecessors. He was more pragmatic, too, because he had been liberated from the responsibilities that had tethered Arthur Fairclough and Dick Ray. As secretary-managers they had to devise and implement budgets. Arthur Crowther, no relation to Hilton, took over the secretarial function and Hampson was engaged as team manager only. The answer would probably be 'no' but at least he could ask the directors for transfer cash. For Fairclough and Ray it had often been pointless, the secretarial angel in one ear always having the stark, economic facts to beat back the managerial devil in the other.

Given his own venerable age when he had his most successful spell as a player, Hampson was keener on grizzled experience than Ray and far more sanguine about buying players in their thirties. Jock McDougall, a Ray aberration when signing the centre-half at 33, became a regular in 1935-

36 as a proper third back, pushing Ernie Hart, the sole survivor from the inaugural campaign, out of the team and away from the club at the end of the season after 472 appearances and eight England caps. Albert McInroy, who had kept goal for Newcastle's 1932 FA Cup-winning side, was even older than McDougall when Hampson signed him from Sunderland in the summer and put him straight into the first team. His one England cap had come nine years previously and he had just spent a year in the stiffs back at Roker Park yet he repaid Hampson's hunch with 18 months' service as a reliable stopgap, even if his face, a careworn victim of his trade and the times, looked more ancient than his thick woollen, ribbed, emerald jumper.

Valiant keeper though he was, McInroy was hardly the kind of symbol Leeds needed to entice disillusioned supporters to come thronging back. Hampson knew it and tried to address the general air of exasperation in an open letter to the fans, a modern technique for Leeds United managers but one which conveyed the same old message.

"I understand that some of our supporters have not seen eye to eye with the directors and management in the past year or two on the question of obtaining new players," he wrote. "I have satisfied myself it is wrong to assume the board are not alive to the needs of the club… [they] have not only been on the look out but have approached many clubs for players who have been fancied. You may rest assured that no effort will be spared to build up a United team worthy of the city of Leeds, a team capable of playing really attractive football. My directors have promised me their wholehearted support. May I now appeal very strongly to all supporters to give me their assistance. Roll up in your thousands to ALL matches at Elland Road and encourage the boys all you can. This without doubt will prove a rare tonic to us and will help considerably to bring success to the club."

It was all a bit Lord Kitchener in its appeal and without any results to back up his claims of a new dawn it was ignored. Only 14,514 turned out for the first Saturday home game of the season and it took Hampson seven games – after four defeats and two draws – to record his first win, a 1-0 home victory over Liverpool by virtue of Jack Milburn's penalty. It was one of nine the left-back 'Penalty King' and 'Dead Eyed Dick' scored that season to add to the six of the season before and it was a crucial element in their recovery from a shoddy start to finish 11th. In September Hampson paid Burnley "a four-figure sum they could not refuse", otherwise undisclosed, for the 32-year-old former England centre-forward George 'Bomber' Brown who had won three titles and the FA Cup during seven years with Huddersfield Town. Hampson used him at inside-right, employing his dribbling and 'Buckaroo' shooting power alongside the less refined skills of the workhorse Jack Kelly, who scored 15 goals to Brown's 18.

A rollicking 7-2 victory over Sheffield Wednesday at Elland Road in which the hosts had raced to a 6-1 lead at half-time put 3,000 on the gate for the next match, a 5-2 defeat of Bolton in November but only the visits of Huddersfield in October and Manchester City on Easter Monday brought in more than 30,000.

In any typical Leeds United season, the increase in average attendance by almost 4,000 would have been a cause for celebration. The board, however, was still concerned about the amount of griping in the stands and on the letters pages. It was also preoccupied with organising a couple of charity matches – an 8-5 victory over Dublin City in October and a 4-1 win against FC Wien in December. United hosted a gala dinner for the Austrian club after the match, decorating the banqueting hall at the Griffin Hotel in their opponent's red and white colours and adorning the walls with Viennese proverbs, including the bleak 'Life is like a hen ladder, covered in muck from top to bottom'. For Alf Masser, the Leeds chairman, it rather encapsulated a campaign which brought him into direct conflict with the Football League as the improbable leader of a rebellion.

By February 1936, 13 years after the first coupons had been sold outside Old Trafford, the football pools were bringing in £800,000 a week during the season to Liverpool's Littlewoods and Vernons and the London-based Zetters. The fantasy of a grand pay-day is never more seductive than during a depression. "Above all there is gambling, the cheapest of all luxuries," wrote George Orwell in *The Road to Wigan Pier*. "Even people on the verge of starvation can buy a few days' hope ('Something to live for', as they call it) by having a penny on a sweepstake." The coalition National Government had tried to ban them under the Betting and Lotteries Act in 1934 and was forced to capitulate under concerted public protest but the Football League clubs, pulling in combined weekly receipts in January 1936 of £48,000, began to covet a slice of the vast turnover and handsome profits the three companies were raking in. So, the League used the only tool it had; the management committee asserted copyright on its fixture list, demanded a significant increase for the licence to use it and called the pools companies "a menace to the game". When put to a vote of its members, 65 backed the proposal to weaponise their hand in the dispute after failing to reach a compromise with the firms, 12 voted against and eight abstained. Masser, one of the 12, then listened to the strategy the League advanced as their next move with something approaching incredulity: if the fixture list was the cash generator for the pools companies, the League should shred it, draw up a new one in secret and inform clubs who had to travel a long way only 48 hours before the match and the rest on Friday mornings to prevent leaks. How could people possibly bet on the pools if existing coupons were void and there would not be time to gather the information from all 88 clubs by Friday lunchtime to print new ones for their army of agents to distribute and collect when they had been filled in?

It was a ploy of quite irreproachable logic and comprehensive stupidity. How could the teams prepare for their opponents, organise travel and possibly accommodation, never mind the obstacles it placed in front of fans, with such short notice? The flaws were pointed out but the majority decided to harm themselves for the greater good.

Masser was joined by Sunderland and Manchester City in opposing the resolution and the Leeds chairman mustered further clubs behind him via 'telephonic conversation'. He said he had received scores of letters from the public "hinting at boycott of matches and expressing extreme disgust with the action which was threatened". The United board backed him wholeheartedly, stressing it was "an issue for the parliament of people not the parliament of football". The League would not budge. Orwell was surveying the slums of Sheffield, Leeds and Barnsley that month and was derisive about people's priorities: "I happened to be in Yorkshire when Hitler re-occupied the Rhineland. Hitler, Locarno, Fascism, and the threat of war aroused hardly a flicker of interest locally," he wrote. "But the decision of the Football Association [sic] to stop publishing their fixtures in advance (this was an attempt to quell the Football Pools) flung all Yorkshire into a storm of fury."

On Friday, 28 February, Leeds received a letter telling them they were playing Sheffield Wednesday at Hillsborough the following day, a mercifully short journey in a snowstorm. It was freezing and only 6,316 turned up, more than 12,000 down on their average for the season. "The weather conditions were appalling," Masser said. "But it would appear that a certain percentage object to interference with their liberties." He called a meeting of clubs in Leeds to discuss the clandestine fixture list and only 36 bothered to send anyone, 26 of them passing a weasel vote of confidence in the League Management Committee and simultaneously calling for the reinstatement of the old schedule. The following Saturday Elland Road hosted Brentford and the gate was 8,000 down on the mean. To gauge the feeling, Leeds balloted the 10,509 present with the question 'Are you in favour of the League fixture list which was issued in May?' Of the 3,584 papers returned, 3,544 voted for the proposition. The age of secrecy could not last and the growing ranks behind Masser spooked the Football League into passing the buck to parliament and restoring the original fixture list. "The rescission of the 'menace resolution' moves the battleground from the football field to the Hall of Westminster," Masser said. The Commons debated the issue in April and trounced the private member's bill which was trying to put the pools companies out of business. The clubs still elected Burnley's Charles Sutcliffe, the management committee member responsible for the fixture list and whose idea the mystery match ruse was, as president during the summer and denied Masser a place on the ruling body. Leeds United had beaten the establishment and would always pay some price.

Hampson's second season at the helm began in a similar fashion to his first. This time it took five matches to register their first victory and they never really recovered save for three successive wins in November and a 5-0 cakewalk over Middlesbrough on Christmas Day. Age withered Willis Edwards and McDougall while injuries struck Bert Sproston, Eric Stephenson, the Northern Ireland left-half Bobby Browne and the tiny 18-year-old winger Aubrey Powell, who suffered a compound fracture of the right leg, broken in a front-on tackle with a sickeningly audible crack, during a defeat at Deepdale in March that shoved Leeds into the bottom two. Powell was left behind in Preston Royal Infirmary for a month and was told his injury was so severe he should retire. It took him 18 months of painful rehabilitation to recover and, though he lost six more years of his career to wartime service with the Army Physical Training Corps, he played on well into his thirties.

North End's victory was Leeds' third loss in a sequence of four that had started away with a 7-1 rout by Everton and the run extended to six defeats and two draws. By Easter Tuesday Leeds were bottom and three points from safety with seven to play. The board had given Hampson a total of £10,000 to buy four players at different crisis points of the season – the centre-half Tom Holley, left-winger Arthur Buckley, inside-right George Ainsley and the veteran South African former Liverpool centre-forward and Lancashire opening bowler Gordon Hodgson, who had met his new team-mates for the first time at Lime Street two hours before kick-off at Goodison. Yet there was no immediate stimulus to jolt the team out of its spiral. United's blemishes were plain to see – they were too flimsy to hold on to the ball, too quiet, lacked leadership and, wedded to a neat passing game even on porridgey pitches, had no variation in play. The *Evening Post* emphasised Hampson's credentials as "one of the most considerate and conscientious managers in football" who would get "the timepiece ticking". The supporters, however, did not believe adjusting the mechanism would suffice. Having suffered three years of anaemic play without him, they longed for Copping's bite and willingness to 'get some blood on thi' boots'.

In early March the Press Association reported that the Leeds board had given up on Hampson and appointed QPR's manager, the pipe-smoking, tweed-suited Scot Billy Birrell, as secretary-manager. Rangers confirmed it and the news was all over the London evening papers. In the West Riding there was bafflement. Hampson certainly had not been told and Masser, collared as he left the station, refused to make a statement. He was no more forthcoming after a board meeting on 9 March, saying only "nothing is settled" and promising to let them know just as soon as it was. The 'curious incident' had left the players "mystified" according to the *Yorkshire Evening Post* and it was left to Birrell, whose resignation had been accepted and compensation agreed at Loftus Road, to enlighten everyone a couple of days after the Leeds directors went to ground. "I was approached and interviewed by the board of Leeds United and offered the post of manager. After further negotiations I accepted the position of secretary-manager, but at a later date differences arose, which prompted me to revoke the decision and remain with my present club." That was that, Hampson was retained and no mention of it was made again. One would presume that it unsettled the team but given they were already in a tailspin it is impossible to be certain and Masser bridled at anyone trying to pin it on him. "I think it only fair to say," he pointed out, "that I accept no personal responsibility for the present position. The decisions have been the decisions of the board." Right there: the genius of collective liability at play.

Hodgson turned 34 in April and ultimately proved the tonic with six goals from centre-forward, while Billy Furness' comeback for the final two games reintroduced steel and tenacity at shielding the ball which brought the other forwards into play. Milburn belted in penalties in those last two matches, Furness scored in each and the four points nudged them ahead of Sheffield Wednesday and Manchester United. Hampson played up the reserves winning the Central League as green shoots heralding a revival and, once more, asked the public to show more support through the turnstiles. "I should like to anticipate an average crowd of 20,000 spectators," he wrote in an advertisement selling season tickets. "And whilst recognising the loyal support we have always had from the 'bob side', I should like those enthusiasts to bring along a 'pal' to enjoy the fare which I am sure our boys will do their best to provide this year."

This time his call was answered and in 1937-38 gates averaged more than 20,000 for the first time for nine years in response to a much tighter defence and Hodgson's enduring class up front. Leeds garnered the dividends of a settled side – nine players featured in 30 or more games by contrast with only three the year before, Bert Sproston's splendid form made him England's regular right-back and the left side, so often United's vulnerable flank, flourished with Milburn and Browne shutting down attacks, while Stephenson and Buckley acted as the perfect creative foils for an ageing but deadly striker.

Hodgson was tall and brawny and had not had much pace to lose in the first place. What had made him Liverpool's record scorer, the unrelenting physicality that left defenders feeling they had been violated by a barbed-wire octopus, a mastery of all forms of heading – cushioned, precision ones, bullets from the brow and snide little glancers – and, like Bobby Charlton, such powerful shooting with both feet it was difficult to tell which one he favoured, served Leeds similarly well. In 1937-38 he scored 25 League goals and all four in a 4-4 draw with Everton in February when they surrendered 2-0 and 3-2 leads and rescued a point in the 86th minute with Hodgson's bludgeoned header. His two goals in a 5-3 Christmas Day victory over Middlesbrough had driven United up to second place but they could not push on. Two wins from the next 16 games ruined their chances of rivalling Arsenal's title bid and they fell back to ninth.

At the end of the season Sproston, the fearsome 'winger eater', was selected for the England squad's continental tour and travelled by train to play in all three matches, the victories over Germany (and essentially Austria since it took place two months after the Anschluss) and France that sandwiched defeat by Switzerland in Zurich. It was in Berlin on the eve of the match against Germany – the infamous game where the players were used by Foreign Office diplomats and the FA and were made to salute Adolf Hitler like good, obedient Nazis before salvaging some dignity by thrashing the 'Master Race' 6-3 – that Sproston uttered the single greatest quotation ever associated with Leeds United. The wise words of Harry Reynolds, Don Revie and Billy Bremner have been turned into slogans by the club and employed to nourish an identity. They cannot, however, turn what Sproston said to Stan Matthews over a pot of tea in a café when they caught sight of Hitler's passing motorcade into a pithy phrase to sell replica shirts. Yet it speaks for the integrity of a man and his trade that were about to be exploited by smoothly craven officials of the state and the game. "I'm just a workin' lad from Leeds. I've not 'ad much of an education and I know nowt 'bout politics and t'like. All I knows is football," Matthews reports Sproston saying. "But t'way I see it, yon 'itler fella is an evil little twat."

So what did Leeds United do with such an upstanding citizen, a wonderfully tough international footballer and their best player? They did what they always did with their greatest young talent – they sold him. Within the month Sproston had joined Second Division Tottenham for £9,500. Ernest Pullan, the builder, had replaced Masser as chairman in the summer of 1937. The alderman had been the ideal man to make the league see sense over the pools and had fulfilled all the formal duties of his role with impeccable decorum. It was Masser who addressed the crowd on the death of King George V in January 1936 and he enjoyed the pageantry of foreign visits and guests. In the end, though, his legal practice and council work, including a daring scheme to bring the FA Cup Final to Roundhay Park, proved too taxing and he vacated the seat at the middle of the boardroom table for one downwind. Where Masser had used collective responsibility over Billy Birrell, the phantom manager, to shield himself from criticism, Pullan abandoned it for the same purpose. Tracked down on holiday in Filey on the day Spurs announced the transfer of Sproston, Pullan told the press: "I was definitely against the transfer. When I was put in the chair I said I would look after the supporters' interests. This, I think, is going against it and I voted against it. The directors, thinking of the financial gain of £10,000, outvoted me."

Said directors seemingly did not hold it against him, at least not in public at the AGM where the board announced a trading profit of £3,872 because of a transfer surplus of £9,000. Leeds were third in the table at that point after three successive victories in November and there was an air of congratulation about proceedings, specifically in their pride at finding a winning formula on one of the lowest incomes in the division. Their gate receipts were only £30,000 while Division Two Aston Villa and just-relegated Manchester City had taken in £80,000 and £60,000 respectively. To break even after paying interest on the debentures was a minor triumph that necessitated cashing in on their assets. Leeds had lost Copping's best years to Arsenal but they used some of the Sproston money to fulfil their supporters' deepest fantasies by bringing him back in March 1939 for £5,000. He returned at the age of 29 after winning two titles and the FA Cup because he sensed war was imminent and wanted his family to be back home in Yorkshire when he joined up.

Willis Edwards, only intermittently fit for the past couple of seasons, played three final games with his erstwhile half-back partner and Leeds United's two best pre-war players went out together for the last game of the season, a 0-0 draw with Stoke that confirmed a 13th-place finish. Once again United had fallen victim to a winter slump, winning merely one of the run of 15 matches from the end of November. The bright hope nurtured by racking up eight against Leicester for the second time that decade, Hodgson's five goals helping to thrash the visitors 8-2 in October, dissipated when their stylish passing game was hobbled by sludge, wind, ice and mud. "It can be said without fear of contradiction," wrote the *Yorkshire Evening Post* in December, "that Leeds United are one of the happiest clubs in the country, and nowhere will you find a more likeable body of men." That could not be said once Copping and his snarl had returned but it was precisely what the team needed. All the best Leeds teams have prospered when a manager has acted on the belief that success with young players can hinge on a transformational signing. The key transfers for Don Revie, Howard Wilkinson and David O'Leary – Bobby Collins, Gordon Strachan and David Batty respectively – brought direction to squads that had promise in abundance but lacked the experience and leadership to turn potential into achievement. Copping could have been that man for Hampson's Leeds United. Sadly, "yon evil little twat 'itler" had other plans.

The new season was only three matches old when Neville Chamberlain declared war on Germany at 11.15am on Sunday, 3 September 1939. The government, using the Emergency Powers (Defence) Act, forbade the gathering of large crowds, which forced the League to abandon the competition quickly, unlike in 1914-15 when its decision to carry on provoked hysterical criticism. Leeds were bottom of the First Division at the time and struggled throughout the wartime regional substitute leagues and tournaments. Player availability was a continuous problem even allowing for guest players stationed at Catterick and other Yorkshire barracks. The temptation to overcompensate their ringers, the Leeds City vice, was resisted by United and was impossible anyway because the crowds – 500 for Hull City's visit in June 1940, 200 for Newcastle's a week later – were appropriately minuscule.

On 22 March 1941, a week after the Luftwaffe's 'Quarter Raid' dropped 25 tons of explosive bombs on the civic centre, Beeston, Armley and Bramley, 1,500 fans made their way to Elland Road for a 3-2 victory over Sheffield Wednesday. The Army's requisitioning of the pitch, stands and offices, which United were permitted to use on matchdays, helped cut overheads but the directors laboured under enormous financial strain and had to ask the debenture holders for assistance to pay an income tax bill from the accumulated funds. In 1944 the trustees agreed to extend the maturation date to 1954 to relieve the immediate pressure and though the club sought a loan from the FA in 1945 to settle the outstanding £26,000 and end the annual drain on income to pay the interest, they were turned down. Therefore for fully 30 years of their existence, Leeds United's potential was hobbled by the need to service the debt accrued to pay off Hilton Crowther.

The war claimed the lives of several who had taken to the pitch in United's colours. In July 1944, Alan Fowler – who had scored eight goals for Dick Ray's team 10 years earlier before leaving for Swindon Town – was killed in action during one of the most horrific and arduous battles of the Normandy Campaign as the Wessex Division tried to capture Hill 112. Fred Mills had retired at the outbreak of war to enlist with the King's Shropshire Light Infantry after five years in and out of the first team. He lost his life in December 1944 at Blerick in the Netherlands and his remains lie in Venray War Cemetery.

The death of Eric Stephenson was marked on his temporary gravestone by a line from his favourite poem, Rupert Brooke's The Soldier, "forever England". The corner of Major Stephenson's foreign field is in Burma where he fell in September 1944 attacking a bunker, killed by a soldier of the Japanese 55th Division while trying valiantly to assist comrades in mortal danger. Stephenson was a Cockney who moved to Leeds as a teenager in 1930 when his unemployed father found a rare job in the city during the depression. A staunch Methodist, he was spotted by Ray and signed for United initially as an amateur. He was a skilful inside-forward, small, sinewy, a bright, enterprising passer and scored twice on his second start in 1935. After overcoming injuries, he was a regular in the last two seasons before the war and vital to Hodgson's Indian summer glut of goals. Stephenson was a regular speaker at Sunday services and wrote a syndicated column even before he made his England debut in 1938. On joining the Army at Manchester Free Trade Hall in 1939, Private Stephenson was assigned to the Physical Training Corps in Aldershot where he served for two years, rising to the rank of Sergeant Instructor. But he wanted to do more than train soldiers for combat and was accepted on the Officer Training Corps, passing out at Sandhurst in 1942. He was posted to 3rd Battalion, the 2nd Gurkha Rifles in Bombay and spent months of hard fighting on the Irrawaddy River Operation with other Chindit units during his first year of action.

In 1944 he was promoted to the rank of major and sent to the Arakan, thick jungle in a miserably punishing monsoon season, to fight for control of the port of Akyab. He was killed on 8 September after ordering the majority of the company he was commanding to remain in position while he set off towards the sound of heavy gunfire with a handful of men.

Stephenson was beloved by the entire regiment and his daughter Jan, who lost her father at the age of five, titled her biography of him The Happy Warrior to encapsulate his engaging temperament and profound sense of duty. Leeds United have had finer players but no greater hero. It was with an abject sense of loss that a battered and almost broken club tried to pull itself back together in 1945.

8

BRING 'EM BACK ALIVE

Candidates for the lowest point in Leeds United's history typically focus on off-field turmoil, financial ruin or some of the chancers who, in recent years, have darkened their door. The club's poor fortunes in any given season – relegation from the Championship in 2007, humiliating defeats en route to going down in other years and periods of risibly stone-broke, sterile mediocrity in between – all have the capacity to make one wince at the recollection. The scars run deep.

On the pitch, however, nothing rivals the two immediate post-war seasons for ceaseless, rank destitution. Never was hope extinguished so swiftly, never the prospect of redemption so remote. It was true, too, that those nominally responsible are entitled to compassion rather than condemnation. Rebuilding the team after six years of war, never mind a club and its ground in dire need of renovation and repair, was a tall enough order without the constraints of their debts and the persistent tithe on income from soaring entertainment tax and interest on debentures. Doing it with surviving players, who had lost half their careers to service, coming home in dribs and drabs from every theatre of war, with their youngest players vulnerable to the National Service call-up, proved impossible. One of the First Division's most beggarly clubs cannot merit much stigma for failure in such dicey circumstances.

The regional professional football leagues restarted on 25 August 1945, 10 days after VJ Day. The toll among registered Leeds players numbered four who had not played in the pre-war Football League: Sergeant Vernon Allen, Pilot Officer Robert Montgomery, Trooper Maurice Lawn, and Sergeant Leslie Thompson, alongside Major Eric Stephenson. Several more, including Jim Milburn, the youngest of United's three Geordie brothers, had been wounded. Guests were permitted and Billy Hampson used 50 players in the 42-match Football League Northern Section season, understandably failing to find any cohesion or fluency. They lost their first five games by fairly respectable margins but sustained mortifying clobberings throughout the season. Leeds lost 6-0 at Bolton, 8-2 at Preston and Manchester United beat them 6-1 at Maine Road. Having been defeated by Sheffield United

4-2 at home, they went to Bramall Lane the next week and went down 6-2, and in March, they took on FA Cup quarter-finalists Bradford and were mullered 9-4.

The black magic of the FA Cup had its usual hexing effect on United even in its emergency two-legged format. After drawing 4-4 at home with Middlesbrough, they were knocked out at Ayresome Park where they went 1-0 up but nevertheless warmed their hands on the half-time tea urn 7-1 down. There was no consolation from keeping a clean sheet after the break as an 11-6 defeat on aggregate marked the final appearance for the wartime stalwart amateur centre-half Frank Butterworth, who was plainly out of his depth.

Twenty-second place in a 22-team league, behind eight who would start the resumption of the Football League in Division Two, ought to have had everyone around the club in brown trousers. While Chelsea and Arsenal proposed another season of regional league competition without relegation to give them the breathing space to fix damaged grounds and get all their players back from overseas, Ernest Pullan, the Leeds chairman, argued forcefully with the majority for a rapid return to peacetime fixtures. "I think we ought to get on with it," he said. "By next August all our players ought to be back and we should have the prospect of a good team."

In prospect instead was the worst season in the club's history. United won only six games, lost 30, conceded 90 goals and earned 18 points, a record top division low for a season of more than 30 games that would stand until Stoke City with 17 burrowed beneath them 38 years later. They had re-engaged every player from the 1938-39 season who was fit to carry on his career, signed a couple more to pad the squad out and worked with the Ministry of Labour and National Service on the release of those who had been in the armed forces and others who had been in reserved occupations, such as the goalkeeper John Hodgson who had been working as a miner in Durham. There were the usual financial obstacles to buying players in the summer of 1946 – the standstill agreed in 1940 on interest payments to the debenture holders at 5 per cent, three points higher than bank rate, was due to expire that year – but also the severe housing shortage meant the club could not guarantee anywhere for a player and his family to rent when they moved.

Hampson's first two seasons in charge, more than a decade before, had begun poorly and 1946-47 was just as bad with one point from United's first five games until a 4-0 victory over Bolton in late September took them off the bottom for the first time. The team was made up of the rump of Hampson's pre-war side but Tom Holley was now 32, Aubrey Powell 28,

George Ainsley 31, Bobby Browne 34, Ken Gadsby 30, Jim Twomey 32 and Davie Cochrane, the pigeon-catching quick right-winger, 26. All had played some form of football intermittently during the war, whether for the Army, RAF or as guests for other clubs but seven years away from their profession left more than just a few cobwebs to blow away. Pre-season had been designed to shake off the rust but they had been held together when young men in their last season before the war by the experience of Willis Edwards, Wilf Copping and Gordon Hodgson – all now retired – and the flair of Stephenson. Without them they were a much older and weaker team bereft of genuine quality, canny knowhow and aggressive physicality.

After misleading back-to-back wins in October, they were simply swept away. The only thing that saved them from relegation by the end of February was the terrible winter which caused scores of postponements and pushed the end of the season hard up against June. Blizzards hit the country in January and it was so cold in north-east Europe that the Leeds-Liverpool canal froze solid as temperatures plummeted beneath -10°C, drifts as high as 7ft were present until March and the roof of Wakefield railway station collapsed under the weight of snow. Fuel shortages led to blackouts, potatoes were added to the list of rationed goods and the football season bunny-hopped to a halt. Leeds United sent their players to Cleveleys, just north of Blackpool, for three weeks to sit out the worst of the freeze and train on the beach. But it did them no good. They had won the last game before the great storm of 21 January, beating Chelsea 2-1, and, although still bottom, the two points had cut the deficit to the safe haven of 20th place to three with 17 matches to play.

On the ice and after the March thaw, which burst the banks of the Aire, Derwent, Ouse and Wharfe in the West Riding, piling anguish on to misery, Leeds drew two and lost 15. They had tightened up the defence and got through games without being mauled but each position in the side apart from Cochrane on the flank had a basic flaw: they were not First Division class and neither were the men Hampson chose to augment them.

The directors kicked the manager upstairs at the end of April, appointing him as the club's first-ever chief scout, and gave his old job to Willis Edwards, who had qualified as an FA coach and had been in charge of the reserves. In the announcement the board refused to add any comment about why they had taken the decision and why they had gone for Edwards rather than a more experienced man but they cryptically emphasised that he would be in charge of the discipline and control of all players. In a less salacious age there was no hint in the newspapers abut why player discipline should be a problem. Disillusion, however, can be contagious and Hampson, for all his geniality, may well have seemed like yesterday's man to those who had been away to serve 'King and Country' and been shaped by all the enlivening and frightening things they had seen and done. Nothing was salvaged, least of all pride, from the final five defeats of that awful season supervised by Edwards – and the pint-sized centre-forward Harry Clarke, bought from Darlington for £6,000 in February, ended a costly, short stay at Elland Road goalless in 13 of his 14 appearances.

Leeds' two earlier relegations had been redressed by promotion the following season but the team had never looked quite so threadbare as it did when Edwards gathered them in July to prepare for Division Two. When they crashed out of the top flight in 2004, United exiled themselves from the Premier League just as it was entering its imperial phase. In 1947 they dropped down at the start of the golden age of the post-war attendance boom.

United's six wins in 1946-47 had all come at home but even so they had lost 10 times at Elland Road. Despite that, average gates were more than 26,000, almost 4,000 more than their previous best. The game's drawing power after the war caught the board by surprise. In October 1946 when they were in last place, the chairman Pullan asked anyone who felt goodwill towards the club to attend a meeting at the YMCA to discuss the hand-to-mouth predicament, particularly those who are "actuated more by a desire to see the club as flourishing as possible than to hold an inquest". When they assembled they were given forms at the instigation of the chairman of the financial committee, John Bromley, urging the holders of the unredeemed £28,000-worth of bonds either to surrender them to the club in the spirit of generosity or convert them into ordinary shares. He spelled out that he was legally stipulated to put 10 per cent of all receipts into the trust fund to service interest payments of £1,400 a year while ring-fencing the excess to pay them off at term and that this was killing the club. A few of the largest debenture-holders, he revealed – including Joshua Tetley and Son, John Smith, the Tadcaster brewer, and the publisher of the *Yorkshire Post* – had all agreed to turn their £1,000 bonds into shares while three more had converted £500 each. Now he appealed for everyone else to do the same. Moving from debt management to fundraising, Pullan invited suggestions from the floor and promised to investigate the feasibility of proposals ranging from selling season tickets for the popular side, expanding supporters' club branches beyond the city, asking fans to subscribe a shilling every time the team scored and using the ground to stage a boxing tournament. The only thing he ruled out was abandoning Elland Road and with good reason – in each of the first four post-war seasons attendances grew until by 1950 they breached 30,000 for the first time. It was the ground's capacity and football's popularity that eventually pulled United out of the hole.

First though, the majority of Leeds United's bondholders could still prove their loyalty to a 'nice little earner', even after 15 years of interest payments from 1925-39, was stronger than their loyalty to the best interests of the club. At the beginning of the relegation season, it had been reported in the *Evening Post*, presumably from a board tip-off, that 100 Leeds businessmen were willing to subscribe £2,000 each to the club, a sum which would have then made them the richest in war-ravaged Europe. In its front page story the YEP called the statement "highly optimistic". It was more than that, a fantasy rather than a fabrication, which kept recurring over the next 70 years. It is the myth of multiple messiahs, the fabled Yorkshire consortium, philanthropically bailing out their hometown club and establishing it with the status required for the greater glory of the city. Harold Marjason, a fruit and vegetable wholesaler who had joined the board, did lend the club £2,000 but 99 others pinched their pennies tight. In December 1949 the club announced that £18,000 was still outstanding on the debentures which shows that the returns were still valued more highly by the remaining holders than cauterising the wound that was bleeding the club dry. In the past trading losses of £12,783 in 1947 and £5,895 in 1948 would have jostled United to the brink of bankruptcy but salvation was at hand by the very thing the club had always craved – sheer weight of numbers clicking through the turnstiles.

One of the reasons for the magnitude of the loss announced for the relegation season was the £6,000 the club had paid in benefits to players who had been with United for 10 years. The board deserves credit for counting the war years as service to the club and not solely the nation – not everyone did – and for making a contribution to the benefit fund set up to help Eric Stephenson's widow and children. Always the best policy when making a kind and noble gesture is to proceed modestly, do it because it is the right thing to do without thought of gratitude. But Pullan, in one of his final acts as chairman, could not resist turning it into a stick when asked to account for why they had gone down. "The players have let us down badly," he told the annual general meeting in December. "Yet no club treats its men better than we do. We have given them £6,000 in benefits this season. I am upset they have not responded better. We found them homes. We take great care of them in every way." In similar vein, the vice-chairman, Stanley Blenkinsop, chimed in: "There is a lack of team spirit and enthusiasm at Elland Road." Their frustration is forgivable but their tactlessness unpardonable. Quizzical looks were exchanged throughout the game and the *Evening Post* noted "directors of several clubs said they thought Pullan was, to say the least, a little indiscreet".

It was his misfortune that the meeting fell two days after the first-team had lost 2-0 at home and 6-1 away at Luton Town in the Christmas double-header and the reserves had been spanked 7-0 by Manchester United. One contributor to the postbag, 'Fed Up', recorded the droll sarcasm of another spectator on Boxing Day: "He said to me he was coming there no more. I asked why and he said 'the excitement is getting me down. I'm afraid I shall die.'" Watching Willis Edwards' United could seriously ruin your health. After that heavy defeat at Kenilworth Road, United were 16th in the Second Division, three points above the relegation places. In that respect Pullan's reprimand made sense but the players, sensitive to scorn after 16 months of inadequacy and the feel of the crowd's hot howls of despair on their necks, resented being put in the stocks by the chairman of all people. "I may be unpolished as a player," said the captain, Tom Holley, after handing in an immediate transfer request. "But I have always played for United with every ounce I have. I resent the chairman's criticism." Pullan scrambled down to training on New Year's Eve to apologise for impugning their integrity. "I did not mean to infer the players were not trying and have made that quite clear. I was merely expressing my disappointment in the technical ability of the men in view of the extra training they had had from Willis Edwards." A shot across his players' bows had careered into his own foot.

Pullan did not say it out loud but his target logically moved from players to manager. Edwards had been a curious choice in the first place. A fine footballer and a good man, in his brown, engineer's overall coat and with his easy manner, he was the ideal No.2, a bridge between staff and players. He had been cherished for his ability during his 14 years in the first team and as an international right-half. He had captained Leeds and played for England but while you can captain by example, you cannot manage without articulating what you want in clear and forcibly persuasive language. It was not that the players did not listen to him, it was that he could not find the words to sound like war drums in their ears, to sell them a system and style they believed would work for them.

In truth Hampson and Edwards had inherited weak hands but they also played them atrociously. Albert Wakefield, a veteran of the Italian campaign, had scored 16 goals by the end of March but 18 defeats and only 12 victories had left Leeds in 18th and in serious need of an initiative – any kind of anti-depressant that would invigorate the team to meet the public appetite for football. It was the club's worst-ever season and yet once again they set a new record for average attendances of 28,943. Imagine the numbers they could have attracted if they had been any good. Elland Road gates increased from 1939 to 1948 by 9,000 but from much better starting points Newcastle, in the Division Two promotion race all season, had gone up 24,000, Manchester United, in the league above, by about the same (albeit at Maine Road), Sunderland 20,000, Chelsea 17,000 and Arsenal 16,000. Just as League football was enjoying its big bang, Leeds United were a wet fart. In the Forties the club squandered its premium opportunity to establish a broader base.

The scale of the problem and the feeling that Edwards was not up to it had not escaped the board, and finally they attempted to do something about it. Major Frank Buckley, or "Bring 'em Back Alive Buckley" as Cassandra of the *Daily Mirror* called him, had been the most charismatic and PR-savvy manager of the Thirties. He had bought himself out of the King's Liverpool Regiment at the age of 21 in 1903 where he had reached the rank of Gymnastics Instructor (First-Class) to pursue a career in professional football. He played intermittent first-team games for Aston Villa, Manchester United and City but mainly for their reserves before decent spells with Birmingham City and Derby County just before the First World War. He was playing for Bradford City when he stood up to volunteer at Fulham Town Hall as the first recruit to the 17th Middlesex 'Football Battalion' which he went on to command. Buckley was hit by shrapnel during the battle for Delville Wood in July 1916 and was thought to be close to death by his men when he was carried away with wounds to his shoulder and lungs but he survived the loss of blood and threat of infection to return to the front line in January 1917. He remained there until he was invalided out following a gas attack.

'The Major', as he now insisted on being called even by his wife and daughter, joined Norwich City of the Southern League as manager in 1919, although he left on a point of principle before they were elected to the Football League in 1920, giving up his smallholding for the life of a commercial traveller selling Maskell's confectionery. In three years traversing the country with his sample case loaded with bullseyes, rhubarb and custards and jelly babies, he recuperated from his injuries and sense of betrayal by Norwich. Blackpool enticed him back into the game and his success in scouting and developing players for sale, more than anything he achieved on the pitch, recommended his job application to the directors of Division Two Wolverhampton Wanderers, who appointed him manager in the summer of 1927. In Buckley's first season at Molineux, the year Leeds were promoted for the second time, Wolves finished 16th and though they progressed he did not get them up until 1932, right on schedule with the five-year plan he had outlined over tea and toast at his interview. What he brought them as well as a physical fitness regime straight out of the Army and a players' code of conduct, was at first solvency and then profitability earned by talent development and a farmer's knack for the right time to harvest said talent and take it to market. Their direct play flourished at the end of the decade when they were runners-up in the First Division in successive seasons and lost the 1939 FA Cup Final, beaten 4-1 by Portsmouth. The build-up to the match at Wembley provides Buckley with his enduring fame – the stunt he spun to the press about doctoring his players with monkey gland supplements outlives 12 years of solid achievement with Wolves. In fact the injections were more likely to have been extracted from bulls' testicles and administered with an amphetamine chaser. They did nothing for the favourites on Cup Final day yet the legend lives on.

In 1939 he had tried to join up for a third time but was rejected because he was 56 and he spent the Second World War commanding a Home Guard unit. In 1944 he asked to be released from the 10-year contract he had signed with the club in 1938 and moved to Notts County as the highest-paid manager in the country and from there to Hull City after the briefest of stays at Meadow Lane. Throughout the game he was known as the 'club-builder' so when Leeds heard he was in dispute with Hull over a feeder team in Doncaster, they invited him to a meeting at Alf Masser's Park Square offices in October 1947. Buckley played along with the necessary subterfuge by telling the press he was there to discuss the purchase of Jim Twomey and the wooing lasted three days. Additional grumbles from Hull, impatience over the serene pace of progress his methods demanded and his determination to sell every crowd favourite were aired but he ultimately decided to spurn United's offer and Edwards was left to soldier on. "The publicity Leeds have had over Buckley," wrote Phil Brown, "aroused greater interest in the affairs of the club than ever before in its history." He did not even have to join the club to hog headlines and have the press eating out of his hand. 'Publicity Pete' Ridsdale could not hold a candle to the Major and the board recognised he was too much of a boon to take no for an answer.

For a while they turned their attentions to figures who could inflame similar interest. In February 1948 an advertisement was placed in the national press seeking a player-manager for an unnamed Second Division club which everyone in the game assumed to be Leeds. That same month United made a £15,000 bid for the Middlesbrough and England captain

George Hardwick to come as player-manager and when they were turned down offered £6,000 to Derby County for Raich Carter, the elegant and mercurial England and former Sunderland inside-forward. If Stanley Matthews was the wizard of dribble out wide, Carter's passing, immaculate control and swivel-hipped feints made him his equal in the box. The silver-haired forward, still an England player, was one of the most distinctive, famous people in the land and was soon spotted in Leeds. Within hours he had agreed a salary with the board who promised him complete control over team affairs including recruitment and a three-year contract. Carter asked for five years and while United thought they were still negotiating he accepted the Hull board's offer to become player-assistant manager to Buckley. Hull, however, had not consulted Buckley, who was angry at losing his long-standing assistant, Frank Taylor. The Major stayed for one more game and then resigned. "I am out of work now and would be prepared to consider anything, including an offer from Leeds," Buckley said. The only impediment was Ernest Pullan, the chairman. The board was split between progressives and what the *Yorkshire Evening Post* diplomatically called "others" and Pullan was in the latter camp. On the same day that Buckley quit Hull, Pullan walked out of a board meeting having resigned the chairmanship after 11 years and the seat on the board he had held since 1925. The progressives had won. "The air has now been considerably cleansed and I think I can say that certain policies and methods of running the club, which have proved so signally unsuccessful over a long period in the past will now go overboard," wrote Brown.

By the beginning of the following week Buckley had agreed to take over at the end of the season. Sam Bolton, the Hunslet haulier who replaced Pullan as chairman, was ecstatic. "This was a great day for Leeds United," he said. "The directors have every confidence in the ability of Major Buckley to make Leeds United the Arsenal of the north." Buckley wasn't quite so bullish, limiting himself to saying, "I am sure I shall enjoy the task of making Leeds into the stronghold of the game the club and its public would like it to be." He set about his task in his usual manner with the demoted Edwards as his assistant. There was never any magic wand with the Major, just hard graft, gimmicks – such as the Heath-Robinson kicking machine he brought to Elland Road to fire shots at keepers and ballroom dancing training for the players – shrewd recruitment and sales. Within weeks Buckley sold Aubrey Powell to Everton for £10,000, Con Martin to Aston Villa for the same amount and Ken Chisholm, who had been at the club for less than a year, to Leicester City in a swap for Ray Igglesden plus another 10 grand.

At Wolves Buckley's player trading had brought the club a profit of more than £120,000 in 12 years. He may have been 65 but had lost none of his acumen and by May 1950, two-fifths of the way through his new five-year plan, he had brought in enough revenue combined with an increase in gate receipts that the board was able to pay off the outstanding debentures of £18,000. At last Leeds United could remove the albatross necklace it had been wearing for 26 years.

Buckley's immediate impact on the pitch was not so rewarding. His first season at Wolves 21 years before had ended with them one place worse off than the previous season but at United there was at least forward momentum, if only from 18th to 15th. They began with a 6-2 defeat at Filbert Street where a certain Don Revie scored twice for Leicester and they finished the season with fewer victories – 12 to 14 – than they had under Edwards. Fewer losses and more draws highlighted an improved defence but while Buckley could trumpet it as a staging post, it was all rather flat. Vital work was being done to restore the club's financial health, training was modernised, discipline enforced and organisational structures were put in place that addressed the casual approach of the past. The shop window, though, remained all too scruffy. Buckley professed himself happy with the churn of players, consistently high crowds and a centre-half he had found who "would be as good as Stan Cullis", the linchpin of his Wolves team and the pre-war England side. "I was sitting in my office when they brought in a giant of a boy," he said. "He told me he was 15. He stood 6ft and weighed more than 11st. He wanted a trial at my club. I thought: 'They don't come that big very often – it may be too good to be true.'" The boy's name was John Charles and he was as good as he looked. Indeed no one has looked any better.

9

OUR JOHN

To corrupt a line from *Pulp*, John Charles was not Jesus Christ though he had the same initials. As a footballer he was acclaimed by Nat Lofthouse as the best defender he had ever faced and by Billy Wright as the finest striker he had ever seen. Indeed, in 1959 a Fifa poll for an Earth XI to take on Mars picked him at centre-half and centre-forward. It was his goals in 1955-56 that eventually ended nine years of Division Two football for a club the press was by then calling 'John Charles United' more frequently than its official nickname, 'the Peacocks'. Moreover his 38 the following season earned him a record move to Juventus, the proceeds of which once again pulled Leeds United out of a financial crisis.

A simple man with extraordinary physical charisma, power and outrageous skill, Charles remains the club's greatest player. United, however, were never in a position to use him as anything other than a bulwark or an inspiration, someone whose quality and example could only do so much to offset the general mediocrity around him. During his first spell, he was happily trapped at Leeds for all but one of the years by his loyalty to the club and love for the city. The maximum wage meant he could not earn any more legally elsewhere in England nor move to a more competitive team unless the directors chose to sell him. Instead the chairman, Sam Bolton, slipped him cash bonus payments and called the bluff of bidders by placing such a large fee on his head that they quailed. To the supporters he was something far more significant than a 'star'. He was a symbol of hope, not in the least remote, 'Our John' and inevitably 'Big John' before 'King John', which was later more widely adopted. He was an extraordinary man with whom ordinary people identified and also invested in, a shining figure whose legend persisted long after his gullibility and lack of business acumen squandered his fortune by his final years. Unpretentious to a fault, Charles spent an entire chapter of his first autobiography running through the price differentials in groceries between Leeds and Turin, noting the inferiority of Italian jam and the Tuscan housewife's dexterity with veal.

The diet rich in artichokes and olive oil he later struggled to stomach were years away the day he was deposited at digs in Beeston in September

1948, three months shy of his 17th birthday. After a distinctly uncontinental breakfast of "eggs, bacon, sausages, black pudding, baked beans, the lot" from his landlady, Daisy, he strolled down the hill to Elland Road to start his fortnight's trial.

Jack Pickard, a native of Leeds and manager of a gents' outfitters, had been appointed the club's part-time scout in South Wales by Billy Hampson. He discovered that Charles, a left-half on the ground staff of Swansea Town, had, crucially, been registered as an amateur in their Welsh League rather than their Football League set-up. He sent him north to the Major in a slightly covert manner because they sought to exploit the loophole of his ambiguous status at Swansea. He had to play the trial matches in borrowed boots. Charles was disheartened to be asked to start the first of them at right-back and the next at left-back, alien positions for a boy who had only ever run out in the No.6 shirt. He met Buckley about halfway through the trial and learnt that it had been the Major's decision to employ him in unfamiliar roles to test his versatility. "His footballers," Charles said, "had to be able to trap a ball with both feet, shoot and pass equally well with both feet, position themselves equally well on both sides of the field and tackle and attack with the same precision from all angles."

Buckley took to him straightaway and, uniquely, insisted on calling him 'Jack'. Charles had precisely the traits Buckley most prized. "I was confronted by an Adonis of a youth," he said. "I liked his bearing and his respectful approach. Somehow he looked like a footballer. He looked like a fine, upstanding young man but he was far too shy and modest to say much for himself."

Charles was engaged on the ground staff and turned professional on £6 a week, along with Grenville Hair, a full-back from Burton-on-Trent, in December 1948. Noticing that Charles had shot up even more during his three months in Beeston and had begun to fill out, Buckley made him an appointment at his tailor's and made sure the club paid for a new suit for matchdays and trips home. If the Major was a stickler for parade ground-standard smartness, he was intuitive enough to realise how mortifying it was to be caught stranded, a boy with half-mast trousers and forearm-freezing cuffs among working men.

Swansea were livid and contested Leeds' right to sign him but the Football Association found in United's favour. John Barr, Don Revie's Scotland scout, took Peter Lorimer, Eddie and Frank Gray, Joe Jordan and Gordon McQueen to Leeds and is rightly celebrated as one of the architects of the club's rise. Even he, though, would have to yield to Pickard for the finest coup in the long history of United's scouting department.

Charles played at right-back for the A team in the Yorkshire League and the reserves and was moved to centre-half in the new year. In April 1949 he was selected to play in a first-team friendly at Elland Road against Queen of the South, Buckley pitting him against the sturdy, swashbuckling Scotland centre-forward Billy Houliston who 10 days earlier had given England's Neil Franklin such a beasting that the Scots left Wembley as 3-1 victors. Tom Holley, United's captain and regular centre-half since 1937, sat out the match but was an attentive and quickly fatalistic spectator. "When the first Scottish cross sailed over," he told the *Mirror*'s Mike Langley years later, "this unknown kid soared above everyone and controlled the ball with his head, then killed it on his chest before bringing it down and beating four challengers on a run from our box to theirs. That was enough for me. I turned to the trainer and said: 'Ta-ta. As from this minute I've retired.'" Holley was as good as his word and from that day on, injury and National Service duty absences apart, Charles was never out of the side.

Buckley had worked tirelessly on him for six months and continued to do so, putting on drills to enhance his left foot, making him wear a plimsoll on his right and a boot on his left so he would have to strike the heavy ball with his weaker foot for fear of bruising the other. One miscalculation was enough to serve as a permanent reminder. He introduced long one-to-one sessions honing his heading and working to improve his leap, something that kicked on prodigiously in Trooper Charles' two years with the 12th Royal Lancers, based at Barnard Castle, where he was corralled into playing basketball, or that 'girl's game' as he first dismissed it. At one point, in an exercise that would make neurologists wince and have personal injury solicitors legging it down the civil court, Buckley had Charles jumping up to head the crossbar itself.

After only three Football League games Charles' wages were doubled and he was taken on the post-season tour of the Netherlands where the Major, in his tweed plus fours and jacket, would stand the team drinks, encourage them to relax and enjoy goodwill games against the top Dutch sides who were still five years away from abandoning their amateur status. Charles relished the happy times on those annual trips to Holland. "It was good fun with the bars, late dinners and lots of ladies," he wrote of a place where the manager would show he was not always a tyrant. In truth he rarely was to Charles. Back then the players still trained on the pitch and Buckley would sit in the main stand with a microphone hooked up to the tannoy and tell them where they were going wrong in the most direct terms. Bobby Forrest, the Leeds inside-forward, told Charles' biographer Mario Risoli that Buckley went easy on his best player. "If you played a bad pass he would shout, 'The fucking ball won't go through the man!' But if John made a bad pass it was always, 'Hard luck, John.'" On another occasion his cry of "You're fucking useless" at Forrest forced the directors to ban his broadcasts after complaints from residents of the Heath housing estate opposite the ground.

Where others would receive a broadside for the slightest sign of distraction during team meetings, Charles was left unmolested by the Major when he regularly nodded off. Sir Alex Ferguson with Eric Cantona was not the first to understand that otherwise stern disciplinarians cannot prosper by treating all personalities with the same rigidity. But Charles did not escape his manager's other eccentricities, including the return of weekly "monkey gland" injections and supplementary pills in 1951, of which Buckley said "it enables a player to think and act a split-second more quickly". He also had the team sniffing neat Bovril as a livener – Buckley"s beefy poppers became Elland Road's version of amyl nitrate. One last whim, instructing his trainers to massage whisky on to his players" arms and legs as an embrocation against the cold, had them trotting on to the pitch reeking like Glasgow"s Barrowland ballroom at fighting time on a Saturday night. They were doused in it at Old Trafford in the fourth round of the FA Cup in 1951, getting through eight bottles of Scotch, and, possibly pissed on the fumes, lost 4-0.

In 1949-50, Buckley's Leeds had finally enjoyed a respectable run in the FA Cup, qualifying for their first quarter-final at the 23rd attempt. Cup fever was rampant in the city – 51,448 turned out for the fourth-round tie against Bolton and 53,099 for the 3-1 fifth-round victory over Cardiff City. The latter match came in the middle of a six-game winning streak in Division Two which pushed Leeds up to fifth and a point off second place.

Tottenham, 10 points clear at the top, had visited Elland Road in early January and Arthur Rowe's 'push and run' side went back to London having been beaten 3-0 by a Buckley team that had abandoned 'kick and rush' for a more quick and skilful short-passing style. It was some achievement given the same players – White Hart Lane gods such as Alf Ramsey, Bill Nicholson, Eddie Baily, Ron Burgess and Len Duquemin – went on to win the Second Division championship and the Division One title the following year.

United's defence of Jimmy Dunn, Charles and Jim Milburn thwarted every Tottenham attack that day, and they restricted Cardiff in the FA Cup to one goal, and that a penalty awarded for reasons that bewildered the correspondents. United were 2-0 up in the 11th minute after a diving header from Charles' tiny friend and compatriot, left-winger Harold Williams, and a shot from the outside-right Davy Cochrane. They were "irrepressible" and "irresistible" throughout, wrote the *Daily Herald*, and rounded off the victory with a sensational goal created by Jim McCabe dribbling 40 yards and round three opponents before teasing a pass through. Ray Iggleden RSVP'd the invitation with a screamer.

On the Monday there were queues for the mid-afternoon edition of the *Evening Post* to find out Leeds' fate in the draw. In the safe knowledge that his words were unlikely to feature in the northern papers, Arsenal's manager, Tom Whittaker, on hearing that Second Division Leeds were heading to Highbury said "Oh! Good!" before adding the more diplomatic: "Only good sides reach this stage of the competition and we will take the match very seriously." His earlier sentiment was echoed just about everywhere else: Fortune had favoured 'lucky Arsenal' yet again. Two hundred coaches and two special overnight trains transported about 8,000 Leeds fans to Highbury on Saturday, 4 March. "Men of the white and red roses clashed in friendly rivalry" when supporters met Stamford Bridge-bound Manchester United fans in Trafalgar Square, according to the news agencies in a sentence that would have had its author sectioned had it been written in the past 50 years. There was not much time to kill before boarding the Piccadilly Line to Highbury and the 62,273 crowd reached capacity long before kick-off. "It was something of a red letter day in the life of the Yorkshire club," wrote *The Times*' Geoffrey Green. "The fates might have been just a little bit kinder to Leeds United on this rather special occasion."

United more than held their own in the first half but could not make the breakthrough during the 10 minutes Leslie Compton, Arsenal's veteran centre-half, was absent having his head stitched after a collision with Leeds centre-forward Len Browning. United's wingers, Williams and Cochrane, were enterprising against the former England right-back Laurie Scott and the Wales left-back Walley Barnes and were given plenty of opportunities to run at them by Jim McCabe and the captain Tommy Burden, United's wing-halves whose aggressive running penned the illustrious Joe Mercer and Alex Forbes inside their own half. While Leeds dominated everywhere bar Arsenal's 18-yard box, a replay looked certain until the home side seized on a moment's inspiration from Forbes. The Scotland right-half cleaned out Cochrane with a Copping-brand tackle, bullocked forward past Iggleden and McCabe and slipped a pass down the left for Don Roper to centre. Denis Compton flicked a header on at the near post and Charles almost did the splits in straining to reach it but Reg Lewis got there first and poked a shot past Harry Searson.

Leeds rallied, Iggleden hit the bar, Arsenal's goalkeeper George Swindin, a wartime United guest, had to dive head first at his feet to stop another effort and Williams almost managed to gull him with an inswinging corner which he saw late and just scrambled to smother. Buckley, so often stereotyped as an advocate of an unfussy style of direct play that frowned on dribbling and promoted long balls up the flanks for wingers to chase, win and cross, was undone at Highbury, wrote Green, because the old dog had learnt new tricks. "Close passing pays no sort of dividends against this Arsenal defence in depth," he concluded, "and Leeds should have realised it long before the end." Whether it was ability or experience they lacked to improvise is not recorded. It would be unfair to say it was an absence of testicular fortitude to defy Buckley's iron rule. It simply wasn't done back then as became embarrassingly apparent when Hungary ran rings round England in 1953 and left them looking even more backdated the following year.

Green picked out Charles for praise – "in command down the centre and living up to all the good things said of him" – as did Denis Compton who went over to the 18-year-old at the end of the match to congratulate him on his performance. Only 11 months earlier Billy Houliston had called Charles on his first-team debut the best centre-half he had ever played against and the exposure he received at Highbury, playing for the first time in front of the national press, established him as a public figure, rumour at last made flesh.

Though well-placed for a promotion charge when they left Highbury, Leeds won only four of their last 11 league matches and finished in fifth, a position they matched in 1950-51 when the first year of Charles' national service often involved him playing a match for his regiment on the Wednesday, a game for the Army on the Thursday and one for United each Saturday. Buckley's third season began brightly, endured an autumn slump and was twice revived by four successive victories over Christmas and seven wins and a draw from their final eight games.

In his first 83 appearances for Leeds Charles had scored only once, a penalty against Plymouth Argyle, but the Major, responding to four games without a win before they played Manchester City away, decided he was the answer to their malfunctioning attack which had provided only 51 goals, the fifth-worst in the Division. To emphasise his point he also put three of the starting forwards, inside-right Iggleden, inside-left Ernie Stevenson and winger Williams on the transfer list as well as sending Charles out in the No.9 shirt. "The shock must have shown on my face," remembered Charles, because he smiled, patted me on the shoulder and said, 'Don't worry you'll be all right. Jack, you just go out there and play, and that's it. You know all the tricks the centre-forwards use against you – now you can use them yourself."

Charles set up his housemate Peter Harrison's goal in the 4-1 defeat on Easter Saturday and kept his place up front for the home match against Hull City on Easter Monday. The *Yorkshire Post* previewed it by saying it would be an intriguing and strangely engaged battle between the best two centre-halves in the Football League, Neil Franklin who had been England's regular centre-half for the five years after the war until he was seduced by the renegade Colombia league and walked out on Stoke City in May 1950, and Charles, who was moonlighting as a striker. Franklin had been banned on his return and sold to Hull but he was only 29 and remained a tremendous player until he succumbed to knee trouble later in his career. Managed by Raich Carter and with Don Revie in the side, Hull had better individuals than Leeds but were less of a team and Charles scored twice in a 3-1 victory. He scored again on his next outing at centre-forward in a 1-0 victory over Grimsby but resumed at centre-half for 20 of his 23 appearances in 1951-52 when Leeds dropped a place to sixth. Cartilage operations on both knees ruled him out until December and on his return he helped them stay in contention with masterly performances at the back. By February United were fifth and only one point off top but three defeats in their next seven games was the catalyst for Buckley to gamble again and make his best player move up. He did not score in those three matches and though Leeds were unbeaten their chances of sneaking into second place were undone by defeats by Swansea and Cardiff.

When Charles was demobbed from the Army he was 6ft 2in and weighed 14st. Such physically imposing players are vulnerable to lazy categorisation and Harry Gregg, the Manchester United goalkeeper and hero of Munich, summed up how it helped him at centre-half. "Trying to get around Charles was like trying to get around a double-decker bus," he said. Yet it was the timing and fairness of his tackling, vision and passing with both feet as well as indomitability in the air that enhanced his stature in defence. As a forward he was built like a heavyweight except he was lithe and intrepid, roving from wing to wing in emulation of the opponents who had given him most trouble when he had played at the back. He may have looked like a battering ram, and was so brave and powerful a header that he had a calloused bump on his forehead from the scuffing of the lace, but he was also a slippery manipulator of defenders, keen as Colman's once he had wrong-footed them. He also struck the T-ball so hard with both feet it's a wonder he did not break a goalkeeper's fingers. He was never particularly sure of himself in attack and there was a sense for a while that he was only doing it because Buckley insisted he should. In the Major's last season, though, he began to emerge as a thoroughbred No.9, no longer feeling like an impostor, a Buckley PR punt or a stopgap.

For three successive campaigns Leeds had missed out on going up by five points or less. If Buckley was to replicate his achievement at Wolves, the fifth season would be the one where all the spadework would bear fruit. Except one thing was different: his 70th birthday fell in November 1952 and he had been growing increasingly tetchy about the constraints placed on him by the lack of funds. He had generated transfer profits in three of his four years, brought in enough to allow gate receipts to liquidate the bonds and gradually pay back the overdraft. Buckley had done exactly the job he had been hired to do, signing young players, non-League talents such as Eric Kerfoot, and flipping those he didn't ultimately fancy to bring in more money. The board had used some of the income on 'sanitary improvements' though the bogs in the Kop remained notoriously disgusting until the late Sixties. In general they let the ground fall into shabby disrepair until the West Stand caught fire in 1956 and even put the prices up in 1951 and 1952 to cover the drop-off in crowds after the 1949-50 peak.

One can understand that having rid themselves of the debenture, the board would have been determined to dilute their own liabilities and bow down before the god of self-sufficiency. They were Conservatives after all, even Sam Bolton who won a ward by-election in Beeston and spent a fractious term on the council. When complaints about the cost of entrance mounted in 1950, the chairman addressed the supporters club, asking them "to stamp out any grumbling they heard and put the grumblers on the right track". If solvency meant a dilapidated ground and having to piss in a concrete trench clogged with fag butts, it was still solvency. Buckley, mindful of his time running out, was understandably fed up and, for the first time in his career, longed for a shortcut. In the end he prevailed and the board let him buy George Meek, Don Mills and the dashing and dapper Yorkshireman Albert Nightingale for a combined £32,000. He had to sell Browning to Sheffield United for £12,000 to offset some of the outlay, and the loss of the leading scorer from two of the past three seasons had consequences for Charles.

Ken Hastie, Frank Fidler and Barry Smith all flunked their auditions in the No.9 shirt and on 11 October 1952, when Leeds were 19th after 13 games, Buckley named Charles at centre-forward again. He did not score in the defeat by Sheffield United but he did in each of the next six matches, including two hat-tricks in a run of 10 goals in five matches when none of his team-mates got on the scoresheet alongside him. His three against Hull and Neil Franklin were, wrote Ronald Crowther in the *Yorkshire Evening News*, the result of "one of the finest displays of devastating marksmanship that I have ever seen from an Elland Road leader in post-war times", which only sounds like extravagant praise if you discount the very low bar.

In 28 appearances in attack that season Charles scored 26 times and struck up a good chalk-and-cheese partnership with Nightingale. Charles was strong but valued fair play, even if Jack Charlton reckoned he "ran with his arms and elbows high and when he went on a surge he left a trail of human devastation behind him. Bloody Gentle Giant indeed!" Nightingale, by contrast, was all spite and needle, a fine incisive inside-forward with a streak of devilry that another United No.8, Allan Clarke, would share. His gamesmanship became notorious, practising an 'anything goes' philosophy when out of the referee's sight, nipping his marker's ankle with his studs to buy time in the box, going over the ball in the tackle and exaggerating fouls. "He'd get tackled on the halfway line and fall down in the area," said Charles while Charlton put him amongst the most unscrupulous players he ever encountered. Buckley's Leeds had hitherto been characterised by an honest absence of guile or cruelty. Nightingale fixed that singlehandedly, scoring eight goals, creating more for Charles and so consistently getting up opponent's noses he established squatter's rights.

It came too late for Buckley. His signings promised much but it was clear by Christmas that the team would take more time to become genuine contenders, not least because Charles' emerging brilliance at centre-forward left a chasm at centre-half. On 6 April after three consecutive defeats he announced he would leave at the end of the season and take the manager's job at Walsall who were about to finish bottom of the Third Division North for the second year running and apply for re-election. Even at 70 he was a glutton for a challenge. "This will be my last job in football," he said. "But it will be my best." He was half right.

Gimmickry and rigour will always define Major Buckley's image but what he achieved at Leeds United outlived the kicking contraption, whisky rub-downs and his tyrannical nature. If all he had done was recruit and nurture John Charles and Jack Charlton, he would deserve to be among the best of Leeds' 37 managers. Yet he did far more than that. His entrepreneurship put the club on the road to financial health for the first time in its existence, he raised its profile throughout the country immeasurably just by being there and he built the foundations of a successful side. His successor ought to have dropped to his knees in gratitude at his legacy. Be that as it may, Frank Buckley knew better than anyone that Raich Carter was congenitally incapable of honouring any debt that would eclipse his own star.

10

A TASTE OF HONEY

The moment John Charles clapped eyes on the city of Leeds in 1948 he was overwhelmed by a steepling sense of anti-climax. "My first impression from the window of the train was what a dirty old place it was," he wrote in his final autobiography. "And Elland Road was not nearly so grand as we had anticipated." Two years later 15-year-old Jackie Charlton arrived at the ground for a trial, following the trail set by his uncles Jack, George and Jim Milburn. "I had the wind knocked out of my sails when I saw the place for the first time," he noted in his testimonial programme. "The terraces were made from ashes, not concrete, and there was more than a liberal sprinkling of weeds. [It] had a look of untidiness and I was disappointed." And these were sons of Swansea and Ashington, not Heidelberg and Florence. Anything that was grotty by their standards must have been miserably dingy.

The post-war city centre gradually became more vibrant as the Forties turned into the Fifties, the shops replaced functional drabness with colour and their range of consumer goods broadened ever more, while at night the dancehalls, cinemas and Greek and Italian coffee bars were rammed. But in 1953 Leeds United lacked any iota of glamour. Of course they had the 21-year-old Charles, the finest prospect in the country, even though centre-halves, including the best, do not draw the casual fan. His triumphant conversion to centre-forward would certainly help convince United's vast band of 'casual' fans to turn out more frequently yet nothing inspires more effectively than hope. If the directors were unwilling to hazard the hard-won financial stability Major Buckley had achieved by buying their way to promotion, they were not averse to employing a manager with sheen and prestige who could use his aura as an attraction – cynics would say distraction – until the team matched the city's budding renaissance.

Raich Carter had been their second choice in 1948 and his reluctance to accept a three-year contract and choice of Hull instead conveniently triggered Buckley's move to Leeds. He had been player-manager of Hull for three seasons, taking them up from the Third Division North at the first attempt but he resigned just after the start of the fourth for reasons he and the City directors never divulged and retired to run a tobacconist's. Hull retained his registration and he returned as a player in December to help the fight against relegation. Carter was back behind the counter the following summer, regularly visited by journalists seeking his forthright opinions on the game as well as 20 Senior Service, but was enticed by Cork Athletic to play in the League of Ireland for the last three months of the 1952-53 season for £50 a match plus expenses. At the age of 39 he won the Irish Cup, and before the coronation in June Carter was appointed to succeed Buckley for the second time. Tragically, during the couple of weeks while he was putting his shop on the market and looking for a house in Leeds, Carter was widowed when his wife, Rose, who had suffered from heart problems since giving birth to their only daughter, died at the age of 38.

On the surface it was a shrewd appointment. There could be no sugaring the fact that frustration had driven Major Buckley to leave Leeds for Walsall, the worst professional club in England, a side so poor his tireless and trusted methods had no discernible impact. Walsall finished 24th and 23rd in the Third Division North in two seasons under 'the club builder supreme'. Leeds' hiring of Carter, 30 years Buckley's junior, camouflaged his predecessor's reasons for walking away – he had envisioned solvency as a launch pad, the directors saw it as a sanctuary.

"Silver-haired and senatorial," according to one newspaper, Horatio Carter had been a magnificent player, as skilful as he was demanding, impeccably turned out in his trench coat, a contemporary contrast with the Major and his tweed bonnet and knickerbockers. He had captained Sunderland to the title in 1936 at the age of 22 and the FA Cup in 1937, winning the Cup again with Derby in 1946. He may not have preened like some of the most arrogant footballers of subsequent generations but 'the Maestro' played with a swagger and upbraided those he felt weren't up to scratch with a dismissiveness that could be construed as contempt. Even when playing alongside internationals he was prone to shouting criticism, gesticulating and mugging for the crowd. At Hull City Carter had bought Don Revie, who idolised him, ostensibly as his own replacement as a scheming inside-forward. Pretty soon Carter decided he preferred himself, played Revie out of position and sold him on to Manchester City where he prospered. It smacked of a reluctance to share the limelight.

There are two types of taking responsibility in football and Carter, as a player, had the rarer one in abundance. He was a leader who had the courage to demand possession when seemingly boxed in and seized the onus of carrying his team forward. But the normal, human quality of acknowledging mistakes, he lacked. Even recognition as a truly great player did not cure his sly habit of deflecting blame. It should have alarmed Leeds. Yet Sam Bolton, the chairman, blithely accepted the recommendation of "a very well-known coach [who] told me that he knew nobody who could better impart his knowledge to other players, professional or amateur".

The sole problem with that glowing reference is that Carter was not a coach in any meaningful sense, nor did he even believe in the value of coaching. Years later he told *The Guardian*'s Frank Keating that his philosophy had always been "you're either a player or you're not" and Keating, sometimes sentimentally indulgent of his boyhood heroes, did not suggest it as a reason for his managerial career petering out in failure.

Leeds United congratulated themselves on the appointment of their first 'tracksuit manager' while neglecting to notice that the reason he had his training togs on was to take part in the sessions, particularly the games on the treacherous and unreliable gravel and ash of the car park, not conduct them. "No one ever coached you, there was nobody you could talk to about your game," wrote Jack Charlton who had made his debut at centre-half as a 17-year-old in Buckley's last match. "The only training we used to do [under Carter] was to run the long side of the pitch, jog the short side, sprint the long side and so on. We used to have five-a-side and eight-a-side matches on the cinder surface of the car park. We never really had team talks or a run-down on the opposition. Leeds United wasn't what I would call a professional club in those days."

The tone was set, said Charles, when the players reported back for pre-season. "On his first day, he called us into his office, told us to sit down and then started showing us photographs of his playing career," he recalled. Carter also incorporated a portrait of himself into wage negotiations, Charles revealed, the manager hooking his thumb over his shoulder at a picture on the wall behind his desk and saying: "You'll get no rise until you play like him." Carter's conceit contrasted starkly with Charles' modesty. Right until his last breath, politeness guided Charles' stated opinions about his clubs and colleagues but he made an exception for Raich. "He was never happier than when talking about himself," he wrote, "and he often took the credit for others' achievements. I always felt he was in love with himself." His team-mates agreed and were convinced that 'The Maestro' was seduced by the green-eyed monster when attention was focused on star player rather than his manager.

Carter made one signing, Eddie Burbanks from Hull, an outside-left he had played with at Sunderland and Derby who was 40 years and four months old when the season began. The best decision he made was to retain Charles at centre-forward and he scored four in the opening game, a 6-0 victory over Notts County, and a hat-trick in the next, a 4-2 defeat of Rotherham United. Albert Nightingale, the spit of George Orwell, playing Dr Jekyll off the pitch, Mr Hyde on it, also scored in both games and between them in Carter's first season they scored 59 league goals, the No.9 bagging 42 and the No.8 17.

A flying start and prolific forwards ought to have made United genuine promotion contenders but their form was sporadic and they foundered away from home, letting in four at Swansea and five at Leicester by the end of August to crash that bandwagon. A six-game winless streak in the autumn meant they could not get it rolling again. More worrying still was the extent to which the entire club was now reliant on Charles. When the news that he would miss the home game with Bristol Rovers in October due to tonsillitis was published in the evening papers, the crowd fell by 9,000, a fraction under a third. What the struggling team needed was coherence but they were left to their own devices. Perverting the old adage, Carter neither gave starving men a fish nor taught them how to fish. Indeed he once told Keating that his old Sunderland manager, Johnny Cochrane, would not even know the identity of their opponents when he went into the home dressing room before matches. When they informed him he would reply, "'Oh, you'll piss that lot boys' and clear off to watch. None of this blackboard nonsense." Some common sense would have been useful. For players craving organisation and strategy, Carter's approach, lifted straight from the Thirties, left them to work it out for themselves and if they sank, well, too bad, it would prove they were simply not good enough. After all, he could not play the game for them.

Or could he? The main reason Carter had been restricted to one signing and that of a player eight months his senior was that the United board had finally decided to erect floodlights. The Football League would not sanction their use in games until 1956 but four Southern League clubs who had taken the plunge were attracting double the number of spectators for midweek night matches than for their Saturday afternoon kick-offs. Lights may have been outlawed for domestic competition but it did not mean they could not be used for other matches and Bradford Northern, who had installed them at Odsal, had demonstrated that the West Riding public had a keen appetite for floodlit sport. In the capital, Highbury's lights had enticed enormous crowds to essentially meaningless matches such as London FA vs Berlin, which brought in 55,000.

United had discussed purchasing some in 1952 but backed out. By 1953, however, they had been persuaded of the considerable returns their investment was likely to realise and sanctioned what were then the most expensive and powerful set in the country, £7,000 for 70 bulbs across four pylons emitting 90,000 watts. These were not the landmark 1973 towers, the tallest in Europe that lasted 20 years and became the ground's distinguishing feature, the diamond lights summoning those of us of a certain age out to play more effectively than any bat signal. The original four were about half the size of their iconic replacements and were ready by early November, right on time for a Monday night friendly against Hibernian.

It was just the occasion for Carter to pick himself at inside-left and he scored two and made one of Charles' double in a 4-1 victory. It was such a success – 31,600 turned up – that they repeated the experiment over the next four Mondays with Carter continuing to play in attack alongside Charles, beating Dundee, in front of 34,500, Falkirk before 17,000 on a filthy night, Park Avenue in the West Riding Senior Cup semi-final to a crowd of 18,800 and, going for one squeeze of the lemon too many, East Fife when 12,000 saw their manager "playing almost at walking pace" lead them to a 3-1 victory. In just five weeks they had attracted an extra 112,000 paying spectators though the gates and even after deductions for match fees and travel costs, the club pulled in £18,000 from the games, turning a loss of about £4,500 in 1953 to the same amount in profit the following year. Where there was light there was hope. "Floodlit football could well be a shortcut to our League ambitions," proclaimed Bolton after the healthy gate for the Hibs match. "I have hopes that the inauguration of the floodlights will be the start of a new era at Elland Road."

Yet, try as they might to economise, scrimping on ground maintenance, cutting the training and medical budgets in half, the overdraft was growing because of the fall-off in crowds for Second Division matches which fell from an average of 30,200 in 1949-50 (boosted by the FA Cup run) to 21,800 in 1953-54 as well as the punitive entertainments tax. In 1954 the club continued to be scandalously undercapitalised – only 19,000 worth of shares had ever been issued – and left them with very thin bedrock. Carrying assets worth £56,000 comprised of ground, land and club houses which depreciated every year, the books were startlingly unbalanced. So when contractual loyalty payments of £750 for five years' service fell due – and in 1952-53 Charles, Ray Iggleden and Grenville Hair were all paid out – directors' loans and the bank were their only means of bridging the gap. Issuing more shares threatened a loss of control and it was an option the board continued to reject in spite of the financial strain. Perhaps if Carter had come out of retirement in the League instead of stealing the show on Monday nights they might have broken 30,000 on a Saturday afternoon and helped him in his desire to raise £20,000 for new players. There was some clamour for it but Carter resisted, restricting himself to friendlies. The passing was as incisive as ever but his legs had gone and, according to Charles, the loss of nip made him "a bugger. He used to kick his own players in training".

United's form under the lights was not replicated in day games and even after Charles' fourth hat-trick of the season in a 4-2 victory over Rotherham on 19 December, they were only ninth. As a sales pitch, then, Carter's speech at the AGM that month was hardly constructive. "I am no creeper and we have not got a good side, but we have a useful one," he said. "One that will not be relegated and one that will do quite well." The players thought him smug but the board doubtlessly wished he would be more positive about his power to effect change in public. Again it was an appeal to supporters' better nature, a plea for understanding, the story of the past 33 years, a switch-back ride between bollocking them and asking for sympathy. "When I was a mere 'bob-side' supporter I thought I saw the faults of the board," lamented Bolton. "Now that I am on the board I am finding it very much more difficult than I have ever thought." Tellingly, only 90 of 900 shareholders bothered to turn up to hear his overture which ended with a request for the supporters' club to get weaving towards greater fundraising targets. Six years in the Second Division and constantly being reminded that the road to the promised land was a test of endurance rather than patience had bred an apathy that was smothering Leeds United to death.

In January they beat the leaders and eventual champions Leicester City 7-1 but promptly lost their next three games and dawdled to the end of the season in 10th. Jack Marsden stepped up from the reserves to take Charles' place at centre-half and Carter even recommended him to the Football Association for an England B cap. But he could not cover as much ground as Charles and was four inches shorter, a handicap he could not overcome with his spring. Jimmy Dunn and Grenville Hair were solid full-backs, Eric Kerfoot and the captain Tommy Burden dependable wing-halves with drive, good passing and heft in the tackle, and Jack Scott a reliable goalkeeper who had the misfortune to be kicked in the head and carried off during Leicester's earlier resounding win. Together, however, and under Carter's lack of guidance, Leeds United were a colander, letting in 81 goals, only eight fewer than they scored. Charles finished with 42, a number yet unsurpassed nor likely to be, but he was missed at the back in an era when headed goals were commonplace. "If there was a corner kick John just told me to stay on the line and said he'd head it down to me," Scott told the

Yorkshire Evening Post. "No one could jump as high as him. It was a piece of cake playing with him."

The following season the limit of Burden's tolerance was breached by Carter blaming Scott for conceding a goal against Bury in one of five successive defeats over a fortnight in August and September. The captain rounded on his manager in the dressing room, forcefully informed him he was the one at fault and had his transfer request on the manager's desk by Monday morning.

Carter made the sensible decision to give Charles the captaincy in Burden's place and sent him out at centre-half. He made a mistake in his first game back in defence that cost Leeds the goal in a 1-0 defeat by Stoke but from then on he was largely imperious. Even though they won six of their next seven games it was not enough for Charles and for the first time he formally asked to leave. Buckley had once contemplated selling him to Cardiff, who kept sniffing about and tried to play the Wales card. The Major said he would release him if they offered a record £35,000, telling Burden, who doubted his sincerity, that football was a hard-headed business and, favourite son or not, cash in the bank to guarantee his own wages was always his priority. In 1952 Cardiff had jibbed at the price. This time they joined Arsenal, Sunderland, Sheffield Wednesday, Blackpool and Chelsea in declaring their interest at £40,000. After Charles stated his preference for going home with Cardiff, City's chairman travelled north prepared to meet the fee and the *Yorkshire Post*'s Eric Stanger pointed out the pros as well as the cons of letting him go, principally the opportunity it would afford them to end their reliance on him and strengthen several positions. The board called a meeting to make the final verdict and Bolton emerged to say that they had agreed unanimously not to sell, telling the crowd over the tannoy before that night's repeat friendly against Hibernian. A poll in the *Evening News* recorded that its readers were split 51 per cent to 49 in favour of his staying which exposes the pointlessness of asking uninterested parties because the supporters at Elland Road, 'Yelland Road' in the Fifties pun, roared their approval. The *Daily Mirror* accused Leeds of restraint of ambition if not of trade, predicting trouble: "[They] have an unhappy player as they have tried to avert the inevitable." It would not be the last misreading of Charles' character or misunderstanding of the fatalistic attitude footballers had towards their lack of agency under 'retain and transfer' regulations. "I'm still anxious to play in the First Division," said Charles. "But what can I do?"

What he did was commit himself to the cause with exemplary class. During six games at centre-forward that season, United conceded 20, in the 34 he played at centre-half, they let in 31. His presence at the back galvanised the team and they won 12 and drew four of his first 17 games as captain. They were 20th after his first match in the job and second on Christmas Day, level on points with the leaders Blackburn. His reading of the game, nose for danger and ability to eat up the ground as he smoothly accelerated to intercept a pass was as important as his stature. In his place up front, the 33-year old utility forward Harold Brook, bought from Sheffield United for £600 in the summer, was not as prolific as Charles but chipped in with 16 goals including both in the 2-0 victory over Blackburn Rovers at Elland Road in their penultimate game of the season that took them to the top of the table. They won the last match, too, a 3-1 victory over Fulham but the old football equation – points in the bag are better than games in hand as Leeds so harrowingly proved in 1972 – did not work in their favour in 1955. Luton, Birmingham and Rotherham all won their rearranged matches and Leeds were left in fourth, one point behind them. Superficially, the poor start was culpable and yet it was those defeats that forced Carter to sacrifice Charles' goals and make them a more effective team. Losing at Lincoln City, in 13th, and Plymouth, in 20th, during the second-half of the season caused the most significant damage. Switching Charles resulted in United conceding 28 fewer goals than the previous season but every action has an equal and opposite reaction and they also scored 19 fewer. Each choice with Charles had consequences. Without cloning him or the money for an upgrade on his stand-ins in either position, it was the yang Leeds were forced to accept for the yin of his defensive brilliance.

Since his debut in April 1953, Jack Charlton had played only one more first-team match in two seasons because of his long absences on national service in Windsor with the Royal Horse Guards. Buckley's military connections may have swung him a place in a Yorkshire barracks and the proximity to play on Saturdays but he was long gone and Charlton benefited immeasurably from his time away. In September 1955 Carter made him his regular centre-half after an erratic start of four wins, a draw and three defeats threatened to spoil the momentum of their upswing. It was not a ploy that was immediately designed to liberate Charles for centre-forward duty because he was needed at right-half. Mercifully, after four games with the four on his back he went up front for the last match in October and stayed there for the remainder of the season. During Charlton's time in the Army he had captained the Guards to the Army Cup, the first private to do so, and he returned to Leeds with far more self-assurance about his own ability than ever before. Growing up in the shadow of his younger brother,

Bobby, 'Our Kid', even his football mad mother doubted his chances of making it as a professional. Charlton yearned for instruction and the little he received came from Charles who taught him how to face up an attacker on the half-turn and how to deceive opponents about the direction of headers. The Army had not square-bashed the bolshiness out of him and he was not afraid to tell Charles off during a match when he felt he was in the way at a corner. Being throttled by the 'Gentle Giant' in the dressing room at full-time taught him to choose his targets with more discretion.

From a position of ninth at the end of October, they began to pick up. Six successive home victories before the year's end were undermined by heavy defeats at Plymouth, Leicester and Middlesbrough who together put 14 goals into Royden Wood's net. Jackie Overfield on the left wing and Harold Williams or George Meek on the right blossomed after the autumn and set up good chances for Charles. "You couldn't miss John with a cross," Overfield told Mario Risoli, "he was like a lighthouse". He also relied on Nightingale's passes and his own initiative to thump in shots from outside the box or swerve past defenders like a one-man armada. One win from their first eight games of 1956, and that a 2-1 victory over the leaders Sheffield Wednesday before their biggest home League crowd for six years, consigned them to ninth, five points off second. It was the old problem, bolstering their firepower with Charles and playing Carter's direct style left them vulnerable at the back to quick opponents bombing past the wing-halves and into the channels either side of the centre-half. Charlton had moments proving his great promise but was only 20 and had his hands full most of the time.

On Easter Monday, something remarkable happened. It was a day late for a conventional resurrection but it was sorely needed because Leeds' defeat on Easter Saturday after heartening back-to-back victories had punctured all optimism. As ever Charles was to the fore with a hat-trick against Fulham in a 6-1 victory, the first of six consecutive wins to end the season. He had been playing at inside-right since the middle of February and had taken no time to adjust. Putting the hard-running Brook back through the middle and Nightingale's recovery from injury gave Carter the perfect blend. Having romped past Leicester and beaten Doncaster they went up to third for the visit of Bristol Rovers who were one place above them with two games left while Leeds still had three to play. For the Fulham match on a Bank Holiday 20,115 had backed them. For the crunch game 19 days later 49,274 pitched up, emphasising once more their potential with a bit of encouragement. United went 1-0 down after three minutes before Charles equalised with an acrobatic, roundhouse volley and set up the winner for

Overfield with a foray to the byline and fizzing, daisy-cutter cross. The two points put their destiny in their own hands with two away games in Yorkshire to come. A win and a draw would send them back up after nine years and they took 10,000 fans to Rotherham, where Nightingale scored both in a 2-0 win, and 15,000 to Hull, Carter's adopted home town, on 28 April 1956. A point would be good enough for the runners' up position against a side that had already been relegated and Leeds duly laboured to 1-1 at half-time. United did not play with any fluency, the tension was palpable, and they needed a penalty that Charles scudded into the top-corner, after giving the keeper the eyes, to take the lead. The captain was also instrumental in helping Brook to score two late on and though the number of his 'assists' were obviously not recorded, poring through the match reports suggest they were about half as many again as the 28 goals he scored in 29 games at centre-forward and inside-right. What cannot be computed are the chances he created for his team-mates just by being in attack and occupying two, sometimes three defenders, on his own.

There is a famous photograph of the players after the match in a state of semi-undress being served Moet & Chandon champagne by Carter and toasting promotion from their Boothferry Park dressing-room issue, ceramic, utility-ware teacups. Charlton, with a plaited loaf of curly hair like a Postcard Records bass player, Carter, Jimmy Dunn and Kerfoot stare straight into the camera. Charles, the waistband of his white shorts rolled down so he could hitch them up to free his thighs, teeth discoloured by a defender's elbow, looks off to the right as if even in such company, and at such a moment, he was reticent. They returned to Leeds that evening to an official reception at the Civic Hall and a couple of thousand supporters gathered on Calverley Street and Portland Crescent to hear the Lord Mayor, Sam Bolton and Carter address them. Tiring quickly of the formalities, a shout of "Two-four-six-eight, who do we appreciate?" and "We want John" quickly spread and Charles at last bashfully approached the microphone. "With the support you have given us, we have done very well," he said. "Promotion is a great thing." It was more young Mr Grace than Eric Cantona at the Town Hall 36 years later but typical of a man for whom fuss was a curse. It was why he protested so vehemently about the press' "King Charles" of "Charles United" caricature and always spread the credit. Never mind the lines, what mattered was the stage and promotion now gave him one to match his talent. There would be no more bushels for Leeds United to hide his light under and, victims of his success, their hold upon him had never been more tenuous.

11

TOO HOT TO HOLD

There were no summer signings for the usual, by now tedious, reasons and Raich Carter loyally spun no investment into a vote of confidence in the men who had earned promotion. "We're a young team," he said, "and individually the players will be able to reveal their skill more openly in the higher class." There was some debate over where John Charles should play during the summer of 1956. Derek Wallis of the *Daily Mirror* was convinced that he should stay in the forward line because "Charlton had become a second Charles at centre-half". It was a case of premature acclamation and excessive, too, yet Carter ruled on the eve of the season that Charles would stay in the No.8 shirt and Jack Charlton, the cocky kid his team-mates tried to tame by calling 'Turkey' or 'The Giraffe', would be a Division One centre-half. "For me inside-forwards are always the key men and Charles, with the necessary ability, will be our main link as well as our most dangerous spearhead," Carter said. And his captain concurred, explaining duties that would have made Superman blanch, incorporating a diplomatic tickle for Carter's ego: "You are expected to help in attack, fall back in defence and in my case get goals. The gov'nor used to do all these things but footballers of his mould don't come along every day."

If there were no new players, they could at least wrap the old ones in new clothes. Major Buckley had ditched the jerseys of contrasting halves and put them in a yellow approximation of gold in 1948, going so far as to change the white shorts to black, presumably in homage to his beloved Wolves rather than Roderick Spode. Carter increasingly favoured the blue change shirts and in 1954-55 they were used more frequently. On opening day Charles led the players out in sleeker, lightweight, v-neck versions in the new official colours of royal blue shirts with gold trim, white shorts and blue-and-gold-hooped socks. In blue, Harold Brook, who worked during the week as a hardboard salesman and trained alone on a Sheffield works ground, set up Jackie Overfield to score the first goal in the second minute against Everton, crossed for Charles to head in unmarked and then scored a 21-minute hat-trick himself as Leeds walked back up the Elland

Road tunnel at half-time 5-0 ahead. They played with pace and crisp, long passing to counteract the sodden, heavy pitch, eased off in the second half as both sides, reduced to 10 men in the first period when Derek Mayers and Albert Nightingale were injured, succumbed to tiredness and trotted in 5-1 winners.

Next United beat Charlton away 2-1 with two goals from Charles, or "the towering terror" as the *Daily Herald* was now calling him, to go top of a meaningless table. It was a breathless start and could not last. They stayed in London after the Thursday evening visit to the Valley to play Tottenham. Leeds equalised after 32 minutes with an own goal but were hammered 5-1, shredded by Charles' Welsh friend Terry Medwin. The London papers were quick to crow about Spurs piercing the hype. "Hitherto unbeaten Leeds, the hotdogs up from the Second Division, were made to look anything but a dangerous pack," wrote *The People*'s Maurice Smith. "Not wolfhounds but King Charles' spaniels. Leeds were as docile as that."

The spaniels recovered their regal spring to beat Charlton 4-0 in the return and racked up three successive victories in September, Charles scoring in each, to sit comfortably in second, a point behind the Busby Babes, after a 2-0 away victory over Wolves who were the only team capable of going toe-to-toe with Manchester United and had been champions in 1954 and would be again in 1958 and 1959. After all these years United were on a roll. Would the good times follow?

Just before 2am on the Tuesday morning after Charles' two goals had delivered the win at Molineux, Arthur Price, proprietor of the fish and chip shop opposite the main gates on Elland Road, was trying to get to sleep. "I was sitting up in bed when the sky lit up," he remembered. Opening his curtains he gazed across the road to see the West Stand ablaze. "I ran out in my pyjamas to a telephone box and called the fire brigade. The stand went up like wildfire and within a few minutes was a raging inferno." It took five fire engines and 10 hoses to put it out, leaving only the warped skeleton of the roof girders, scorch marks on the concrete terrace and a brown, singed apron of the pitch as relics. The wooden seats, cushions, pitch and bitumen roof, the club's offices, dressing-rooms, archive, physio equipment, pennants, tournament trophies, goalposts, footballs, groundsmen's tools, shirts, shorts, jockstraps, socks, training kit and boots had been destroyed when a spark from an electrical fault turned the predominantly wooden stand into a tinderbox. The morning after players helped clear the rubble and walked across the car park for a smoke and a meeting on the two pitches opposite on Fullerton Park that Major Buckley had had the foresight to buy when the speedway stadium closed down after the war.

The club scrambled around for new kit and boots, asked local residents to let players change in their front rooms and pressed ahead with preparations to play Aston Villa on the Saturday in front of the gutted shell. It was arranged for the two sides to strip at the Whitehall Print factory premises behind the Kop and then brought to the ground by coach for kick-off. Charles disembarked in his hastily sewn jersey, walked his team through the tunnel with the blackened steelwork overhead and led them to a 1-0 victory in front of 35,388 spectators watching from the other three sides. The club had put on its bravest face, but inside it was quaking.

Having written down the 51-year-old stand's value year on year since the last major upgrade, the lower part of the barrel roof added in 1923-24, the directors knew that the insurance payout would be pitifully short of the £180,000 estimate to replace it. As it always has in times of crisis, the board approached the council for help, but instead of a loan they jointly launched a public appeal. It proved the easiest fundraising initiative in the club's history and contributions flowed in over the autumn and winter, totalling £60,000. It enabled the club to arrange the swift demolition of the upper part of the stand, make the lower terrace safe enough to reopen and put design and construction contracts out to tender. "In adversity came solidarity," wrote Simon Inglis in his seminal *Football Grounds of England and Wales*. Perversely, the average gate would be the highest in the club's existence and that in a year when those of Everton, Newcastle, Manchester City and Chelsea all fell.

The architectural firm of Braithwaite and Jackson won the job and the reinforced concrete and steel structure, eventually housing 4,000 seats in the top tier and room for 6,000 to stand in the bottom paddock, was built by Robert R Roberts Ltd, rising out of the ashes as the spring and summer progressed. After decades of neglect, it is to the directors' credit that they opted for such a forward-looking design with a sweeping, cantilever roof, superior sightlines, a revitalising splash of modernity in its blue steel façade with white Leeds United AFC sign that finally gave Elland Road a chic focal point to divert attention from the ramshackle stands around it. At last the board seemed to understand that this was a place the devoted treasure, a secular shrine, rather than a once-a-fortnight revenue generator, the cost of whose upkeep peeved them. It gave the ground and the club an identity. The sign and fascia were taken down in an act of cultural vandalism when the ugly Brookside Close-style brick banqueting suite was bolted on to the back of the stand in 1992, but for 35 years it symbolised the club and was visible from the train heading north into town and the motorways. Back then United's quest for commercial revenue would always trump heritage.

Five games without a win after the euphoria of beating Villa advertised the team's callowness and the loss of Nightingale, who did not recover from his cartilage injury, mangled their attacking balance. Charles often made up for it on his own, performing with unbeatable aerial power and unstoppable vigour, scoring two hat-tricks, 10 doubles and almost bursting the net with his torpedoed free-kick in a 2-1 defeat by Manchester United. His 38 goals made him the division's most productive striker and his irrepressibility was rendering him irresistible. He was sensational in the 3-2 victory over Newcastle at St James' Park, helping the flash-in-the-pan debutant Frank McKenna to two and scoring the other himself, and he and Brook steamrollered Blackpool 5-0 on Boxing Day. Charlton, however, suffered a dramatic loss of form and focus, lost an argument with Carter and then his place, and the old defensive frailties set off a lurch down the table to eighth after four defeats and only one win from their last six games.

In August 1956 a spokesman for the Italian Soccer Federation, noting rumours that Charles was contemplating a move to Serie A, pointed out that all but Torino had registered their one permissible overseas player and hence it was "unfounded". Throughout the 1956-57 season, as Charles proved himself so thrillingly a forward of Division One quality and with the knowledge that after the fire Leeds were unlikely to be so obdurate, inquiries were received from Internazionale, Juventus, Lazio and Real Madrid. The catalyst, obviously, was his staggering form and the mind-bending contradiction between the broadness of his beam and dainty touch, thunderous shooting, lithe speed and supreme balance. But a change in Italian regulations allowing Serie A clubs to field two foreign players also sparked the rush.

Gigi Peronace, a man for whom any job description would be inaccurate and restrictive – a polymath fixer, agent, scout, general manager, executive, interpreter, sounding board and liaison officer – had first been to watch Charles in training at Elland Road in 1955 and made contact with the player in April 1957 after a Leeds defeat at Highbury. Umberto Agnelli, the president of Juventus, who were enduring a woeful season and were flirting with relegation until they sacked their manager, Sandro Puppo, in mid-April with six matches to go, then travelled to watch Wales play Northern Ireland at Windsor Park. A week later Agnelli cabled the Leeds chairman, Sam Bolton, telling him to expect his arrival in the city to discuss the transfer.

A revisionist view that Charles was reluctant to leave has taken hold since his death but his own words tell a contrasting story – however much he loved Leeds, he loved his family more and thus embraced such a lucrative opportunity: "I should regret it all my life as a married man, with two children and a third due at any time, if I turned it down," he said. "I could never hope to earn that sort of money here, however long I played." When David Batty left for Blackburn in 1993, a similar myth proliferated, that he had been sold against his will to pay for a new stand, this time on the East side. Yet in his autobiography he explicitly states that he was fed up at Leeds and had told Kenny Dalglish he "would love to" join Rovers when contact was initially made. There is no dishonour in that. Both can still be heroes. We do not have to make them martyrs.

Charles' agent, Teddy Sommerfield, took the train to Leeds on 18 April with the BBC's Kenneth Wolstenholme to advise him and booked into the Queen's Hotel where Charles, dodging photographers and entering through the kitchens, met them in room 222. The hotel's Italian waiters, Charles reported, proceeded to do the best promotional work for Juventus possible, even before Agnelli and Peronace arrived, extolling the beauty of the country and the potential of the team.

The first meeting between the two clubs took place at the Waddington's games factory on the outskirts of the city before reconvening in room 233 at the Queen's. Was the Leeds board trying to send a signal about Monopoly money? After an hour with Juventus starting at £45,000 and Leeds at £70,000, agreement was reached at a British record £65,000, £55,000 for United and a £10,000 signing on fee for Charles. Sam Bolton, Raich Carter and the vice-chairman, Percy Woodward, were off as soon as the deal was signed. After telling Charles how much they adored him all week, they took the money and ran. The talks between the player's representative and Agnelli were more protracted before Sommerfield settled for £70 a week for his client, a £25 away and £15 home win bonus, a car and apartment of his choice.

Charles finished the season with Leeds, playing three more matches and scoring four more goals, bidding farewell at Elland Road by captaining them to a 3-1 victory over Sunderland. At the final whistle fans steamed on to the pitch from all three sides and converged on him, patting him wildly on the back and yanking his kit so forcefully for souvenirs it was a wonder he maintained his decency. Hundreds waited for him to emerge from the temporary dressing room huts on Fullerton Park afterwards, chanting, "We want, John" and engulfed him all over again. He could not speak, fought his way to a car and headed off on his adventure.

His considerable skill and particularly his strength – "he seemed to hover over opponents looking like an eagle among sparrows, a predator surveying lunch," wrote Michael Parkinson – had recommended him to Juventus but it was his self-effacing and placid character that won the hearts of the fans. He never retaliated, was never cautioned or sent off. He used his wealth unwisely over the years until it was frittered away and in the 1980s and 1990s he could be found once a fortnight in the unpretentious West Stand bar that bore his name, but no one deserved a peaceful pint there more. In 2004, after his death, they named the stand after him, as it always should have been – after all it had been his transfer fee that enabled United to pay the last instalments.

"Leeds without John Charles," wrote the *Yorkshire Post*'s Eric Stanger as early as 1953,"are like Hamlet without Sir Laurence Olivier." Jack Kelsey, the Wales and Arsenal goalkeeper, said his departure left Leeds looking "like London without the Tower". Given his height, 'Big Ben' would have been more suitable and it almost became a cliché to mint new aphorisms in that vein after Leeds lost five of their first seven games the following season, then lost five in succession in November. Writers did not really require any metaphorical flourishes. Leeds without Charles were poor with a decent defence, "a lot of quite good players who didn't always fire together" in the words of the genial right-back Jimmy Dunn. They lost 19 games and scored 51 goals, the lowest in the top flight, but conceded 63, the same as the year before. Despite the grand opening of the new stand for the visit of Leicester City in August 1957, average gates fell by 8,000 and with greater velocity than United's slide. It had to be a very precise and fiery kind of adversity, it seems, to bring solidarity.

At first Carter was allowed only £12,000 to replace the irreplaceable and he went for Airdrie's Hughie Baird, a nimble finisher who scored 20 goals, a touch more than half Charles' return. A 12th defeat from their 21st game caused tremendous concern and though Carter was allowed to spend £7,000 on the Ulster Footballer of the Year and Glenavon wing-half Wilbur Cush and £5,000 on the slight Irish inside-right Noel Peyton, improvement was only relative. Farcically they were drawn against Cardiff City for the third consecutive year in the third round of the FA Cup and were knocked out for the third time by two goals to one, meaning that Carter, whose contract was allowed to expire without renewal after finishing 17th, never won a cup-tie in his five years as manager. The poverty of what he was able to send out, a team that was thrashed 5-0 by Manchester United and 4-2 by Manchester City, was only emphasised by the return of Charles in October for a floodlit friendly against Juventus. He scored twice in a 4-2 victory and ended the season a champion and top-scorer in Serie A.

Carter was astounded by the decision not to grant him a new contract, a board resolution that Bolton said had driven him to tears. The manager departed arguing, not unreasonably, "This season could never be any more than a holding season once a player like Charles had gone." Nevertheless, he was not well liked by the players, the directors had lost faith in his ability to improve them and his aversion to coaching could not cover up the multitude of sins Charles' exit had unmasked. They should also have wondered with the 5ft 3in George Meek, 5ft 4in Cush and 5ft 5in Peyton in the starting XI whether Carter was managing Leeds United at all or assembling a troupe of diddymen.

Carter departed, his dignity conspicuously wounded especially since he had turned down an approach from his former club Derby County and chosen to stay at Leeds, but United had no plan about what to do next. Bolton was preoccupied with the financial strain of the overdraft which had supported them through the season as income was diverted to pay for the stand. He recruited five new board members to help him, including Harry Reynolds, owner and managing director of a successful engineering firm, and Bob Roberts, whose company had built the new stand. It left little time for a beauty contest so the board settled for the most convenient option and appointed Bill Lambton, Carter's coach, as caretaker. Hints were also dropped to the press about the high-profile names they were pursuing, the most prominent of them the Manchester United assistant and Wales manager Jimmy Murphy, although there is no evidence to prove whether contact was ever made.

Lambton had been hired by Carter from Grimsby Town in November 1957 where he had been assistant manager. He had been an Army PT Instructor and described as a renowned 'fitness fanatic' or 'glutton for fitness' as if it was something highly suspicious. He had earned a reputation for innovative training routines centred on suppleness, bounce and explosive pace, using trampolines and sprinting drills in place of stamina work. In the December of his last season, Carter said "the new training methods of Bill Lambton should produce immediate results" but they had not had any noticeable effect. He must have interviewed well because he certainly seems to have impressed the board, much in the manner of a tieless, barefoot, 'hug a polar bear' Tory strategist who dazzles the gullible with bullshit.

The board let him take pre-season training and then drifted into the season with him still in caretaker charge. Leeds lost 4-0 at Bolton in the first game and won only two of their first 13 matches. With almost a third of the season gone, United were 21st, second bottom. "Bill was a nice enough man," wrote Jack Charlton, "but he wasn't a player, he wasn't a coach, he wasn't anything. If you ever saw Bill walking about he always had a piece of paper in his hand – nobody ever found what was written

on that paper but it made him look as though he were doing something."
Jimmy Dunn later said that Lambton was "a bloody comedian".

Leeds had swapped a manager the players did not like for one they did
not respect. The board, whether out of confusion, desperation or plain
negligence, had given free rein to a spoofer in a double-breasted blazer.
And yet the directors, growing jittery because of the dismal results,
allowed him to splash more money in eight weeks than they had given his
predecessor over five years. He spent £8,000 on Burnley centre-forward
Alan Shackleton, £5,000 on the winger Billy Humphries and, the week
after a 4-2 away victory over Blackburn took them out of the relegation
places, £14,000 on Sunderland's former England forward 'Roaming' Don
Revie, 'soccer's happy wanderer'.

Earlier, during the summer of 1958, Lambton and Harry Reynolds
had driven to Stirling after watching a schoolboy international between
England and Scotland, the second half of which had been televised live by
the BBC. Arsenal, Chelsea and Sheffield Wednesday had already beaten
a path to the door of 35A Weir Street, a three-bedroom council house in
Raploch. So had Rangers but on discovering that the object of their interest
was a Catholic, they quickly scuttled away. The 15-year-old boy had never
heard of the city of Leeds, let alone United, but he was taken by Reynolds'
sincerity, passion and persuasiveness as well as the prospect of a fortnight's
jolly on trial playing football at, what he discovered to his shock, was a
First Division club.

The boy's name was Billy Bremner and he, together with Revie and
Reynolds, would deliver Leeds from four decades of barren toil. They
would not know it for a couple of years; purgatory would detain them for
a while yet. But salvation was at hand.

12

'WEKKEN UP!'

Bill Lambton's incompetence as a coach did not prevent him from making a third wise decision during his spell in caretaker charge. While the players were dumbfounded by his demand that they play a practice match in track spikes, the manager apparently oblivious to the hazards of tackling in lethal footwear, the signings of Don Revie and Billy Bremner were astute. He could not have had the foresight to appreciate the long-term consequences of his sound judgment in those two cases, but he deserves to be commended for reviving the youth policy instigated by Major Buckley that Raich Carter had allowed to slither towards dereliction. Indeed Bremner was its first beneficiary or, more accurately, Leeds United have cause for eternal gratitude that Bremner was the principal bequest of Lambton's structural revamp. It is strange, though, that someone who recognised Carter's negligence towards homegrown players during the rise and all too brief ascendancy of Manchester United's 'Busby Babes', and addressed it, would also behave like a prize chump with his first-team players. The story of how one training session was interrupted because the balls had been overinflated and the casing so hard they felt like cannonballs is notorious. In the telling of the tale by Jack Charlton and Jimmy Dunn, Lambton accused them of being soft, pontificated that anyone who called himself a professional should be able to cross a ball in bare feet and, foolishly, when dared to do so, took up the challenge. Lambton was in his mid forties and had played merely four League matches as a goalkeeper a decade before. In the course of showing his players how to kick a ball 'properly' he bruised his feet so badly that he had to limp down the steps from the training ground with their hoots of derisive laughter ringing in his ears. Footballers as a collective can be monstrously cruel but they can smell out an impostor double-quick.

Revie was 31 when he joined Leeds United from Second Division Sunderland in the fourth move of a career that had taken him from Leicester via Hull, Manchester City and Roker Park to Elland Road for combined fees totalling £76,000, the most ever spent by clubs on one player. He had been Footballer of the Year in 1955, when City instituted the 'Revie Plan' and were runners-up in the FA Cup, and returned after a dispute with his manager to drive them to victory over Wolves at Wembley in 1956, the year he won the last of his six England caps. Revie had been a great player, enigmatic certainly, but also elegant, smart, brilliant in possession with his head up and scanning the field to pick out long, penetrating passes. The deep-lying centre-forward role he and City devised was by no means original but it took his skill to make it work, combining his creative flair with the need to be on the ball that had previous managers shuttling him between inside-forward and wing-half. He sometimes termed the position 'advanced centre-half', a licence to roam ever deeper, which is something Nandor Hidegkuti, the Hungarian prince of 'False 9s', would never call himself, but it involved broadly the same tactics, dropping back to instigate moves and using the right-half as an auxiliary, late-arriving attacker thrusting into the space vacated. He was very much a schemer, a prompter, a conductor. But after City, each subsequent move took him to a worse orchestra. Revie managed to get a tune out of Leeds for his first three games at inside-left, steering them to victories over West Ham, Forest and Bolton. His skill and locksmith passing were intact but there was a distinct stateliness to his running by now, a legacy of a triple-fracture of the ankle in 1946 that had reduced his chances of playing professionally again, according to his surgeon, to "a thousand to one against". Each game was won by the tightest of margins yet after the second of them the board had seen enough to upgrade Lambton from caretaker to actual manager.

It was an odd business. Bolton had summoned Headington United's manager Arthur Turner, who had guided Birmingham City to promotion then on to the 1956 FA Cup Final and their highest-ever Division One finish, to Elland Road for an interview and he championed his candidacy. His board, however, was dismissive, outvoted him and elected to put Lambton's employment on a more durable footing. It was a disaster. In 1974 Brian Clough walked out of Elland Road after being sacked and memorably, with piercing, nasal, Teesside pithiness, said: "I think it's a very sad day for Leeds and I think it's slightly sad for football." He strolled away under the north-west floodlight pylon back to the company Mercedes that was now his as part of an extraordinary pay-off settlement. In the early evening he headed for the Yorkshire TV studios. During the *Calendar Special* debate about what had happened where he sat between Don Revie and Austin Mitchell, he portrayed himself as the victim of a player coup as if it was not only heinous but unprecedented. Lambton could have disabused him of that notion. There were differences: the Leeds directors exploited the players to deliver the killer blow to Clough.

In April 1959, they were forced by the threat of mutiny and defections to act.

When Leeds gave him a long-term contract in December, the *Sheffield Star* extolled Lambton's qualities so gushingly and mistakenly one might almost think its motive was sabotage. "Lambton has given proof in recent months that he has imagination, ability and enthusiasm," the anonymous correspondent wrote. "He is rapidly gaining the other virtues of tact and experience and with those, United may have in him their best manager for years." They were right about the enthusiasm but one virtue could not pardon the other sins. After the early impetus of Revie's transfer, Leeds reverted to their patchy and exasperating inconsistency. They managed to attract a sizeable crowd for West Brom on Boxing Day, second only to the season's high of 48,574 for the visit of Manchester United, and responded with another tight victory but then lost three on the trot. The stalwart left-back Grenville Hair had already asked for a transfer in September and in the spring he put in another request, saying his health was being affected by worry about the team's weaknesses. Hair had been a first-team regular for six years and that such a loyal servant of the club could take no more is damning. More recent recruits, Chris Crowe and Jackie Overfield, both first-team regulars under Lambton, followed Hair and formally asked to leave.

Problems were rearing their heads like a whack-a-mole injected with amphetamine sulphate. The end of Wilbur Cush's tether had been reached by mid-January, and the tenacious midfielder, Leeds' original pocket battleship, resigned the captaincy. Lambton tried to solve that one by holding a vote to show that he was not a dictator and the players duly elected Revie to replace Cush. Next up the manager alienated Jack Charlton by refusing to allow a couple of his relatives to cross London on the team bus after a match at West Ham, pompously saying it was for employees and officials of Leeds United only. But on a later trip to the capital Lambton invited some waiters from the team hotel to travel with them. Charlton, predictably, lost his temper at his manager's hypocrisy and stormed off the coach in protest. Lambton told the driver to leave him by the kerbside and drive back to Leeds and the directors had to intervene and overrule him. On another occasion Lambton went to war with a ravenous Charlton over whether he was allowed soup and melon as a pre-match meal starter, telling the centre-half that he should wind his neck in and order only one like the rest of them. Charlton, pointing to the set menu which clearly stated he was entitled to two choices should he please, was stung by the injustice and the manager's culinary put-down that his choices did not work together and simply wasn't done. Only a complete hobbledehoy would order fruit and soup together. Charlton, feeling belittled, told him to "stick it" and walked out in fury. Lambton's inability to enforce discipline shredded the last remnants of his credibility.

It was another ostensibly petty dispute adding to the weight pushing Lambton off his flimsy toehold. Gravity would have knocked him off soon enough but the players could not wait and gave one last shove. Dunn and Eric Kerfoot made formal complaints about his ineptitude after a 6-2 defeat by Wolves in February and three defeats and a draw from the following four games. Home gates had been steadily dropping since Christmas but 14,900 for Portsmouth, in what turned out to be Lambton's last home match, was turning a farce into a crisis. In early March the directors convened a full meeting of the board, the manager, his staff and all the players. What ensued was a full-scale rebellion, an airing of grievances. For all his bluster Lambton did not seek to confront the mutiny with the defiance of Charles Laughton's Captain Bligh. Instead he made a pathetic plea for a clean slate. The players had found him out long before but when the scales belatedly fell from the directors' eyes Lambton's contract was terminated the same day. Each player had been given the floor and not one of them argued his merits. Mass denunciation is a blunt, cowardly method of dismissal, just as Clough's would be, and, maybe realising it, Leeds United at least granted him the fig-leaf of resignation as a sop to his dignity. Lambton left telling the press that the board's interference in his training methods had been the trigger. How myopic Bolton and co must have been to demand an end to the insanity of five-a-sides in spikes and with iron-hard, metatarsal-cracker footballs. Bob Roxburgh, the 62-year-old physiotherapist who had been Billy Hampson's assistant, was entrusted with the last nine games of the season and five wins and a draw from them was enough to raise United nine points above the second relegation place.

Five games before the end of the season, the *Daily Mirror* had splashed the news that Arthur Turner, "back in the big time", had been summoned to Leeds a second time, interviewed again and agreed a contract to manage United. "Headington have been very good to me," he said. "But the Leeds job offers me so much opportunity, apart from the money, that I would be crazy not to take it." Turner was an attacking manager during his years at Birmingham and had fostered a great team spirit on the road to Wembley, uniting players and supporters in song, belting out *Keep Right On* with such catchy vigour that it became the club's anthem. His verbal agreement with Sam Bolton lasted 10 days but he never turned up for work and on 13 April he announced that he would remain at Headington and fulfil his mission to take them into the Football League, something he finally achieved in 1962 after they had changed their name to Oxford United. It was a profound humiliation: a First Division club could not attract a non-League club's manager, nor match the enhanced salary they were paying him to stay. If they could not persuade Turner, their approaches to incumbent managers – Charlie Mitten of Newcastle United, Bob Brocklebank of Hull, Dundee's Willie Thornton and Archie Macaulay of Norwich City – were essentially fool's errands. Bolton also offered the job to former captain Tommy Burden, who had left for Bristol City after falling out with Raich Carter and was still leading them with inspirational midfield drive at the age of 35. He had spent most of his six years at Elland Road commuting to Leeds and staying in digs because his wife refused to move up from Somerset. Hearth and home won out.

After such a run of dispiriting rejections, a candidate was found who was willing to take the job on. Jack Taylor had done little to recommend himself in seven seasons managing Queens Park Rangers, all of them in the Third Division. There was no consistent upward curve from 20th place in his first campaign to 18th, 15th, 18th, 10th, 10th and 13th. In 1954-55 they had been knocked out of the FA Cup by Walthamstow Avenue, who had beaten them 4-0, and two years later they were thrashed 6-1 by Southern League Hereford United. Taylor had kept them afloat financially and had once been a trusted servant of Major Buckley, who had signed him for Wolves and Hull, and Carter, whose Hull side he had helped to promotion. He was a Barnsley man, thrifty, conciliatory, which was an important quality after his provocative predecessor, and came as a pair with his younger brother Frank, an FA-qualified coach. Ian Gamber, the writer and lifelong QPR supporter, says Taylor "was a nice guy, liked by the board and the players. He had great difficulty in making decisions and sticking to them and was rarely seen on training days, preferring to let others get on with it. He had a reputation for liking his suits and a warm office. My father once described him as a comfortable pair of slippers with holes in that you didn't want to get rid of". Between Lambton and Taylor, Leeds United seesawed from Porridge's Mr MacKay to Mr Barrowclough.

Taylor made no new signings until the middle of September and, although his brother impressed Jack Charlton on the training field by introducing drills to refine the players' skills, they won merely three of their first 15 games. They were hammered 6-0 under the lights at Old Trafford in September in spite of Manchester United having an injured Albert Quixall hobbling in isolation out on the right wing for most of the game. Selling Alan Shackleton, their highest-scorer from the previous season, for a profit of only £250 was another penny-wise call that reduced United to improvising with the leggy Revie through the middle for six matches until Taylor used the £10,000 he received from Southampton for the inside-forward George O'Brien to buy Bradford City's John McCole. The centre-forward was just what Leeds needed, a stout-hearted, bubbly finisher with plenty of Glaswegian bite. He may, they say, have been a lively tippler, but his 22 goals from 33 appearances were the only thing that gave Taylor's Leeds a puncher's chance of staying up.

Gerry Francis, born to parents of African and Asian heritage in Johannesburg and who had been signed by Carter in 1957 after paying his own way over for a trial, was given a run on the right wing by Taylor in the autumn and he scored in draws with Everton and Blackpool. "I used to like playing best on the side where the old Lowfields Road Stand used to be," Leeds United's first black player remembered on his return to Elland Road in 1998, 25 years after emigrating to Canada. "The fans there loved me and if I didn't get a lot of the ball the fans used to give some of my team-mates a hard time for not passing it to me." Francis was a buoyant figure, less scarred by doubts about his self-worth than his friend and compatriot Albert Johanneson who had been subject to traumatic racist violence during his youth in the Germiston township. Francis was direct, good at picking his time to arrive in the box to meet left-wing crosses and could impart blistering power on concussively heavy caseballs with his heading and shooting. Yet the winger could not hold down his place even though the Leeds defence was much further away from clicking than the attack. In four games straddling November and December they conceded 15 and their vulnerability became the season's defining motif, keeping only four clean sheets in 42 games, 43 if you count the ritual third-round humiliation in the FA Cup.

Norman Hunter, who had been engaged on the ground staff at the age of 15 in September 1959, recollected a crisis meeting called by Taylor to address their problems. "It was just before Christmas," he said, "and all the players were there from the first team down to the newcomers. He was a very polite man but to my surprise no one took a blind bit of notice of what he was saying. Several first-team players were throwing streamers across the room while he was talking." Ronnie Blackburn, a forward in the youth team at the same time as Hunter, remembers that Taylor was "kind and encouraging but he delegated everything to his brother and never cracked down hard on anyone if they were mucking about". Revie, ever the professional, set the example as captain by giving his all in training and chivvying his colleagues to step up but without the authority to enforce standards. Charlton continued to act the renegade with a seditious attitude and prickly contempt for anyone who dared to be critical of his self-indulgent and impetuous performances that were in danger of writing off his talent before he had the opportunity to express it properly. Leeds United were again drifting towards the rocks.

In January 1960 Revie took it upon himself not to allow the malaise to infect the club's brightest prospect. On the evening before they played Chelsea at Stamford Bridge, Revie appointed himself Billy Bremner's room-mate and ensured that the 17-year-old debutant would not be polluted by the permissive attitude of the manager and resentful indifference of some players. Bremner was tormented by homesickness for his first three years at the club and, not for the last time, was about to ask to leave when called up to play on the right wing. "Right from the start, it was as if he sensed my mood," Bremner recalled. "He made sure that it was bed at 9pm sharp for wee Willie that night, and that I was up at 7am, set to get in a long walk before the streets became filled with the fumes of exhaust pipes. And all the time he talked football... football... football." The 15-year age gap between the outside- and inside-rights was bridged by their common obsession and Revie not only prepared Bremner, he coaxed him through his first few games, too. He did not do it with any foresight about their imminent roles. He took Bremner under his wing because he had been a teenage prodigy himself and remembered the debt he owed to the rigorous tutelage of veteran England half-back Sep Smith.

Revie set up one of McCole's two goals in the 3-1 victory over Chelsea, their third win in London that season, and the two points took them up to 17th, a spur which should have given them some confidence but somehow instead they lost their next four games. West Brom and Blackpool put four past them, Fulham five, in a run so galling that only 8,557 souls turned up at Elland Road to witness its end in a draw with Birmingham City.

In desperate need of a defensive wing-half to help Charlton, Taylor sacrificed Chris Crowe, the England Under-23 winger he had been using at inside-left, selling him to Blackburn Rovers for £25,000 and investing £10,000 of it in Manchester United's Freddie Goodwin. The lanky Mancunian was solid enough in his early career at Old Trafford yet suffered by comparison with memories of the much-missed, snake-hipped sprite Eddie Colman. His introduction and particularly his no-nonsense attitude to clearances tightened Leeds up considerably but not sufficiently to get off the canvas unless they could win their final two games and hurdle over Birmingham City. McCole missed a penalty in their 3-2 defeat by Blackburn in the penultimate match which rendered their 1-0 win over Nottingham Forest on the final day in front of 11,699 mourners meaningless.

The Guardian's Eric Todd summed up United's failings witheringly in his match report of April's 3-0, "shoddy, scrappy" defeat by Wolves under the devastating headline: "Leeds United's play conforms to no logic." Todd describes their tactics on a day when the hapless Taylor sent out Wilbur Cush in the No.9 shirt as "wholly inexplicable", and points out that the only hope for their diminutive forwards was passes to feet "yet Charlton and his backs booted it to such ridiculous heights that only a giraffe could have hoped to beat Slater in the air... Goodwin once or twice realised that the forwards were not operating from helicopters." He concludes by quoting an overheard remark from a fan not bemoaning the policy of lumping Route One balls for a tribe of Ronnie Corbetts to chase but their ponderous build-up. "The unkindest remark of the afternoon – and there were quite a few – came from a partisan who entreated United to 'Wekken up. We don't want no Revie-plan 'ere.' One feels disposed to ask why not? It would be better than none at all." Wekken up? It would be easier to arouse Rip van Winkle. A club bedevilled by vertigo and no money, had sunk into debilitating lethargy. Where were the people who cared enough to do something about it?

In the boardroom the Fifties had been more about death than renewal. Alf Masser was the first of the founding fathers to die in 1950 at the age of 73 and Hilton Crowther followed seven years later in Blackpool where he had been spending his retirement years. Sir Albert Braithwaite, knighted after losing his Buckrose seat in 1945, had been re-elected to serve Harrow West in 1951. He was still sitting for the constituency in 1959 when he killed himself with an overdose of barbiturates after suffering from kidney disease for a number of years. The men who replaced all three on the board had yet to demonstrate an iota of their problem-solving vigour, sharing only their exasperation with the public and appetite for status. As John Charles pointed out about the years after the debenture had been repaid but before the fire: "We regularly had over 30,000 at Elland Road so there was good income and very little paid out in wages. Where did it all go? Certainly not on players and definitely not on ground improvements until our stand burned down. But the chairman and his directors used to drive around in nice cars and have very good dinners." One decade of squandered opportunity now seeped into the next.

'Jovial' Sam Bolton, entering his 13th season in the chair, still talked a good game and hope and bluster kept the show on the road in the summer of 1960, most of which was spent keeping the bank at bay because the overdraft had mushroomed beyond £30,000. On the surface the signing of the Scotland and Celtic midfield terrier Eric Smith for £10,000 suggested that Taylor had identified United's greatest weakness and solved it in a savvy and purposeful manner. Smith had an abrasive quality, an intolerance for the laziness and casual commitment that players call 'cheating'. His transfer – and the news that Charlton was staying because Liverpool's board had balked at the £20,000 asking price – convinced the *Mirror's* Bill Holden to tip Leeds for the Division Two title. Indeed, at another club Smith would have stiffened spines but it did not take him long to discover that Taylor and Bolton had conned him into signing for a wreck. "The club was fifth rate and the players were undisciplined," he told Andrew Mourant a couple of years before his distressingly premature death in 1991. "It wasn't their fault. Jack Taylor had let things go. I thought beforehand I was coming to a top club. I found out otherwise in the first three or four days. We would go on long training runs and at the end some players, quite senior players, would walk in with ice lollies in their hands." In any case he broke his leg in the second game of the season and Taylor was robbed of his drive.

The season was a disaster financially and Taylor's investment in Smith and Colin Grainger, the former England left-winger who had scored twice on his international debut against Brazil in 1956 and had enjoyed a dual career as a recording artist in the Vic Damone-mould, changed nothing. Only the visit of Huddersfield Town brought more than 20,000 through the gate and over the season the average was down by 8,000, around 35 per cent. When Revie was injured in October, Bremner moved into his No.8 shirt and thrived, scoring eight goals at inside-forward as Francis filled in regularly at outside-right. By the end of the year, nine victories from 24 games left them in 10th but a minor rally was followed by four successive defeats during a dismal February and March, leaving them squarely in limbo, trapped in 10th. Obviously a better position would have stayed the board's hand; paradoxically, it is likely that a worse one would have also paralysed them for fear of drastic consequences. Inertia, though, was the perfect incentive. On 13 March 1961 Taylor was invited to a board meeting after training and given two far from palatable options. "After discussions Mr Taylor offered to resign his position in the hope that a change would be in the best interests of the club," said the chairman. "I accepted his resignation."

Harry Reynolds was not going to give Bolton free rein to choose another manager. Buckley, Carter and Taylor had all been his candidates while Lambton had been forced on them by expedience and a deficiency of imagination. Twice before, when Dick Ray had resigned and Lambton binned, Leeds had soldiered on with the coaching staff until the end of the season and such was the absence of any positive signs emanating from the club that it was commonly assumed that they would do so again. While Bolton was preoccupied with preparations for Elland Road's staging of an FA Cup semi-final, Reynolds made his move. He had retired from an executive role at HL Reynolds Ltd, his steel and engineering company, in 1959 and had progressively become more involved in club affairs. When Don Revie had been sidelined by injury the previous autumn, Taylor had sent him with Reynolds on a scouting mission to Bolton, the two men had found common ground in their thoughts about the game and a warm, personal empathy. The self-made millionaire was something of an eccentric who continued to live in his two-up two-down at Hough Top, reserving his adventures in the high life for polo and Cunard cruises. Revie, too, was not without his singular foibles and each found in the other qualities that inspired trust. "Don Revie came to my house a lot after that and we talked about many things connected with football," Reynolds said. "I liked him."

In the spirit of *The Man Who Shot Liberty Valance* the custom is to print the legend over Revie's appointment. It is certainly true that he had applied for the Bournemouth and Boscombe Athletic's player-manager's job in February 1961 and had even sounded out two reserves, Jimmy Ashall and Peter McConnell, to go with him. Moreover he had asked Reynolds for a reference but it is a myth that it was while writing it for his friend that he had a 'Eureka!' moment, tore it up and gave him the Leeds job. For a start their courtship, if we can call it that, was not *amour fou* – it had been a gradually deepening relationship. Even more pertinently Bournemouth had already been quoted £6,000, his value as a player, and backed away, possibly with a view to making a counter-offer. Revie had also been approached by Tranmere Rovers, Chester City and Adamstown, a semi-pro side based in Newcastle, New South Wales. There was no single reason, the trigger was both Leeds' dreadful form and crowds, Revie's amenability to the idea of going to Bournemouth plus the impression he had made on Reynolds over the winter. Within three days of persuading Taylor to do the honourable thing, Reynolds had convinced the board to give his protégé a chance. Small wonder, given his inheritance, that Revie felt a combination of pride and apprehension when he accepted. He did not need to send a car to Blackpool to fetch Gypsy Rose Lee just yet to tell him there were more sleepless nights than red letter days in his immediate future.

13

THE FAMILY WAY

There is a statue of Don Revie on Lowfields Road now, paid for by public subscription and unveiled in 2012, 51 years after he was appointed as Leeds United's ninth full-time manager. It captures him at his zenith, cast in bronze, wearing the shorty sheepskin he favoured in his final couple of seasons at Elland Road. He is smiling and punching the air, his arm more horizontal than the traditional uppercut of delight, more restrained, as if conveying a prim 'you little beauty' rather than the earthier 'fucking get in there' one would expect his inner voice to be bellowing at the moment of triumph. He is smiling, baring his teeth, eyes fixed on the back of the East Stand, quiff immaculately swept back, sideburns inching south of his earlobes.

This is Revie as matchday manager, barathea suit, every hair combed and palmed into place in front of the dressing room mirror, his shoes immaculately shiny even if they had to be rubbed against the calf of his trousers to stay so spick. It's the public Revie, the reassuring bear of a man, who mostly keeps his guard up in the 1974 documentary *The Don of Elland Road*, despite being filmed propped up in bed like a sultan in crisp cotton pyjamas beneath a psychedelic peach and rose quilt as he chats away on a Sunshine Desserts ivory-white telephone.

It is, understandably, a heroic representation yet it does not reflect the man at work. The Revie his players treasure most is not suited but adidas booted. He is not wearing the finest Huddersfield worsteds – he sports a drill training top or a yellow rugby shirt or heavy, slate-grey fisherman's knit jumper, his hair stands proud, there is perspiration on his brow and colour in his cheeks. He is the Bill Haley of *Oh Boy!*, not of *Pebble Mill at One*. Revie was, in the famous words of Arthur Hopcraft, written in 1968: "A big, flat-fronted man with an outdoors face as if he lives permanently in a keen wind." He was a manager who never forgot what it was like to be a player, a manager who built his team on the training ground and built a club by involving himself in every detail, from midnight dashes to Dundee to sign young players to making sure the sisterhood of the tea urn had a couple of bob to play the horses on Saturday afternoons. In March 1961 he refused to be cowed by the handicaps that were all too obvious to a man who had lived with decay and disorder for 18 months. He was bright, conscientious and dauntless. Best of all he had a patron and a handful of dedicated disciples.

As a player Revie had been something of a dandy, though contrary to perceived wisdom that type of player is far from soft. In truth they have to be resilient to weather the disappointment whenever their creative impulse does not pay off, tough enough to carry on being audacious regardless of groans, never cheating their talent with conservative, cop-out passes. This fortitude served him well after a very shaky beginning to his spell in charge when Leeds won only one of the last nine matches of the season and slipped down to 14th.

"If we get back into the First Division in five years, we will have done very well," he had told the board on accepting the job. Having agreed a deal for £1,900 a year, the same as his playing salary after the abolition of the maximum wage three months earlier, it was the conditions rather than the terms of his employment that invested him with authority. "I have full power on selection, transfers in and out, training – all aspects of the work necessary to get a good playing staff," he said. "If everyone pulls together from the directors down, and is Leeds United-minded, then we shall get somewhere."

In his first 11 months in charge he ran through a few novice gambits. Alchemy had seemingly worked for Major Buckley in turning John Charles into a centre-forward so Revie gave it a punt with his towering centre-half, Jack Charlton, who, by his own admission, blundered his way to 15 goals in 25 games in the No.9 shirt spread over two seasons. "I didn't know what to do," Charlton recalled, "and nobody showed me. I remember Joe Shaw of Sheffield United laughing at me, I was making such a mess of it." Revie picked his friend Peter McConnell in a number of roles, let Gerry Francis and John McCole leave prematurely, even put his boots back on and played his last seven games as a professional without improving Leeds United's fortunes.

The only transparent key performance indicators – results and attendances (6,975 on an April evening, 9,360 on a September Saturday during Revie's opening six months) – were universally depressing, and yet behind the curtain the new manager and Harry Reynolds were laying sound foundations. Later Revie would enjoy a fond friendship with Bill Shankly, but Old Trafford was his first port of call in the spring of 1961 to seek Matt Busby's advice. The Manchester United manager told him there was only one way to establish an institution and that was with a youth policy that allowed a manager to mould the core of his playing staff and define a club's identity, not necessarily with local talent but ones who would come of age faithful to its values and their comrades. The second commandment, Revie said, was to establish a style of play, "defensive systems and attacking systems that will operate throughout all our teams" so that the A-team left-half could play for the reserves or first team in that role without having to change anything significant.

To help him set the pattern and entrench it throughout the club Revie had the support of three men added to the coaching staff by Jack Taylor: Bob English, who had come from QPR, Syd Owen, England centre-half at the 1954 World Cup, player-manager and captain of Luton Town in the 1959 FA Cup Final and Footballer of the Year at the age of 37, plus Les Cocker, the former Stockport and Accrington Stanley forward, who had moved north from Kenilworth Road with Owen in the summer of 1960 when his boss fell out with the Luton board.

English was a Northern Irishman from Antrim, not just a sergeant major-type, as Queens Park Rangers' players remembered him, but a real sergeant major in the PT Corps for more than 20 years who served Leeds as physiotherapist for two decades. Cocker was a rare bird in 1960, a fully qualified FA coach, abrasive, obstinate, shrewd, innovative, a lifelong learner who was so far ahead of his contemporaries that within a year of joining United he had also been picked as trainer to the England Under-23 squad. He subsequently moved up to work with Alf Ramsey and the senior team, becoming Leeds' third World Cup winner in 1966 with Jack Charlton and Norman Hunter. He was, Brian Clough once said, "an aggressive, nasty little bugger", traits that Clough could recognise in anyone but himself. He was also instrumental to everything Leeds United achieved, honing muscles, physiques and minds to withstand the most gruelling fixture lists in English football over 10 seasons at the top. He used every psychological ruse required, from placebos to moral blackmail, to get Revie's preferred XI on the pitch but he was a man of science, too, a workaholic, the implacable, unfailingly loyal No.2, indispensable to two hall of fame managers.

Owen was a perfectionist, "a difficult man to please, very cutting with his remarks" according to Norman Hunter. Revie installed him as first-team coach, harnessing his drive and intelligence. Even the manager, had to admit that his inability to sugar-coat any criticism along with a provocative lack of tact was ultimately too antagonising for his senior players and he redeployed him to mentor and chivvy the youth and reserve sides. "I think he felt that the harder he came down on a young lad," Hunter said, "the harder his 'victim' would try to prove him wrong." Eddie Gray appointed Owen as his chief scout when he became the second of Revie's old boys to become Leeds manager in 1982 and says "he was the person who helped me most to become a professional though there were times when he almost reduced me to tears". He was uncompromising in his standards, the kind of slave driver that was once commonplace in football, a man for whom a pat on the back and a kick up the backside were only ever inches apart. Nonetheless, "everything [Les and Syd] told me was for my own good", said Billy Bremner, "and any improvement I ever made was thanks to their constant attention to detail".

Revie rounded off his core staff by bringing the decidedly more avuncular Maurice Lindley back as his assistant and chief scout. Lindley had played for Everton and managed Swindon and Crewe before working for Jack Taylor at Elland Road as first-team coach. He had been sacked along with Willis Edwards in the summer of 1960 following relegation from Division One and was working for Harry Catterick at Sheffield Wednesday when Revie persuaded him to return. "The board made him the scapegoat for the club's lack of success," Revie told Jason Tomas. "There was a stony silence when I told them I wanted him back, but I was determined to do the job my way or not at all." Lindley's man-management skills were the velvet glove that cushioned the iron fists of Les and Syd and his warmth and reassuring manner were employed alongside Revie's vision of what the club could become on recruitment trips all over the country. They would emerge from Revie's Ford Zephyr in fugs of smoke from the manager's cheroots and Lindley's pipe to drink endless cups of tea until their charm seduced a young player and his family to commit to Leeds United, a Second Division club that had never won a damned thing. With one team assembled to his satisfaction, Revie turned his attention to the more taxing one.

At the end of the 1959-60 season when Leeds had needed victory over Blackburn at Ewood Park in the penultimate game to have a chance of staying up, Bremner remembered them stopping on their way to the ground to have their pre-match meal at a hotel they had never used before. "On the menu was steamed chicken," he wrote. "There was also toast, and it had been badly burned. We were certain it wouldn't live and we doubted if we would, either, if we ate much of it. The very sight of it put us off and turned our stomachs." He claims that they were so nauseated that it affected their performance and contributed to their 3-2 defeat, but the point of his anecdote is not to post a scathing TripAdvisor review 60 years too late. It was important because the club's ad hoc approach to preparation disgusted Revie and once he became manager, he changed it.

"Although the club was heavily in debt," he said, "I insisted upon the players getting the same sort of star treatment as those at clubs like Manchester United and Tottenham. Everything about Leeds then was second-class, from the balls we used in training to our hotels for away games. I just felt that we had to start thinking big and the lead had to come from the top." From the day he took the job and held the routine, formal meeting with his players, in which he informed them that he was no longer 'Don' but 'Gaffer' or 'Boss', he put his players first because he believed that they were Leeds United, not the plot of land on which they stood. He told Hopcraft that he had taken over a "dead club" and proceeded to resurrect it by demonstrating how much he cared for them.

"Leeds United-minded" meant treating them like family and his first act was to tear up the petty rule book and replace it with what he called "the common sense rule". Ronnie Blackburn, who could not graduate further than the reserves, says that no trouble was too trivial for Revie. It was not just insisting that the first team stayed in four-star hotels before away games or sending the youth team off to play in prestigious overseas tournaments or his famously solicitous approach to players' parents, wives and children, Blackburn remembers receiving baskets of fruit when he was injured, the manager providing sherry and eggs to build Norman Hunter up and Revie personally lending a player money when a request for a club loan to ease a financial embarrassment had been rebuffed. Youth players babysat for Revie's children, Duncan and Kim, and they were taught table manners, how to run their bank accounts, mortgages and even about sex.

"He built Leeds," Don's wife Elsie told *The Telegraph* in 1996. "They were his second family. Don's players came to him as boys. We hardly saw him. He was always away scouting for the team and waiting for the boys to develop... Billy, Eddie, Peter, Norman, Paul. I used to joke to my two children: 'That man who just walked past the window with his hat on, that's your dad!' But I didn't resent it. That was his life."

On the field he implemented the four main principles he had learnt from Sep Smith:

1. When not in possession, get into position.
2. Never beat a man by dribbling when you can beat him more easily with a pass.
3. It is not the man on the ball but the man running into position to take the pass who constitutes the danger.
4. The aim is to have a man spare in a passing move, then soccer becomes easy.

Right away he had a plan, but he did not have the players. Grenville Hair had been first-choice full-back for 10 seasons and had a couple more years of solid service left in him, 'King' McCole was a prolific penalty-box predator, Bremner was electric, a once-in-a-generation talent, an athlete with ceaseless energy and invincible spirit, a fine passer, tackler and goalscorer. He was fearless and ebullient as a player but was also headstrong, hard to handle and, when Revie took over, determined to move back to Scotland to be with his girlfriend, Vicky. It took his manager a couple of years of cat-and-mouse play, agreeing to allow him to go on the transfer list while surreptitiously rejecting all offers, until Leeds' progress and Revie's recruitment of Vicky as his ally convinced Bremner to stay.

His other key asset was arguably of dubious value. Revie recognised that Jack Charlton had considerable ability while also thinking him an insufferable pain in the arse. "I said to him one day that if I ever became manager of this club I wouldn't [even] play him in the reserves," he revealed in 1968. "Because I felt at that time he was an undisciplined player who only went out to enjoy his game and he wasn't bothered about the team performance and how they carried on that day." Charlton, clearly nettled, had been just as brusque in his response. "Well you're not the manager," he said. "So what the hell?" Now that he was, though, Revie kept him in the side at first until irritation at his arrogance, temper, truculence and gross positional indiscipline forced him out. The manager understood, however, that Charlton's spikiness masked a craving for acceptance and respect. That he was in 'Our Kid's' shadow was obvious yet it was not the main reason for his contemptuous attitude. He harboured a fatalism about the inevitability of his career being squandered playing for a mediocre team with no prospect of redemption. "It didn't worry me at all when 'Our Kid' used to get write-ups as the greatest thing since the Archangel Gabriel," he said in 1970. "All I was jealous about was the club he had joined – Manchester United. I was jealous about their success, their traditions, the way people thought about them as a team. That's the way I wanted people to think about Leeds."

'Jackie', as he was publicly better-known back then, had earned his FA coaching badges and had an inquiring, enterprising mind, constantly involving himself in successful business ventures to occupy the time he wasn't wasting training with people who scorned technical and tactical work. "There was no method about he way we played," he said about the eight lost years since his debut in 1953. "You just ran your guts out." After several false starts in their manager-player relationship, Revie used Charlton's passion for coaching and learning to win him over, turning the man his closest friend, Bremner, once called "a nuisance" and "a one-man awkward squad" if not into a model pupil, then something far better, a great defender. "I called him in and told him if he screwed the nut he would play for England," Revie said. "I told him he would have had as many caps as Bobby if he'd knuckled down when he was a youngster." All along Jack had needed someone to believe in him. As he gradually stopped wanting to fight Cocker and Owen and listened to them instead, a load was lifted off a squad which was no longer polluted by his sourness.

During his first pre-season, Revie revamped the wage and bonus structure and devised a new competitive approach to the necessary fitness and conditioning work. He even changed the location, taking them out to Farnley Hall Park where they were split into teams of six to compete against each other for prizes in everything from cricket and golf to cross-country running, rounders, five-a-sides, relays and transporting telegraph poles. "We trained harder than any other side," Willie Bell, a utility half-back signed by Taylor who would flourish at left-back under Revie, told Leo McKinstry for his biography of the Charlton brothers. Most of all, though, it was enjoyable and the pictures of the squad show them smiling as they were put through their paces. Revie understood that they responded best to variety, short, sharp routines, positivity and purpose. Charlton was so impressed after a doomed romance with Manchester United, who had balked at his £26,000 price tag, he asked to come off the transfer list, signed a new contract and was appointed captain. He did not last long, forsaking it in the short-term after arguing with Revie over gallivanting off upfield and in the long-term by succumbing to a superstition that he had to be the last man out of the tunnel.

Other changes followed. Ever since United had been formed, on a weekday night before their first fixture the directors had held a formal banquet at one of the city centre hotels for the players and staff. Revie scrapped it in favour of a party for the players, their wives and children at the Ringway Hotel where he outlined his vision of a family club, emphasising how grateful he had been for the sacrifices Elsie had made to sustain his career and pledging that they were no longer to consider themselves as detached and unappreciated but part of one family that looked after its own. He, as the father figure, would never let them down.

Revie's final innovation that summer was the most striking. After 27 years in multiple combinations of blue and gold, he ditched the club colours and sent Leeds United out in the all-white strip of Real Madrid. It proved one of the most successful rebranding exercises in history and has been rationalised as a gamble fraught with potential humiliation. Equating journeymen players such as Derek Mayers and John Hawksby with the five-times European champions was patently ridiculous, more chutzpah than tribute. Revie justified it as an aspirational move, not that 'the clothes maketh the man' and something magical would rub off on his players, but a goal for them to attain the highest standards. It demonstrated his flair and his nerve, giving them such a fresh and distinctive overhaul yet in truth it was driven as much by practicality as cheek. United had played in white shirts away from home the season before and the manager, still then a player, had been reminded from his England days how much easier it was to pick out a team-mate in his peripheral vision than when they were wearing the drab royal blue.

This brand-new start for club and players produced victories over Charlton and Brighton in the first two games of the 1961-62 season before they endured a sobering afternoon at Anfield where Liverpool gave them a 5-0 hiding. Their evisceration by Ian St John and Roger Hunt, who scored a hat-trick, triggered a run of six defeats from their next eight games, a sequence that punctured all the pre-season buoyancy and left them with crowds dipping down to four figures by mid-September. Revie's first signing, Albert Johanneson, the South African winger, lost form and fitness during the deluge of defeats and was sent back to finishing school in the reserves. Albert was a thrillingly direct runner, a grand dribbler who had a seat-of-the-pants quality that made it seem he was playing at the very limits of his capability, which made occasional mistakes in control an ineradicable element in his game. But he was also a prodigious finisher, scoring a goal every three games, quick, unstoppably strong and his crosses were belted into the box like guided missiles. Pleas from the crowd of 'Giyit, Albert!' were routine in the mid-Sixties as he provided the glimmer of glamour in a tough and pragmatic team hardened by battle and only too willing to overpower an opponent before outplaying them. His family have worked tirelessly to rehabilitate his memory after his death in such pitiful circumstances, to recalibrate our view of Albert the man rather than Albert the player or Albert the alcoholic, driven to the bottle by self-doubt, dislocation and the demons of his treatment in his childhood under apartheid in Johannesburg. Would that he knew the affection in which he was held – now, posthumously, he is receiving the recognition, too. It would take a year after his debut for 'the Black Flash' to become one of Revie's key men and his vigour and dazzling skill would give Leeds a touch of off-the-cuff improvisation to embellish their structured play. In 1961 there was no such respite.

Once in the slump, they found it difficult to break their fall, losing 17 and winning only eight of their first 31 games. After defeat by Huddersfield at the beginning of March they hit the bottom of Division Two. It is hardly surprising that Revie revealed that he, too, hit rock bottom. "There were numerous occasions during that period when I'd tell Elsie that I'd had enough, there was no point in carrying on," he said. "I found it very difficult to sleep. More often than not I'd be up half the night sitting in our lounge drinking pots of tea." Yet he did not pack it in and the main reason was Reynolds' unwavering faith in him. The poor attendances – an average of 13,607 for the season – had pushed already parlous finances into the crisis zone and the board would announce record losses for a campaign of £72,000. At the AGM the supporters' club chairman, Mr Dixon, acknowledged: "Revie had a terrible and Herculean task. We know his plans but a youth policy takes time and, looking at the league table, that is something we haven't got."

In November the bank had refused to extend an overdraft bloated by the axing of pay differentials and the investment in superior equipment, travel arrangements and hotel accommodation. Sam Bolton, the chairman, revealed he and the directors had lent the club £3,500 each just to survive the summer and he begged the wealthier supporters to come on board. It had been a familiar refrain for 40 years but this time two men responded to the call, Albert Morris, who ran Morris Wallpapers, and Manny Cussins, the owner of the John Peters Furnishing Group. After serving in the chair for 13 desolate years, Bolton admitted his time was up in December and stood aside for Reynolds who immediately put up £50,000 and persuaded Morris and Cussins to weigh in with £10,000 apiece. Leeds United had a survival kitty but almost left it too late to use it.

Revie appeared to be biding his time with a nonchalance that was almost suicidally bold but he was looking not for bodies or reinforcements but a truly transformational player. It was not until they slipped into 22nd place with 11 matches to go that the perfect man became available. Only a cock-eyed optimist, however, would think that Bobby Collins would leave Everton and the First Division for a side not simply flirting but virtually making out with the drop into Division Three for the first time in their history. Collins, a 5ft 4in inside-forward, had won the league and Scottish Cup during 10 seasons at Celtic as well as 27 Scotland caps and was coming to the end of his fourth year at Everton when Harry Catterick hurt his pride by circulating his availability through friendly journalists. As soon as Revie heard the news he drove to Liverpool with an offer of £25,000. Collins had been upset to learn Everton were contemplating selling him but was livid that they were happy to let him go at the age of 31 to the worst team in the second division. At their meeting before morning training Collins informed Revie that he was minded to hold out for a top-flight club and would speak to him again in a couple of days. The Leeds manager turned around on impulse a short while into his eastbound journey and parked up outside Collins' house. He waited five hours in his car until 'the Wee Barra' returned and he then stayed until 2.30am to talk him through his plans, how integral Collins was to them, until he relented and agreed to sign for Leeds.

United were never the same again. The Goodison Park 'Pocket Napoleon', instantly galvanised the struggling club and during his four-year spell in the first team he shepherded the club to promotion, an FA Cup Final and the runners-up spot in the league. His only real rival as the best captain Leeds have ever had, his protégé Billy Bremner, gave a succinct account of his mentor's qualities: "I always felt confident that so long as Bobby was in the team, he would bully, coax, cajole, cool us down when we were in danger of losing our heads, encourage and praise us whenever we did anything good, and generally look after us like a father." It helped Collins, of course, that his team-mates were, in a sense, terrorised by the fear of falling short of their volcanic captain's standards. Even Jack Charlton, a good foot taller than Leeds' new captain, was wary of Collins. "I got on all right with him but I didn't like to play against him," he said. "When we were playing five-a-side, you never knew what he was liable to do because he wanted to win so much." Collins also hectored his colleagues throughout a game, teaching them the value of communication he had so assiduously learned at the highest level in Scotland and England. In March 1961 all that followed would have seemed fantastical, though possibly not to Revie and certainly not to Collins. At their lowest point, they at last had a leader in the boardroom, in the manager's office and on the field. The second half of their name was convincingly reflected in the unity of most of the essential elements of success. Only mass support was stubbornly absent.

14

FIRE AND SKILL

Not for the first or final time, Leeds United would have genuine grounds to be grateful for Don Revie's patience and persistence. Had he not turned his car around and driven back to Merseyside for one last try, United would probably have been relegated and Revie's managerial career, for all Harry Reynolds' patronage, may have been beached. Like Lieutenant Columbo, but without the shabby mac, Revie's tenacious pursuit of 'one more thing' cracked the case. Within hours of Bobby Collins completing the transfer to Leeds, Bill Shankly rang him at home and wished him well, rueing the missed opportunity to sign the Everton captain for Liverpool, the runaway Second Division leaders. A cross-city move would have allowed Collins to continue living in Aintree and afforded him the perfect stage from which to cause Harry Catterick maximum embarrassment and remorse. Everton fans might argue that Collins would never have betrayed them but this was the age before rivalry turned rancid and it would be foolish to underestimate just how sore he was. Instead it was Revie who harnessed his sense of rejection and injured pride into a one-man crusade; it was Leeds United who provided the vehicle for Collins' vindication.

Revie sent him out in the No.8 shirt for his debut against Swansea and he scored the opening goal in a 2-0 victory that prised United off the bottom and to within a point of safety. Fellow new signings Ian Lawson (£20,000 from Burnley) and the bald left-back Cliff Mason (£10,000 from Sheffield United) helped to inspire a remarkable uplift in the attendance, doubling the 8,500 who had watched them lose to Plymouth. The number on Collins' back was no constraint, he popped up everywhere in midfield and attack, constantly demanding the ball and using it expertly, both mop and prompter. He was still impishly quick and swept passes with great precision to the outside-forwards and up to the No.9. But it was his aggression in scavenging for possession, lancing his right leg into tackles like a Doberman's mouth snagging a postman's ankle, which captured the crowd's hearts. His quality was evident but his almost psychopathic drive was the clincher in convincing fans and players that no cause would ever truly be lost with Collins in the team. And anyone thinking of giving in

THE BIOGRAPHY OF LEEDS UNITED

would be advised to think again or he might just rip your head off. The logic was faultless: Leeds United could not be losers because Bobby Collins was a winner. It was as simple as that. Revie hadn't merely transformed his team, he had transfused its spirit with Glaswegian grit. Endeavour alone used to endear players to the Elland Road terraces. From this point on Collins was the avatar. Leeds fans adore all kinds of players but they worship those who can play and intimidate the opposition with a 'What the fuck are you looking at?' strut.

They lost just one more match all season and won three and drew six of their final nine games, battling Bury twice and Derby County to draws over five days at Easter. The double-header against Bury, beginning at Gigg Lane on Good Friday, would later form part of the case the *Daily Mirror* put forward to allege Revie was corrupt in September 1977 after he had quit the England job to take up a position with the United Arab Emirates. The newspaper quoted Bob Stokoe, the Bury player-manager, saying that Revie had offered him £500 if his side "take it easy today". It was an allegation he made many times from 1977 until his death in 2004 and all who knew Stokoe intimately portray him as a man of irreproachable rectitude. While the most significant component of the *Mirror*'s claims concerning the title decider against Wolves in 1972 can be discredited and, when exhumed by the *Sunday People* to smear Billy Bremner, were judged to be libellous, this one cannot be disproven. Stokoe says it happened between the two of them without witnesses and as such can also never be substantiated.

Yet there can be no doubt that he held a sincere contempt for Revie for the rest of his life. What we can say is that if Revie indeed did have "£500 in his pocket", as Stokoe said, it was unlikely to have been his, a man with two young children, 14 months into a managerial career on £36 10s a week. If it was not his, as would be plausible should we take Stokoe at his word, then it would have had to have been a far deeper conspiracy involving Leeds United in either some sort of slush fund or a bung. Since no one else has ever been implicated, there is no corroborating testimony, no evidence to suggest Stokoe ever reported it to the Football League or Football Association during the 15 years before he went on the record, nor any insinuation that Revie sought to fix any of the other equally important matches in the run-in to the end of the season, the Leeds United manager can neither be convicted by his numerous detractors nor exonerated by his supporters. To report it as fact, as so many obituaries did at the time of Stokoe's death, is to give his accusation greater weight than Revie's denial at a time when his toxic unpopularity after leaving the England job put a fat thumb on the scales against him.

One last word on this, as reported in Lance Hardy's definitive history of the 1973 FA Cup winners, *Stokoe, Sunderland and 73*, is Stokoe's assertion that when he was Blackpool manager in 1971 he refused to entertain Leeds' offer for his transfer-listed playmaker, the dazzling dribbler Tony Green, and scrambled to secure him a move anywhere else. "I tried to get Liverpool interested," he said. "When Bill Shankly asked me why I was set against the offer from Leeds, I told him about the thing with Revie at Bury. Bill went silent. I don't think he ever again saw Revie in the same light." For the next six years, however, the two old friends, Revie and Shankly, continued their habit of a weekly phone-call every Saturday night or Sunday morning and in April 1975, when Shankly held his testimonial at Anfield to bid farewell to the Liverpool supporters, it was Revie whom he asked to pick and manage the International Select XI who took on his Red Men. The two embraced in the dressing room and on the pitch and Shankly continued to serve as Revie's most influential England scout after his retirement from management, providing his often withering assessments – "Forget all about him, he couldn't trap a bag of cement" – with typical candour. "I have always found Bill a very good friend, very straight, very honest," said Revie that year. Would the unimpeachable Bill really have continued to be firm friends with Revie four years after Stokoe's briefing had he believed he was bent? Would his integrity have allowed him not to confront Revie if he thought it was true? That part of Stokoe's story simply doesn't wash.

The three Easter draws gave Leeds a one-point lead over Bristol Rovers in 21st place and Revie took his team to play Newcastle knowing that a draw, given their superior goal average, would suffice to save them. With 3,000 fans making the journey to St James' Park on Saturday morning, Leeds romped to a 3-0 victory inspired by the recently restored Albert Johanneson on the left-wing and Billy Bremner, reluctantly outcast on the right to make way for Collins in the middle. Even Billy McAdams scored, one of three goals the former Manchester City team-mate of Revie's contributed in 11 starts at centre-forward in a barren year. With Collins patrolling in front of them and Charlton 'screwing the nut' at its heart, the defence conceded only four goals in their final nine games, proof that it was starting to click. McAdams' shortcomings at centre-forward, however, in a season when Leeds were the division's second-lowest scorers and Charlton was the most prolific No.9 with seven goals in his fish-out-of-water role, prompted outlandish action over the summer.

The 'King Over the Water' had been growing restless in Italy. In 1961 John Charles had signed only a year's extension to his Juventus contract and at the end of it, a poor, injury-ravaged season during which he was violently assaulted by Real Madrid during the European Cup quarter-final play-off, he announced he was determined to come home for his children's sake. In fact it was his wife, Peggy, who was needling him to return, having already sent their eldest son to stay with Charles' parents to be educated in Wales. Several factors coalesced in the spring of 1962: the restaurant in the centre of Turin in which he had invested was an expensive flop, after back-to-back titles Juventus had collapsed to 12th and Charles, characteristically placid, wanted to do the right thing by his wife. Given a straightforward choice between Leeds United and Cardiff City, the two clubs who spent June and July not just declaring their interest but mounting PR campaigns with daily bulletins for a breathless public, Charles plumped for his wife's home town over his homeland. The negotiations took Revie, Harry Reynolds, Albert Morris and Percy Woodward to Turin where they agreed terms with Charles but could not nail Juventus down. Umberto Agnelli, mindful of the status of the man Juve's supporters would later vote their greatest foreign player, resigned rather than sanction his sale which forced Charles to go public with an open letter to the fans outlining his desire to leave. He claimed that he did not wish to outstay his welcome and pointed to his ageing parents and children as the reason the love affair should end. It took five weeks of telegrams, transcontinental telephone calls and sweat before Juventus relented and agreed to let the 30-year-old go back to Leeds for £53,000.

For Leeds it was an opportunity they could neither afford nor afford to miss. "We'll get the money somehow," said Reynolds at the start of the summer, "if Juventus will let him leave." They gambled that their coup would serve two purposes – bring back the 20,000 paying fans they had lost since Charles' last season and provide the goals that would propel them into the First Division just as he had done before. The deal was finalised in July and Charles reported for the signing ceremony in the second week of August, only 10 days before the start of the new season. Publicity photos were taken with Revie's arm around the tanned Charles and he then changed into his new all-white strip to pose in front of the West Stand. There had been a delay of a week between registering him and photographing him because they did not have a shirt big enough for his Mr Incredible physique. He still looked like a magnificent athlete from the waist down but with too much, hopefully temporary timber, up top.

When Leeds had sold Charles in 1957, they had insisted that the money be paid up front in one lump sum rather than allowing Juventus to follow the English custom and pay in instalments. Juve, naturally enough, insisted that this arrangement be reciprocated and it caused severe cashflow difficulties at Elland Road. In October United would report a loss of £72,000 for the 1961-62 season, further payments were about to fall due for Collins, Lawson, Mason and McAdams in the autumn and they had also signed Jim Storrie from Airdrie for £15,000. The directors met the Charles fee between them and also bought him an £8,000 triple-garaged house off Wetherby Road in Collingham. Now that they had him, they proceeded to rain on their own parade. In an effort to spread the load, the board announced its 'Everyone Pays' strategy. Had they doused themselves in petrol and struck a match it is doubtful whether they would have been more badly burned. First they put up the season ticket prices by 45 per cent to 10 guineas, arguing that they were "giving the public the chance to show the firmness of their promises to support the club if the board embarked on a policy of team building and bringing personalities to Elland Road". Yet the only promises they had ever received were nothing of the sort. There were nebulous approving words, the type that some committed fans habitually pledge when radicalised by the euphoria of a supporters' club or annual general meeting. Without a broad, coherent subscription drive to sign people up to the scheme, what people consent to with a nod of the head or roar of endorsement can be contradicted by what they actually do. Had the history of Leeds United taught the board nothing? It is never clever to test the supporters' honour and sincerity by contrasting it with the investments directors had made. When they compounded the error of raising season-ticket prices without consultation by hiking standard charges for the standing areas from 3s to 7/6, a 150 per cent rise that made United the most expensive club to watch in England outside the capital, the directors provoked a revolt.

The *Yorkshire Evening Post* was deluged by letters of protest, one saying it was "the first nail in the coffin of Leeds United", another pointing out that "King John's shilling has turned into 4/6" and a third sarcastically congratulating the club's ingenuity for bringing back their hero and making it impossible for people to watch him. United had put kiosks in City Square, the Headrow and Briggate to sell tickets for the first two home games against Rotherham and Sunderland, hoping for a rush. Instead business was slow and only 6,000 were sold in advance, a number that made Reynolds, in the sole major misjudgement of his time in the chair, irate. A future chairman would denounce protesters as "sickpots" and "dissidents"; Reynolds chose "nigglers" and "summat for nowters". Phil Brown, the *Evening Post*'s football correspondent, caught in the crux between his readers and the club whose workings he was briefed upon and understood, tried to explain the board's predicament. When they paid Charles' fee, he wrote, the club's borrowings would exceed £200,000, "a record in the history of professional football in this country". Clawing some of it back, he said, was the only way to lighten the substantial burden they were carrying. Critics saw it differently, surmising that the board demanded the praise due to saviours while taxing the supporters to fund salvation.

Storrie, a quick, incisive pest of a forward who ran his balls off, scored the only goal in the opening day away victory over Stoke City in which Charles made his second Leeds debut and was praised by *The Times* for his "skilful and authoritative approach work" at No.9. A commendable performance by United and their star was not enough to coax more than 14,119 through the gates for the home defeat by Rotherham four days later and only 17,753 came for Sunderland's visit on the Saturday. Predictably, Reynolds was enraged and, in a Gerald Ratner moment, told reporters: "The Leeds public disgust me." Realising he had gone too far, he apologised early the following week and, after a board meeting, slashed admission prices back to more modest levels. Despite their patchy form, two wins, a draw and two losses from their first five games, the board's surrender boosted the crowd for the third home game against Bury to 28,313. Charles, who had never been blamed, was truly back among his people. And yet his wife, who brought the children over from their holiday apartment in Diano Marina some weeks after John arrived in Leeds, felt homesick for Italy the moment she walked through arrivals at Manchester airport. When she confessed this to him, he admitted that he felt the same way and had made "the biggest mistake of my life".

It didn't help that he was ponderous, overweight and could not adjust to the way Collins was pulling the strings, calling the wingers back to help out in midfield and leaving only him and Storrie to forage up front. He wouldn't do the speed and stamina work prescribed by Les Cocker and could not acclimatise to the hectic pace. He had spent most of the previous season playing at centre-half and would have prospered had Revie moved him back. But if Leeds could not really afford a £53,000 striker, they certainly could not justify spending £53,000 on a defender, especially not when they had Charlton. After the 2-1 defeat by Bury in which he was injured and reduced to limping up the left wing as a luxury passenger, he played only five more games, letting his manager and subsequently the press know that he needed to go back to Italy. Roma, alerted to his distress at such a comprehensive loss of form, made a bid that Leeds initially turned down. When they returned offering £65,000 and Charles begged to leave, United reluctantly took the £12,000 profit and let him go. There was no shame in it. He had been away too long and taken too many knocks to hit the ground running as a centre-forward in Division Two. His subsequent failure in Rome and his family's unhappiness in the Eternal City suggested something more profound was wrong with his marriage and his constitution. By returning to Leeds Charles had hoped to please his wife and ended up making them both miserable. It tarnished nothing, only emphasising that for club and player alike, going back is mostly laden with disappointment.

Charles was a ghost of the striker that had once graced Elland Road and his second coming had incited the board to declare war on the fans, even so the signing had not been in vain. It had illustrated United's ambition and his fleeting presence left a profound mark on a remarkable crop of young players Revie was ready to blood. Charles' transfer was the quick-fix, messiah route to promotion. In his absence after his injury against Bury, Revie opted for the more sustainable approach. Not that he thought so at the time. On the Thursday before the away match against Swansea, the manager summoned Gary Sprake, Rod Johnson and Paul Reaney, all 17, and Norman Hunter, 18, and told them they would be taken along with the first-team squad on Saturday for the experience. Sprake, alone, had already made his debut, as a 16-year-old rushed to Southampton by an aircraft chartered for £80 on the morning of the game to replace the sick Tommy Younger the previous season. Reaney and Hunter had established themselves in the reserves only recently, the former a centre-half converted into a right-back by Syd Owen and Cocker, the latter an inside-forward turned into a left-half. Revie told them an hour before kick-off that they were, in fact, playing and though Johnson, a slight greyhound of a centre-forward, stood in for Charles and scored in the 2-0 victory it was the other three who would retain their places and each make more than 500 appearances for Leeds.

This was the moment 'the Revie team' we all know was born but the clouds did not part above the Vetch and a heavenly light illuminate Revie's tyros. The manager felt relief rather than vindication because he had told Reynolds that he feared ruining the four kids if his gamble had not paid off. "I know I have made mistakes but I think I have done something really bad this time," Jason Tomas, Revie's ghostwriter, remembers him saying. "I have put in four kids who are just not ready for this level of football." But the kids were alright. When Charles recovered to play his final five games for Revie, it was alongside the teenagers who were galvanised by his advice and example.

The relationship between Bremner and Revie is usually characterised in the father-son mould and it is true that the manager forged a bond with Bremner and the clans of Scots he recruited for the club based on admiration for their vitality. His loyalty weathered Bremner's cheek and wayward discipline because he knew he represented the fire and skill at the heart of his team. Hunter, by contrast with the prodigal Billy, was the model son. He was Revie's favourite and had been the first apprentice to whom he awarded a professional contract on the Monday morning after becoming manager, obliterating Jack Taylor's lack of faith that Hunter could make a career in the game. "His tracksuit hung on him because he was so thin," Revie wrote in 1975 for Norman's testimonial. "I was struck by his keenness to work hard and to try and impress... even over-eager to try and make the grade." Revie went on to say signing him gave him the "confidence-boosting jolt" he needed. He admires the tremendous strides he made because he was "still working overtime at improving". He concluded by calling Hunter "the best sweeper that's ever lived", praising "the timing of a 21 jewel Swiss watch" that was the hallmark of his tackling and called him "perfection". It's the tribute of someone brimming with paternal pride and while it may read as though Revie was laying it on thick, it reflects his abiding affection for a player who grafted his way to greatness.

With Sprake, Reaney and Hunter in the side and Charles in Rome, Leeds gradually began to climb the table from 14th in early October to 10th after their defeat by Sunderland three days before Christmas when the Big Freeze hit the north. The winter of 1962-63 was the coldest on record in England during the 20th century, temperatures fell to -16°C and snow lay across the country for three months. So many hundreds of football fixtures were cancelled that the pools companies inaugurated the Pools Panel to keep their income flowing. Leeds United, having reduced their overall debt to £140,000 by selling Charles, were dependent, like every other club, on gate receipts to pay the players' wages but were unable to play home or away for 70 days. They tried to defrost the pitch using straw and braziers, enlisting the labour of the ground staff boys to tend to them overnight. Revie and his staff hosted these evenings by showing young players such as Jimmy Greenhoff, Terry Cooper, Paul Madeley, Terry Hibbitt and Peter Lorimer films of great European Cup Finals in one of the West Stand lounges when they had finished their shovelling shift and gathered for hot soup before bedding down. It worked wonders as a bonding exercise even if the ground could not be made fit for play until the thaw arrived in late February.

Deprived of income for the whole of January and February, Reynolds, Manny Cussins and Albert Morris had little option other than extending their personal guarantees to the bank and issuing further loans to the club. Yes, their loans were secured and over the next few years all their investments would make returns, but it is to their credit that for the first time in the club's history it found three directors who were prepared to go 'all in'.

When Leeds finally returned to action on 2 March 1963, their progress continued. Charlton, who had suffered a relapse to his unruly worst in August when throwing a teacup at his manager after being blamed for a goal, was revelling in the responsibility of organising the defence along his preferred zonal lines and acting the grouchy mother hen to Hunter and Reaney. Further forward Storrie, moving to No.9, was enjoying the most prolific season of any United striker since Charles Mk I had departed in 1957. Conducting all this was Collins, a dervish with a demonic temper targeting anyone who might be foolish enough to try to hide. He taught them all the value of courage, emphasising their duty to make themselves available, to have the confidence and technique to take the ball in the tightest of spaces, encouraging them by example to put their bodies and their opponents' on the line and to never back down. "He really was quite frightening at times," said Bremner. "People don't appreciate how much power he had over the team."

Leeds won seven of their first 10 League games after the thaw to advance to eighth place, six points off a promotion spot but with three games in hand on Chelsea due to the winter backlog and as many as six on Plymouth from the balmy south-west. Miracle of miracles, they even won their first FA Cup tie for more than 10 years by beating Stoke 3-1, Stanley Matthews and all, in front of a crowd of 36,873 at Elland Road and followed it up with a 2-0 victory over Middlesbrough in the fourth round. Forest knocked them out in the next round, Leeds' sixth match in 16 days as they tried to cram in the remaining fixtures before the mid-May cut-off, and congestion also did for their promotion push after Easter when they had to play nine games in 27 days, winning only four of them to finish in fifth.

During their long hiatus between games, Les Cocker had drilled them in the gym every day and it was apparent when they went back on the field that they now had the stamina to overwhelm teams with a hard-running, harrying game that cured them of their tendency to ship late goals. Bremner was the one player who had hit a rough patch after the break, playing so poorly at inside-right that the crowd got on his back and he was understandably 'browned off'. His treatment instigated a third transfer request after he had ben dropped but Revie spent all summer avoiding contact with bidding clubs and subtly manipulating his asking price so that they could never pin him down. After another long chat with Billy and his fiancée Vicky, in which he again made the point about Bremner's importance to his grand design, he encouraged their wedding plans and teased out commitments that they would stay down south. The hours he spent building a rapport with players' parents and his natural empathy with working-class people and their concerns attracted the cream of Scottish schoolboy talent to sign for a nothing club. They could tell that it was not an act because it was all drawn from personal experience of the loneliness and financial and emotional anxiety he had suffered as a boy when he lost his mother to cancer at the age of 12. His willingness to extend the same care to wives, girlfriends and children emphasised his vision of Leeds United as a family with him at his head, fostering tremendous club spirit.

Bill Shankly and Brian Clough usually treated their injured players with an insensitivity that bordered on cruelty, irrationally behaving as if injuries were contagious, and both Shankly and Matt Busby acted as if every penny of their club's money were their own, frequently shafting world-class players with absurdly low salaries. Revie was always on his players' side, understanding their doubts and needs far better than the two sainted sons of the Ayrshire and Lanarkshire coalfields. For Busby and Shankly, ultimately it was all about the institution, for the greater glory of Manchester United and, in the latter case, Liverpool and their congregation. For Revie, however, it was all about his boys. That's why he was never aloof, always making himself available to them, truly hands-on even down to the soapy massages he and his staff administered on Thursdays.

In August 1963 in a friendly against Roma that had been arranged as part of the Charles deal, Bremner, about to get married to his Stirling sweetheart, played magnificently in midfield, restraining his natural impetuosity through greater discipline and fear of Collins, and flourishing with greater involvement on the ball. He was 20, had always been supremely confident and Revie decided that he had come of age to play in his rightful position, opening a spot further forward on the right side of attack in an increasingly settled side. Grenville Hair played only a handful of games, another Scot, Willie Bell, slotted into his left-back role with Johanneson ahead of him while Sprake, Reaney and Hunter continued to be schooled by Charlton. With Bremner dropping back, Revie used Storrie as centre-forward until he was hurt in early October, improvised with Ian Lawson and Don Weston in attack while Collins was everywhere, a William Wallace in size four boots.

To fill the gap on the right, Revie made a second pilgrimage to Old Trafford to see Busby and offered him £33,000 for Johnny Giles, a sublime passer off both feet, a streetwise inside-forward who was sick of the dressing room politics at Manchester United and his manager's lack of trust in him. Unusually, too, for a footballer of the early Sixties, he refused to

ABOVE: *The United squad for the 1920-21 season, the club's first in the Football League, having been elected to the Second Division on 31 May 1920*

LEFT: *Leeds United's first-ever captain, Jim Baker. A resolute centre-half, Baker followed his manager, Arthur Fairclough, from Huddersfield to Elland Road and was a mainstay of the side that won the Second Division in 1923-24*

ABOVE: *The Earl of Harewood, whose son would serve as the club's president from 1961 until his death in 2011, shakes hands with United's Irish outside-right Harry Duggan before the match against Arsenal in 1932*

ABOVE: *The hugely influential Major Frank Buckley poses for the camera at his desk. His unconventional methods included broadcasting dance music through the public address system during training days*

ABOVE: *The imposing figure of John Charles, the greatest player in the club's history*

ABOVE: *Officials survey the damage to Elland Road's West Stand following the 1956 fire*

ABOVE: *Don Revie took charge of United in 1961 and ushered in a truly golden era for the club*

ABOVE: *The Leeds squad and supporters in jubilant mood after securing the Second Division title in 1964*

ABOVE: *Billy Bremner waves to the crowd following the 1968 Fairs Cup triumph*

ABOVE: *Revie's ability to harness the talent of Jack Charlton was a huge factor in United's success*

RIGHT: *Champions of England at last! Bremner sits on the shoulders of Gary Sprake and Charlton while the rest of the squad gets the celebrations underway*

ABOVE: *The battle-hardened Leeds players are all smiles after winning the 1971 Fairs Cup Final against Juventus on away goals*

LEFT: *Allan 'Sniffer' Clarke celebrates United's 1972 FA Cup Final victory over Arsenal, having scored the decisive goal in a hard-fought 1-0 win*

ABOVE: *The Leeds squad brandish the league trophy in front of a packed Kop in 1974*

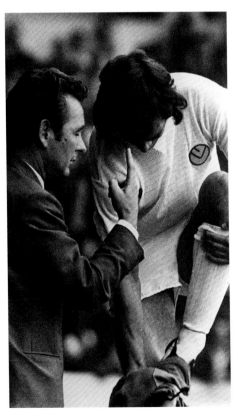

ABOVE: *Brian Clough's time at the Leeds helm was as turbulent as it was brief*

ABOVE: *Billy Bremner can't hide his sorrow following the 1975 European Cup Final defeat*

ABOVE: *Excited Leeds supporters make their way through Holbeck Park on matchday*

ABOVE: *Fans flock into the stadium under the imposing figure of the East Stand*

ABOVE: *The bronze statue of Don Revie that stands opposite the East Stand was unveiled in 2012*

ABOVE: *An array of scarves showcase the club's traditional colours of white, yellow and blue*

RIGHT: *The statue of Billy Bremner is always lovingly adorned with scarves on matchdays at Elland Road*

LEFT: *In the words of former player Shaun Derry, "You don't choose to play for Leeds United, Leeds United choose you," a sentiment that this fan would surely agree with*

RIGHT: *An array of evocative memorabilia, programmes and magazines can always be purchased in the club car park on a matchday*

LEFT: *What trip to Yorkshire is complete without a helping of fish and chips?*

LEFT: *A young fan lights a flare in the ground, demonstrating that Alex Ferguson was perhaps right when he said: "Elland Road is the most intimidating venue in Europe"*

RIGHT: *Supporters young and old drink in the matchday atmosphere*

LEFT: *The words of club icon Billy Bremner proudly adorn the East Stand and remain a sentiment that lies at the heart of the club*

LEFT: *The architects of United's third league title: chairman Leslie Silver (left) and manager Howard Wilkinson. The pair established a great partnership from the off*

RIGHT: *The Leeds squad, with (from left to right) Gary Speed, David Batty and Chris Fairclough in the foreground, celebrate the club's promotion back to the First Division*

LEFT: *The club mark promotion as well as acknowledging the chaotic scenes down in Bournemouth that followed the crucial match*

ABOVE: *Wilkinson playfully grasps the collar of new signing Lee Chapman, whose goals would ultimately fire United to the First Division title*

ABOVE: *Gary McAllister joined the club from Leicester and became the lynchpin of one of the club's greatest-ever midfields*

ABOVE: *The talismanic Gordon Strachan acknowledges the fans after the 1991-92 title*

ABOVE: *Dominic Matteo heads home at the San Siro as David O'Leary's young side rattle Europe's finest*

ABOVE: *South African international Lucas Radebe was a hugely popular figure amongst the Elland Road faithful*

ABOVE: *Adam Pearson (left) and owner Massimo Cellino pose at Elland Road in 2014. Cellino's regime would prove... controversial*

ABOVE: *Players and manager Simon Grayson celebrate promotion to the Championship in 2009-10*

ABOVE: *Marcelo Bielsa atop his famous bucket for a game against Norwich*

ABOVE: *Cardboard cut-outs fill the ground as the 2019-20 season is devastated by Covid-19*

ABOVE: *Back in the big time! The triumphant 2019-20 squad celebrate their achievement*

ABOVE: *Kalvin Phillips and Pascal Struijk in fine form amidst the jubilant scenes at Elland Road*

be cowed by Busby's aura and platitudes. He knew he deserved an integral role in the side and was enraged by being essentially quarantined from the main battleground out on the right wing. Giles had won the FA Cup only weeks before and his team-mates thought his mind must have been temporarily twisted by bitterness towards Busby even to contemplate leaving Manchester United for a Division Two club. No one would ever question Giles' resolve again, indeed he told his wife: "I am going to haunt him." Revie secured his man and drove back over the Pennines convinced he now had everything he needed to push for promotion.

While Giles had been impressed by Revie's words and what he had heard on the grapevine, what he found at Fullerton Park and Elland Road was, he says, "manna from heaven. There was method, there was a fierce hunger you could feel, a huge desire and work ethic. Don was always out there, supervising, and Bobby Collins setting the highest standards". It was that will to win that influenced him the most, a consoling assurance that together they would defy almost any odds. Giles, driving two hours there and two hours back for training from his home in Manchester every morning until he found a house in Leeds in December, took time to settle in and play with his old verve. The team had no problems accommodating him, Revie simply left the cleverest player Leeds have ever had, 'Brains' as the 1972 FA Cup Final song *Leeds United* calls him, to adapt to them rather than vice versa. There was nothing silky about the style, it was all about efficiency and endeavour, Johanneson's speed, serpentine dribbling and shooting providing the champagne moments that lingered long after the results in supporters' minds.

They were unbeaten at Elland Road throughout the 1963-64 season, laying the seeds for the conviction Leeds fans of a certain age maintain – that it should be considered a disgrace to lose a home match. Their rugged tackling, gamesmanship, hyper-aggressive gameplan and sometimes naked provocation from Collins set the tone for which they would become scapegoated in the summer of 1964 as 'Dirty Leeds'. Yet the question of whether Revie advocated hard play conducted at the very limits of legality, condoned it or simply put up with it as it developed organically in the jungle of Division Two football lingers. It is telling that Bremner's three-game suspension in February for persistent dissent was defended in public by Revie. In front of the dressing room he gave him such a bollocking that Bremner admitted he felt humiliated. He would always step in if their behaviour was self-harming. Only later would he recognise reputational damage as equally detrimental... once he had finished using the London press' censure as an 'us against the world' motivational tool.

United lost only one game in their first 24, a charge to the top of the table that had crowds nudging towards 30,000 that allowed the board to make inroads into the overdraft and eventually, over the next decade, pay off the debts they had incurred. Success would usher in a brief age of self-reliance when the club would be entirely funded by its supporters but although the board became less important if not less prominent, their misjudgements in the Seventies would once more put them on the hook. A draw with second-placed Sunderland on Boxing Day brought an attendance of 41,167 to Elland Road and a point that kept them three points clear at the top. Losing the return at Roker Park two days later after his makeshift forward line of Lawson, Weston and a patently unfit Storrie failed to fire convinced Revie to make one more move in the transfer market and in February Leeds signed the England centre-forward Alan Peacock from Middlesbrough for £53,000, the same amount they had paid for Charles. In this case there would be no chance of recouping their investment – while Peacock was a thoroughbred No.9, outstanding in the air, he was only available and affordable because he had recently undergone a difficult cartilage operation which had reduced his mobility.

Peacock was not an immediate hit and, like in 1990 and, sadly, 2019, the division frontrunners stumbled in spring, allowing Sunderland and Preston to narrow the gap after a run of four draws and a defeat. Four games into Peacock's Leeds career, however, Giles and Johanneson began to find the centre-forward's range and Leeds banished the stutter for fluency, winning eight and drawing two of their final games to win the Second Division championship by two points. It was a title built on defence. Leeds conceded 34 goals and scored a mere 61, Weston, Johanneson and Lawson crawling into double figures and Peacock returning eight from 14 appearances.

"They have obeyed my orders perfectly on and off the field," said Revie after their last game, a 2-0 victory over Charlton. "We have not always played popular football and the players have been denied gaining the flattering headlines that they would have because of their style. They have never grumbled once." What he said would take five years had taken him three. It would take far longer to persuade critics that the stigma attached to them for the manner of their triumph was a distortion devoid of any sympathetic context. Worse still, the agent of their tainting was the Football Association. Not long after the Town Hall bunting came down in the summer of 1964, the governing body was painting Leeds United's name black.

15

MAD MEN

An 18th century English proverb that applies to Don Revie's Leeds United has lost its pay-off in modern usage. Robbed of its concluding three words it reflects only the fact of the stain they were made to bear, decoupling it from the consequences. In full, however, "give a dog a bad name *and hang him*" explains the entrenched prejudice against them, the kind that allows a journalist to condemn them as "dirty, cheating bastards" decades on from Revie's death, preaching to a choir echoing "We all hate Leeds scum" back at him. Whether United's fans make a virtue of necessity and embrace this 'Dirty Leeds' cheap-shot cliché, resurrected by cretinously puerile, lad-mag, man-child Tim Lovejoy in the Nineties, is by the by. Dismissing or defying it cannot restore fair recognition to those players for what they achieved.

During the 10 years from their promotion in 1964 they won two league titles, were runners-up five times and never out of the top four. They played in four FA Cup Finals, winning one, and five European finals, winning two as well as the League Cup once. Over that period they amassed more points than any club, 48 more than Liverpool in second, won more games and scored more goals. Defensively, they lost the fewest matches and conceded the fewest number of goals. Three United players – Bobby Collins, Jack Charlton and Billy Bremner – were named Footballer of the Year, Norman Hunter became the inaugural Players' Player of the Year, 19 were selected for international honours and Revie himself was Manager of the Year on three occasions. They never sought garlands and do not want praise from halfwits as reparations now. The surviving members of that side have the only thing they craved, as John Giles says, the camaraderie and unbreakable bond forged by the "satisfaction of sticking together through the dark days", of overcoming disappointments and bile to savour the sweetest victories. They also enjoyed the respect of their peers, elders of the tribe of fabled 'Football Men', Bill Shankly, Bill Nicholson and Frank McLintock among them. 'Dirty Leeds' is meaningless shorthand now, asinine and undeserved. It once did genuine damage, though, and stung even more because it was facilitated by the Football Association giving the snipers of the London press ammunition to fire at Revie and his team.

It started in August 1964, a fortnight before the opening match of Revie's first Division One campaign, when the FA News published a report on the "depressing record" of misconduct during the previous season. In fact it outlined improvement among First and Second Division clubs and deterioration in the third and fourth while pointing out that the FA would be writing to clubs who had accrued 12 or more offences against their players. Published alongside the report was a table, showing that Leeds United had the worst record and Ipswich Town the best. It all looked pretty damning bereft of context and yet, as Leeds were quick to point out, there had been no dismissals and only one of their players had been suspended in 1963-64. Billy Bremner was banned for a fortnight after his second booking of the season while Manchester United, for example, had had Denis Law, Paddy Crerand and David Herd sent off for violent conduct against Aston Villa, Burnley and Willem II respectively. It transpired, though not explicitly stated, that Leeds owed their blackguard status to their record as a club because the figures were compiled from first team, reserves, 'A team' and schoolboys. It was a serious issue and one that needed to be taken in hand by Revie immediately but that was not how it was spun. The sins of the sons were visited upon the fathers, the notoriety was attached to the first team, the standard bearers, and they were hung for it alone.

Revie was furious and used his anger to counter-strike, warning referees that he would be hyper-vigilant for any sign they were being influenced by Leeds' reputation. "We maintain that the 'dirty team' tag which was blown up by the press could prejudice not only the general public but the officials controlling the game, and, to put it mildly, could have an effect on the subconscious approach of both referee and linesmen," he said. "To say nothing of the minds of spectators, especially some types who are watching football today. It could lead to some very unsavoury incidents." Sir Alex Ferguson will tell you how much he learnt from Jock Stein and Sir Matt Busby. But his use of the pre-emptive word to the wise was pure Revie.

The new label did not earn United any rancour at first as they began the season at such breakneck pace that the manager, according to Bremner, had to tell them to "stop running round like a set of mad men" and calm down. Once they caught their breath and abandoned that hectic approach, they fought back to win at Villa Park on the opening day, beat the champions Liverpool 4-2 at Elland Road and defeated Wolves to make a perfect start. And all without any signings save for the most significant when Revie eventually turned down approaches to move to Sheffield Wednesday and

Sunderland. He went as far as accepting the Sunderland job in October until a demo following Leeds' 3-1 victory over Tottenham obliged the board to offer him better terms.

Leeds arrived at Goodison Park in early November in fourth place, having acclimatised like natives to the rarefied air. That they had done so without Alan Peacock, injured during pre-season, and with the workhorse, reserve 19-year-old centre-forward Rod Belfitt, filling in proved the effectiveness of the system. Leeds United were the most heavily coached side in the League while Revie was manager, and pioneers in the meticulous attention to detail they paid to the opposition, illustrated by the scouting reports or 'dossiers' compiled by Syd Owen, Maurice Lindley, Les Cocker and Revie himself. It was here that Owen's perfectionism was a pure positive – no one was more sharp-eyed at spotting a players' weakness or ruthless at working out ways to exploit it. In *The Glory Game* Hunter Davies speaks to one of the authors of these reports before Tottenham's FA Cup quarter-final at Leeds in 1972. He doesn't name him but it can only be Owen from the tone. "His report was very damning," Davies wrote. "Each Spurs player sounded like a condemned man about to be sentenced for life." What benefited Leeds was not Owen's verdict, it was the case he made for the prosecution: "I wouldn't have [Martin] Peters on my side... he lacks the strength to contain the opposition in midfield when things are going badly. I wouldn't have [Ralph] Coates in my side either. All he can do is run, usually into people or through people. He has no distribution." At the time he said it, the World Cup-winning Peters was captain of Tottenham and England and Coates, a £190,000 signing from Burnley, had four caps, none of which, sadly, he put to use to constrain his Trumpian combover. It is true that Revie continued using the reports long after his team were bored by them and skilful and mature enough to adapt off the cuff. To his players' detriment in the late Sixties, the manager's caution kept the handbrake on. But the dossiers were vital during these early years and, after Owen's reserves were drilled to mimic Saturday's opposition during the Friday morning run-through on the training pitch, ideal in helping the players visualise and learn exactly how to react to the things the scouts had spotted.

A dossier from a United Nations rapporteur would not have prepared them for what they encountered at Goodison Park. There had been a sense for a few weeks that the kettle had been boiling away – Tottenham had four players cautioned at Elland Road and Sheffield United's Len Badger had been sent off there the week before Leeds played Everton. Both sides left complaining about their treatment but were referees really ignoring what Leeds were up to in terms of foul play and provocation? It seems unlikely and contemporary match reports by national newspapers of United's home games do not bear this out. On the road, especially in London, they were often damned for their sins while those inflicted upon them were ignored – Eddie McCreadie's wild hack from behind on Johnny Giles at Stamford Bridge in September that put Giles out for four weeks with knee-ligament damage a case in point. One of the reasons, as Giles said, that some of the matches turned into roughhouses is that Leeds' reputation preceded them: "They seemed determined to do unto us, what they thought we were going to do unto them." The other reason is Revie and his handbrake. Having moulded a formidable defence over the preceding three years, away from home the strategy was to score and then go into lockdown, holding what they had with positional discipline and hard tackling. With Bremner cockily strutting around midfield and Collins needling opponents, they almost invited retribution from those they were frustrating.

Revie's warning about unsavoury incidents was borne out four minutes into the match when Giles, dribbling towards the penalty box, was scythed down by Everton left-back Sandy Brown. Before they picked themselves up, Brown punched Giles in the belly, right under the referee's nose, and was promptly and deservedly sent off. An already hostile crowd was incensed and for the next 34 minutes pelted the Leeds players with coins, fruit and any number of missiles as vicious running battles, over-the-ball fouls and shoving matches erupted all over the pitch. After Derek Temple collided with the man who had given Leeds an early 1-0 lead, Willie Bell, and both were pole-axed by the mid-air impact, the referee Ken Stokes was hit by a projectile while the casualties were receiving treatment. For the first time in a Football League match, the referee led both teams off the pitch for a cooling off period. He spoke to the managers and players in their dressing rooms, telling them to cut it out or he would abandon the match and said the same thing to the crowd over the tannoy. Ten minutes later he led the players back on to the field where they turned it down a touch to a spiteful simmer and Leeds completed a 1-0 victory marred by more violent flare-ups, missiles and the racial abuse of Albert Johanneson. In the second half the rhythmical chant "Dir-ty Leeds, Dir-ty Leeds, Dir-ty Leeds" resounded out from the fuming home supporters. At least the pitch invasion, which seemed imminent on several occasions, never came, yet the United bus was barraged as it pulled out of Goodison Avenue and Stokes had to barricade himself in his changing room for several hours until the police could guarantee his safety on the streets.

Condemnation was swift and severe. Hand-wringing in the broadsheets and summary calls for a crack-down were accompanied by cries of "Dirty

Leeds" at away grounds after almost every United tackle. Geoffrey Green in *The Times* was one of the few to acknowledge both reasons it had been such a tinderbox. "Goodison Park," he wrote, "has already gained an unsavoury tribal reputation for vandalism: Leeds United, too, more recently have earned black marks for ill-temper on the field. The marriage of those two dangerous elements sparked off the explosion." That sounds about right: neither the venue nor the visitors were entirely to blame but in combination, especially when Leeds refused to yield even though their infamy had hyped opponents up to blitzkrieg them, it blew up in the referee's face. "I feel we are not being allowed to settle down to play the football we are capable of playing," said Revie. While it was the truth, his Leeds teams never let the opponents settle down either. "I am disgusted by these attacks on us," he continued, "and I ask that we be judged fairly and squarely on each match and not on this unfair tag that we have got."

Fat chance! When the Football Association disciplinary committee met to consider the referee's report, Brown was banned for 14 days and Everton fined £250, up from the usual levy of £100, for the misconduct of their supporters. No matter, Leeds United have always been censured for winning 'the Battle of Goodison Park' rather than responsibility being shared or, in accordance with the official findings, Everton taking the blame. As another less catchy proverb has it: 'He that has an ill name is half-hanged.'

The victory over Everton was the fifth in a run of seven which in itself was the starting stage of a tremendous sequence of only one defeat in 27 matches from the end of September until the middle of April. Leeds went to the top of the table for the first time at the turn of the year when Jack Charlton and Norman Hunter headed goals to defeat Sunderland 2-1 at Elland Road, having broken clear with Manchester United and Chelsea for a three-way title race. Teenagers Paul Madeley, Jimmy Greenhoff and Terry Cooper were ready to fill in and each made contributions during the run. Winning, in Peacock's absence, had not been much of a problem but there was a staccato quality to the play without him leading the line and dominating centre-halves. They were second by the time he returned in February and he scored four in five successive victories that directed them back to the top just in time for the visit of Manchester United on 17 April.

It was the fourth time the two Uniteds met that season and the matches sparked a rivalry that has been mottled by hatred for more than 50 years. Some analysts have tried to claim that the poisonous animosity dates back to some visceral remnant of the Wars of the Roses but a more accurate assessment locates the origins of this relatively modern football feud to on-field events in the spring of 1965, four months after Leeds had won the first League match at Old Trafford 1-0. With both sides going for the Double, they were drawn together in Leeds' first-ever FA Cup semi-final at Hillsborough and it turned into a ragged, violent draw. Nobby Stiles' early dreadful tackle on Johanneson set the tone for a game which quickly degenerated into a series of skirmishes on and off the ball between Jack Charlton and Law, and Bremner and Crerand. The ill-feeling spread to the terraces and scuffles, fights and assaults were reported by the city constabularies of Sheffield and Nottingham after that game and the replay four days later at the City Ground that Leeds won with Bremner's 89th-minute goal. "I just darted in," said Bremner, " and headed the ball through the only gap I could see. But as soon as I saw the ball in the net I thing I went delirious. Certainly my eyes were full of tears of joy." The goal decided a riveting match, much removed from the kicking carnival on the gluey Hillsborough pitch. Manchester United, after picking up two cautions in the first match and committing 24 fouls to Leeds' 10, attacked with urgency and fluency "as good for 20 minutes," according to Jack Charlton, "as they have ever played". But Leeds withstood waves of attacks, Collins' hectoring voice resounding around the ground organising his team-mates, until they took a late grip and sealed it when Bremner tracked the flight of Giles' deep, floated free-kick with his back to goal, as if he expected it to dip quickly and demand an overhead volley. When it kept going, he managed to improvise and leap backwards then twisted his neck to flick it with the left side of his forehead around Bill Foulkes and past Pat Dunne. If ever a moment embodied Bremner's brilliance, it was this. His technical skills and swagger delighted supporters, especially when combined in those reverse, right-foot passes that would have dislocated most mortal players' ankles. But it was his never-say-die spirit and timing of those deadly incursions into the box that made him Leeds' supreme match-winner.

Tellingly he was serving a week's suspension for receiving a fourth caution of the season when Manchester United took them on again at Elland Road where a home victory would have lifted Leeds five points clear at the top with four games to go. John Connelly scored the only goal in a gale and Collins' inventiveness was not matched by the finishing of Peacock and Don Weston. The top two had enticed a record crowd of 52,368 to watch them and *The Observer*'s Tony Pawson, a former star of the Pegasus side famed for their sportsmanship, was struck by how something in Leeds' style had forged a bond with their audience. "Every team that has met them," he wrote, "has had to put its head down and battle against their relentless drive. From the first game they have played it hard but with perhaps two exceptions they have tried to play it fair. Such rugged determination has offended the purists but enthused the city."

Leeds had four games in eight days to redress the damage but an away defeat by Sheffield Wednesday gave Manchester United an initiative they did not cede. Leeds remained top by one point with one match to play while Manchester United had two games left and Revie's team fought back from 3-0 down at Birmingham City to draw 3-3. Manchester United's victory over Arsenal was enough to put them ahead on goal average, an advantage their subsequent defeat at Aston Villa in their final match could not dent. Each had won 29 games, drawn six and lost seven but Man Utd had scored six more goals and conceded 13 fewer. By the time they received the trophy, Leeds were two days into a five-night stay at the Selsdon Park Hotel near Croydon, preparing to take on Liverpool in the FA Cup Final.

It was a mistake to go so early. It suited Revie to have so much time with his players and retain complete control. Like his peers, particularly Jock Stein, he was the beneficiary of a secret army of snouts throughout the city who would nark on his players if they saw them out and about after a Wednesday yet Revie still preferred to take them away, usually up to the Victorian spa hotel, Craiglands in Ilkley, before home matches. He would fill their time with the much-derided bingo, cards, carpet bowls and putting competitions to counter boredom and the players, who are bemused by the amount of attention these twee diversions attract, bought into it because they enjoyed each other's company and there was nothing else to do. In 1965, however, he had not worked out his full compendium of games and five days was far too long for them to dwell on the match.

None of them recall the final with any fondness. The hype in the city around the scramble for tickets was tangible yet Charlton recognised a strange reticence when he saw a group of his friends on Wembley Way a couple of hours before kick-off who were reluctant to show their rosettes. The vibrancy of Liverpool's support and the almost hysterical longing to win their first FA Cup defined the coverage. Collins, the Footballer of the Year, led Leeds out in his yellowing woollen socks and inside the ground United's fans did make their excitement felt with some soprano yelps to punctuate the throaty bass bellows of 'Leeds!' It was a dog of a game, ruined by rain and injuries sustained by Storrie and Liverpool's Gerry Byrne. Johanneson, the first black FA Cup finalist, suffered abuse from the stands and his day was wrecked by anxiety while Bremner vividly remembered the game as a nightmare in which he could never escape from someone chasing him down. Only Sprake kept Leeds in the game, thwarting Liverpool whenever they escaped the midfield meat-grinder, and his three magnificent saves kept it to 0-0 at full-time.

It improved in extra-time when Roger Hunt's goal strong-armed Revie into throwing Charlton and Bremner up front and the latter scored another spectacular goal, spearing a rising half-volley into the top corner after 100 minutes. Leeds held out for another 17, three minutes short of taking it to a replay at Maine Road, until Ian St John's flying header from six yards deservedly won it for Liverpool. Sixty thousand people greeted their return to Leeds on the Sunday to mark their achievement as runners-up in League and Cup, the unwanted 'double' that was nonetheless the finest season the club had known. There was no bashfulness as they took the applause, their torsos popping up through the open skylights on the top of the single decker coach as they made their way down Boar Lane, up Briggate and the Headrow to the Civic Hall. Collins, Harry Reynolds, and Lord Harewood all spoke to the crowd and were cheered. Revie's words were the most prophetic, however. "To be a big club we have to take set-backs and carry on," he said. "If we can't take defeat we will never be a club." He had taught that lesson to his team and now he nurtured it to the city. "If you give support like this year's we will give everything in our power to pay you back."

The next three seasons were ones of consolidation for Leeds United at the top of the table, seasons where crowds fluctuated around an average of 35,000, which allowed the club to rebuild its finances, settling debts with the bank and directors. Wages were increased and budgets for travel and hotels were improved. The temptation to spend some of it on transfers was resisted, Revie instead promoting Cooper, Madeley, Greenhoff, Lorimer, who had made his debut at 15 in 1962, and Eddie Gray. He was not against buying players – indeed he made illicit approaches to both Alan Ball and Frank McLintock, turning up at their houses unannounced to tap them up, but nether could persuade their clubs to sell. Yet the quality he now thought would improve Leeds was not readily available. He was no longer in need of stopgaps. The tyros in the youth teams he had so diligently assembled were ready and he recognised that their talent cried out for opportunity.

Greenhoff would thrive after leaving Leeds and is remembered best for his graceful play at Stoke and Manchester United but he shone for Leeds as well in the years when their forward play was mostly functional. He had terrific balance, control and struck the ball with blistering force. He was also diffident and drifted out of games. The other four broke the mould.

Cooper, a left-back converted from outside-left, would redefine his position. His exuberant overlapping and neat link-up play was a nod to the great Brazilian pioneer of marauding full-backs Nilton Santos, who became such a devastating attacking threat during the 1958 World Cup.

Week after week he pinged the ball about with Hunter, Giles and Gray before storming forward to deliver marvellously menacing crosses.

Madeley's versatility has been lauded for six decades, movingly so after his death in 2018. It barely did him justice though because it underplayed how integral he was – he was never the 12th name on Revie's teamsheet, he was usually the first, the only question being where he would play. He was an outstanding right-back and central midfield player, superb in the air, utterly unflappable in possession and, given his upright style, deceptively quick with a smooth change of pace. He played a season up front, making those leg-sapping channel runs as if he was born to it and ended his career as the most stylish of sweepers and centre-backs, rarely letting a fleck of muck taint his pristine white kit throughout 90 minutes of exertion. "The imprint of Paul that remains," wrote Geoffrey Green in Madeley's testimonial programme, "is of a guardsman doing his job wherever required and doing it to the last ounce without raising a fist or foot to an opponent in anger." Revie called him the Rolls-Royce but he was even more elegant than that. He was a Lagonda.

Lorimer and Gray, still thick as thieves in the seventh decade of their friendship, provided contrasting talents to the flanks. The bright-minded Gray, really a central midfielder, brought his sinuous dribbling to bear on the left where his dazzling feints and swivelling, Presley-esque pelvis turned full-backs into a conman's marks. On the right Lorimer, famed for 'the hottest shot in football', was the most dynamic player in the side, bustling past defenders and, with uncanny precision, flaying in crosses or shots that would whistle like Stukas en route to their targets. All were naturals, each of them handpicked by Revie and schooled by Owen and Cocker. Cooper, Madeley, Lorimer and Gray rewarded that faith by playing 2,355 games between them.

Their chances came quicker than Revie had wanted when, in Leeds' first European campaign, he lost his captain Collins. United had been greatly influenced by their experiences playing Italian opposition in friendlies that had begun as part of the Charles' deal. It was in those games that they were first subjected to the concept of 'marking the inside of a player's shirt'. In the Sixties Serie A defenders made nuisances of themselves in any way they could, from pulling an opponent's hair, nipping, twisting his knackers, in one famous players' horror story, jabbing a finger up his arse, and the ubiquitous bumping to knock them off balance. There was nothing so subtle when Leeds took a 2-1 lead over Torino from the home leg and two chartered aircrafts' worth of fans to Italy for the second leg. Leeds held on for a 0-0 draw with 10-men to go through after Fabrizio Poletti, the right-back, took his chance when Collins was on the ground, 10 yards away from the ball, to jump on him with both feet, shattering his femur. The man who had done more than anyone to shape his team-mates, who had taught them how to be winners, lay grievously injured with a broken thigh-bone, screaming with such piercing anguish that the wives of Willie Bell and Billy Bremner burst into tears. He was 34 and, typically, would fight his way back to play again with a 15 inch pin in the bone, ploughing on for another seven years, sometimes in excruciating pain, his compromised mobility ending his days as a Division One regular. Poletti, along with his team-mates, went to apologise at the Turin hospital in which Collins was confined for two weeks. While Bremner admitted that he had murder in his heart after the incident, Collins simply said: "You live by the sword…"

In Collins' absence Giles moved inside to form the midfield axis with Bremner that would become the finest duo in the land, the perfect blend of cool calculation and raw emotion. Giles was an even better passer than Collins and over a couple of seasons the attacking style evolved because he could pick out any of seven forward options. Leeds finished a good second in the league behind Liverpool in 1965-66 while never really running them close for the title. They had faced off on successive days over Christmas, Leeds smashing and grabbing a 1-0 victory at Anfield, Liverpool winning 1-0 at Elland Road 24 hours later. However, when Peacock broke down again to join Johanneson and Collins as long-term absentees, United ran out of steam when going deep in Europe and lost too many games in the spring to creep up on Bill Shankly's side.

The Fairs Cup treated Revie's men to a thrilling ride in 1966 and again in 1967 when they made it as far as the semi-final and final respectively. They were both arduous campaigns, taking them into the heart of Eastern Europe and Fascist Spain. Revie tried all manner of tricks from sending out his players in numbers not corresponding to their positions to flooding the Elland Road pitch for the semi-final replay against Real Zaragoza, a ruse which bit him on the backside when his side went down 3-1. During an earlier home tie against Valencia, Charlton was so incensed by a punch when the score was 1-1 that he chased the offender, Francisco Vidagany, and tried to bray him. It had started when Charlton rattled the keeper and in the melee had been surrounded by Valencia players who kicked and punched him. It ended with police on the pitch to break up the scrap and the referee sending both off in the dressing room where he had dispatched the teams to calm down. Leeds could not find the winner against nine men after another Valencia sending off but nonetheless won in Spain.

They picked up stamps in their passports from Italy, East Germany, Spain and Hungary en route to the semi in 1965-66 and a year later went to Holland and beat DWS, triumphed again in Valencia, drew with Bologna on aggregate and went through on the spin of a disc. They played Kilmarnock in the semi-final and won 4-2, Belfitt scoring a hat-trick to cap a frustrating season in which United finished fourth, five points behind Manchester United, and were knocked out of the FA Cup in the semi-final by Chelsea at Villa Park by virtue of a refereeing decision of baroque fastidiousness from Ken Burns. Trailing 1-0 with a couple of minutes to go, Lorimer had smashed a free-kick past Peter Bonetti before the wall had retreated the full 10 yards. Even though Chelsea's dawdling had been to their advantage, Burns ordered a retake and Lorimer could not strike twice. Their season ended when they knocked Kilmarnock out and Uefa decided to hold over the Fairs Cup Final to the beginning of the following season. Crucially, because Leeds' desperation to win something had made them fight on all fronts, fixture congestion hobbled them with fatigue every season. At the end of 1964-65 the FA Cup Final was their sixth match in 15 days, in 1965-66 they ended with seven in 22 and in May 1967 it was eight in 25. Playing a final at the start of a season should have been ideal and allowed a fresh side to cure the impatience of their supporters and the abuse of critics who were bandying around slurs such as 'muffers', 'lemons' and 'losers'. The players tell us that they did not care about all the snarking, that they retreated into the comfort and insularity of the family. Revie cared all right, cared enough to want to ram all the put-downs up his nearest critic's nose. If 1964-65 was supposed to be the beginning of something not the end, paradise had been postponed long enough.

16

MAKE THE RAFTERS RING

Every summer since the foundation of the Premier League in 1992 the build-up to the new football season comes earlier and with yet more hype. From June onwards we are treated to freshly minted advertising slogans such as 'football is our religion', 'once in a lifetime', 'are you ready?' and even 'it's theatre, art, war and love' delivered by a rainswept and pensive Sean Bean in moody black and white. The burst of clamour and drama that accompanies the trailers from Sky was expertly parodied by the comedian and football sceptic David Mitchell in a sarcastically telling skit lampooning the ubiquitous nature of the game in England and how deeply Sky has striven to embed it in the national psyche during the past 28 years. Marching up the touchline, captured by a hand-held camera performing a giddy dance copied from American cop shows and whipping himself towards hysteria as he previews the coming fare, Mitchell approaches self-combustion as he reaches the peak of his sales pitch. "All the football all the time," he hectors. "Thousands and thousands of hours of football, each more climactic than the last. Constant dizzying, 24-hour, year-long endless football, every kick of it massively mattering to someone presumably. Watch it all here, all the time, forever. It will never stop. It's officially going on forever. There is still everything to play for and forever to play it in. Watch it, watch it, watch the football. Watch it, it's football."

Mercifully, priorities still lay elsewhere in the summer of 1967. Leeds United's players were enjoying their seven-week break when most of the nation tuned in to *Our World* in late June to see John Lennon in his paisley and brocade psychedelic finery put down his pint of milk and sing *All You Need is Love* to a global audience of 300 million. The game was not so intrusive back then, not so determined to colonise the media, and when Leeds United regrouped for five weeks' pre-season training, they did so away from the scrutiny and rumour that plagues elite footballers today. The variety and intensity of the training routines left them tingling with energy and alert, ready to redress the mistakes of the previous season and steamroller opponents from the off with their usual urgency.

An uncharacteristically slow start had left them far too much ground to recover in the closing weeks of the previous season to catch Manchester United and they stuttered again in August 1967 without the injured Giles. A draw and two defeats from their first three league games sent them to Zagreb to play Dinamo in the first leg of the Fairs Cup Final at the bottom of Division One. They lost 2-0 in Yugoslavia and were unable to make amends at home where the conduct of the crowd and Bremner had taken a troubling turn. Between the two legs they had managed their first victory of the season by beating Fulham at Elland Road during which Bremner, now the captain, was sent off for using obscene language after being booked. His dismissal sparked a fight between supporters and police officers were also attacked when they tried to break it up, resulting in three arrests and two people being taken to hospital.

It was not the first time there had been punch-ups on the terraces, as early as their first home match in Division One against Liverpool in 1964, three 'juvenile delinquents' had been collared for wading into the away fans and there had been arrests over the years for drunkenness, profanity, throwing toilet rolls and significantly less absorbent missiles. While Bremner played on waiting for his FA hearing, *The Observer* sent Arthur Hopcraft to discover whether the captain's ill-discipline was a catalyst for the crowd's. He found compelling evidence during the second leg of the Fairs Cup Final, which Leeds drew 0-0, while trying to watch both the game and its effect on the Scratching Shed, where the most unruly fans gathered. Under the headline 'How a footballer can set the crowd on fire', Hopcraft wrote in an astute evaluation: "If the compulsion in watching football is largely a matter of identity-transference, [Bremner] does duty for the fighter in us... Spectators can afford as much murderous thought as they can muster, without personal danger and possibly with some therapeutic value. Players feed it at their peril." A few supporters took the opportunity to take sly shots at the police during the cup presentation at the end of the draw with Dinamo Zagreb that confirmed Leeds' fourth runners-up spot in three seasons and in November the FA banned Bremner for a month.

A year before Harry Reynolds had addressed the crowd after some carping following a 7-0 defeat by West Ham in the League Cup and a 5-0 battering by Liverpool in the League – caused, Norman Hunter said, by an experimental system which left him a fish out of water at left-back and Willie Bell overwhelmed in an ineffective man-marking job. The clamour from the crowd for signings had begun to needle the board but Reynolds firmly put them in their place. "We haven't exactly been idle," he said. "Signing new players is the job of the manager - and it's the job of directors to find the money. We're backing our manager now as we always have done – and we'll foot the bill when the time is right." On the back of profits exceeding £130,000 in the two years to August 1967, Revie went out and bought Mick Jones, a centre-forward from Sheffield United who had been capped twice by England, and made him Leeds' first £100,000 player. Regrettably it was the last deal overseen by Reynolds in the chair as he was forced to step down due to the larcenous effects of arthritis which had slowly stripped him of mobility and left him in severe pain right on the threshold of 'the glory years'. He was not only the best chairman Leeds United have ever had, he was the transformative presence who deserves a statue every bit as much as Revie and Bremner. His two maxims – "you get nowt for being second" and "management in any job demands common sense and the courage to apply it" did as much to shape the character of the Revie side and hence the club as anything else. He would live to see Leeds win trophies but was not well enough to enjoy them in the manner his contribution merited. By March 1968 when Leeds were at Wembley again, he managed the journey to watch the League Cup Final but could not conquer the stairs to reach his seat in the royal box. For seven years there had never been any doubt that he had Revie's back. Once he stepped down, though, some of his successors would come to resent not sharing the credit and gratitude bestowed on Revie. "At a football club there's a holy trinity – the players, the manager and the supporters," Bill Shankly once said. "Directors don't come into it. They are only there to sign the cheques." Reynolds, to purloin another Shankly-ism, was "much more important than that" but as for those who followed him into the chair, it would be fair to say that Revie and his Anfield friend were kindred spirits.

Jones was an unusual choice but a shrewd one. *The Guardian* had diagnosed United's flaws back in August as the "lack of a schemer and a finisher". While Giles' return from injury midway through the season would resolve the former, Jones was not a prolific goalscorer. He was a tireless, hard-running and enabling No.9 possessed of foolhardy courage and a selflessness that he put at the team's disposal. His sacrifice to the principle of 'teamship' masked a surfeit of skill – he had a thunderous shot, a leap to match Jack Charlton's and terrific touch in the extended dribble, seen to best effect in his goal in the 1970 FA Cup Final replay and the running cross for Allan Clarke in the final two years later. He played but did not score in the 7-0 victory over a shambolic Chelsea who had just sacked their manager, Tommy Docherty, and when he overcame the ankle injury that he brought with him from Bramall Lane and returned to first-team action in December, he led the line in a 13-match unbeaten run that drove United from fourth to first by Easter.

Jones was cup-tied and played no part in the League Cup campaign in which Luton, Bury, Sunderland, Stoke and Derby were brushed aside. Madeley played at centre-forward in the final against Arsenal in a pig-ugly match ruined by caution and too many fouls. Charlton, who had scored only six goals from centre-half in his first eight seasons at Leeds, ended up with 95 by the end of his career, only 15 of which were bagged during that long-abandoned experiment up front. What turned him into a regular contributor was his controversial innovation of standing directly in front of the goalkeeper for inswinging corners, an infuriating but legal ruse that he had cooked up during England training. Having noted how much it annoyed goalkeepers, he asked Revie to trial it and credits his manager for not being at all precious about trying other people's hunches out. It worked a treat and provoked many goalkeepers to counter it by jumping into him knees first or punching him in the head as they soared to clear the cross. Strangely it was criticised when he used it for Leeds but not for England where it was more profitable, and in the League Cup Final it set up Terry Cooper's winner. From his customary position Charlton sandwiched Arsenal's Jim Furnell with Madeley under Eddie Gray's corner and Cooper volleyed the clearance back past the goalkeeper. The goal came on 17 minutes and was its only highlight. Arsenal complained vociferously and with justification but the referee awarded the goal and the match descended into a forlorn bore of sideways passing and constant retrenchment. Madeley was withdrawn into midfield, Arsenal tried to get their own back by buffeting Gary Sprake at a corner and Leeds' 'all for one' rule kicked in, prompting a mass shoving match that was more action-packed than the football. Nonethless Leeds grimly held on, not risking anything but not needing to either. When Les Hamer blew his whistle, United's players were almost uncontainable, wheeling their arms and whooping with joy while Bremner did a forward roll in the centre circle before climbing up the steps to the royal box. After 48 years the club had won its first cup and its significance did not pass anyone by. As they supped champagne from their winners' tankards, Charlton said: "We came to win and not put on a showpiece. We will take some whacking now we have got one under our belts. Now we know we can win trophies." Fifteen years a professional, Charlton at last added a club honour, albeit a drinking vessel, to his World Cup winners' medal.

He had also jumped the gun: Sprake, who had punched Bristol City's Chris Garland and been sent off a week after Wembley in an FA Cup fifth-round tie, was hurt during the semi-final against Everton, played on and shanked a clearance straight to an Everton player which directly led to the penalty that knocked Leeds out. Back in December at Anfield he had thrown the ball into his own net, the adhesive effects of chewing gum-laced spittle enhancing his error. It was there that he was serenaded with Max Bygraves' *Careless Hands*, a quip that he would never live down though he would redeem himself in the eyes of his team-mates and Revie, as he always did, this time by winning a key tie almost alone at the beginning of the following season. Sprake's injury kept him out of the final three matches of the league campaign, all of which Leeds lost, and they tottered from second to fourth to let Manchester City exploit Manchester United's late slip and take the title.

"One under our belts" did not have the immediate galvanising effect Charlton forecast in terms of victories at each of the four fronts on which they were fighting. There was no question whatsoever of prioritising the FA Cup over the championship, Europe over the League Cup. For the first seven years of their Division One life under Revie, they gunned for everything each season until, impossibly stretched in the spring of 1970, something had to give. Until then their mission was to go as deep as they could in every competition and typically they would manage to do so in at least three.

Having enjoyed their continental excursions in the Fairs Cup during the previous two seasons, happy to be together and toasting their success at all the formal post-match banquets which were still an essential part of the experience, they were punished with a 'staycation' in 1968. Having beaten Spora Luxemboug 16-0 and Partizan Belgrade 3-2, the draw, farcically, compelled them to play Hibernian, Rangers and Dundee. The 'Anglos' – Bremner, Lorimer and Gray – who were looked down on by the Glasgow press because they had never played in their native land, were desperate to do well and inspired their team-mates to home victories and battling away draws to go through to the final for the second year in succession. They played poorly at Ibrox in front of 80,000, apart from Bremner who, according to *The Times*, "was indefatigable... his strength of purpose, his dogged refusal to be beaten, covered the gaps". There were casualties during the match at Elland Road due to overcrowding in parts of the ground and from bottles hurled by Rangers fans when Leeds took a two-goal lead. "Leeds always had the edge," wrote Geoffrey Green, "and they had it by their quenchless spirit, their fire and hard brand of teamwork." It was the first and not the final time that Alex Ferguson would leave Leeds on the losing side.

One feature of this story is that one should never be surprised by the obtuseness of the Leeds support – the attendance for the semi-final against Dundee was nearly 27,000 fewer than the 50,500 who turned up for Rangers' visit. Yes, Rangers had turned the city into a suburb of Glasgow when they came and the crushing may have put some people off, but even so the year before 43,000 had come to the semi-final versus Kilmarnock and the drop-off frustrated the manager and his players. "I say: give us a chance!" wrote Bremner in a puzzled lament. "All we ask the supporters is that they come and judge for themselves, as to whether or not we are worth the price of admission." He wondered if it was a generational thing, saying some supporters "will admit, grudgingly, it sometimes seems, that the present-day lads at Elland Road are not a bunch of complete scrubbers but, still, it seems, we cannot hope ever to compare with men like Willis Edwards, Wilf Copping and Ernie Hart". It would not have been much comfort to him but the truth is the public did not roll up in any significant number to watch the Thirties side either. Capacity was never an issue, enthusiasm was and Bremner concluded that if there is hope, it lies in the youth. When they "marry and have families," he wrote, "they will still come down to Elland Road to watch the lads and when the kids get old enough they'll bring them down with them. So that one day we'll have a real family of fans on the terraces and a full house". Patience was required on the pitch, too, after a gruelling spring. Eddie Gray scored the winner against Dundee in United's 66th match of the season and fortunately Uefa, once more, postponed the final to August – not so much because they wanted to give Leeds and Budapest's Ferencváros time to draw breath but to clear the decks for the European Championship Finals in Italy. Whatever the motive, it was welcome.

Madeley was again upfront when the first leg of the final was played in August. Live TV coverage, summer holidays and the usual apathy suppressed the crowd to 25,000 for a drab match and anyone who had marvelled at the performances of Florian Albert and Gyula Rakosi for Hungary at the World Cup two years previously in England were sorely disappointed. In a game full of niggly fouls and attrition, Leeds scored the only goal when Jones bundled in a corner that Charlton had flicked on from under the bar. The second leg was delayed for five weeks because, as a member of the Warsaw Pact, Hungarian forces had taken part in the invasion of Czechoslovakia on 20 August. For a while there was a chance that the match would be voided and Leeds would be awarded victory but Revie argued that the game should go ahead and on 11 September his players walked out at the Nepstadion to defend their lead. In Sixties football language, at times the match resembled 'the Alamo' as Leeds United repelled waves of attacks yet there was nothing fluent about Ferencváros' game. Yes there were plenty of shots from Zoltan Varga and Albert, and Sprake had the game of his life, saving vitally with his feet and turning a dipping, torpedo of a free-kick round the post. He saw it late and the ball was slightly behind him when he slapped it back. The volume of chances Ferencváros created was misleading because too many were taken on from distance as Leeds successfully disrupted their movement.

This final is United's peak as primarily a defensive side, one that suffocated the opposition and treated defeat as a worse sin than not winning. It was hard, professional, trophy-winning football and well-drilled, skilful players fighting for each other, sacrificing their own flair for the good of the team, secured their second cup in six months. The party in Budapest carried on into the following morning with every man performing his party piece and Bremner even called Lord Harewood, the club president, to the microphone to sing. "I wouldn't put him in the same class as Caruso," the captain recalled.

Another trophy meant another parade and they partook in it while second in the league with a game in hand. The reason Arsenal, at the top, led by a point was because Leeds' match against Nottingham Forest at the City Ground had been abandoned at half-time and halfway through Revie's team-talk when the Main Stand caught fire. As Sprake tried to raise the alarm, Eddie Gray remembers Bremner telling him to shut up because "the boss is speaking". Single-minded to the end. Everyone eventually made it out safe.

In the summer of 1967 Revie had set them the goal of 'two cups". Now he focused on the League, not that you could tell in Europe, where he consistently picked his strongest side and made it through three rounds. Instead he made a couple of changes in the domestic cups and did not take elimination as badly as he had before. Lose in the league and he would stand in front of the dressing room mirror furiously combing his hair and muttering to Cocker about it being high time to buy some new players. In the cups, for one season, he was sanguine about defeats.

They lost only two matches all season, both in the autumn, going down 3-1 at Maine Road when beaten by the champions and, more surprisingly, 5-1 at Turf Moor. In the dying minutes of that match Burnley's Ralph Coates, who had played a blinder, dribbled the ball into the corner quadrant and sat on it, much to the crowd's delight. "Ralph was just taking the piss," wrote Giles. "We didn't forget about it." Those last four words from Giles tell you all you need to know. They are not menacing in themselves but they convey a warning just as much as his famous, possibly apocryphal, utterance to Frank Worthington who had tried to nutmeg him: "Take the piss out of me or Leeds United ever again and I'll break your fucking leg for you!" There was no physical retribution taken on Coates at Elland Road, a 6-1 home victory and constant barracking from the Scratching Shed sufficed. The purchase of Jones proved pivotal, his running and strength in possession allowed Leeds to create and exploit space for the wingers, Mike O'Grady and Gray, to flood into or Lorimer, in and out of the side as a support striker, to attack. He also contributed 14 goals himself, not a total to give Jimmy Greaves night terrors but absolutely crucial for a low-scoring side. In midfield Madeley patrolled the area in front of the defence, allowing Giles and Bremner more leeway to attack, while occasionally overwhelming opponents with a burst of acceleration on a third-man run, like a windjammer in full sail. A sequence of seven successive victories starting in January gave them an eight-point lead over Liverpool with nine games to play. All they had to do was hold their nerve and Revie gave them the same message before every game: "If we get anything today we will win it." Giles' goal earned them victory over Manchester City and he scored again in a 2-1 win at Highbury yet they only shook off Liverpool when they went to Anfield in their penultimate match, needing a point to seal their first league title right on cue for their 50th anniversary.

Sprake was lucky to play in it. At Highbury he had thumped Arsenal's Bobby Gould but had been let off by the referee on the spurious grounds of provocation because the burly, chirpy striker had kicked him in the balls. Instead he was allowed to finish as an ever-present even if he was barely required at Anfield where midfield and defence combined perfectly to stalemate Liverpool. They had been unbeaten for 28 games, kept 24 clean sheets and won the championship with a record 67 points. They celebrated in front of their own fans and Revie, in a gesture that has become part of the club's folklore, told his initially reluctant players to go down the other end to acknowledge the Kop. To their eternal pride, they were saluted and cheered by the Liverpool supporters and stayed on the pitch for 20 minutes to savour rare, objective acclaim as shouts of 'Champions!' rang out from the home supporters. Back in the away dressing room Bill Shankly raised a glass to them and, after tickling his audience by opening his remarks with "the best team... drew", went on to call them "a great side" and "worthy champions". After 50 years of almost constant turbulence, Leeds United had clawed their way to the top.

17

LOST AND FOUND

Leeds United lived the Sixties the wrong way round. When the years were swinging, Don Revie's team were grafting; when the dream darkened towards the end of the decade, corrupted by debauchery, paranoia and cruelty, they lightened up. Revie was a picture of elation in the summer of 1969, his broad smile softening features most frequently captured in stern, tense, absorption, the expression of a man with entrenched suspicions about the game, the men who ran it and his accursed, rotten luck. He felt satisfaction rather than vindication, saying United's successes "made the past failures more easy to bear, and to look back upon without anger or anguish".

Most of the sneerers had been silenced by their success if not exactly won over, although a couple emphasised that their record of having more points than goals (67 to 66) disbarred them from consideration alongside the truly great champions. That was not the only reason Leeds broke the transfer record to sign the Leicester City striker Allan Clarke for £165,000 in June but his purchase ingrained a ruthlessness in attack that was already present in defence and midfield. Clarke was a magnificent player, two-footed, clever, nimble, quick and callous. On Jimmy Greaves' plane as a one-to-one finisher, he seemed to get a kick out of tantalising goalkeepers, putting them in a position from which they could not make a quick enough adjustment then poking the ball sadistically out of reach as if he were goading them. He was bought, Revie said, "because he has the kind of skill that can bring us a greater dimension in attack", adding: "It's not a question of altering style but scoring more goals."

This was the start of the phase that has become known as Revie 'letting them off the leash', allowing his players more leeway for creative play, to express the skill they had hitherto stifled for the cause of efficiency. It was not quite as straightforward a step-change as it seems in retrospect. He would continue to brief the players on their opponents in intricate detail until the day he left the club and never said to them: "We're Leeds United, we'll let them worry about us." He was too fastidious in nature, too cautious to play with abandon. Revie needed control like a vampire requires blood. The significant difference between the team before its first title and the five years it took to win a second is that Peter Lorimer, still only 22, became a regular in the outside-right position in which he would make his name and with Clarke playing off Mick Jones they were better at taking their chances. The confidence it brought them, combined with their resilience and maturity, made them a more dominant team. It was this, more than anything Revie specifically changed in his instructions, that made them increasingly play with a panache that was irresistible to all but the diehard critics.

They had bought Clarke, too, because he was the best player on the market and they could afford him. They had spent several years' profits on rebuilding the Kop in 1968, opting for a much steeper rake to improve the sightlines, replacing the vast earth bank with concrete terracing and finally protecting its denizens with a roof after 48 years at the mercy of the elements. New stands would be built in the northern corners over the next seasons and, in 1974, the Scratching Shed would be torn down and replaced by the boxy South Stand. It was boom time at Elland Road and Revie, recognising the dangers of complacency, took the reckless route of publicly announcing his targets for the forthcoming season. Attacking the idea that his team had already reached its pinnacle, he revealed that he had set his players the goal of not only retaining their league title and winning both the FA and European Cups but of going through the season unbeaten. "We lost twice on our way to the League Championship last season," he told the *Mirror*. "This time we don't want to lose at all."

It is a reflection of the esteem in which his players held him that no one carted him off to the nearest asylum. The Double was all but impossible; only Tottenham in 1961 had managed it all century. But a 'Triple', as Revie initially called it? That, surely, was preposterous. Indeed, the 'Invincible' dream had lasted only as far as the end of August when their record top-flight run without defeat was terminated by Everton at 34 successive matches. And yet as late as early March 1970, with only six weeks left of a season brought forward to accommodate England's preparations for defending the World Cup in Mexico, Leeds were top of the league with seven games to play and in the semi-finals of the FA and European Cups. Clarke, playing with more conspicuous effort and dedication than before as the arch-individualist found a team he deemed worthy of his talent, was an instant hit and Leeds surpassed the goals tally of their championship-winning season with 10 games to go. Progress, however, had come at a price and their programme had become so congested at that critical stage of the year that Leeds' club physician, 'Doc' Adams, had warned Revie that six of his shattered team were on the verge of physical and nervous exhaustion. This left Revie facing a dilemma and he solved it by jettisoning the league and cramming his team with reserves for their remaining games.

Revie's second-string picked up only three points from a possible 12, earning the club a £5,000 fine for fielding an uncompetitive team from the Football League who refused to believe the manager's claims of an injury epidemic. The nine points squandered in this spell was the precise difference between themselves in second place and Everton in first at the end of the season. This sacrifice at such a late stage was understandable but it required the winning of at least one of the other two competitions to prove that such a cold-blooded compromise would not blow up in their faces.

The European Cup, somewhat paradoxically given its status, was the least gruelling of all the major tournaments to win in the 1960s and 1970s, with only four rounds in total before the final. That season Leeds had cruised past Norway's SK Lyn Oslo 16-0 on aggregate, twice thumped their old Hungarian adversaries Ferencváros 3-0, and beaten Standard Liège 1-0 home and away. Their semi-final opponents Celtic, by contrast, had required a huge slice of luck to get past Benfica in the second round, winning 3-0 at home but losing by the same score in *Estádio* da Luz. With no replay scheduled, Billy McNeill twice correctly called heads at a coin toss in the referee's changing room, the first time to determine who actually called first in the deciding spin, the second time to win the tie for Celtic, thus reaffirming his club's love affair with the city of Lisbon that had begun three years previously. Qualifying for the semi-final by beating Fiorentina 3-1 over two legs, Celtic set off by train to Yorkshire to face the overwhelming favourites with the wise-cracking comedian Lex 'Sexy Lexy' McLean, 'The master of the belly laugh', in their private carriage to help take their minds off their daunting assignment.

The game at Elland Road, on April Fool's Day, was Leeds' sixth match in 12 days, a pile-up caused by their failure to see off Manchester United until the second replay of the FA Cup semi-final. Missing Norman Hunter through injury, Leeds were taken apart in the first half by Jimmy Johnstone's ability to beat Terry Cooper at will, a memory that Cooper admits can still give him the 3am tremors, and by Bobby Murdoch and Bertie Auld's dominance over Billy Bremner and John Giles in midfield. Conceding their first goal in the competition to George Connelly in the first minute, Leeds never recovered and though they somehow contrived to keep the deficit to one goal despite Celtic's onslaught, they were never in the game at all. Late in the second half Bremner was concussed when his head hit the ground and spent the last 20 minutes of the game wandering dazed and bewildered up and down the tunnel. He was eventually found by the club doctor in the Celtic dressing room. It was symbolic of Leeds' uncharacteristically dislocated performance but there was little sympathy for either Bremner or his team when Everton secured the League title that night. *The Daily Mail* gloated that Leeds had only themselves to blame for abandoning that prize for Europe and getting stuffed twice in the process.

The second leg took place a fortnight later at Hampden Park in front of an official attendance of 136,505, the biggest in the competition's history and still the largest crowd to watch a match featuring an English club side. Both teams had played in cup finals four days prior to the decider, Celtic losing 3-1 to Aberdeen, Leeds, playing at the top of their game for the first time in weeks, throwing away a 2-1 lead carved out by a scintillating performance from Eddie Gray on a Wembley gluepot, infamously ruined by the Horse of the Year Show, to allow Chelsea to equalise in the 87th minute and force extra-time and a replay. Gray – in his first incarnation as a Leeds player, a sinuous dribbler with glorious balance, his tongue sticking out like a child concentrating on colouring between the lines as he lined up a full-back to diddle – was at his peak in the spring of 1970. At Wembley he was irresistible, the splash of golden syrup streaking across the porridge, but a week earlier against Burnley, as one of only three regulars in the XI, he scored two of the greatest goals in the club's history. The first, which he prefers, was a 35-yard chip that arced over the keeper, an artful strike made possible by a velvety first touch. In 1972 Les Reed would call him 'The Last Waltz' in the FA Cup Final song *Leeds United* and no one who has seen Gray's second would need to ask why. There was a touch of Stanley Matthews in it, a dash of Harry Houdini and a dollop of Fred Astaire. Boxed in by the goal-line, he embarked on a serpentine dribble replete with jinks, shoulder-feints and drag-backs which initially took him out towards the corner flag and back, gliding by two defenders, nutmegging another and sitting the fourth down before stabbing a surprise right-foot shot, a kind of Panenka on the run, past Peter Mellor. It was one of those goals that makes the spectator give their head a shake and burst out laughing and Gray himself says it had a "slapstick element". If you play *Bag o' Rags* over the footage, the Burnley players' resemblance to the Keystone Cops is undeniable.

Predictably, it was another winger on Revie's mind during his pre-match briefing in Glasgow – how to stop Johnstone inflicting the same sort of damage for a second time. With the left-footed Hunter now back to support Cooper on the exposed side of United's defence, the two players were told to drop off to cover the winger, forcing him to pass inside rather than dribble, hit the byline and cross. Initially it worked and Johnstone was far less penetrating. Leeds began well, playing with authority and menace and even gained the upper hand momentarily when Bremner thundered in a 30-yard shot after 15 minutes to level the tie and silence all but the 3,000 travelling Yorkshiremen in the enormous crowd.

Not for long, however, as Celtic came back at them with almost hysterical intensity, peppering the Leeds goal with relentless frequency. Sprake, who had been at fault for Peter Houseman's equaliser at Wembley when he let a pea-roller shot from 30 yards burrow beneath his dive, was keen to amend for his mistake. The keeper was inspired but even he could not stop the tide forever and Celtic sneaked back in front with a John Hughes goal just after half-time. Shortly afterwards, Sprake was stretchered off after a collision with the goalscorer. David Harvey, his replacement, had little chance with Celtic's second – the only time Johnstone was left one-on-one at the back, crossing for Murdoch to turn it in from close range. With two goals required in less than half an hour, totally shagged out and flattened in the face of Celtic's pressure, the match petered out into a comfortable victory for the Scots. Essentially, it had been lost in Leeds but that didn't stop the disappointment on the night, a disappointment that was exacerbated by the fact that Celtic succumbed to the rank outsiders Feyenoord in the final.

For Leeds, after 61 intense games, and with a team on the verge of collapse, they'd come up short in two of their three targets. Their whole season hinged on the 62nd game, the FA Cup Final replay at Old Trafford. It was lost in extra time after 105 minutes of viciously foul-strewn football when David Webb headed Chelsea's winner. A TV audience of 28 million watched the ridiculously lax referee, Eric Jennings, a supply teacher at Bash Street, allow a staggering number of filthy challenges, retaliatory blindsiders, rakes and kung-fu lunges. Chelsea committed 35 fouls, including a pre-meditated hobbling of Gray by Ron 'Chopper' Harris, to Leeds' 11 but the notoriety inevitably clings to Revie's side more than Dave Sexton's. At the end the players trudged up the tunnel, the slow clack-clack of their studs on the concrete sounding out the death march. On the floor, physically and psychologically, they could barely raise themselves to collect their medals.

Nine months on from Revie's original target, they had fallen agonisingly short of every goal. "Leeds, like Sisyphus, have pushed three boulders almost to the top of three mountains," wrote Geoffrey Green by way of Albert Camus in *The Times*, "and are now left to see them all back in the dark of the valley." It had been their greatest ever season but Leeds had won nothing. Ultimately, it had proved too tough an ordeal. Learning his lesson, Revie vowed never again to be so unrealistic. Five years later, with Revie now at Lancaster Gate, his team, in its dotage, finally made the European Cup Final. Coincidentally, they were joined there by Michel Kitabdjian, who had refereed the Elland Road tie with Celtic in 1970. It was not a happy omen.

Consolation, however, was not impossible. "I only remember the appalling pain of losing," wrote Giles. "The devastation of ending the season with nothing after we had come so close, played so hard and so long. So long, we thought it would never end. But it was in such moments that I feel the real greatness of this Leeds team would always emerge. Don would tell us that we'd have to start again, that we could come back from this. *Only* Leeds could come back from this." It would be this, their Chumbawamba quality, their ability to sing the songs that remind them of the best times to fortify their defiance and get back up again that made them special. It was not the cups or swagger or style. It was their spirit. "It's better than not being involved at all," said Revie and told his players to put their shoulders to the boulders and begin afresh.

Leeds recovered their verve so comprehensively in 1970-71 that they should have won the League but their season turned, after one of the most indelible of FA Cup upsets in the fifth round by Division Four's Colchester United, in the 39th League game, at home against West Bromwich Albion. At the start of that bleak April Saturday Leeds held a two-point lead over Arsenal who had two games in hand, one of which was at Elland Road. With 20 minutes to go, West Brom were leading 1-0 by virtue of a Tony Brown goal and a questionable decision from the referee, Ray Tinkler, to rule out a Mick Jones equaliser. In the 70th minute, with Charlton posted up front, Hunter tried to force a pass that wasn't really on and flapped it to Brown whose interception knocked the ball over halfway and gave him a clear path to goal. Up went the flag of linesman Bill Troupe, running up the West Stand touchline because Colin Suggett was miles offside though not interfering with play. At that moment Brown slowed to walking pace, looking back at Tinkler who hesitated. Leeds stopped the chase until Tinkler waved play on, enabling Brown with his headstart enhanced by the confusion to accelerate and roll a forward pass to Jeff Astle who slipped a shot past the stranded Gary Sprake and flashed the insouciant smile of an undetected bigamist. All hell broke loose, men in sheepskins and suits, collars and ties, walked on to the pitch to remonstrate with Tinkler who was protected by a couple of dozen police officers. Revie followed them on, clutching his tartan lap rug, turning on his heel, shaking his head and, in Barry Davies' words, "a sickened man, looking up to the heavens in disgust". It is one of Davies' great commentaries, just about staying on the tightrope between "Leeds have every right to go mad" and "the Yorkshire spirit coming to the fore" on one side and "the disgusting action" in which the other linesman was struck by a missile thrown from the Lowfields Road stand. Clarke scored to make it 2-1 in the 88th minute but West Brom held on to win and Leeds essentially forfeited the title by a point in spite of beating Arsenal in their final home match.

No Leeds player begrudges Arsenal the championship – all are united in their praise for Frank McLintock and the character he and his team-mates showed to keep grinding out their victories until they seized the initiative given to them by Tinkler. And you do not have to be a renegade Leeds fan to concede that Suggett was not interfering with play – yet it is not the point. The fact is that Tinkler and his linesman were guilty of ambiguity. Had the referee instantly overruled Troupe, it would at least have been a clear signal. It was the lack of clarity more than the conflicting interpretations of the two officials that caused confusion and provoked the crowd. David Miller of *The Sunday Telegraph*, perennially Leeds' most vehement detractor, called their behaviour "the definitive moment of moral corruption in English soccer, from which point the domestic game moved steadily downwards. Leeds United stood for everything that was reprehensible in sport. Revie and his chairman, Percy Woodward, disgracefully suggested that Tinkler's performance – which I have to say was lamentably inadequate – had justified the crowd's reaction". Davies, his former colleague on *The Times*, who had explicitly said "Leeds have every justification for going mad", mysteriously escaped being trampled by the hooves of Miller's high horse. Revie had actually said he regretted "the crowd scenes like anybody else, but I can understand why they cut loose". Explaining it is not the same as condoning it. Nonetheless, the Football League and FA did act, closing Elland Road for the opening four home games of the following season, forcing Leeds to carpetbag their way from Leeds Road to Boothferry Park and on to Hillsborough.

Revie found solace in the Fairs Cup and for the first time they completed the two-legged final in the same season in which they had entered it. The tournament took them to Norway, East Germany, Czechoslovakia, Portugal and Anfield, where a half-fit Billy Bremner's diving header after seven weeks out with injury, was enough to seal a 1-0 victory over Liverpool. Nothing ever came easy for them: the first leg of the final against Juventus was abandoned after 51 minutes during a biblical deluge and they reconvened two days later to come from behind twice to draw 2-2. The away goals by Paul Madeley and Mick Bates compelled Juventus to attack at Elland Road and their unusually adventurous approach stimulated a cracking game. Allan Clarke gave Leeds the lead, Pietro Anastasi equalised and Leeds' defence with Terry Cooper to the fore on the counter, held firm until Juve ran themselves into the ground.

In another season of fine margins at the top, United were both winners and runners-up by the tightest of divides. "It was the right place for us," said Giles. "The only place." By the end of the following season, "the only place for us" became a refrain that echoes across five decades and ushered United back to glory and the brink of despair, the two fates excruciatingly, eternally, intertwined.

18

THE GREATEST IN
THE LAND

For a notoriously superstitious and sentimental man, Don Revie could also be jarringly hard-nosed. In terms of his irrational fears and rituals, Leeds United's manager came as close to anyone in football of going the 'full Peter Sellers'. The great comic actor was petrified of green and purple, insisted on giving anyone who handed him something sharp a penny, believed that walking between two nuns would bring him good fortune and evolved his litany of tics and rites into a fascination with mysticism, séances and the occult. Revie, too, was vulnerable to suggestion, allowing charlatans and his own whims to make a trial of each match, from his habit of precisely sequencing his routine of inhaling from his cigar (three puffs), sucking on a mint (60 seconds) and chewing gum (10 minutes) during games to soothe his unease to a display of genuine petulance when John Giles made the mistake of putting a pair of his boots on a table. He came to believe that birds were unlucky and had United's owl badge replaced with the cursive LUFC script for the Fairs Cup Final against Juventus and he stuck with the same suit all season even when the arse fell out of them and forced him to wear his overcoat to hide his embarrassment on sunny days.

He carried lucky charms, happily explained his need to promenade from his hotel and circle a set of traffic lights on every visit to Anfield or Goodison and, in 1971, brought Gypsy Rose Lee over from her kiosk on Blackpool's Golden Mile to exorcise a hex on Elland Road. Revie claimed that he had received a letter informing him that Romani people had cursed the ground when evicted to make way for the football stadium at the turn of the century and he acted upon the tip, even though there has never been any evidence to support the idea that there had ever been a settlement there. Ms Lee spent some time on the pitch, scratched the grass on the centre-spot and laid some seeds there before doing the same in the four corners. When she joined Revie for a cup of tea afterwards, presumably taking the opportunity to interpret the leaves in any dregs he left, she told Revie that the curse had been lifted and success would follow. Would that it were that simple. All his little foibles proved infectious among some players who became neurotic about repetition, turning dressing room circumstance – bathing in lukewarm water, throwing the ball between them 20 times, putting their shorts on last – into custom. They have been held up to ridicule him but essentially they were harmless tics that comforted him and he was never precious about explaining them. It is discernible from his droll voice during such interviews that he, more than anyone, was aware of how daft he appeared. However, he continued to see his little ceremonies as a significant part of his match preparation, refusing to leave anything he might be able to control, however illogical, to chance. Even Giles, the most practical of footballers, would break his journey if he ever spotted a solitary magpie to hang about by the side of the road until he had seen another. "It wasn't unique to Leeds," he says of the contradiction between their ultra-professionalism and the supernatural obsessions. "It's human nature."

Revie's belief in ju-ju contrasted with a more cold-blooded approach when it came to the players he trusted. Although he always sent them telegrams wishing them luck before international matches, he always signed off with "DON'T GET INJURED = THE BOSS" as if he thought it a dereliction of duty. Revie was always the mother hen, combining pride in their achievements with alarmist anxiety about the perils lying in wait beyond home. Yet he was far more cavalier when he needed them. He had Les Cocker strap up a virtually lame Norman Hunter to start games on several occasions, encouraged Billy Bremner to play with a hairline fracture of the shin, once instructed Doc Adams not to tell the captain he was suffering from appendicitis until they had finished the season and, after a run of three defeats and a draw from five games in the autumn of 1971, rushed back Allan Clarke and Mick Jones at least a fortnight early to stop the rot. They had been unbeaten during their four-game exile from Elland Road and defeated Liverpool there on their return once the suspension had expired, but defeats at Arsenal, Huddersfield and Coventry without his favoured forwards spooked Revie and recalling them far too soon for their long-term benefit was the least drastic of fixes he had contemplated. "At the final whistle, I turned to Les Cocker and said: 'I've never seen a sloppier performance from our lads. They look as if they have gone.' I told the players: 'If you reckon we have gone as far as we can together, I am quite willing to move on.'" He had considered leaving before and would twice be tempted by sizable offers over the next two summers but this time he took Elsie to Jersey for three days after the match and came back placated.

Peter Lorimer reckons it was around then that he began to lose the players a bit. "It was there, that little seed of doubt," he said. As they grew up they were less spellbound by him, wanted to see more of their families instead of being sequestered in hotels and were sick to death of the dossiers. Revie did not bend to them immediately and subsequently regretted that he had not done so but their desire and ability to play with more of a flourish were unstoppable. After a patched-up Clarke and Jones inspired a 3-0 victory over Manchester City, Leeds recovered their poise and by the end of winter hit such a dominant vein of form that they stood public perceptions of the club on their head.

The sluggish start kept them off the top for all but a week of the season, though they continued to stalk the leaders with ominous persistence and beat Liverpool 2-0 on New Year's Day, the hosts' first league defeat at home in 22 months. After also knocking Bill Shankly's side out of the FA Cup, over a fortnight in February they beat Manchester United 5-1 at Elland Road and destroyed Southampton 7-0, both in front of the Match of the Day cameras and a palpably besotted Barry Davies. It was Leeds' great good fortune that it is Davies' pitch-perfect commentary on these imperishable clips rather than John Motson's, the former's poetry trumping prose in establishing their distinction. The Manchester United of Charlton, Best and Law were pretty much derelict by 1972 and the manner in which Leeds ran rings around truly great players emphasised their own vitality and how much more they still had left to give. "Gray took it off Charlton as though he wasn't there" stands as testament to Leeds at their imperious best and when Gray nutmegged Best in front of the dugouts it made Davies gasp. "The spectacle was almost that of the matador toying with a weary bull, the delighted roars of the crowd at each new piece of virtuosity the equivalent of the Olés of the bullring," wrote Brian Glanville.

At their next home game, when Leeds were 7-0 ahead, there was no need for "the equivalent of Olés"; the real thing rang around the ground as Leeds, with a rare peacock strut, played keep-ball for 30 passes, incorporating reverse passes, feints, back-heels and juggles that inspired Davies into a rhapsody. "It's almost cruel," he said between yelps of ecstasy he would later reserve for Wimbledon's Centre Court. United's 90 seconds of showboating was endlessly reshown by the BBC a generation later but it does not capture the devastating impact of them at their freewheeling best. That came when Norman Hunter galloped up the left wing and centred for Jack Charlton to score, one centre-back teeing up the other in a microcosm of Total Football, West Riding style. By the end of March they had beaten the champions Arsenal 3-0 and Nottingham Forest 6-1 to move to within two points of Manchester City with a game in hand.

Their run in the FA Cup as well as those crushing victories were exploited by Revie's friendship with the artist Paul Trevillion who devised a series of gimmicks and stunts that helped transform 'Dirty Leeds' into 'Super Leeds' by bypassing the press and making a direct appeal to the public. It involved marketing ploys such as numbered sock tags, vigorous group callisthenics designed to whip the crowd into a frenzy during the warm-up, kicking plastic footballs into the stands and saluting as the players pirouetted through 360 degress on the halfway line while wearing gaudy mauve track suits with their names emblazoned on the back. It worked, too, when they unveiled them for the first time before the home FA Cup quarter-final tie against Tottenham which they won 2-1 in an electric atmosphere generated by their routine and glittering performance. "Their football was breathtaking in its scope and fluency, alive with dazzling improvisations," wrote Hugh McIlvanney. "The full intimidating depth of their quality has never been more manifest than it was in those early minutes. Only bigots can now bet against them in the competition."

United romped past Birmingham 3-0 in the semi-final at Hillsborough but a defeat at the Baseball Ground before the tie had left them fighting with Derby and Liverpool for the title after Manchester City imploded following the March signing of Rodney Marsh. Leeds also lost Terry Cooper to a broken leg during a victory at Stoke which kept him out for almost two years and consigned him to watching the FA Cup Final against Arsenal in plaster and waving his crutches to spur on his team-mates.

The Centenary Cup Final was Leeds' penultimate match of the season and they went into it knowing that wins at Wembley on the Saturday and against Wolves at Molineux 48 hours later, the Football League and FA having refused them an extra day's grace, would earn them the Double. "We played so many games we never had too much time to get nervous in the week," remembers Giles. "There was no let-up. But FA Cup Final day itself is nerve-racking. You try to get control of your nerves as best you can and I remember getting up early to go for a stretch-out in the park near where we were staying. Arsenal was always a difficult match, but I had my lucky mascot there, as I always joke with Frank McLintock. I played in three winning cup finals at Wembley – in 1963 for Manchester United against Leicester, the League Cup in 1968 and the FA Cup in 1972 and Frank was on all three teams against me. He was a terrific player, a great lad and captain."

It was a typically dour match between the two sides, one which would not have recommended a hasty return to Wembley for the Queen who was compelled to make one of her rare visits to the FA Cup Final for its 100th birthday. After what seemed an interminable build-up – a parade of past winners, the band of the Royal Marines treating the crowd to *The Theme from the Virginian, Moon River* and *Spanish Flea*, Tommy Steele leading *Abide With Me* and presentations to the Queen and Duke of Edinburgh – the game got off to a constipated start and never loosened up.

In the first half McLintock forced a fine save from David Harvey, who had replaced the injured Sprake the month before and kept his place, Jones whistled a shot past the post and Clarke headed on to the bar as United progressively took control. Ten minutes into the second half Jones roasted Bob McNab, reached the byline and whipped over a cross that dipped suddenly, forcing Clarke to adjust by the penalty spot and arrow a diving header past Geoff Barnett low down at his left post. "We got a hiding," says McLintock. "After that they ran us ragged at the back."

Leeds had enough chances to quadruple their lead but the tension never entirely left them and they were content to hold Arsenal at bay and hit them on the counter. In the 88th minute Jones dislocated his elbow in a collision with Barnett and was still receiving treatment as his colleagues leapt in jubilation at the final whistle. He eventually made it up the stairs to the Royal Box with the help of Hunter five minutes after the Queen had presented the Cup to Bremner. "I think she said, 'Very well done, you have earned it,'" Bremner hazily recalled. "But you don't really take it all in when you've got thousands of people just waiting for you to lift the trophy." When he raised it, a guttural roar, seven years in the stifling since Liverpool beat them in 1965, greeted their achievement. The players felt relief and, because of their pressing engagement in Wolverhampton, a profound sense of anti-climax. While their wives and parents went to the banquet at the Savoy, they were taken to Scratchwood services for a cup of tea and a sandwich before Revie spirited them off to their hotel in the Black Country.

To win the Double Leeds had to draw with a Wolverhampton side who were 10th in the table. Defeat would enable Liverpool, playing on the same night against Arsenal, to leapfrog both them and Derby to take top spot if they won. In the absence of Jones, Bremner played up front with Mick Bates taking his midfield role and the captain was as incisive as ever. Clarke and Giles had both needed painkilling injections for longstanding groin injuries to play while Gray's perpetually troublesome thigh was wrapped in a bandage from knee to groin, yet they managed to create chances and had three penalty shouts, two for nailed-on hand balls by Bernard Shaw, turned down by the referee, Bill Gow. For all their possession, corner count and supremacy in chances created, United went 2-0 down in the 65th minute when Derek Dougan scored and though Bremner got one back and Terry Yorath, who had replaced the ailing Clarke, had a chip scrambled off the line by the full-back Gerry Taylor, Leeds could not find the equaliser. At Highbury Arsenal held Liverpool to make Derby County and Brian Clough, holidaying in the Scilly Isles, champions.

The mood on the three-hour journey back to Leeds was understandably solemn and when the coach stopped at the Queen's Hotel, where their Double party had been due to be held, all but one player said he could not face it. Peter Lorimer, the scorer of 28 goals that season, was spiritually offended that their near-miss in the League had shrouded their maiden FA Cup win. He stood up and said, "Fuck this, I'm going in for a drink." Giles, his big pal, who had been sitting next to him in "the pall of gloom", conceded he had a point and followed him in. "You don't win the FA Cup every year – it's the only time Leeds won it – and obviously once it's done and dusted you have a good night but we couldn't afford to do that, we had to go straight on the coach to Wolverhampton," Giles says. "It doesn't matter. Winning it is the most important thing, it never goes down in history that you have a good night out after the FA Cup Final, only that you won it. That's the big thing.

"Peter always had a great philosophy and it was his idea, not mine. I would have got off the coach in a bad mood to be honest. I was sitting beside him on the coach and everybody was down after the Wolves match, only two days after winning the cup and Peter said: 'Ach, we've had a great season. If somebody said at the start we'd win the cup and finish runners-up in the league, come on, it's a great season.' The way it finished was a disappointment but we'd had to play four matches in eight days. Wolves had a good rest. It was a great season. If we'd lost the league the week before it wouldn't have been so bad. Had we finished the season with winning the FA Cup... instead we lost the league in the space of two days. I think Peter was looking at it in the right way. We'd had a great season and we should go in and have a drink on it. It was true. We sat in the banqueting room, food all around us on the tables and had a drink just the two of us. It was something that just had to be done. Peter was great. Always had a terrific, cheerful attitude."

Five years later, when Revie had left the England job for the UAE, Richard Stott of the *Daily Mirror*, the man who would subsequently write the headline "The Man Who Saved the Mirror" upon the death of Robert Maxwell, used the Wolves game as the main thread in another tranche of 'evidence' that the Leeds manager was corrupt. The report, employing a statement from former United player Mike O'Grady, alleged Revie had offered the Wolves players £1,000 each to throw the game. When they turned it down, according to Danny Hegan, the Wanderers midfielder,

Bremner shouted an offer of "a grand" during the match to concede a penalty. Sprake was paid £15,000 by the newspaper for his contribution, alleging he witnessed Revie trying to fix a match against Nottingham Forest in 1971 and that his manager had once given him a bung not to play for Wales. Terry Hibbitt, who was not paid, told the reporters, "I cannot deny what you have put to me" when asked to corroborate rumours that he had been approached following his move to Newcastle from Leeds to arrange for his new team-mates to take it easy in a game between the two in April 1972. However, when the Football Association and police investigated the stories after they first surfaced on the eve of the Wolves game, they found that Revie had no case to answer. Further allegations have predictably been made since the deaths of both Revie and Bremner, who sued the *Sunday People* in 1982 when the paper rehashed the story and explicitly named him as a conspirator. Giles, Clarke and Charlton all gave evidence on his behalf, describing the allegations as nonsense, Sprake said he couldn't remember anything about the alleged incidents and the man who scored Wolves' second goal on the night, Derek Dougan, appeared for Bremner and said he had no knowledge of them and no reason to doubt his integrity. The jury awarded Bremner a record £100,000 in libel damages, an enormous sum but no compensation for the taints his character had to endure. Mud sticks and the immunity provided by the deaths of the captain and manager continues to allow anyone who feuded with either, or more generally critics of Leeds, to bandy about all manner of wild, unverifiable accusations. It was the bane of their lives and a curse since their deaths. So much for Gypsy Rose Lee.

Three days after their shattering defeat at Molineux, they paraded the FA Cup around Leeds and, to their astonishment, were greeted by 35,000 fans at Elland Road. "I just didn't believe it would be like this," said Revie who had long felt disheartened by the Leeds public's blasé attitude to the club. It was his Sally Field 'you like me' moment, when it finally dawned on him that they had won them over. It proved a short consummation. By mid December, when they had recovered from a patchy, injury-stricken start to consolidate in third, three points behind the leaders Liverpool, only 25,285 bothered to show up for their 4-0 victory over Birmingham. Hammering the champions Derby 5-0 in October suggested the old fluency was returning, but Charlton, at the age of 37, was creaking, Cooper absent and Jones prone to the chronic knee pain that would finish his career within 18 months.

Revie had bought Trevor Cherry from Huddersfield to reinforce his defence and he slotted in solidly at left-back without matching Cooper's charisma and verve. Joe Jordan had been signed from Morton on Bobby Collins' recommendation in 1970 and had been filling in more and more when Jones was too sore to play and, on the recommendation of chief scout, Tony Collins, he was joined in digs in 1972 by the centre-half Gordon McQueen, "a gangly nutter of a lad, big and raw" according to the scout's report, from St Mirren. All three would become pivotal players though only Cherry featured prominently on the return road to Wembley.

In Europe they were kicked from pillar to post during an away draw with Ankaragücü in the first round of the Cup Winners' Cup and they easily overcame Carl Zeiss Jena and Rapid Bucharest to qualify for a semi-final against Hajduk Split. Allan Clarke scored the winner at home before being sent off for retaliation when he was flattened from behind. His two-match ban ruled him out of the away leg, which Leeds drew 0-0 in a masterly defensive performance that Revie rated as the equal of anything that had preceded it, and the final against AC Milan in Salonika. Before they went to Greece, a 2-0 defeat by Liverpool at Anfield on St George's Day secured Shankly's side the title and Leeds, recalling 1969, gave their players a guard of honour at the end of the match. Still, they had the consolation of a return to Wembley for the FA Cup Final by virtue of a vengefully enjoyed win against Wolves in United's sixth FA Cup semi-final in nine years when Bremner scored the winner with a left-foot half-volley and slid on his knees at Maine Road in celebration.

Leeds' opponents in the final were Second Division Sunderland, managed by Bob Stokoe who used every opportunity he was gleefully afforded by the press to needle Revie and his team. First he marked the referee's card, warning him not to be influenced by Bremner's politicking during the game, then complained about Leeds being put in the 'home' dressing room and their supporters given the tunnel end. In the build-up Stokoe pointed out "we are playing a real professional team and, let's face it, the word professionalism can embrace a multitude of sins as well as virtues". It was a Trumpian trick, accusing others of things you were actively engaged in as he readily admitted after the match: "I'm not saying the referee was influenced, but he didn't let Bremner get at him." If that isn't the kind of 'professionalism' Stokoe claimed to denounce, Sir Alex Ferguson never once tapped his watch in his life.

It had no significant impact on the game, only that it allowed Stokoe the opportunity to gloat after running on the pitch at the final whistle in his curious outfit of trilby, tracksuit and flasher's mac. Leeds never clicked, Gray had a poor game on the stage he had twice graced, Dave Watson, Sunderland's centre-half, was outstanding at the back and created Ian

Porterfield's 31-minute goal with a Charlton-esque masterclass of chaotic, distracting incursion at a corner. Jack himself, who had ben injured in the semi-final, his 772nd and penultimate game for Leeds, was working as a TV pundit. If ever they had needed his 'set a thief to catch a thief' nous one last time, it was then. Even so Leeds would have equalised except for an astounding double save by Jim Montgomery who clawed away Cherry's diving header into the path of Lorimer who scudded a shot seemingly beyond the keeper's reach. Montgomery managed to twist in mid-air and tip it on to the crossbar, confounding the BBC's David Coleman who had already proclaimed with an air of finality: "And Lorimer makes it one each." He hadn't and no matter how many times Leeds fans can stomach rewatching it, the Montgomery miracle scotches them still. "The better team won on the day," Revie said. Sunderland were not so magnanimous: at their homecoming six supporters carried a coffin with 'Leeds died 1973' written on the side as part of the official Roker Park celebration of their FA Cup triumph. The remains of Europe's most consistently strong side were laid to rest in the centre-circle. Sunderland AFC: classy to the end.

Obituaries were forthcoming and only intensified over the following week despite rounding off their season with a 6-1 thrashing of Arsenal. On the eve of the Cup Winners' Cup Final, Revie answered his hotel door in Salonika to a delegation led by Giles, Hunter and Bates and confirmed the rumour that he would be leaving the club after 12 years following the match. He had been insisting that fools had been writing them off prematurely as 'shot', too old and scarred by falling short, and yet here he was, poised to abandon them for a £20,000 a year contract instead of leading the campaign to end the orgy of schadenfreude and shove the carpers' words where the sun does not shine. Revie burst into tears, as he had done at the Savoy after Wembley, and was so preoccupied he forgot to bollock Giles for turning up with an injury sustained playing for the Republic of Ireland. Giles remains sympathetic, noting that Leeds had never paid their manager more than £15,000 and appreciating that the defeat by Sunderland "brought the day closer when he would have to tell some of us our time was up and he couldn't face it".

To compound injury with insult, Christos Michas, the Greek referee for the final against AC Milan, produced a display of such manifest bias that a campaign for the result to be voided smoulders on almost 50 years on. He facilitated Luciano Chiarugi's goal, awarding a free-kick for a perfectly timed Paul Madeley tackle, turned down penalties for a flagrant hand ball and obvious fouls on Lorimer and Jones and sent off Hunter, justly, for retaliating after Gianni Rivera had attempted to amputate his legs with his studs. Leeds, the darlings of the home crowd who knew a bent referee when they saw one, were applauded off. Milan and Michas ran the gauntlet of jeers. Twice Leeds supporters have petitioned Uefa to investigate the game, citing Michas' life ban from consequential games for his performance, both times the governing body has told them it is unable to review cases that are more than 10 years old. Italian clubs' systemic corruption of referees during the late Sixties and early Seventies was brilliantly exposed by Keith Botsford and Brian Glanville in *The Golden Fix* but the only thing Uefa ever managed to nail AC Milan for was making gifts to a referee in 1978.

For Revie it seemed an unkindly fitting way to bow out. Exhausted, feeling jinxed and fearing the men he had relied on were on the wane, it was time to take the money and run. If the outlook was bleak, no team was better equipped with mental resilience to rage against the dying of the light. The world had underestimated them. Their manager, who knew them best, had too. But there would be no sweet surrender to time and fate. Like *Carrie* an arm would rise up from the rubble and chillingly invade their enemies' nightmares. It was not over unless they gave up on each other and they never have yet.

19

'IF WE HAD TO GO, WE WOULD GO HARD'

Two unlikely heroes came to Leeds' aid in May 1973 and granted them a year's reprieve. Without them Don Revie's record-breaking Indian summer at Elland Road could never have happened and the tears of Wembley and Salonika would have functioned as the funeral for 12 years of dedication. The first of them is the fleet car manager at the Leeds Mercedes-Benz franchise who persuaded the club's manager to accept a vehicle in maple yellow; the second is Dennis Skinner, the Beast of Bolsover, then a 41-year-old serving his first term as a member of parliament. The distinctive colour of Revie's saloon when he stopped to ask directions to the Liverpool suburb of Freshfields led to a tip-off to the newspapers that he had been heading for Sir John Moores' house to discuss the Everton job. As Revie had a contract with six more years to run with Leeds plus a further five years' consultancy agreement handcuffing him in white, yellow and blue bracelets until 1984, the story of a clandestine meeting exposed Everton to accusations and possible charges of tapping-up.

When it emerged that Moores had offered Revie a £50,000 signing on fee and an eight-year deal at £25,000 per annum, 1,200 per cent more than the average UK salary, Skinner demanded that the Secretary of State for Employment in the Heath Government submit the case to the Pay Board, set up under the Counter-Inflation Act. Its purpose was to review executive salaries to ensure new hires were not paid more than the people they were replacing. The football pools magnate could easily afford a tax-free golden hello but not the hit to his reputation of two investigations into the process and detail of his agreements with Revie. Moores backed down. Revie, who had returned to Greece for a sailing holiday around the islands on a yacht owned by the president of Olympiakos, rang Leeds to tell them he would be staying after all. While players contacted for their reaction expressed their delight, rancour split the board.

Bob Roberts, whose company had built the West Stand, believed that Revie had received credit that was the board's due for building Leeds

United into a proper elite football club and advocated forcefully that he should be allowed to go. Percy Woodward had quibbled repeatedly about the team's expenses, hotel bills and the like, while Manny Cussins, Sydney Simon and Sam Bolton remained loyal to Revie. They knew it would not be as simple as carrying on as before. In 1969 after winning the league title, the club had bought one of Cussins' houses, the grand Three Chimneys on Sandmoor Drive in Alwoodley, for £18,000 and given it to Revie to kill off an approach from Torino. Revie had moved Elsie's elderly Scottish relatives in with them and lived happily there until selling up and building his own house on the Harewood estate on a plot given to him in gratitude by the Earl, the club's president and the manager's staunch friend and ally. Before he returned from his holiday, he had informed the press that he had received offers to manage the Greece national side for £20,000 a year and, for the second time in four years, Panathinaikos for £28,000, both sums net of tax. It was the ideal ammunition to tickle the board for a raise, which they conceded – Roberts, most of all, resentfully.

John Giles says no set of players "were ever as determined to put all the things right" as the Leeds squad that reassembled on Fullerton Park for pre-season training in late June 1973. "You lads are good enough to ram the criticism back down the throats of all those who have denied you the respect you deserve," formed the beginning of Revie's opening address, according to Joe Jordan. "You must go out to show them all what you can do, what good footballers you are. I want the title – I think you're more than good enough to do that. I also think you could go through the season without losing."

It was not the first time he had told them to focus on finishing invincible, a dream that had lasted only seven games in 1969. Now he told them the league would be their sole focus and they were duly knocked out of the League Cup in their first tie. The players would have been just as happy to be eliminated at the same stage in the Uefa Cup but despite picking reserve-strewn sides they made it through to the third round by virtue of Stromgodset's feebleness and a remarkable performance by Billy Bremner at sweeper against Hibernian and an unwanted victory in the penalty shootout. The captain had insisted on starting at Easter Road because he wanted his family to see him play and the old competitive urge and desire to entertain his tribe took over. At one point defending a corner he blocked a goal-bound header on the line and stood, like the Wembley statue of Bobby Moore, with his foot on top of the ball and invited Hibs to try scoring as he rolled it around under his sole for several seconds before he feinted and cleared. Then, in the shootout, he pointed to one corner but hit one of those swivel-hipped reverse shots – cutting his foot across the ball in a manner that would put most men in traction – into the other. Small wonder Revie left him out for the third-round second leg against Setubal, on the morning of which the squad played a round of golf before going down 3-1 to ensure their campaign was over before Christmas.

In the league Leeds United built a monument to their manager, as awe-inspiring for what it represented as much as for what it was. They began with brio, winning their first seven matches. Gordon McQueen replaced Jack Charlton, who had retired to manage Middlesbrough at the age of 38, and once Norman Hunter, Giles and Bremner had employed sharp words to curb his enthusiasm for undisciplined, gallivanting surges upfield in the spirit of a young, headstrong Jack, he had an outstanding debut season as a regular. United went 29 games unbeaten, building a nine-point lead over champions Liverpool, until losing from 2-0 up at Stoke on 23 February, sinking to a 3-2 defeat. By that stage some of their dash had been eroded by injuries – Giles and his classy understudy Mick Bates both missed months of action and the rugged Terry Yorath filled in with wholehearted commitment and defensive abrasiveness but with less finesse. Terry Cooper managed only two games, Eddie Gray eight and, though Mick Jones top scored with 14 goals, his knee was crumbling and he had to endure chronic pain to turn out 28 times.

After a 4-1 victory over West Ham in November, Ron Greenwood, the opposition manager and no fan of Revie, said: "Leeds are the equal of Manchester United in their heyday. They play with such imagination and flair. It looks as if they are out on their own, playing the sort of football I would love to play." Yet by the turn of the year they were more austere, the flamboyance of their display at Tottenham, where they raced to a 3-0 lead inside 30 minutes, had been replaced by serious grind and late equalisers. The charisma of that golden autumn that had won over away fans, referees and even the FA, who had hit them with a suspended fine of £3,000 for too many bookings the previous season, gave way to character in midwinter. From champagne football to Pomagne.

Revie's team required all the resilience accrued over 10 years at the top after three successive defeats in March gave Liverpool, whose run to the FA Cup Final had left them with several games in hand, an opportunity to clamber over them if they won all those matches. Giles came back for the injured Clarke against Derby and with Bremner pushed up front as an emergency striker, the captain scored in a 2-0 victory. They scrabbled to draws with Coventry and Sheffield United and 24 hours after the latter played the Blades again and beat them 2-0 at Bramall Lane, both Lorimer goals coming in a tension-racked second half. Ipswich's comeback from 2-0 down at Elland Road in the penultimate game of the season must have given the players the shudders but the crowd lost its bottle before the players did and Clarke, playing only after an injection for his injured Achilles, scored the winner. Liverpool's draw in the Merseyside derby meant they had to win each of their three remaining games and hope that Leeds would lose at QPR in order to win back-to-back titles.

Mounted police had to break up a near-riot after the Ipswich victory on the Elland Road forecourt as the queue for tickets for the trip to Loftus Road the following Saturday dissolved into chaos, jostling and a crush. By the Wednesday night what could have been an excruciatingly stressful match in west London was transformed into a coronation when Arsenal won at Anfield and Leeds United captured their second title while sitting at home. "I feel as though someone has come along and lifted six tons of coal off my back",," said Revie who had been out at a friend's house to watch the transmission of *This Is Your Life* for which he had been ambushed by Eamonn Andrews and his big red book at the Queen's Hotel on the Sunday evening. The show featured Bill Shankly and Sir Matt Busby paying tribute to him as he sat there beaming surrounded by the Duncan clan and the United squad. Shankly was back in touch after the Arsenal game to congratulate Revie on his finest achievement. Once the season was over, neither of the two friends would manage in league football again.

For most of May and June 1974, while Bremner, Harvey, Jordan and Lorimer were playing for Scotland at the World Cup in West Germany, the identity of the successor to Sir Alf Ramsey as England manager was a backpage obsession. In fact Revie had already put out feelers to the FA and had received encouraging signals. His candidacy quietly moved from one committee to the next in the Lancaster Gate bureaucracy. It took him until 4 July to announce his resignation and a few days before his 47th birthday he became only England's third full-time manager on £20,000 a year, almost three times his World Cup-winning predecessor's salary. He had spoken of his burning desire to win the European Cup with Leeds but the honour of England offered him an escape route from taking his team to the breaker's yard and, in the essentially part-time nature of the role, more time with Elsie to pursue their mutual infatuation with golf.

"This must be any manager's dream. I also have a feeling of sadness," he said at the time. "I have tried to build the club into a family and there must be sadness when anyone leaves a family. [With England I will] try to develop the same family spirit that we have had at Leeds." It would prove to be a disaster, ruined by indecision, a prickly relationship with his employers that degenerated into toxic buck-passing and an inability to generate an affinity with players he had for at most 25 days a year. In 1973 he had outlined why his job still entranced him after more than three decades in professional football without a break. "The game offers so much tension and excitement it tears your guts out," he said. "When you get the smell of embrocation and hear the roar of the Saturday crowd your stomach turns over." Without that he was lost and all the grandeur of Wembley and his position could not compensate for the loss of a way of life that consumed him.

Before leaving he attempted to protect his legacy by fixing the succession. The outstanding candidate was Giles, universally respected and admired for the severity of his focus, his cleverness and wit. He was the only one with any experience of management, having been player-manager of the Republic of Ireland for a year, and had shown he could handle the transformation of his status among familiar faces with the necessary diplomacy and detachment. He did not want the job and would have preferred Revie to stay but was willing to take it on to preserves continuity and allowed, as a consummate politician would, his name to be put forward. He was telephoned after a board meeting to be told he would be appointed the next day but the announcement was cancelled because Bremner had got wind of it and demanded the right to be interviewed. Despite Giles being the best man for the job, a man with the calculating rigour and streetwise nous to cope with it, Bremner's typically emotional intervention put the wind up Cussins and his directors and he requested, with pre-season about to start, to delay the decision. Giles promptly withdrew, reckoning that any board that hemmed and hawed over something so consequential was not worth his time. He foresaw years of unnecessary trouble and wisely walked away. Bob Roberts, the director who had antagonised Revie the most over the years, is widely suspected of sabotaging the manager's last request by leaking the news to Bremner in a bid to restore the board's authority. Indeed the players cite an incident at White Hart Lane when Revie ordered the coach to leave after the match at the appointed time and not wait for Roberts to finish his schmoozing as the final straw for the director. If it was something so petty, it proved to be myopic and disastrous.

Cussins, seeing himself as heroically heading off a civil war that actually existed only in Roberts' mind, turned instead to the 150 outside applications for the post. The board drove to Scotch Corner to interview Motherwell's Ian St John and gave him the impression that the job was his, although they did say that they had one candidate left to meet, Brighton's Brian Clough, Revie's loudest and most trenchant critic. The news that he was on the shortlist provoked an anti-Clough petition that attracted 400 signatures on the first night of canvassing in the Merrion Centre for the simple reason that the former Derby manager had spent five years needling Revie and his players in ever more strident and damning terms. During the past two years alone Clough had said United's poor disciplinary record warranted automatic relegation, accused Bremner of tyrannising referees and provoked a walk-out at a Queen's Hotel banquet by delaying his toast to the guest of honour with a shit-eating smirk, saying: "You can wait. I'm off for a piss." When he returned he laid into Peter Lorimer for his "falls when he hasn't been kicked and protests when he has nothing to protest about". Boos drowned out the rest of his character assassination.

Clough and his assistant Peter Taylor had resigned from Derby in October 1973 and spent eight months at the Goldstone Ground, endured humiliation in the FA Cup when thrashed by non-League Walton and Hersham 4-0 and ended their season in 19th place in the Third Division just two years after winning the title. In Clough and Taylor the Leeds board felt they had found a pair with the pedigree to win the European Cup, gradually overhaul the squad and build on the £2m cash in hand at the bank Revie's 13 years had bequeathed to them. Clough's desire for the job was palpable once he had been tapped up in Mallorca. He felt isolated on the south coast and seemingly could not feel comfortable among people whose heritage was not derived from heavy industry. Taylor, by contrast, loved it and informed United via the Brighton chairman at a meeting with two Leeds directors in a Hove hotel that he would not be leaving. Cussins and Roberts, who had expected to be recruiting a management partnership that had only ever operated together in the professional game, were not given a chance to back-track because Clough marched out of the room at 2am and, on the basis of a verbal offer to him and Taylor, announced to the journalists he had tipped-off to turn up: "Gentlemen. I've just been appointed the manager of Leeds United."

"Despite the unfortunate publicity he gets, he is a first-class manager," Cussins said. "I'm certain United's players and fans will soon take to him. Although his contract is for four years, I hope he will stay with us for life."

Even though the Leeds players had been back in pre-season training for almost a fortnight on the day of his appointment, Clough immediately flew back to Mallorca to resume his summer holiday. When he finally turned up at Elland Road nine days after accepting the job he brought his two sons, Simon and Nigel, with him in a bid to deflect any hostility. He kept his distance for the first four days, letting Jimmy Gordon, the Scot he had brought from Derby to replace England's new assistant manager Les

Cocker, take training. He staked out his approach to the press even before he addressed the players, sounding conciliatory and outlining where he and Revie diverged. "Leeds have been restricted by their intense approach in the past, I feel," he said. "If a flower has nothing but water it dies, if it has only sunshine, it withers. It has got to have a combination of both to bring it to full bloom."

"On the fifth day God blessed them, saying 'Be fruitful and multiply'". On Clough's fifth day at Elland Road he settled for an earthier "fuck off". His behaviour that morning was so extraordinary it is tempting to interpret it as deranged. We know from the scores of books that fete him that he had a singular sense of humour and an iron nerve but his decision to air his grievances showed such little understanding of the temperaments of the men he insulted – battle-hardened by 10 years at the top having again and again overcome crushing disappointments – that it reads like kamikaze, self-generated constructive dismissal. Abrasive rudeness was his fondest weapon and it often worked with young players and those who owed him their careers. But in the players' lounge he royally squandered his only bequest of an elite side because Taylor was not there to play the diplomat and leaven the choleric denunciation that Clough had been waiting years to get off his chest.

"Right, you fucking lot," he said. "You might have been wondering why I haven't said a lot this week. The reason is that I have been forming my own opinions." He then proceeded to rattle them off. To Norman Hunter, he said: "You've got a terrible reputation in the game and I know you'd like to be liked." Hunter returned his gaze and said: "I couldn't give a fuck." He moved on to Lorimer, the king of "making a meal" of tackles and Giles, "another with a bad reputation". Following Hunter, they stood up for themselves, pointing out how often Clough's Derby had rough-housed them on their gluepot pitch. Clough paused to praise Gordon McQueen and Allan Clarke before rounding on his final target, the much-loved Eddie Gray. The winger's long-standing thigh injury had restricted him to 67 league appearances over the past four seasons, which prompted Clough to say: "If you were a racehorse you would have been shot years ago." Why Clough, a man whose own career had been wrecked by injury, waded in with such a spiteful quip on a sensitive subject defies rational analysis. Perhaps he got carried away, perhaps, in his own favourite phrase, he was just "a shithouse". He finished with his mic drop moment before scuttling back to his office, an arsonist who had set a fire under his own job: "As far as I am concerned you can all throw every one of your medals in the bin over there. You never won any of them fairly."

Forty days later he was gone having overseen one victory, three defeats and two draws in his six league games. He hadn't been helped by Bremner's 11-match ban for his epic brawl with Kevin Keegan in the Charity Shield and their churlish response to being sent off but it is doubtful if even Leeds' talisman could have saved Clough from himself. Over 10 days in early August he spent £380,000 on Duncan McKenzie, John O'Hare and John McGovern, more than Revie had spent in his last 10 years at the club, but none of his signings had any positive impact though the trick-laden McKenzie entertained the crowd and infuriated his team-mates in equal measure.

Shortly after a home draw with newly promoted Luton Town during which the Kop had turned on McGovern, who was wearing Bremner's shirt, and jeered his every sideways pass, Clough struck a deal with Forest to sell them Terry Cooper, who had recovered from injury after two years but had lost his irrepressible zip. "I have little choice but to leave," Cooper said. "Brian Clough has declared his hand in my case. What is the point in staying at a club when it is apparent you are not wanted?" But he was still wanted by the board, who used the fact that they had not been informed that his sale had been agreed as a catalyst to address United's decline. At a meeting on the Monday night, they discussed low crowds, the hostility of the fans and the club's lack of direction. Spooked, the majority voted to act, overruling Roberts whose candidate Clough had been. Yet they did not have the stomach to wield the knife themselves and, recalling Bill Lambton's demise, sought to hide behind a proxy – the players.

Cussins convened the squad and Clough in the players' lounge on 10 September and asked: "Why are things going wrong?" After a stilted debate, Paul Madeley, usually taciturn, suddenly piped up with all the dramatic weight of Chief Bromden in *One Flew Over the Cuckoo's Nest* and said to Clough: "I just don't think you can manage." It gave Sam Bolton, the vice-chairman the ammunition he had sought. The following afternoon the *Yorkshire Evening Post* reported that a "vote of no confidence" from the players had left Clough's job "hanging by a thread". He was sacked the next day. He left Elland Road on 12 September with a pay-off of £100,000 and his club Mercedes, grinning for the photographers and lamenting that what had happened "was a very sad day for Leeds and for football." Cussins refused to elaborate further and walked to his Rolls-Royce, saying: "We've been spoilt by Don Revie."

Apportioning blame for this episode is straightforward. It wasn't the players' fault or Clough's for taking such an unsuitable job. It rests solely with the board for hiring a man who had sneered at them for years and then professing shock when he acted in entirely predictable fashion. His subsequent success with Nottingham Forest – crucially, at first, with Taylor – provokes wistful revisionism: had Leeds shown more backbone, two European Cups could have been theirs instead. It's rubbish. It wasn't a case of the right man at the wrong time, Clough was the wrong man at any time for Leeds. United's 'sliding doors' moment in the currency of counterfactual speculation was not sacking him; it was not appointing Giles.

Given the chance to rectify their error, they blew it a second time because Roberts and Woodward were still opposed to Giles taking the helm and he refused to accept it from a board split three to two. Maurice Lindley was put in temporary charge, winning two and losing two of four games, while Cussins sought a replacement. Bolton's Jimmy Armfield had been on the original shortlist but was hesitant when approached. The Leeds delegation who travelled to his Blackpool home to offer him the job "were four men in a flap", he said, and he asked for time to consider. It was then that the England manager intervened and asked him to drop into Lancaster Gate for a chat. "All you have to do with those players," Revie said, "is send them out on the field. They'll do the rest. You'll be able to sit in the stand and pick up your bonus. They're the best players in the country."

Armfield took the job and almost proved that the 'best players in the country' were capable of a glorious swansong. In the League Armfield's light touch and Bremner's return on 9 November after injury and suspension galvanised them. Indeed, with Clough gone and Bremner back, they rallied to such an extent that they climbed from 18th to finish in ninth, eight points behind the champions, Derby County. They had been seven points behind them after six games when Clough was sacked, truly an indictment of those shambolic 44 days.

United also survived humiliation in the FA Cup after drawing with non-League Wimbledon when Dickie Guy saved Peter Lorimer's penalty and Richard Stilgoe commemorated the bearded keeper in a spoof Wombles song on *Nationwide* which took the piss out of Leeds' decline. But they won the replay and were only knocked out in the quarter-finals after a third replay with Ipswich Town. By that point they were already in the European Cup semi-final having beaten Anderlecht home and away in the preceding round.

The first leg had taken place in swirling fog at Elland Road that was thick enough at times to have the fans in the South Stand imploring the Kop to let them know what was happening when Leeds were attacking that end. At several points the match could and probably should have been abandoned. The clearest picture came on TV and there it was plain to see how Bremner and Giles combined magnificently to open up Anderlecht's flanks and provide a series of centres for Joe Jordan and McQueen to exploit. Both Scots scored, as did Lorimer, before Bremner won the away leg in a mudbath with an impudent chip.

Prior to United's European Cup semi-final against Barcelona, the League and FA fell back on established practice and refused to ease fixture congestion, forcing Leeds to play six matches in 12 days. For once, it didn't have its usual effect. The home leg against Barcelona was the greatest atmosphere at Elland Road this author can ever recall, with more than 50,000 roaring Leeds on to a 2-1 victory. Bremner and Allan Clarke scored but as so often John Giles was the inspiration, while Paul Madeley made a telling contribution by stalking Johan Cruyff all over the field. They drew the away leg 1-1 after Peter Lorimer gave them an early lead and then fought skilfully and doggedly, a man down following McQueen's dismissal, to protect it in front of 110,000 whistling supporters at Camp Nou. "This, I think we all sensed, might be the last of the team the football world had come to know for their winning instincts," Jordan wrote afterwards. "And if we had to go, we would go hard. No blood or sweat would be withheld. The 10 men of Leeds refused to break." Once again Leeds had Bremner's remarkable ability to make decisive contributions in semi-finals to thank for delivering them from peril when he ran behind the reserve goalkeeper David Stewart to kick a shot from Johan Neeskens off the line with only two minutes of the game left. The reward for his tireless endeavour was to lead the team out in the European Cup final.

Leeds had 28 days rest between their 64th match of the season and 65th, the final against Bayern Munich in Paris. Armfield, whom David Lacey praised for "his calming influence on the disturbed Leeds psyche following the Clough cataclysm", arranged four friendlies over the month to keep the players in shape.

Ten years on from their first-ever Fairs Cup tie against Torino, more than half of that side – Reaney, Bremner, Madeley, Hunter, Lorimer and Giles – walked out at the Parc des Princes for the biggest game in the club's history. Leeds, cheered on by Revie who was alongside David Coleman in the BBC's commentary box, dominated the match for an hour, putting on a performance full of aggressive, fluent and incisive football that put Bayern Munich, who finished only 10th in the Bundesliga, on the back foot. The single favour the referee Michel Kitabdjian did Leeds was to allow Terry Yorath to stay on the field after his brutal foul that shattered Bjorn Andersson's knee. In the first-half alone Kitabdjian turned down two penalty appeals, the first for a Beckenbauer handball, the second when the Bayern captain slid in, missed the ball and wrapped both legs around Allan Clarke.

Twenty-one minutes into the second half Lorimer thundered a volley past Sepp Maier and, after celebrating, Leeds walked back to the halfway line. The referee had signalled a goal but Beckenbauer then asked him to consult his linesman and it was disallowed for Bremner being in an offside positon - a marginal call given he had been pushed there and was not interfering with play. Even before Bayern had picked them off on the counter-attack to score twice a section of the Leeds support had begun to tear out the plastic seats and shower them down on the French riot police. "These were scenes only known in South America," wrote Beckenbauer somewhat hyperbolically. It escalated beyond the final whistle and got so out of hand that Bobby Collins, the club's former captain, was assaulted outside the stadium by a Leeds fan who mistook him for a Bavarian. Outrage at the larceny – two years after they had lost the Cup Winners' Cup final to AC Milan after an even more aberrant refereeing performance – persists and is given defiant vent at every game in the 'Champions of Europe' chant, which originated after their first Fairs Cup triumph but owes its longevity to Paris. "I felt exactly as I did when our home was burgled," Armfield said afterwards.

Two years on from the defeat by Sunderland, the press could rework those premature epitaphs, portraying defeat as the last of Leeds' bold failures. They were right that the team had at last run its course. Armfield was a conciliator not a rouser. He could not make his words resound like a battle cry as Revie had. This was the end of Revie's team – Giles would leave that summer, Bremner and Hunter a year later. And, with a four-year European ban imposed on them for their fans' behaviour, it was the end of Leeds as a European force, a surprise, exhilarating Champions League run in 2000-01 notwithstanding. Revie left the BBC box to offer words of consolation to his players. The dream was over.

20

KINGDOM OF RUST

During Don Revie's 13 years in charge at Elland Road, Liverpool won three league titles to his two, two FA Cups to his one, one European trophy to his two and zero League Cups – which they couldn't give a fig about – to his one. Bill Shankly's record is superior but in 1974 there was barely a whisker between United as champions and Liverpool as FA Cup winners. In retrospect the Charity Shield strikingly symbolises two clubs meeting each other while passing on adjacent escalators – Liverpool ascending towards 10 further titles and four European Cups in 16 years while Leeds, after Paris, plummeted towards the depths of incoherence, relegation, financial ruin and the ignominy – not for the last time – of having to sell the ground and become tenants to stay afloat.

Why the two diverged so radically defies one simple explanation but it is rooted in Liverpool adhering to the principle of continuity and their directors understanding they were guardians more than owners. When Shankly left Liverpool they appointed Bob Paisley to replace him, a man steeped in his mentor's methods. It did not matter that they replaced the game's greatest communicator with someone who was often unfathomable: Geordie riddles succeeded the gnomic wisdom of Shankly, who made Norman Vincent Peale sound like Eli Woods. The board knew its place, trusted the structure and accepted that vanity and meddling were indulgences they could not afford.

Leeds' directors, in contrast, wanted more executive control and credit that had been, in their view, monopolised by Revie. They acted as if they thought that the only thing they needed to do was recruit a suitable man: that they could drive the vehicle that Revie had built if only they could find the right mechanic. For a while their formula seemed to be that the new manager should have as little in common as possible with his predecessor's approach. Over 14 years they almost destroyed the club with this behaviour. It was never a messiah they needed but a plausible plan and the means to do what it took to make it work.

The period between Paris and Howard Wilkinson tends to be characterised as the 'wilderness years' for Leeds United, one long uniform recession. Yet there were moments even during spells beset by financial problems and a torrent of crowd disorder and violence when decline was avoidable and revival seemed thrillingly imminent. The directors recognised Brian Clough's ability and thought it pardoned his flaws. Instead of the 'genius' they hoped they had recruited, they got a suspicious mind in his imperial gobshite phase. To redress their mistake they went for the urbane, emollient and thoroughly decent Jimmy Armfield to undertake the sensitive dismantling and renovation work. His poignant assignment all but complete, they spun the top again, sacked him and appointed the greatest of all British managers, Jock Stein. Blinded by his prestige and charisma, they congratulated themselves on their coup and passed over his motivation. Driven by resentment at Celtic for making him a glorified pools agent, he wanted to show his former employers that he wasn't past it. Stein was conflicted from the start – the offer of £30,000 a year seduced someone who had been poorly paid at Parkhead but he was incapable of thriving alone away from his wife, his friends and his kind. When the Scotland job he had wanted all along fell into his lap, he became the second of the '44-day men'.

From imposing aura and high priest of 'Big Man' management, Leeds immediately switched their criteria and chose someone renowned as the best technical coach in the game. Jimmy Adamson had refused the England job in 1962 and built a fine side at Burnley before falling out with the chairman, the obnoxious anti-semite Bob Lord who baited Leeds' Jewish directors and sold Adamson's key players. He left Turf Moor when Burnley were stuck at the bottom of Division One in 1976 and was relegated with Sunderland a year later. Ignoring that, and presumably having not researched him thoroughly enough to pick up rumours about his drinking, they appointed on an obsolete reputation and saddled themselves with a whipping boy for the supporters' venom. No Leeds manager has exasperated the public more and some, with a malicious and black-humoured bent, denounced the Wearsider as the Yorkshire Ripper when the 'I'm Jack' hoax tape hoodwinked desperate but gullible senior West Yorkshire police officers in 1979.

Chastened by that experience and criticism of their guilt by association, Manny Cussins and his colleagues turned to men who carried a shield. The enduring affection of Leeds supporters for Revie's players sheltered them from the kind of vitriolic derision that had haunted Adamson. Allan Clarke arrived promising the European Cup and in 18 months took United down after 18 seasons in the First Division. Eddie Gray was bumped up to player-manager and shrewdly followed the Revie template of youth development before hitting the buffers of impatience. Finally Bremner was brought back to instil the intensity of his drive and pride into the club but was undermined by a lack of imagination from above and his inability to broaden his horizons from his time in charge of Doncaster Rovers. Quality was rationed and the age of the journeyman descended. Armfield and Adamson never managed again. All three 'old boys' were attracted by the opportunity and their sense of duty; all three essentially ruined promising managerial careers in the process. The job had become the kiss of death.

Yet in January 1976, only a few months after Armfield had brought in Don Howe, the man who had coached Arsenal to the Double in 1971, as his right-hand man, a run of eight victories in nine games took Leeds up to second, a point behind Manchester United with a game in hand and all without the injured Gordon McQueen and Joe Jordan. It was Revie's team with Frankie Gray now established at left-back, Terry Yorath in for Johnny Giles and Duncan McKenzie up front, but as soon as Bremner was hurt in an embarrassing FA Cup defeat by Third Division Crystal Palace, they faded. The captain was only 33 but there were an awful lot of miles in those legs and a cargo-load of Virginia tobacco had passed through his lungs. Nonetheless he defied both to perform superbly in the winter, fuelled – one suspects – by embarrassment at being banned for life by Scotland over a drunken stramash in Copenhagen. His reflexes remained electric and his savvy made up for the corrosions of age and his lethal habit. Sadly, the dramatic finale the romantics craved, the veteran gunslinger leading his posse on one last heist, dimmed to black as Leeds ultimately slipped to fifth.

Bremner was sold to Hull in September 1976 after four more games at the beginning of his 18th season with the club. The manner of his departure, mirrored when most of those hall of fame players left, symbolised everything that was wrong with the way the club was run. He had been equivocal about going, as Johnny Giles and Terry Cooper had been and Norman Hunter would be when he followed him out of the door a couple of months later. At least Bremner and Hunter had enjoyed testimonials, heading the queue of the long backlog as several players hit 10 years' service at roughly the same time, but all found that Amfield and Cussins prevaricated when asked to confirm verbal offers of contracts or reassurance that they had roles to play. Armfield fiddled away at his pipe to buy time, Cussins gabbled. Both Bremner and Hunter were first-team regulars when they were sold during the 1976-77 season. When he visited the dressing room Cussins actually pinched the players on the cheeks like a berserk maiden aunt in a no doubt affectionate but condescending and proprietorial gesture the players despised. He will have contributed to buy a piece of silver or crystal to bid them farewell but he also made sure Leeds received a standard transfer fee for players who had given their all. Cooper, Hunter and the captain had cost Leeds nothing yet despite the combined 43 seasons they had given the club, United took in £125,000 when they left. It is significant because those fees suppressed the signing-on bonus the players would have received from their new clubs. Even so, each found himself on more money from his new employer, discovering too late that their salaries had not kept pace with the game's wage inflation since Revie left.

Giles, meanwhile, had to take the nuclear option and retire midway through the run to the European Cup Final, missing training and a match until Cussins caved and put in writing the offer of a testimonial. Then, when his request for a new contract was mired in the limbo of Armfield's indecision and the club accepted a £50,000 offer from West Brom to hire him as player-manager, he stalled because Cussins refused to pay him his due. It was only his threat to stay that forced the board's hand and their attitude caused bitter resentment that resonates still. There is a telling vignette Giles records from a couple of years later at a reception after Paul Reaney's testimonial:

"[Cussins] did that thing of his, pinching my cheeks as he said, 'I say, I say, I say, we should never have let him go, should we?'

Fortified by a few Bacardis, I turned to Manny and said: 'Weren't you the chairman who sold me?'

'Yes, that's right,' he said.

"Well you were the one responsible for me going. So fuck off and don't ever annoy me again."

No wonder their bond is principally to each other rather than the club. They knew they could rely on their team-mates, not on Leeds United. That is not to say Liverpool or Arsenal had a more sympathetic approach, only that it grated so bitterly with Revie's stalwarts because he had specifically run a 'player-first' policy. "That's the nature of football and you accept it," says Eddie Gray. "People who own football clubs make the decisions and you've got to abide by them. You don't necessarily agree with them." It is perhaps Revie's least appreciated achievement that he held that 'natural order' at bay for so long. When it bit back, it put the club on the return journey to where it had been in 1961.

The crowd played its part as well, barracking Terry Yorath so poisonously that he asked to leave. His crime? Not being Johnny Giles, which evokes Sir Michael Parkinson's anecdote about Sir Leonard Hutton's son, Richard, the England all-rounder who was told by one mean-spirited dimwit at Headingley as he walked out to bat: "Tha'll never be as good as this dad." A fair point, indeed, but as Parky pointed out: "Who will ever be as good as his dad?" The same holds for Giles and Leeds. Armfield took Coventry's £160,000 for Yorath to offset the £240,000 he had paid for Tony Currie, an attacking midfielder who tends to get lumped in with the 'mavericks' but was far more robust. At times he was magnificent in an average side and would have thrived in a great one that could have compensated for his bouts of meekness when his forceful dribbling and clever passing should have turned defeats into draws and one point into two. He gave a generation their happiest memories of Leeds, particularly in FA Cup ties against Norwich, Manchester City, and West Brom, and was usually inspired by the presence of Yorkshire TV cameras to score some crackers, none more distinguished than the curling shot against Southampton in November 1978 which was in the same class as any bent by Rivelino, Nelinho and Dirceu at that summer's World Cup. Great players win trophies, the best flamboyant ones make the people happy and ensure that hope is always a companion when they turn up to watch. It was the Elland Road crowd's pleasure and tragedy that Currie was a glittering decoration for three seasons rather than a herald of the second coming.

Currie was instrumental in three runs to semi-finals, one in the FA Cup in 1977 and in the League Cup in the following two seasons. Elland Road hosted Manchester City in a fifth-round tie in 1977, Leeds winning a dramatic game four minutes from time when Trevor Cherry's tenacity drove him to get up from the penalty area mudbath when tackled by Mike Doyle to toe-end a shot past Joe Corrigan, who was trying to make ground to smother the ball. Few present can have forgotten a save Corrigan made from Allan Clarke's header. The goalkeeper's instinctive, acrobatic brilliance when he changed direction mid-dive and veered upwards to palm the ball over the bar while the Leeds striker already had his arm raised in celebration was so mesmerising that comparing it with Gordon Banks' from Pelé at the 1970 World Cup does not flatter it. At the end of the match the Kop, still in the habit of singing *You'll Never Walk Alone*, put up a wall of scarves that seemed to kiss the sky. On that afternoon there was a palpable sense that the good times were back.

The City goalkeeper was back in an FA Cup tie less than a year later. Colin Bell set up two goals before a Leeds fan took umbrage with Corrigan, ran out of the Gelderd End to assault him and ended up with the City No.1 responding with a couple of haymakers of his own. A denser pitch invasion followed but the referee, Colin Seel, told the crowd via the PA that he would not abandon the game and would stay till midnight if necessary to conclude it. After a 13-minute interval ("of shame" as Jimmy Hill called it on *Match of the Day*) City won 2-1, Leeds were fined and Elland Road was closed for the club's next home FA Cup tie as punishment.

It was in 1978 that, for the first time since John Charles left for Juventus 21 years earlier, international players in their peak years began agitating to leave. Joe Jordan had been annoyed that the board had refused to sell him to Bayern Munich straight after the European Cup Final and let his contract wind down, turning down the opportunity to join Ajax, and holding out until Manchester United made a bid in January. He rejected a last minute offer from Liverpool to go to Old Trafford for a fee of £350,000 and doubled his wages to £500 a week. Gordon McQueen, his great friend, annoyed at being left behind, took matters into his own hands during the FA Cup defeat by City and punched his own goalkeeper, David Harvey. Coincidentally Manchester United chose the days after the match, when Leeds were in the pillory, to offer £495,000 for the centre-half. Reluctantly, Armfield let him go. It was these defections that turned a festering, rancid relationship between Manchester United and Leeds supporters into something much worse.

Antagonism and violence between the fans had first flared during an ill-tempered FA Cup semi-final draw at Hillsborough in 1965. A foul-strewn match ended with skirmishes outside the ground and on the streets of Nottingham four days later when Leeds got through to their first FA Cup Final after Billy Bremner's 89th-minute winner in the replay at the City Ground. Leeds held the upper hand in head-to-head encounters over the next decade, losing only two of 21 matches, but all bar their 5-1 shellacking of Frank O'Farrell's side in 1972 were tight affairs and the tension exacerbated the malevolence.

In 1977 they were pitted together again at Hillsborough in an FA Cup semi-final and so many Manchester United fans obtained tickets in Leeds sections that punches outnumbered shots on goal. By the early 1980s the atmosphere had become so febrile, and so regular were the attempts to make the opposition supporters lose face by forcing them to turn tail and run away, that Greater Manchester police and their West Yorkshire counterparts must have breathed a sigh of relief when Leeds were relegated in 1982.

After Jordan and McQueen left, the ill-feeling deteriorated further, exacerbated by McQueen's parting shot: "Ask all the players in the country which club they would like to join and 99 per cent would say 'Manchester United'. The other one per cent would be liars." For the next four years, Leeds fans appropriated the Jilted John song to serenade the pair with "Jordan is a moron" and "Gordon is a moron" and both were still harangued whenever they went to Elland Road decades later, despite being title winners with Leeds and failing to repeat that success across the Pennines. Eric Cantona, Rio Ferdinand and Alan Smith subsequently followed their path and receive equal billing with the two Scots in the 'Judas' hall of shame. Cantona's departure in 1992 was a particularly hard blow to take, the Frenchman becoming an adored talisman at Old Trafford who almost immediately ruined the Leeds fans' boast that they had won the title three times since Manchester United's last championship in 1967. His returns to Elland Road were not always successful but those matches were memorable for the sheer volume of spite he attracted and the manner in which he seemed to revel in it. Whenever the rivalry resumes – on a sporadic basis these days – grievance at these ancient 'betrayals' still kindle the hate.

Armfield did his best to replace Jordan and McQueen but, as so often, his scouting seemed limited to his old haunts in Lancashire and Yorkshire. In three full seasons at the club, he used the proceeds from selling McKenzie, Yorath, Jordan and McQueen as well as Revie's old guard to buy Currie from Sheffield United, Ray Hankin and Brian Flynn from Burnley, Paul Hart from Blackpool and Hull City's John Hawley. Only Arthur Graham, the bustling Scotland winger who joined from Aberdeen, came from beyond Armfield's parochial compass.

After finishing 10th and ninth in his last two campaigns and with his offer for Newcastle right-back Irving Nattrass just lodged, Armfield resigned in June 1978 because the board was split over whether to offer him an extension to the contract that was due to expire in October, four years after he had succeeded Clough. Armfield's kindness and integrity equipped him to do a difficult job without causing rancour and there were times – the two charity pantomimes he wrote and essentially produced for the players at the City Varieties as well as McKenzie's Mini-leaping antics at testimonials – when United were an uncharacteristically jaunty club. He left after producing a trading profit that had funded more ground redevelopment in the northern corners and at the southern end. The words of one anonymous former Revie player (that sound like Clarke), uttered when redevelopment commenced, rang ominously true: "We're a great team playing in a second-rate ground. By the time it's finished we'll be gone, and they'll have a great ground and no team."

Cussins first approached Southampton's Lawrie McMenemy to replace him but was turned down, according to James Mossop of the *Sunday*

Express, a journalist who was tighter with northern-born managers than any other, because "Leeds have a cold, demanding crowd and a board of directors whose sense of direction resembles a maze". Stein was a bigger coup and was pitch-perfect when he agreed a three-year deal for £30,000 a year. "This club is as big as any in the game," he said. "Their facilities, potential and reputation are second to none." He was gilding it a bit – Leeds had started the season with Maurice Lindley in charge because they had not managed to persuade any of their preferred candidates to take it – facilities, potential and reputation notwithstanding. He won four, drew three and lost three of 10 matches in the League and League Cup and used his charm on the dressing room to convince them of his sincerity and vision of a "forward-moving team who will go out to win attractively". Gray and the other Scots who knew him well, however, sensed right away that his heart wasn't in it. He made an unsuccessful bid for Derby's Gerry Daly and an inquiry for Dundee United's David Narey, which showed that he was looking to play a cultured game by identifying a wiry, hard-running playmaker and a Hansen-esque, elegant centre-back to change the style. But when Scotland sacked Ally MacLeod, the homesick and lonely Stein ordered the BBC's Archie Macpherson to put his name in the frame. The SFA took the hint and he accepted their offer, turning down Cussins' counter proposition of a house and a £35,000 cash bonus. Halving his salary to £15,000 Stein went home, leaving the *Daily Express*' David Miller to quip, with a call-back to Revie, that the Leeds chairman should "open an agency for supplying international managers". Lindley filled the breach once again, supervising two defeats and a draw that shoved Leeds down to 14th.

The board's divisions were plain – there was talk of Ron Saunders, speculation that they would finally rectify the mistake of 1974 and ask Giles or try once again for Don Howe, Bobby Robson or McMenemy. Instead they compromised on Sunderland's Adamson, a Geordie from Ashington, Milburn/Charlton country, then managing his boyhood favourites. Wearsiders had not taken to him, though few coaches were esteemed as highly within the game. His achievements at Burnley in creating the 'Team of the Seventies' may have mouldered because Lord annually liquidated a playing asset for cash yet it was hoped that the right environment would nurture his strengths. In three years at Roker Park and Elland Road he proved that Burnley was the only club right for him. Adamson was merely 49 but starting over was a grinding business and almost overwhelming for a man scarred by his recent experiences and employing liquid courage to take an edge off the strain.

Lorimer thought him a prig and while the other players were not so damning, they were disappointed he had forsaken the technical and tactical work that had earned him so much recognition. Now he deferred to his assistant, Dave Merrington, a muscular evangelical who, when not trying to convert them to Christianity, policed perceived examples of 'disrespect' with a hand around the throat. Eye-rolling became the order of the day. Adamson, rarely seen in his tracksuit, spoke to the players individually and collectively, remaining astute at distilling their duties in the pithiest terms. But his words often contrasted with the work Merrington had been doing and left everyone confused. Nonetheless, on the back of Currie's irresistible form, Adamson led United on a 16-match unbeaten run from mid-November to the beginning of March. Brian Flynn, a former Burnley trainee, who looked like cross between an elfin droog from *A Clockwork Orange* and an even-more stunted Bay City Roller, carried Currie's water effectively, Graham made incisive thrusts and the Gray brothers and Madeley maintained their highest standards. It was enough to qualify for the Uefa Cup in the first year they were eligible after the Paris ban but Adamson's summer trading undid the progress they had made under his light-touch start.

The manager told Currie that the fans would lynch him when his captain asked to leave in June because his London-born wife was depressed. Currie disingenuously now says that Leeds should have done more to keep him, allowing him to live and train in London and come up for games, but it would not have been acceptable in 1979 and it was not even an option put on the table by either party. Adamson cannot be blamed for allowing an unhappy player to leave, particularly one who cited his wife's mental health as the only incitement. He can be held culpable for wasting the £400,000 received for him from QPR and more on Brian Greenhoff, Jeff Chandler and Alan Curtis. Worse still was his judgment over Hawley, who had scored 16 league goals in his debut season, and Ray Hankin who bagged 20 the year before. Hawley was sent to Sunderland for £120,000 plus Wayne Entwistle and the burly Hankin, who needed a proper 'beasting' to get him down to fighting weight, allowed to leave for Vancouver Whitecaps a couple of months later. Hawley was merciless in his denunciation of the manager and the man who replaced him: "Jimmy Adamson and Dave Merrington didn't like me so the deal was done involving a Sunderland player whose name escapes me but sounded as if it was a Welsh veterinary disease," he told the website *Sheridan Dictates*. The Sheep Scab virus would have fared better up front than Entwistle, who left on a free transfer 12 months later.

A 7-0 defeat at Highbury in the League Cup emphasised what a lightweight team Leeds had become and Adamson was remorselessly barracked after sluggish, pussy-footing performances propelled them down to 11th in 1980. Indeed for most of the last year or so of his stay at Elland Road the layman could have been forgiven for assuming his surname was "Adamsonout". His personal problems led to so many absences the players started calling him 'Howard Hughes'. Football clubs and the correspondents who make their living reporting about them close ranks to conceal such issues and the rapidity with which he was sinking pints and whisky chasers over the road at the Old Peacock did not leak. Even so, his public image as a clipped, disillusioned headmaster, bemoaning the decline in discipline, could ill-afford further evidence that he was blind to all the mistakes of recruitment and organisation. When it transpired that more glaring and costly transfer errors had been made by selling Frankie Gray and signing Alex Sabella – an enchantingly gifted player who was lost in a struggling side – Adamson was finished. In a little under two years he had spent £750,000 net and left the club with a spineless team and a crowd in open revolt. He had also asked the board for funds to sign Kevin Keegan, Peter Withe and Martin Dobson. It could not have been much of a surprise when they turned him down because they had wasted so much already and there was no guarantee he would know what to do with them any more. After four defeats in the opening five games of the 1980-81 season, following demonstrations during which directors had been jostled and felt the occasional speck of saliva from fans' fury on their faces – and crowds regularly plummeted below 20,000 – he was persuaded to resign for a £30,000 settlement. He had left Burnley at the bottom of Division One in 1976 and drove away from Elland Road four years later with United in the same position. He had always been a solemn man. Now he looked disembowelled.

Maurice Lindley stood up as caretaker for the fifth time in as many seasons, prescribing a period of continuity to rehabilitate the club. His former boss, Don Revie, only midway through his 10-year consultancy deal with United, was the inspiration for the solution. If they could not have him because he had just signed a long-term contract to manage Al-Nasr in Dubai and was enjoying a more relaxing way of life, they decided to go for the next best thing, one of his 'lads'. Giles had become increasingly disillusioned with management and, besides, had told Cussins to "fuck off"; Jack Charlton was ambivalent, presumably mindful of the directors he knew so well. The anti-Revie faction on the board hinted that the former Rangers' manager Jock Wallace was the man for them but a Revie boy would offer them something the intense 'Battle Fever' Wallace could not. They had never considered the other side of the coin. The recognition directors had hungered for when Leeds were flying was also a liability that was causing them hassle and distress as they walked from the boardroom to their Daimlers. Feeling exposed and vulnerable, they sought protection.

21

THE OLD MAGIC

Allan Clarke, by contrast with the two Jimmys, never wanted for certainty. It is still apparent today when he asserts, as he annually seems to do, that the Revie team would easily beat whichever side has just won the Premier League. Arrogance enhanced his technical gifts as a player, making him the prickly and clinical striker of his manager's dreams. Selfishness and a tendency to stroppiness, not helped by his sour Walsall twang, were rubbed off by a united Leeds dressing room of purposeful and forthright characters who chiselled away at his flaws. He retained an intimidating manner, though, which equipped him well when he dropped down to the Fourth Division as player-manager of Barnsley. No lower league brute would dare to clog a player with his reputation for aggressive self-defence and he belied the injury problems of his last couple of seasons with Leeds to score 12 goals and lead Barnsley to promotion, selling out Oakwell as the pit town enjoyed a dose of revival fervour. He built an exciting, youthful team who were poised at the beginning of his third season to mount a promotion run when Manny Cussins offered him the Leeds job. He not only accepted a four-year contract but told the players to expect the European Cup before his deal expired.

The club was in 21st place when he took over and he immediately set about shoring up the defence. Clarke had two priorities: to turn around the slide down the table and arrest the slump in attendances from an average of 31,500 in 1976, the sixth best in England, to 22,778 four years later, 16th in the country. He set about this in contradictory fashion because he believed that the reason fans were staying away had less to do with the historic indifference of the Leeds public to a struggling side and the Thatcher government's instigation of mass unemployment in the north than the scourge of hooliganism.

It is true that arrests had been burgeoning and that there had been riots at Old Trafford in 1979 and at Elland Road when Manchester United were defeated 2-0 in May 1980. Leeds had served bans in every competition bar the League Cup – ground closures for league games in 1971 and then the FA Cup in 1979 which completed the full house alongside the four-year

European suspension for the Parc des Princes disorder. By 1980 hostility and danger were palpable on matchdays as troops of lads with Phil Oakey haircuts but dressed like Bjorn Borg, having liberated Austin Reed of half its stock, went in search of likeminded souls to ambush. Two years later when Leeds fans tore down a fence at the Hawthorns during the match that relegated them and embarked on a spree of vandalism and violence in the teeth of a police baton charge, Clarke would claim not to have seen anything and insisted: "Our fans are the best in the country."

When he first arrived, though, Clarke was not yet turning a blind eye to the evidence and saw it as his job to lead the moral majority in suppressing it. Wearing an Alan B'Stard-esque pinstripe shirt with white collar, he was photographed with the leaflets he had printed to distribute at the ground asking for support for his clampdown. He was only 34 years old but sounded like Rhodes Boyson. "Extreme violence should be met with extreme measures," he said. "The most violent offenders should be flogged in front of the main stands before the start of a home game. I feel so strongly on this matter that I would volunteer to do the whipping." The birch as a judicial punishment had ben abolished in the UK in 1948 when Clarke was two, yet here he was calling for its restitution. He can only have been posturing because even the 'short-sharp-shockers' in the government would have quailed at the opposition to changing the law.

Without being able to attract thousands of sanctimonious sadists to watch the beatings and swell the gates, Clarke could have changed the tactics to promote a more attacking approach to replace Adamson's functional botch-job. It was an extravagance he could not afford, he said: "We must put results before entertainment. You want players to entertain but football is big business and at the end of the day the result is the be-all and end-all." He managed seven victories, six defeats and five draws in the run to New Year's Day, a start for Clarke that took them to 16th after a 0-0 draw with champions Liverpool in their last match of the year.

To tighten up the defence he played 4-5-1, using Brian Greenhoff and Eddie Gray as overlapping full-backs, Kevin Hird, the Jasper Carrott lookalike right-back, in midfield and Terry Connor, United's first black player since Albert Johanneson and a product of Leeds City Boys, as a quick, stylish and raw centre-forward. Connor made a fine start to his Leeds career, confused and conflicted the racist morons who had turned parts of Elland Road and certain city centre pubs into cesspits of National Front debasement, and played throughout with inspirational moral and physical courage. Arthur Graham and Carl Harris fought for scraps on the wings and did their best to create chances in a side set-up to defend. In five years at Elland Road Hird experienced a transformation from derided flop to cult hero but Gray, Graham and the goalkeeper John Lukic apart, Leeds were an anaemic team lacking an identity. They won nine of their last 16 games, including a memorable 1-0 victory at Old Trafford, to move up to ninth but crowds had begun to yoyo alarmingly. If, as Clarke maintained, it was thugs rather than the fare that were keeping people away, one would expect significant drop-offs especially for opponents whose supports travelled in numbers and enough of whom were up for the dance. Yet 39,206 came out for the visit of Liverpool when a fortnight before 15,882 had bothered to turn up for a 3-0 victory over Coventry on a spring Saturday afternoon. Leeds and the country were enduring myriad social and economic problems – scoring only 39 goals all season, their worst-ever return before George Graham, was also a major factor in putting people off. United were boring and going to the game felt like a chore unless there was a genuine rivalry with the opposition.

Clarke had tried to address it as soon as he arrived by making a bid for the First Division's leading scorer, Justin Fashanu, who went to Nottingham Forest instead, and then played a snide trick on Terry Yorath by agreeing a fee with Tottenham to bring him home but allowed Cussins to publicise his friend and former colleague's salary demand to paint him as greedy in the papers. Instead of folding, Yorath, feeling alienated, joined Johnny Giles at Vancouver Whitecaps instead. In the summer of 1981 they scouted Austria Memphis' Walter Schachner and the Uruguay forward Waldemar Victorino, with no mention of how they expected to obtain work permits, asked after Tony Woodcock and Joe Jordan and later made a bid for Wolves' Andy Gray. So why they settled on Peter Barnes, the England left-winger, who was desperate to leave West Brom and move back to Manchester City, has always been a mystery. Clarke had asked for and been given £1 million to spend, and he blew £930,000 of it on a bauble. The directors objected, saying they had expected three players for their outlay but backed down when Clarke insisted and used the media to press his case. Men who were habitually as tight as a trombonist's sphincter when prudently running their own businesses allowed the club's money to be flushed down the toilet. Frank Gray came back from Nottingham Forest where he had won the European Cup that had been denied him in 1975 but Leeds started the season with the Rangers retread Derek Parlane up front, Barnes betraying his dribbling skill with grotesquely inaccurate crosses as the team racked up six defeats, three draws and a solitary victory from their first 10 games.

They plumbed the depths on opening day. On the eve of the season, John Toshack, manager of newly promoted Swansea said "we are capable of frightening some teams to death", and they obliged at the first attempt. Bob Latchford scored a hat-trick, the much missed attacking-midfield colossus Robbie James set up a couple of goals, and at 4-1 the North Bank at Vetch Field began singing *Land of My Fathers*. Alan Curtis, sold back to his boyhood club by Clarke, still had a point to prove, and scored Swansea's fifth and final goal with a vicious right-foot shot into the top corner. Toshack, according to the goalscorer, then turned to Clarke, a person not noted for his humility, stuck both thumbs up and shouted: "Cheers, mate!"

After four weeks at the bottom of the table, having scored only seven goals in 10 games in this, the first season of three points for a win, the board released further funds and allowed Clarke to buy the 1978 Footballer of the Year, Kenny Burns from Nottingham Forest, for £400,000. Burns had once been a tearaway centre-forward, tamed by Brian Clough and Peter Taylor and turned into a central defender of rare composure. At Leeds, like Barnes, Burns was not the leader in word or deed that Clarke desperately needed. His scouting was three years out of date and appeared thoroughly superficial. Anyone in the game could have told him that Barnes was too diffident and Burns was prone to putting on weight and fond of a drink. Without Clough to bully him, all Burns' worst instincts returned. The men who paid the price for these follies were Bob English, Maurice Lindley and Tony Collins, each of whom had given the club and Don Revie years of loyal service. All three were made redundant in a cost-cutting exercise just after Burns signed.

There were moments when staying up seemed possible. Three wins out of four in the autumn took them two places clear of the relegation zone and victory in the return against Swansea in January helped United up to 14th. Straight after that, however, they lost five of the next six and the Grim Reaper had one hand on their shoulder thereafter. Frank Worthington was signed in March and later claimed, contrary to public perception, that Clarke was not a forthright manager and took on board too many opinions from all manner of hangers-on. Greenhoff, meanwhile, blamed the endless fitness work on Mondays, the pat response of a struggling side's manager without a proper answer.

Worthington's flamboyant image enabled him to achieve his principal life goal and sleep with half the adult female population of wherever he was currently laying his cowboy hat, but such antics masked his razor-sharp talent as a forward. Feed the ball to him quickly and he was as fine a finisher as any in the league. At Leeds 'Elvis' scored nine goals in 17 games yet they won only four of them and his tongue and impulse for retaliation meant he was suspended for a Monday night visit to West Brom, the last match of the season, when a draw was required to stay up.

United had limped along on life support all year and owed their chances to a mesmerising away victory over Aston Villa, a month before Villa became champions of Europe, and a 2-1 home win over Brighton in the penultimate game. There had been fights at White Hart Lane in the FA Cup and League and when United went 2-0 down at the Hawthorns, the result, said Worthington, of ceding too much space, some of the 4,000 away fans in the Smethwick End worked the bolts on the fence free to launch a pitch invasion in pursuit of a postponement. Mounted and riot police beat them back and relegation was confirmed in a blaze of condemnation for a renegade club with delinquent supporters. Clarke had started his spell stating, "I'm a winner" and began the year saying "our name is on the FA Cup". He continued the PR game in the interlude before his sacking, praising the fans in spite of the melee and three-dozen arrests. It did him no good. The board sacked his assistant, Martin Wilkinson, in early June, and when that did not force his resignation they dismissed Clarke three weeks later. The age of Sniffer was snuffed out with a whimper after a second season of 39 goals. The sharpest striker Leeds have ever had presided over a drought. In a neatly symmetrical touch, Revie had left them with £2m in the bank – eight years later they went down owing precisely the same amount.

They gave the job to Eddie Gray because he had proved himself an impressive coach when he took on the youth team in 1975, because he so obviously cared and, given his playing contract was already costing them £25,000, it would cost only £5,000 more to make him player-manager. They were favourites for promotion but had never been in more debt. As Gray prepared for the new season he took on a lopsided squad with scope only to asset-strip rather than invest. He remembers arriving at work one morning to find the Inland Revenue appropriating club cars in lieu of unpaid tax. "In relative terms we were big payers so we had a lot of players on good contracts and wages that we couldn't really afford," Gray says. "So one by one you had to try to move them on. No disrespect to them – nothing detrimental to their playing abilities, the club just couldn't afford to keep them. The crowds went down and you try to bring young players in through the system. It's tricky balancing it. In the early days, you introduce one or two, but you need the experienced players to help them along or the club could have fallen right through that division as well."

In the first few months he sent Barnes out on loan, sold Worthington, Parlane, Flynn and Trevor Cherry to get them off the books, ruining a promising start forged by his progressive innovation of using Cherry as a sweeper. Off the field he was forced to become such an authority on hooliganism that he was sought out by senior police offers for advice. The club evaded any sanction for the Hawthorns riot because Ken Bates had established the precedent that he and Chelsea could not be held liable for failing to control their travelling supporters as that responsibility fell on the home club. Relief lasted no time at all – the first game took Leeds to Grimsby where one Leeds fan ran on to the pitch and nicked the match ball, others smashed up a stand and there were regular assaults in Cleethorpes from the Friday night until the Sunday morning. This time there were 57 arrests. There were brawls at Hillsborough in September, affray in Blackburn and an infamous hours-long sequence of skirmishes before, during and after the visit to Stamford Bridge in October that spread, underground and overground, into the West End. During the home match against Newcastle Kevin Keegan and John Anderson were struck by missiles, one chucked out of the Kop, the other from the away section. Play was suspended while police retrieved the evidence – coins and a ball-bearing – and towards the end of the game, which Leeds won 3-1, seats in the Lowfields and South Stand were splintered and hoyed over the rusting skeleton of the never-completed south-east corner on to Elland Road itself.

A week later in response to the FA's ultimatum to stamp disorder out, the following message appeared on the front cover of the programme: "The future of Leeds United Association Football Club hangs in the balance. This must not be taken as an idle threat. Despite repeated pleas and warnings, the mindless actions of a minority of the club's so-called followers last Saturday have placed an enormous degree of uncertainty over this great club. We would ask for the help and co-operation of everyone who have Leeds United at heart – and we appreciate that this is the majority of our supporters – to help rid the club of the 'scab' element who, although small in numbers, have caused the club so many problems and whose loathsome actions now place the very existence of Leeds United in jeopardy."

The FA ordered the terraces to be closed for the following two home games but when they went to the Baseball Ground in January, another £20,000 worth of damage was caused in the away end. Nihilism reigned now, and no matter how often Gray and the board condemned it, they were helpless to prevent it. During his third season, the manager stopped his own children from watching the club after ultra-violence at Huddersfield Town. When they lost the lead at Oxford in another televised match, some supporters picked clean a camera gantry and threw the scaffolding poles and boards on to the pitch, Chelsea's electronic scoreboard was destroyed and taken back in bits on the train and, at the very end of the 1984-85 season, on the day of the Bradford fire, Ian Hambridge, a 15-year-old boy from Northampton, was killed at St Andrew's when a wall collapsed under the weight of Leeds fans fleeing the police. Gray had been asked to make an appeal over the PA when the violence began but found an audience too riled to listen. "It had no effect whatsoever," he says. "I remember going down there to try and quieten them down and they were throwing bricks on to the pitch. Times like that you feel like walking away from it."

Anyone who thought that the lethal consequences of all this posturing and lust for carnage would have a sobering effect would be disappointed 16 months later when Leeds lost at Odsal, Bradford's temporary home, and a chip van was set ablaze. It was the first away game since the FA's decree to make all United's trips all-ticket, there were more than 60 arrests and though there is some dispute about how it came to catch fire, it was a particularly sick twist. It left the board arguing again for greater restrictions to be imposed on their own fans for fear of what they might do next.

Gray's first season went surprisingly well given the churn. Aiden Butterworth, a youth team contemporary of Connor's, a nimble centre-forward who would walk away from the game in 1984, scored 11 goals, and a good run of four wins and two draws from mid-March gave United a sniff of a promotion spot in these pre-play-off days. John Lukic left for Arsenal and was replaced by David Harvey, who answered the call to help his old friend at the age of 35. Never the most vocal of goalkeepers, he nevertheless ministered to a back-four of Gwyn Thomas, Paul Hart, Martin Dickinson and Frank Gray with the same enthusiasm he had given Reaney, Charlton, Hunter and Cooper. The upsurge in form had coincided with the introduction of the 18-year-old John Sheridan, a midfielder who passed with poise and precision, long and short, and cantered forward with his head up like a meerkat sentry, assessing his options. Sheepish off the field, he was a lion on it, conducting attacks, probing away, directing his side into position, gesticulating and shouting to express himself. He had swagger, a physical charisma and just the right amount of petulance which inspired the famous 'Sheridan Dictates' banner when, under Billy Bremner, he was encouraged to shoot more and became an even better player. He broke his leg after nine games of Gray's second season and left a void in a team that was struggling without leadership. The player-manager was injured and had tried to fill the gap the previous season with Brighton's Neil McNab but could not afford the £65,000 to turn his loan into a long-term transfer. They could not find anyone to take on Barnes' wages and he reappeared at outside-left, two Scots, Andy Watson and George McCluskey, were signed with some fanfare and no real impact while punts on lower league talent – Tony Brown from Thackley and John Donnelly from Dumbarton – were sabotaged by a lack of pace and application respectively. From eighth in May 1983, without Sheridan they slid to 19th after defeat by Oldham on 27 December.

Gray had blooded every young player he thought could take the strain and had run out of options. On New Year's Eve, a hunch turned into a masterstroke. Peter Lorimer had been training with Leeds during the NASL off-season and had been made redundant when the league went bust. At the age of 37, five years after his last appearance for the club, Gray named his friend as substitute against Middlesbrough and he came on to secure a 4-1 victory. Over the next 18 months his skill and enduring smartness galvanised Eddie's tyros, a smaller-scale version of Bobby Collins in 1962 without the tyranny. He had lost the dynamism and gained a paunch but remained a magnificent footballer who revelled in the responsibility. "I brought Peter back because I knew he was still fit, he was still playing in America, and I knew his experience and attitude towards the game," says Gray. "All the boys looked up to him and got on well with him. It was a great benefit to the younger players when he came back." With Lorimer back on the right of midfield, Leeds won eight of their next 11 games and finished the season safely in 10th.

Scott Sellars, an 18-year-old, deceptively slight midfielder with a wonderful left-foot, remembers Lorimer's introduction vividly. "That day was where the change-around came. It was a big moment to win that game and to win it so well. Peter, like Eddie, was a great person, a really nice guy, who understood what we were going through as young players because he'd been there and done the same thing. Him and Dave Harvey and Frankie were very supportive.

"With me now in the job I'm in [Head of Academy at Wolves] there's a lot based around my experiences of Leeds as a kid. Because of the history of the club, we were always under a challenge at Leeds. Even in the youth team everyone wanted to beat us because we were Leeds and a big club. It still had that big club feel about it. It was so well organised – everything was there. Don Revie was miles ahead of his time and his structure was still there. Eddie as one of his pupils just carried it on really. Individually he would talk to me a lot. I was lucky because my job as an apprentice was to clean out the staff room after training finished and he would talk to me then about players. Things he said to me then, I now say to young players as a coach myself. Most importantly he is a fantastic person, he really cared about the young players. He had come to Leeds as a young boy and wanted us to have the same support he'd had. Most significant of all, he trusted us, which gave us a lot of confidence. Eddie had a massive influence on me and two crops of young players in that way."

With Sheridan fit at the start of the next season, Leeds made a flying start with four successive victories and with Denis Irwin, Neil Aspin and Andy Linighan joining Sellars and Tommy Wright as first-team regulars. At times they were irrepressible – hammering Oldham 6-0, Notts County 5-0 and Wimbledon 5-2, a match that seemed to capture all the verve of Gray's young side, crowned by Sellars' back-heel, drag-back tackle that set up a glorious, parabolic chip. "Dave Beasant being about 6ft 9in, made it all the better," says Sellars. "It was instinctive. I was creative and wanted to try things and Eddie always encouraged me to do it." And what of Sheridan? "John was one of the best players I ever played with," he says. "I had the pleasure of playing with him again at Bolton later on and I think he was so underrated. His composure, always knowing where the next pass was, always looking like he had time on the ball. He could pick a pass, was aggressive as well, he could dig a bit when he had to. He was just an outstanding footballer."

However, for all the moments of exhilarating play at home, infuriating inconsistency away left them needing to beat Birmingham at St Andrew's to have a chance of promotion. They lost 1-0 on the club's darkest day, an afternoon that still haunts those present.

"Back then the exposure wasn't on the football, more on the crowd and what they were going to do," says Sellers. "I remember at Huddersfield I was trying to score a goal and my shot came off a policeman who had come on to the pitch to chase an intruder, so it was difficult to concentrate on the game, there was so much going on. And at Birmingham someone loses their life, it's quite traumatic [to deal with that]. Someone's gone to a game and is not going home."

Five months later Leslie Silver, the paint magnate and chairman since 1983, sacked Gray after 11 games of a league campaign that had begun badly before a five-match unbeaten run had pulled them out of the dive. The decision provoked uproar and the players put Lorimer up to protest the decision, a role he willingly took but one which cost him his job. There were loud protests and Silver's Rolls was trashed before the next match against Middlesbrough, though by now crowds above 20,000 were a once-a-season feast day and four-figure attendances were embarrassingly frequent. It wasn't that Leeds were dying, specifically. All over the country people were drifting away from the game.

Lorimer reckons the board canned his close pal to deflect blame for their lack of investment. It was, he said, as if they had lost faith with Leeds United. It remains the most myopic managerial sacking in the club's history and uniquely unwelcomed by supporters. Carelessly, Billy Bremner, Gray's eventual successor undid all his good work. Terry Phelan was released and went on to win the FA Cup with Wimbledon, Andy Linighan, sold for £55,000, won the title and scored the winning goal in an FA Cup Final for Arsenal, Sellars – offloaded for just £20,000 – cost Howard Wilkinson £700,000 when he brought him back in 1992, Irwin left for £60,000 and subsequently won the Treble at Manchester United among seven Premier League championships while Sheridan, who stayed until 1989, linked up with Irwin and Phelan in the Republic of Ireland's side at the 1994 World Cup.

"People who knew football could see it was a young team and sometimes with young teams you get ups and downs," says Sellars. "But it was a young team that had a lot of potential and it was proven by the careers people went on to have at other clubs. With a bit more time and support I've no doubt that Eddie would have got that team going. We'd proved it as a youth team around Europe, we'd beaten the very best, the likes of Milan. We just needed more time."

Percy Woodward's son Brian, a director, resigned in support of Gray but the board ploughed on with its search for a successor, once again casting its net near and narrow. After discussions about Revie returning as a kind of general manager to John Giles foundered, they approached Bradford City for Trevor Cherry and Terry Yorath, backing down when they were quoted £200,000 a man in compensation. Jack Charlton, who had recently walked away from Newcastle, was, like Giles, thought too independent, and though the directors considered Derby's Arthur Cox, they turned in the end to Bremner who had led Doncaster Rovers to two promotions from Division Four in seven years at Belle Vue. Stung by negative reactions, once again they went for the safest rather than the best choice. Individuals in a crowd have their own favourite players but collectively Elland Road had anointed Bremner their king in the mid-Sixties. No candidate was more popular as a man and his standing put a buffer of respect, and indeed love, between board and supporters.

If his dismantling of Gray's team seemed like an act of vandalism even before those players went on to make their fortunes elsewhere, it was how he replaced them that was truly disenchanting. In Ian Snodin, his former Doncaster captain, Ian Baird and Sheridan he had inherited three robust, aggressive and skilful players around whom he tried to build a team. Mervyn

Day was a solid goalkeeper, still capable of the sensational, acrobatic saves of his teenage fame, and Andy Ritchie a gifted forward with a Velcro touch. He had the makings of a very good side and Irwin, Phelan, Sellars, Linighan and Tommy Wright, a bright, buzzy forward, were gaining in experience and had a surfeit of potential. There was no money to spend but he needed only one or two additions. Instead he drummed out Lorimer, released the five youngest players and bought mature top-flight reserves, plus Third and Fourth Division nobodies.

Leeds finished in 14th at the end of his first season but began to gel in 1986-87 when he replaced some of the hasty, cheap buys with more considered purchases, using some of the £800,000 he could not refuse from Everton for Snodin on John Pearson, Mark Aizlewood, Bobby McDonald and Micky Adams. He valued character as much as skill but remained besotted by the game, often delaying his journey home by joining the youth team car park kickabouts in his sports jacket, trousers and shoes. Bremner exhausted himself in the job and the overflowing ashtray on his desk spoke eloquently of the stress he was under. "At times I almost expected Don Revie to walk in and tell me to get out of his chair," he once said. "Yet, somehow, the place seemed run-down."

The directors had sold Elland Road to Leeds City Council just before they sacked Gray and used the £2.5m they had received – as well as a 125-year lease – to pay down the overdraft and the loans they had stumped up over the past few years. It had become a shabby place of scarred linoleum and chipped formica, full of ghosts. Bremner was too close to it all to demand the radical changes and investment required. Revie had done so; Howard Wilkinson would make it a prerequisite of taking the job in 1988. Bremner had the power of the people at his back but chose not to use it. He had come to the club at the age of 16 and you could tell. He addressed Silver as "Mr Chairman" with unusual sincerity.

When Brendan Ormsby, the veins in his neck sticking out like steel cables, bulleted a back-post header to win a fifth-round FA Cup tie against First Division QPR the roar was loud enough to make the rafters ring in the Kop for the first time in years. A party started on the south-east corner wasteland and continued in the next round at Wigan, where fans in jubilation slid down the antiquated mud banking at Springfield Park, when a 2-0 victory put Leeds in the semi-final.

This was Bremner country. Three times in semi-finals he had scored the winning goal in the white of Leeds United. But this time they were on their own. The match against Coventry was played at Hillsborough and provoked the biggest run on tickets since the 1977 semi-final at the same venue. Like Liverpool two years later, Leeds were assigned the smaller Leppings Lane End by virtue of geography and many, including this author, bought tickets from Coventry. We were escorted from the Kop and deposited into the overcrowded Leeds standing section to watch a serpentine match in which David Rennie scored the opener and Ormsby's hesitancy made a gift of an equaliser. The late Cyrille Regis was thwarted on at least five occasions and Leeds hung in to score a late equaliser of their own when Keith Edwards, a prolific goalscorer at his previous clubs, finally proved his worth with a near-post header into the far corner. Coventry fought back to win 3-2 in extra-time just as they did in the final. Edwards came off the bench again to score two more important goals in each leg of the play-off semi-final against Oldham.

Seven wins in their last 11 games helped them up to fourth and a place in the inaugural version of the promotion eliminators. Sheridan, Sellars, Irwin and Wright had all been in digs together and when they were old enough to move out continued to share a house. Sellars had gone to Blackburn, Irwin and Wright to Oldham and after Edwards added a 90th-minute goal on the scarily abrasive plastic Boundary Park pitch to his 89th-minute winner at Elland Road to qualify Leeds for the final on the away-goals rule, the three housemates, victor and vanquished, went home together.

In 1987 and 1988 the First Division was reduced to 21 teams and then 20 and the play-offs were instrumental to the scheme. In both those years the team finishing fourth from bottom in the top division earned a place in the semi-finals and it was that side, Charlton, whom Leeds had to face in the two-legged final. Both sides won 1-0 at home (or Selhurst Park where they were outnumbered 2:1 by Leeds fans in Charlton's case) but with only 48 hours between the ties, tiredness and tension led to desperation and an often hysterical atmosphere at Elland Road. Ormsby scored Leeds' winner, stealing it off young Bob Taylor with a goal-hanger's stealth, and try as the crowd did to maintain a berserk, desperate intensity, Charlton held firm.

They met in the replay at St Andrew's four days later, with more than two-thirds of the 18,000 fans behind them. Ormsby's knee injury in the first-half forced Adams into defence and Baird back into midfield to accommodate Edwards because we were still in the days of one substitute. It was an understandably cagey and frustrating game, deadlocked after 90 minutes until Sheridan scored a beauty in the ninth minute of extra-time. Throughout his Leeds career he had a habit of pointing as he ran to show his team-mates where he wanted them to go. Here he used it as a distraction technique, a 'hey, look over there' ploy before blindsiding the victim with a haymaker. As he sauntered up to take a free-kick from 25 yards, he pretended something was wrong, extended his left index finger then took the final two steps and arced his right-foot shot over the wall and beyond the keeper's grasp. Having scored in slow motion he celebrated in a frenzy. But a weak defensive header from Adams allowed Charlton to ping the ball back into the box and their captain Peter Shirtliff to pounce on a lucky ricochet and equalise.

Sheridan failed with a 50-yard chip from the kick-off that kissed the top of the goal and three minutes from time a badly-positioned Aizlewood let a free-kick over his head and Shirtliff, as cursed a name as there would be in Leeds for a couple of years, completed United's misery with an unstoppable header. The police, fearing a repeat of 1985, massed on the pitch at full-time. Mainly, though, Leeds fans simply stood there and only when the players came back out to thank them did they begin to depart. Much was made of Bremner at least reviving the 'Bridesmaid' tag that season. Cruelty, even back then, played better than sympathy. "It took me back to the early days when we were branded as the team who always went close but never actually won anything," said Bremner. "We shut the critics up then and I know we could do it again."

Sadly, because nobody wanted it more than Bremner, he could not do it again. He once told Jason Tomas that when he was a player, "I never thought anybody was better than us, even when we had a crap team" and he carried on with that passion and belief, instilling it in everyone he mentored. But it wasn't enough and without the board's financial support, he could not take the last step. Leeds finished seventh in his third season and they fired him at the start of his fourth after two defeats and three draws from six games, citing dull football, poor recruitment and bad results. He made mistakes – selling talented players, buying a dozen or so duds – yet he gave United their most enjoyable year for more than a decade. When the board dismissed him, it was like the whacking of Joe Pesci's Tommy DeVito in *Goodfellas*. There may have been merit to it, but it was a poignant end for the impetuous, fiery, inspirational heart of Leeds United. Don Revie had less than a year to live but the long tail of the Revie era died the moment Bremner eased his white Mercedes out of the manager's parking space at Elland Road for the final time in September 1988.

In *This Bloody Mary is the Last Thing I Own*, the late Jonathan Rendall perceptively defines why nostalgia is so seductive. "It's what everyone dreams of isn't it?" he writes. "Not to wallow in cherished memories, but for the spirit of those memories to come back, anew, and start living again, as if time were cyclical." Leeds had been intoxicated by its charms long enough. A brand-new start was essential.

22

'FIVE HOURS WITH A STUPID GRIN ON MY FACE'

Bill Fotherby did not live to see Leeds United's centenary, but when the club's former commercial director, managing director and chairman died in March 2019, he was feted with his reputation as high as it had ever been. More brutal than any Twitter takedown, the infamous testimonial spray-painted on the side of a bridge on Gelderd Road – "Fotherby: Liar, thief, crook" – lingered long after he was forced out in 1997. Yet in the last 10 years of his life, journalists sought out Fotherby and left his Harrogate home enchanted by his unfailing enthusiasm and sheer brass neck. Where once he had harnessed his chutzpah to the cause of relentlessly promoting United, now it rehabilitated his image. By contrast with Ken Bates, GFH Capital's tieless spoofers and Massimo Cellino, it was obvious, at least, that the former rag-trade tycoon cared deeply for the club and his city.

As a director he had risen to prominence in 1987 with an implausible scheme to buy Diego Maradona, a kite-flying exercise on an epic scale that was holed by two small technicalities: lack of both money and desire from the Argentina captain to leave Serie A champions Napoli for a Second Division side in a country still vilifying him. Fotherby managed to make contact and was convinced that he could come up with the cash even though Leeds were currently sharing their rutted pitch with Hunslet RLFC because they had been so broke they had sold the ground to the council. In future Fotherby would conjure transfer fees out of nowhere by kicking the can down the road, begging sponsors' money from forthcoming years and trusting a signing would boost income. His 'Hand of God' plan, though, relied on that old staple – a mythic alliance of benevolent local businessmen who, cometh the hour, are supposed to emerge like a ghost army to rescue Leeds. They did not exist then and never will.

Fotherby's ostentatious gambit pulled eyebrows into the Spock position and many shook their heads, admiring his cheek rather than admonishing his bluster. It did establish him as a character in his own right, though, as the showman and dealmaker who put the Ritz on Leslie Silver's reserve and rectitude. "He could sell sand to Arabs," said Howard Wilkinson with an indulgent smile. More importantly, he sold Wilkinson the idea of Leeds United, a concept richer in fantasy than substance. Fotherby could build castles in the air; Silver and Wilkinson dug the foundations – a happy marriage of passion and practicality. For five years they were as good a team as the one they sent on to the pitch.

Wilkinson was not the club's first choice. Fotherby said that they originally approached the England manager Bobby Robson and put out feelers to Howard Kendall, then managing Athletic Bilbao. Robson turned them down but recommended Wilkinson, then the Sheffield Wednesday manager, and a Leeds director, Jack Marjason, fed in the rumour that Wilkinson was unhappy at Hillsborough because his board would not remove his budgetary restrictions. He had taken Notts County into the First Division and kept them up for two years before joining his boyhood club Wednesday in 1983. Promotion at the first attempt was followed in his third year with a fifth-place finish and an FA Cup semi-final. They dropped to 13th and 11th in his final two full seasons. Players can smell a lack of ambition at a club and the better ones invariably leave. Wilkinson was powerless to prevent it. He could not match the wages offered by other clubs for those he wanted to sign or stay. "Wednesday became known," he wrote, "as the big city club with the small town mentality." Disillusionment was one motivating factor as was his club's permission for him to speak to Leeds. Fotherby and Silver still had to persuade him, however, and they did this in typical fashion: Fotherby spoke to him; Silver listened to him.

Once Fotherby had given him the spiel, he agreed to meet Silver at his paint factory in Birstall where he outlined three models for a promotion push. At County, he had no money to spend but coached intensively and, he conceded, had the good fortune to enable a miracle. With Wednesday he employed very modest outlays to enhance his squad when and where possible, ran the players' socks off on notorious Monday cross-country runs through the Derwent Valley, proved the worth of his efficient style and system with results and established a structure to which each player was committed. He had proved he could do both, he pointed out, but there were no guarantees and, one suspects, no point for him in leaving a top-flight club for one fourth from bottom of the Second Division if the policy was to rely on a healthy slice of luck either way. Finally he outlined his preferred option, a more ambitious strategy of investment in transfer fees, salaries and long-term planning, presenting them with a 10-year blueprint on restructuring Leeds United and turning it into a club that would sustain itself among the elite by producing its own players to star in a rebuilt ground. A virtuous circle would ultimately produce a truly modern club.

For a club perennially stuck in the past it must have been a godsend. Silver took notes throughout and pledged his support to Howard's third way. Fotherby was detailed with raising the money through commercial deals, pushing through his plans for corporate hospitality, executive facilities for wealthier fans and merchandising. Wilkinson, after stalling momentarily over Silver's insistence that Fotherby would be his point man, was persuaded that he could develop a positive working relationship with the bombastic Bill and signed the contract. 'Wilky' of Wednesday, as he called himself, was no more. Sergeant Wilko was born.

He almost cocked the whole project up by starting with a run of only two defeats in his first 22 games with Billy Bremner's squad plus a couple of quick, economical signings scouted while at Hillsborough. Before they lost twice in a week against West Brom and Ipswich, Wilkinson had taken them from 21st to eighth and merely a point behind the play-off spots. Crowds were edging encouragingly up and Fotherby was selling the club throughout the city. Going up the Plan B way would have satisfied Wilkinson's competitive instincts but left them immediately vulnerable to relegation. Plan A was designed specifically to negate 'yo-yo' syndrome. Premature promotion with players he felt unsuited to his style – John Sheridan, who was living it up too much around town, Mark Aizlewood, who flicked the Vs and screamed at the Kop to "fuck off" after one too many mass groans at his wayward passing – would have left him with a dilemma. There would be pressure to give some he was unsure about a chance instead of embarking on a costly, wholesale refit in the summer. The spring tailing off benefited him but he did not recognise it at the time.

But that's not to say that it was not a successful season. Noel Blake and Vince Hilaire, two black players who had suffered disgusting racial abuse when playing at Elland Road for Portsmouth, had been signed by Bremner in the summer of 1987 and their presence alongside a concerted campaign organised by the pioneering protest group, Leeds Fans United Against Fascism and Racism, began to drive the National Front away from the ground. Neither had the careers they had hoped for at Elland Road but just by coming to United and their willingness to confront the bigots helped the detoxification process, particularly when the club belatedly got on board and funded a community department under the St Lucia-born former Bradford City right-back Ces Podd. The triumph over the Bulldog sellers and bonehead, far-right recruitment squads plus growing intolerance for the prejudiced poison some still spewed at black players was more valuable work than promotion. Elevating attitudes is more difficult than upgrading a team.

At the end of March, following Manchester United's FA Cup quarter-final defeat by Nottingham Forest, Alex Ferguson rang Wilkinson to let him know that the player he had been trying to buy for the past two years was now available. Gordon Strachan was 32 and Ferguson, who had inherited him twice when taking over at Pittodrie and Old Trafford, now thought him finished as a First Division force. Over-familiarity had blinded both men to each other's virtues and Leeds were the grateful beneficiaries. They had to fight off Wednesday and Strachan's friend and former manager, Ron Atkinson, which they accomplished with a fat contract doubling his wages and their faith in his transformative impact. "Leeds were standing still, I was standing still," says Strachan. "When I met Bill and Howard I thought: 'OK. They've asked me to do something here.' I was given a responsibility to get the team promoted, a leader to get the team into the top league and it was great for me because I'd really been missing that for a couple of years. I believed them because I could tell they also had a real sense of responsibility. Leeds were in a dire way. It really was a last throw of the dice financially. They would have been in trouble if it didn't work."

They paid £300,000 for Strachan and £500,000 for the Tottenham centre-half Chris Fairclough, a smooth, quick stopper who suffered only by comparison to Des Walker, the player who replaced him at Nottingham Forest. There were 11 games of the season to go, enough time to regroup and push on for a play-off place but a side of cliques – the men of the future and those of the past – could not click and they finished in 10th.

A fortnight after the end of the season and on the day Arsenal beat Liverpool to win the title at Anfield by virtue of Michael Thomas' last-minute goal, Don Revie died at the age of 61. He had been diagnosed with motor neurone disease in 1987, two years after returning to the UK following eight in Abu Dhabi, Dubai and Cairo. He first noticed numbness in his legs while playing golf, a hobby that had taken over Don and Elsie's lives in retirement, whether at their homes in Spain, Wentworth or when they moved to Kinross. The family sought experimental treatment in the US and Soviet Union and the *News of the World* used the latter trip to confect a story announcing he had been cured in Moscow. The rag's depravity was well-established long before it was shut down in 2011 but the Revies did not sue. He had been burned by his experiences in 1979 when the high court overturned the FA's 10-year ban on him managing in England for resigning his job with the national team and moving to the UAE. Mr Justice Cantley upheld his appeal against the unlawful ban but used the remarks made in his judgment to lambaste the victor, citing Revie's "disloyalty, discourtesy and selfishness". Revie could consider himself lucky. Six months earlier Cantley had presided over Jeremy Thorpe's trial for conspiracy to murder his former lover Norman Scott and attacked the prosecution's witnesses with such brazen prejudice that Peter Cook turned his summing up into one of the great satirical tours de force of the century. Revie had no such champion and was gravely wounded by the experience. In 1988 he returned to Elland Road, distressingly frail and confined to an electric wheelchair, for a fund-raising testimonial. All his 'sons' bar the pariah Gary Sprake, were there to greet and pay tribute to him but he was too weak to stay to watch the match. When his death was announced, the West Stand gates were festooned with scarves and shirts and became a temporary shrine. A van-load of supporters went to pay their respects at his funeral in Edinburgh alongside his 'boys' and also Kevin Keegan and they were warmly welcomed by Elsie and Don's children. In the 88 years either side of Revie's reign, the club has won one major trophy. Manchester United put up a statue to Sir Matt Busby in 1996, Liverpool to Bill Shankly in 1997. Both clubs enjoyed success before and after their two greatest managers. Yet it took Leeds United until 2012 to honour Don Revie, the man who made them, in the same fashion. Had they ever really deserved him?

One of Howard Wilkinson's first acts as manager had been to remove the memorabilia of the Revie era, the photographs, the trophies and pennants. He wanted the club to stop being a dusty, threadbare mausoleum and become a living, vibrant entity once more. Bremner's protégés such as David Batty and Simon Grayson had hung around doing the boots after training and revelled in the manager's old war stories. But Wilkinson imposed a structure – banishing the homely, ad hoc approach of his predecessor – and drove through sprucing up projects to replace the dilapidated wire around the training ground, sort out the antiquated laundry, generally tart the pace up after years of neglect.

Wilkinson isn't at all how he seems. Yes, the hunger for learning that nourished his teaching career when he dropped down from Brighton into the semi-pro game pigeon-holed him as didactic. His thoughtfulness and tendency to weigh every word fed into his dour public image yet his players remember a tinder-dry sense of humour and his pragmatism. His fitness regime and the sacrifices it entailed enforced changes to the diet while his rigorous drilling of set-pieces and his belief in the importance of the second ball, especially the knockdowns and flick-ons from goalkicks and long punts, lumped him in with the long-ball school. It was part of his make-up, not all of it. He dressed like a dandy, with a fondness for light suits and co-ordinated ties and pocket squares. Wilkinson was well-read, liked good wine, malts and Havana cigars, very much a Mercedes saloon man in contrast to Bremner's station wagon. Above all, though, he had an overriding credo, as outlined by his right-hand man, Mick Hennigan, to the author Dave Simpson. "At Leeds it was about creating chaos, especially in the penalty box," he said. "That was the theory underpinning it all."

In the summer of 1989, Wilkinson set about recruiting the men who could put his ideas into practice, bringing in Mel Sterland, an attacking right-back with a mule-kick shot and belting Doodlebug crosses, Jim Beglin, a bright, quick Double-winning full-back with Liverpool on the comeback trail from injury, the veterans John McClelland and Mickey Thomas (who hardly featured in the following campaign), Scottish winger John Hendrie and the pantomime villain of English football, Vinnie Jones from Wimbledon. Netting off the nine disposals including Sheridan, the only one that was mourned, and adding on Fairclough Strachan and Carl Shutt from the March spree meant an investment of £2.3m funded by Silver with some money fronted by sponsors including Burton Group and Umbro.

Jones attracted all the coverage. The media saw the man who had spat on the 'This is Anfield' sign, twisted Gazza's knackers, executed a brutal hit-job on Steve McMahon in the FA Cup Final and brawled his way to notoriety triggered by inflammatory managers and his chairman at Wimbledon. Wilkinson saw a leader. During a Wimbledon game at Arsenal, Wilkinson had witnessed Jones nearly throttling one of his own players, the midfielder Detzi Kruszynski, for not tracking back and helping out his defence. He turned to Hennigan and said: "That's the man we want." He did not want an enforcer who would go round clogging the opposition, though he artfully used the reputation Jones carried with him as a psychological weapon. He identified Jones as the man who could instil a team spirit of such passionate intensity backed up by fear of retribution that no player would dare cheat a team-mate by not giving everything all the time.

Jones established the new order in the most Vinnie Jones-way possible, by chinning Bobby Davison, one of the Bremner holdovers who was a mainstay of the canteen snipers. That Davison knuckled down afterwards to make telling contributions to promotion is a testament to his own character as well as Jones' initiative. Jones, who actually hated running, set the standard in the arduous cross-country during pre-season, not by winning but because, in spite of obvious exhaustion when he finished third, he went back out to run with a straggler, Chris O'Donnell, and buddied up with someone who was about to sink, chivvying them back into safe harbour.

"Dylan Kerr, who was largely in the background, played every now and then but he was always at the front in training," says Strachan. "And Vinnie led the group along. We didn't need a fitness coach. We had three or four players to drag everyone in their wake. We didn't need anyone to tell us our heart rate was up there. It was always up there but our attitude was 'never mind, we've got to go again. If you feel you can't go, stay with me. I'll be there. Stay with me until you drop'. We made ourselves super fit."

They lost 5-2 at Newcastle on opening day without the injured Jones but he returned from the bench for the first home game against Middlesbrough and was an instant hit, greeted with fervent acclaim when he came on and set up a spawny winner. For a while he was everywhere in Leeds, hooking up with countless commercial partners yet at the forefront in every community endeavour, giving his time to charities and hospitals, taking David Batty and Gary Speed under his wing and behaving with such charm and dedication that the city's affection for him is undying 30 years on. His influence on the field was equally profound. Although he concentrated on winning the ball, giving it and intimidating the opposition with a snarl, his touch grew increasingly assured and he scored some cracking goals, especially an Exocet volley from 30 yards against Hull and a deft near-post finish to beat West Ham in October.

The London papers went berserk after the victory at Upton Park, ascending the steps to their pulpits to blow the dust off their 'Dirty Leeds' clichés. "It was with some justification that Wilkinson expressed surprise at the allegations afterwards that his team were negative, cynical and overtly aggressive," wrote The Times' Clive White. "After all, Leeds have been displaying much of the same 'qualities' on and off for the past two decades." With a further sideswipe at Jones, the ignoble savage, the sermonising ends after burying the salient point that zero Leeds players were booked while three of West Ham's were. Wilkinson defended his players forcefully and attacked the hysterical tone, employing the shrewdness and confidence that made players as diverse as Strachan and Jones devoted followers. In any case it was Leeds' offside trap and their direct tactics rather than the recklessness of their tackling that really offended their detractors. In 45 appearances that season, Jones received merely two yellow cards.

United went top after a 2-0 away victory over Middlesbrough in early December and stayed there for the rest of the season, not without several dicey moments. At appropriate junctures during the campaign Wilkinson stiffened their mettle with the purchase of Lee Chapman and Chris Kamara, who were both in the side on Easter Monday when Leeds walloped third-placed Sheffield United 4-0 at Elland Road. Towards the end of it, and with the insouciance of youth and startling composure, Speed glided up the left for 50 yards, controlling the ball with a velvety instep to sweep in Leeds' fourth roared on by a shamelessly partisan commentary from John Boyd that culminated in a rasping cry of "Go on Gary Speed, get one yourself, son." The memory of it will never fade.

United's first home defeat of the season by Barnsley left them two to play and only a point ahead of the Blades, who had a game in hand, and two above Newcastle. Leicester's equaliser in their penultimate game left them at the mercy of others if they ended the match with only a point and, with seconds to go, that seemed their fate until the captain Strachan, gaunt, he says, with worry, arrowed a left-foot shot from 20 yards into the top corner, his 16th goal of the season. "Every now and then I get a feeling in my left foot that is the same feeling I had when I scored that goal," Strachan says. "Every training session, every run I had to school, every time I threw up and had been sick because of training, every knock back I got, every horrible game I played in, it was all kind of destined for that one moment. It made it all worthwhile. Just for that one moment. I can always live off that for the rest of my life. I don't have any memorabilia in my house but I have a painting by Brian West of my celebration of that goal and it's the only thing I have up."

The energetic and enthusiastic Kamara, the perfect tonic as a replacement for the exhausted David Batty, set up Chapman's winner in the final match at Bournemouth which earned promotion on the south coast during an afternoon of larceny, looting and affray by some of the thousands of Leeds supporters who made the journey down to be able to say, like Max Boyce, "I was there". Five thousand made the trip for the Bank Holiday weekend, 2,700 without tickets. The police made 150 arrests, 50 people sought hospital treatment for injuries and £40,000 worth of damage was inflicted on pubs and shops. For the country, understandably, it overshadowed the team's achievement. This element of 'sick filth' of a club painted as irredeemably degenerate were plastered across the Sunday papers. Over three years there had been a de-escalation in the violence, certainly of the so-called organised variety, as several prominent members of the Service Crew were prosecuted in dubious circumstances. The club had banned more than 100 supporters from the ground but was powerless to prevent anyone exercising their right to lawful assembly or travelling anywhere without tickets. It was why, in August following an FA inquiry, it protested the proposed sanction of a four-match closure of Elland Road for the first repeat of similar disorder and the "withdrawal of the club's membership and affiliation to the Association", i.e. shutting United down, for a second breach. "It leaves us on a knife-edge," said Silver. "Any future trouble could see the club slung out of the League for the actions of people who do not have the best interests of Leeds United at heart."

While *The Sunday Telegraph* chronicled Bournemouth's 18-hour ordeal exhaustively the next morning, its correspondent, Christopher Davies, focused his match report on the distaste he felt for the club and for Wilkinson, giving them no leeway for anxiety or the difficulty of playing on a rock-hard pitch. "Leeds will not be welcome visitors in the First Division," he wrote, "both for the way they play and for the loutish manner in which some of their followers behave... The baddies won and the goodies lost."

Away from the carping and the wounds inflicted by some of their own supporters, the players emerged from their brief dressing-room party to board the coach for the long journey home. "I found myself a quiet spot at the front of the bus and just sat there for five hours with a stupid grin on my face," says Strachan. "I don't think I spoke to anybody. That was my celebration. Winning the top league [in 1992] was a bonus. Most of us who were brought in there, and for Howard and Bill as well, we had to get promoted. It was the main thing. Because of the momentum we built up over a couple of years we were able to go on and win the top league, but for me 1990 was just huge. Winning the Second Division was far, far more important for the club and for me."

Leeds' first season back in the First Division for eight years was the most enjoyable of all Wilkinson's time at the club because they played a vibrant attacking style, pulled off some surprising victories and, compared with the seasons sandwiching it, there was none of the tension generated when winning something is tantalisingly close. Bill Fotherby brokered £1m deals for the return of John Lukic, after seven years at Arsenal where he had won the title in 1989, and for Leicester City's captain, Gary McAllister, an elegant, serenely gifted midfielder whose transfer signposted a change of approach. Leeds had been helped in their pursuit by Brian Clough's rudeness. McAllister, who yearned to play for Clough, was teased for wearing cowboy boots and watched the Forest manager insult his agent. The game had changed, not for the better, and Clough shipwrecked himself on the old attitudes. Fotherby was cannier, buttered the Scot and his representative up, offered him an outstanding contract and threw in his Mercedes which McAllister coveted. The signing broke Vinnie Jones' heart and though he tried to laugh it off with a famous prank involving a 12-bore shotgun, he took his demotion hard, feeling it humiliated him with the peers he had worked so hard to win over, and he left for Sheffield United far too hastily and in a huff. Chrissie Whyte, another former Arsenal player, joined

Fairclough at the heart of the defence bringing the robustness and occasional Jack Charlton-style, Bambi-esque foray to a complementary partnership.

Whyte was one of six players to feature in every League game in 1990-91, while Chapman, McAllister and Speed were also ever present in the six FA Cup and seven League Cup ties. Only Tottenham at Elland Road, with Paul Gascoigne and Gary Lineker in scintillating form three months on from Italia 90, and Liverpool at Anfield exposed a gulf in experience and class as Leeds stormed up the table. The elegant arc of outswinging crosses from Strachan, Speed and Sterland, bent disconcertingly early at full pelt on to the head of Lee Chapman, caught out countless defences and the centre-forward bagged 28 goals. When he landed face first on the cinder path at White Hart Lane and knocked himself out, breaking his nose in two places and shredding the bridge of his nose so severely the bone was exposed, so devout was his determination not to miss the League Cup semi-final against Manchester United eight days later that he took advice from the boxing trainer Brendan Ingle and painted a resin on his wounds to protect the plastic surgeon's salvage job. As Chapman ruefully acknowledged, even Bryan Robson, foolhardy with his courage on numerous occasions, looked at him across the centre-circle as if he was deranged. Wembley ultimately proved beyond them. Manchester United won a raucous, two-legged semi-final 3-1. In the FA Cup, after seven hours of football without a single booking in a fourth-round match and three subsequent replays against Arsenal, who would go on to win the title, they fell behind for the first time in the fourth match of the tie and could not recover.

In mid-April champions Liverpool came to Elland Road and the first half staged the last hurrah of the mainstays of Kenny Dalglish's amazingly fluent attacking team of the late Eighties. John Barnes, Ray Houghton, Jan Molby Peter Beardsley and Ian Rush tore Leeds to shreds. They went 4-0 up after 27 minutes, Barnes tormented Sterland and disappointment had given way to bemusement by half-time. There was very little defiance in the stands but in the dressing room, Wilkinson invited his players to stop fannying about and revert to what they did best. In the second half, Chapman domineered Glenn Hysén so pitilessly that it effectively ended his career in England. He pulled one back, then Shutt scored a second but when Ian Rush made it 2-5 with 12 minutes to go all seemed lost. Not for Chapman though, who bulleted in two headers and had a goal disallowed for a non-existent foul on Mike Hooper. It was the middle of three glorious seasons of frenzied atmospheres at Elland Road, but no matchday was more boisterous, none more enjoyable despite the defeat. Liverpool looked rattled and haunted as they trudged off. Saved by the clock.

So much for being unwelcome visitors, Leeds finished fourth, quietening their critics with their swift, forward passing and audacious commitment to blitzing opposition in the first 15 minutes of games at Elland Road when they attacked with the fervour of an upended wasps' nest. The supporters named Batty, now capped by England, player of the year but he was only one quarter of an exquisitely balanced midfield which possessed each mandatory quality for a League-winning side – inspirational dynamism, grace, grit and guile. At the age of 34 Strachan was elected Footballer of the Year by the Football Writers' Association. There was no talk of goodies and baddies now, only the Leeds captain's brains and craft. Not for the last time a writer afflicted by premature adjudication ended up in an embarrassed mess.

Wilkinson tried to buy Beardsley and Dean Saunders that summer but settled for the twins Rod and Ray Wallace, England internationals Steve Hodge and Tony Dorigo plus two of his old Wednesday trainees, Jon Newsome and David Wetherall. The six cost £4.1m but having sold 20,000 season tickets and signed up to join the breakaway Premier League in a year's time, with crowds now regularly hitting (a much diminished) capacity and a new TV deal inflated by the resurgence in interest imminent, Leeds were ready to go all in.

Wilkinson plotted the fixtures on a wallchart in his office, ascribing each game a value according to his expectation of the points to be gleaned. He saw it as a systematic path to the title and for 11 unbeaten matches at the start of the season that took Leeds to second, it accurately mapped their rise. They hammered Southampton 4-0 and against certain teams Dorigo's graceful acceleration up the left wing, which matched the galloping Sterland on the right, left opponents with no respite. The blistering speed of Rod Wallace and Dorigo was especially incisive away from home, allowing Leeds to strike on the counter but the team's composure and control during 1-0 victories over Chelsea and Liverpool were evidence of an evolution just as crucial as the injection of pace.

United made their live TV debut for the season at Aston Villa in November and won 4-1, Wilkinson cleverly using a flexible defence to switch between 5-3-2 and 4-4-2 to neuter Villa's wingers. All four goals came from crosses and the afternoon, which confirmed Leeds at the top of the table, was the perfect distillation of their style – 'chaos in the box' created by clever set-piece routines, the use of the flick-on to create gaps for the attacking side to invade between defenders and Strachan's off-the-cuff brilliance. They were better still in their next away outing in font of the ITV cameras in the new year, a 6-1 victory over Sheffield Wednesday, again in the yellow away kit but significantly, this time, completed in the absence of the injured Batty and Strachan. Spurred on by a sense of injustice after a brazen dive from Gordon Watson had conned the referee into awarding a penalty, Leeds shredded a side that would go on to finish third, terrorising them left, right and centre with a bombardment of shots and crosses.

Three matches at the turn of the year against Manchester United, who had not won the title since 1967 but had been playing with such brio that they convinced the media, their supporters and army of fellow travellers that their day had come, were portrayed as season-defining for Leeds. The trio began with a draw in the league at Elland Road, Sterland scoring the equaliser from the penalty spot with 11 minutes to go, a point that left Manchester United on top by two points and with two games in hand. Leeds were drawn at home against them in both cups and deservedly lost in the Rumbelows Cup as Manchester United rallied from being thrashed by QPR on New Year's Day. They improved in the FA Cup tie though Strachan's sciatica, which had now become chronic, flared up and he missed a 1-0 defeat in which Chapman shattered his wrist when he fell heavily at the back post while craning his neck to head a difficult chance into the side-netting. Three days earlier he had scored his hat-trick at Hillsborough; now his anguish at the pain and the shape of his arm, nauseatingly fractured in two places and bent as if someone were torturing a pipe-cleaner man, suggested the team's attacking fulcrum would be out for months.

First Wilkinson improvised with Speed at centre-forward for a couple of games then used the loan market to sign Tony Agana from Notts County and Eric Cantona, a 25-year-old France forward from Nimes who had announced his retirement in December following a French Federation hearing convened to impose his eighth disciplinary suspension in five years. He had been persuaded by Michel Platini to try again in England and Wilkinson, striking with the cruelty of an eBay last-second gazumper, offered him a deal while he was ostensibly on trial with a procrastinating Sheffield Wednesday.

Such is the Cantona mystique that what he stood for is more significant than what he did. Manchester United see him as a kind of divine figure with shamanic gifts who healed their club. In some vague sense they are right, he was a transformative signing who had the skill and certainty to allay their neuroses after two-and-a-half decades without winning the League. To Leeds United's title-winning side, made up of tough, seasoned professionals, he was an embellishment whose goals, charisma and radiant smile, like a man emerging from an exorcism, were his main contributions. When he left for Old Trafford, he was cast out as a Judas. For 28 years they have loved to hate him but they would have loved to carry on loving him more.

Cantona had not played for more than two months when he made his debut as a substitute in February during Leeds' second League defeat of the season, a 2-0 reverse at Oldham where the wind-chill compounded the misery. After starting the draw with Everton, he was back on the bench when Chapman returned with a cast to lead the line against Luton. Both scored and Chapman, defying the club doctor's wishes, was ever-present until the end of the season although his wrist did not fully heal for another four months. The victory was vital because Manchester United had now played their games in hand and only had a two-point lead. Strachan missed a penalty in a 0-0 draw with Aston Villa that would have put Leeds back in first place and later in March Sterland, who had been having cortisone injections to mask the pain of a bad ankle tendon injury, broke down and was out for the season. In fact he would make only three more appearances before he had to retire at 32 and Leeds lost their most exuberant player. The game was never as uncomplicated when 'Zico' finished. Speed was moved to right-back in the interim, then Newsome, a centre-half, played in a 4-1 midweek defeat by QPR who inflicted on them the same Ray Wilkins masterclass that had done for Manchester United. Three weeks later, after grinding out draws with Arsenal and West Ham, Manchester City beat them 4-0 at Maine Road when their offside trap stuttered and they were caught chasing the game. "We are not feeling suicidal," said Wilkinson. "It's a question of getting back to work on Monday and making sure that one mistake doesn't lead to another." They were now a point behind Manchester United with five to play while the leaders also had a game in hand.

Talk of 'bottling it' or Leeds cracking from the strain was bandied around. But those three matches against Manchester United did prove decisive as they saddled the victors with five more matches to add to their additional four in the Cup Winners' Cup. Wilkinson resorted to core principles with his selection, told Cantona he would be used as an impact sub rather than a starter and he came on to score a wonderful, ball-juggling goal against Chelsea in a victory that restored their equilibrium. Over the Pennines Manchester United were held in the derby and could only manage a point at Luton despite the plastic Kenilworth Road pitch, a constant Ferguson bugbear, having been outlawed and replaced by grass at the start of the season. The Leeds manager's old-fashioned caution about Liverpool made him set the team up defensively for the trip to Anfield and he was delighted with a point yet Lukic had been called on to make so many saves that Wilkinson's heart must have been in his mouth by the end. Ever the rationalist, he said that the title race had still not reached the stage where desperate measures were called for to chase impractical targets. It was "Don't panic' but without Corporal Jones' flapping.

He was right, too, because before Leeds won at Coventry on the evening of Easter Monday, Manchester United lost their first game in hand against Nottingham Forest. Strachan, by now conspicuously in severe discomfort, soldiered on until they had put the game beyond Coventry's reach and returned Leeds to the top of the table. Two days later Manchester United lost at West Ham and Leeds' title fate was back in their hands, a point clear with two games each left.

Leeds United's Sunday trip to Sheffield United was brought forward to lunchtime to allow ITV to broadcast it and Manchester United's visit to Anfield. Denied the anaesthetic of any time in the pub before the early kick-off, it's a wonder everyone survived the tension of a stressful, chaotic and often farcical 3-2 away victory. When Brian Gayle headed the deciding own goal past poor Mel Rees it was the prelude to the best day any Leeds supporter between the ages of 50 and about 35 can probably remember. Later that afternoon Liverpool beat Manchester United, Howard Wilkinson finished his Sunday dinner, finally accepted that Leeds were champions and stuck on a daft hat to pose for the photographers with a glass of champagne. While the manager had made an ostentatious show of not watching the match because the result was beyond his control, Batty, McAllister and Cantona watched it at Chapman's house with an ITV camera Goggleboxing their words and facial reactions. McAllister is supposed to have been unaware that Ferguson was still hooked up to an earpiece after his interview and could hear the midfielder's ribald objections to the Manchester United manager's lack of grace at losing the title. It was excusable in the situation, however Ferguson's initially choked, colourless tribute to Wilkinson and his players fed into the myth that Manchester United had lost it rather than Leeds deserving to win it. Victory over Norwich in the final game after a week on the lash established the winning margin as four points and Leeds could also point to more victories, goals and fewer defeats. Had Don Revie been so publicly sour when Matt Busby's Manchester United pipped them on goal average in 1965, we would never have heard the end of it.

The begrudging attitude of Ferguson and some of the journalists who craved the better story of Manchester United's long drought ending did not take the gloss off it. The city centre was rammed on the Sunday morning after the last game to greet the players' parade with 250,000 people, far more than had ever turned out to receive Revie's team. Wilkinson's courage and organisational zeal made it all possible as well as the astute recruitment funded by Silver and Fotherby which had seed-funded their rise. Three full seasons into a 10-year plan and United had already won their first First Division title for 18 years. Wilkinson's dry diffidence was nowhere to be seen that day as he saluted the supporters and he laughed along with the payers when Cantona stole the show, coerced by Sterland into reluctantly taking the microphone. "Why I love you?" he asked. "I don't know why, but I love you." There were no hearts left for him to melt in Leeds on that sun-dappled May morning. A club no longer living in the past could now put the old pictures back up. A vibrant present promised a bright future. Optimism was the only currency in town.

23

'WE LOST ALL THE GOOD HABITS WE JUST ACQUIRED'

While the champions of England were scattered across the globe in the summer of 1992, the Conservative government, surprisingly re-elected to serve a fourth term a couple of weeks before Leeds United won the last First Division title, were struggling to contain their vitriolic divisions over Europe. BSkyB, which had won the TV rights to broadcast the new Premier League on their subscription-based satellite platform, placed commercials in the papers, on billboards and on rival, defeated channels, promising a 'whole new ball game', featuring one player from each of the 22 breakaway clubs. The obvious candidate for Leeds' representative would have been Gary Speed, Top Man's poster boy. He had let his hair grow out and now resembled a member of the Soup Dragons but, trying to emphasise tradition and not wanting to scare the horses, the marketing department picked Gordon Strachan, sporting a mullet and the puffy mainsail of the club's roomy new Admiral shirt. Rupert Murdoch's company continued its drive with a commercial boasting that its product was 'Alive and Kicking', which was certainly true of Strachan. Careful management of his sciatica and long rest had reduced the pain and restored his mobility. Howard Wilkinson, understandably, had bargained for his 35-year-old captain fading away and Mel Sterland, Strachan's right-side accomplice, making a full recovery. Consequently he paid £2m for Arsenal's David Rocastle, a beautifully balanced, sinuous dribbler with a forbidding, streetwise resistance to intimidation, to take Strachan's place. Then Scott Sellars was brought back from Blackburn, overloading Leeds' already healthy midfield resources. Neither were needed because of the two title stalwarts, it was Sterland who was finished. He jacked it in after four unsuccessful operations on his shredded ankle tendons, leaving a hole at right-back with Leeds' transfer budget long since blown.

Promotion in 1990 had encouraged the board to resurrect the mothballed plans for the south-east corner and, after 14 years, complete the original design. During the 1991-92 season, supporters were invited to pay £500 to buy an East Stand bond and fund the demolition of the Lowfields Road Stand – circumcised at its exposed end by the erection of the South Stand 17 years previously – and its cavernous, cantilevered replacement. For their investment supporters were entitled to buy season tickets at 1992 prices for the next seven years discounted by £100 each time, which proved an attractive bargain for those who could afford it, plus the honour of having their names inscribed on the new seats in what looked suspiciously like Letraset. The council put up £2m of the £5.5m cost, bondholders contributed a seven-figure sum which fell short of the £2m target, with the rest funded by increased revenues, trading and directors' loans. It took shape over the course of the season, the hulking, predatory steel skeleton expanding week-by-week and looming over the Lowfields diehards enjoying their last few months on the 'Pop Side' terrace.

Sky's 'whole new ball game' was prophetic. Football's function as a driver of income and profit for global broadcasters and advertisers has commodotised the league, turning elite clubs into rootless brands roaming the Earth, searching for markets to colonise. This fundamental change to the nature of the game the birth of FA Premier League presaged was accompanied by a practical one, one which hobbled an integral feature of Wilkinson's tactics. The International Football Association Board had been tasked with redressing the imbalance between defence and attack visible at Italia 90 and latched on to the way back-passes to the goalkeeper stifled enterprising play. Too many teams would fanny around, wasting time with boring passing across the back four before retreating to the safe haven of the keeper's grasp if a forward came close. Wilkinson's Leeds did not use the ball in that way but they were victims of the insertion of a clause into Law 12 prohibiting the keeper from picking up a pass deliberately played to him by a team-mate's foot. Because Wilkinson wanted his players to push high up the pitch to feed on knock-downs from Lee Chapman, when the ball was passed back to John Lukic, only the centre-backs and David Batty would be within 40 yards of him. It is far easier to find the proper trajectory to bypass midfield with precision when punting the ball than it is fly-kicking one that is on the move. It would take time to adjust. Where laws, tactics and personnel had all been in harmony when they won the title, the blend was all to cock in the inaugural Premier League season and the comedown from a progressively intensifying three-season high was like a crash.

Completing Eric Cantona's purchase after his loan deal expired in the summer was unavoidable. Wilkinson had never been truly convinced of his suitability as a starter for a team built on work-rate and a distinct method. Cantona's technical skill and imaginative ability to extemporise added a dimension to the side's attack but there was no room for a free spirit in Wilkinson's system. Strachan and Gary McAllister, as penetrative talents as Cantona, had curbed their instincts. A licence for adventure came with responsibility under Wilkinson. For all the manager's doubts, after the "I love you" moment, Leeds had no choice and agreed to pay Nimes a £1.3m fee. Cantona spoke rarely in public and when he did say something it was usually epigrammatic and elusive. Hence everyone projected colour on to the blank canvas. He answered a yearning for something different from the Leeds United norm where, since John Charles, team had trumped the individual, side had been put before self.

Is it shallow to want a superstar of your own? Possibly, but it is understandable. Cantona made Leeds fans feel special and answered an unacknowledged desire for a touch of sophistication, someone to make other supporters' envious. It was like a self-made millionaire who grafted all his life amid the muck and nettles buying himself a Bentley and pronouncing: "I deserve this." His hat-tricks in the 4-3 victory over Liverpool in the Charity Shield and in the 5-0 home defeat of Spurs before August was out suggested that Wilkinson's misgivings might be misplaced.

They were not. Ten players filled in at right-back over the course of the season including the unfortunate, virtual 'unidexter' Sterland, channelling Mr Spiggott's audition for Tarzan in *One Leg Too Few*. Leeds' vulnerability was an open wound. The 4-1 hammering by newly promoted Middlesbrough at Ayresome Park in the third game of the season was more instructive of the team's state than Cantona's goals. Rod Wallace moved out to the right, Strachan started on the bench and Cantona played off Chapman, operating more as a finisher than the creative hub he became at Manchester United. While Chapman was adept at holding the ball up, Cantona had surer control than Wallace but less pace and Leeds became a mishmash of confused styles that made them particularly brittle away from home, where, humiliatingly, they could not manage a win all season and just seven draws in a year wrecked by a kind of agoraphobia. The other two promoted sides – Ipswich and Blackburn – whacked four and three goals past them at Portman Road and Ewood Park respectively and they conceded four in a total of six away matches of meek ineptitude. Leeds took merely five points from a possible 18 off the clubs who would go on to be relegated and were beaten 3-1 at Elland Road by Forest, who finished bottom, in their first home defeat for 20 months. It proved their only reverse at home and their saving grace was the 12 wins which prevented them from emulating Manchester City in 1938, relegated a year after winning the title. Strachan called a team meeting in April before they played Blackburn at home and bollocked those whom he felt were not pulling their weight. He scored a hat-trick the following day, playing with furious intensity, and the victory, their last of the season, proved vital in keeping them up by two points.

In less than a year they had lost their mojo. Under Wilkinson their foot-to-the-floor drive and frantic starts had been allied with a rigour at set-pieces and the shrewdness of Strachan and McAllister. The coalition cracked because of tactical confusion, a glaring hole and the inevitable staleness of certain players whose achievements had already exceeded their dreams. Wilkinson, too, came over as ratty and dogmatic. Gratitude evaporated and the manager found himself increasingly the butt of criticism. It did not help that he lacked the PR skills to deflect it and favoured sarcasm instead. "He's the last English manager to win the top title," says Strachan. "There are other managers who are given legendary status because they keep a club up from relegation or something like that and you're talking about a man taking a team from fifth-bottom of the second division to winning the top division in three years. It's all been passed over because he wasn't media friendly. Not that he wanted to be a 'character' so he presented himself entirely as he is."

On 16 September 1992, 'Black Wednesday' in the UK, the day the Conservative government hiked interest rates from 10 to 15 per cent in a single day before reluctantly surrendering and pulling the pound out of the Exchange Rate Mechanism at 7pm, Leeds played their first European Cup match for 17 years. The new format, which had been in place for a year, was still confined to title-winners and scheduled two knockout rounds before the Champions League stage began, featuring the last eight teams. Leeds were drawn against VfB Stuttgart and played pretty well in the first half of the first leg in the Neckerstadion. Wilkinson used Batty at right-back, Gary Speed in central midfield and Strachan on the left, giving Rocastle his debut on the right. Rocastle missed a decent chance, Cantona had a lob and a forceful header saved and the keeper also blocked a Strachan shot. In the second half Cantona twanged his hamstring yet instead of booting the ball out of play so he could go off, he tried to arrow a curling, crossfield ball with his damaged leg. Before it had left his boot, Wilkinson could be heard on the TV coverage yelling an exasperated "Fucking hell". When the ball was picked off and sent up to Fritz Walter to open the scoring with a chip,

Wilkinson had hands on both hips. Cantona's apparent nonchalance when substituted must have riled him even more. Walter scavenged a second from a Lukic parry after Steve Hodge banjaxed the offside trap and Chris Fairclough, who had seen his partner Chris Whyte fall flat on his arse to give Walter the space to score the opener, slipped and let Andreas Buck bag the third. In 17 minutes they threw the game away with three cheap goals.

"The last lesson you learn is the first thing you forget," said Wilkinson, who had employed a man-marking system for midfield and centre-backs. "We lost all the good habits we just acquired. Suddenly, we were chasing a goal when there was no need to." Cantona had let the side down and the players opened themselves up trying to make amends for it when they should have settled for a 1-0 defeat.

In the second leg, their sixth match in 17 days, Cantona was back and at his magnificent best, cushioning a superb headed pass for Speed to thunder past Eike Immel on the volley, scoring himself to make it 3-1 in the second-half and carving out numerous chances. While Guido Buchwald, the 1990 World Cup-winner, wrestled Chapman for the entire match, Cantona tormented the sweeper, Slobodan Djubicic. When Chapman headed the fourth Leeds had 10 minutes to find the winner and continued to bombard the goal but could not squeeze the ball past Immel who had earlier clawed one out that looked over the line. If only another moment of timid defending had not allowed Buck to score, it would have been the perfect performance, Wilkinson's Leeds at their very peak, one last hurrah for a side going over the top, roared on by an ardent crowd. At the end, though, they were eliminated on the away goals rule. They went out on their feet; Stuttgart's players lay supine on the pitch. Less than 24 hours later Leeds were still in Europe when Uefa, alerted by a TV viewer, accepted that Stuttgart had broken the tournament regulations by fielding four non-German players, one more than their allowance. As ITN's Alistair Stewart wryly put it: "They've got more foreign reserves than the Bank of England." Wrangling went on over the weekend and a Leeds delegation returned from Switzerland with the news that the match had been voided and awarded to them as a 3-0 victory, which conveniently set up a replay at a neutral venue the following Friday.

Camp Nou was chosen as the host and about 5,000 Leeds and Stuttgart fans, marooned in the second tier, were the only spectators. The 115,000 empty seats made for a strange atmosphere and after Leeds took the lead through a Strachan 25-yard strike, they went in level at half-time following another goal scored when a makeshift right-back was caught out of position. Cantona, who had not trained all week because of tonsillitis, was taken off after 80 minutes and within 60 seconds of his entrance, Carl Shutt headed a clearance, raced 80 yards upfield, played an inadvertent one-two off Buck's instep and ignored the urgent, profane yelling of the untracked Strachan to square it. He jinked to the right, suddenly tacked left and speared a low-shot across the keeper and into the centre of the goal. "He started in non-League, I took him to Sheffield Wednesday and now he ends up scoring the winner in a European Cup-tie," said Wilkinson. "It is *Roy of the Rovers* stuff."

'Roy' did not play in Europe again. Cantona started against Rangers in the second round at Ibrox. The Scottish champions had banned away supporters so Gary McAllister's dad, a lifelong Rangers fan, was one of the few to pierce the hostile cacophony when it was momentarily silenced by his son's first-minute goal, a rocket volley from 18 yards. Lukic, who had made several stunning saves to hold Stuttgart at bay, then punched in a corner, claiming to have been blinded by the floodlights and Leeds conceded a second from a corner before half-time. With the lesson of Stuttgart foremost, they focused on holding what they had in the second half, prizing their away goal above a draw.

Before the home leg, Coventry City's Stewart Robson crocked Batty, ruling him out for seven weeks and without him Leeds' creaking defence was left dangerously exposed. Mark Hateley scored a marvellous early volley and, when Leeds started to chase the game in the second half, dummied a pass to lose Newsome, raced down the left and fizzed over a back-post cross from which Ally McCoist scored. Leeds had reverted to the long ball too early and it took Strachan to calm them down and prompt more intelligently. Andy Goram made a string of fine saves in both halves, Cantona eventually broke through with a half-volley and set up Wallace late on with the deftest of flicks with the outside of his foot, a chance that Goram again blocked. Leeds were out, beaten by the better side over two legs. It should not be forgotten that Rangers in 1992 were the richest club in Britain and had invested £40m in players and facilities in the preceding four years. Elimination meant Leeds missed out on the £4m windfall six group-stage ties would have brought and left another chasm in the budget. To put that sum into perspective, Leeds had won £100,000 in prize money for winning the League Championship, 40 times more was on offer simply for qualifying for the last eight of the revamped European Cup.

That goal was Cantona's 14th and last for Leeds. He played one more game, picked to play up front in a 4-0 defeat by Man City, and hostility between him and Wilkinson, which had been quickening for weeks exploded in a transfer request. The manager had already sent him home from a trip to QPR and tried to arrange a discreet disposal back to the Continent where any damage he might inflict would be contained. But there were no offers until Bill Fotherby called Manchester United and asked to buy Denis Irwin. Alex Ferguson, working on information furnished by the France manager turned deep throat, Gérard Houllier, scoffed at the proposal then inquired whether Cantona was for sale. After some bluffing it transpired that he was and the deal was quickly struck for £1.3m. The backlash was immediate and rancorous. There was anger, of course, that it was 'to them' and a sadness because it seemed that under the stern headmaster Leeds were not entitled to beauty as well as success. The truth was that Wilkinson had taken him in desperation, never intending it to be a long-term deal and the more he was exposed to Cantona's indifference to authority and convention, the less he liked him. He tried to bend and play a more expansive style but Cantona would not meet him halfway and it left him in a bind with the other players. If a manager cannot impose discipline on one player, he cannot impose it on anyone. Something had to give and two stubborn men were relieved to be shot of each other. Fotherby's Micawberish approach to funds – "something will turn up" – also played its part. An instalment of £500,000 owed to Nimes fell due in November and the Champions League bounty had been cut off to them. It made sense to take the money and for Manchester United to exploit Leeds' predicament to pay only £1.3m for a leader who came to symbolise the club's sense of exceptionalism. "Eric likes to do what he likes, when he likes, because he likes it – and then fuck off," said Wilkinson. "We'd all want a bit of that." Stung by the criticism, Leeds refused to divulge why they had sold him, foolishly allowing innuendo to fill the breach. 'Sgt Wilko' had always been a tongue-in-cheek but affectionate nickname until 1992. From then on it spoke to perceptions of his rigidity. By contrast with Phil Silvers, Howard's platoon seemed to be part of the anti-fun regiment. A 17th-place finish after three seasons of tireless improvement fuelled dissent.

Travel psychosis and distinct signs of wear and tear in the first-team fabric were Wilkinson's first significant debits in the ledger book though the manager could point to a couple of major credits to complement those already accrued. The first was the building of the East Stand, undertaken by the construction firm owned by Peter Gilman, the key boardroom ally of Leslie Silver and Bill Fotherby. It seated 17,000, increasing Elland Road's capacity back to 40,000, would be fully functioning for the start of the new season and was brought in under budget. The second was the success of Paul Hart's academy whose senior team won the FA Youth Cup for the first time in the club's history, beating the defending champions Manchester United 4-1 in the two-legged final. Gary and Phil Neville, David Beckham, Paul Scholes, Nicky Butt were beaten home and away yet solely Noel Whelan of the victors had anything approaching a lasting top-flight career. Over the next couple of seasons Wilkinson tried to integrate Jamie Forrester, Kevin Sharp, Whelan, Mark Ford, Andy Couzens and Mark Tinkler into the first-team squad without the impact of Batty and Speed nor the crop of graduates who succeeded them four years later. It did not reflect badly on Wilkinson – Manchester United's 1992 team and Leeds 1997 side were the anomalies and the 1993 group the norm.

Leeds let Chapman and Whyte go in the summer of 1993 for nominal fees. The centre-forward had been top-scorer for three successive seasons but was 33 and Wilkinson explained that it was time for him to call it a day with Leeds. He bought Sheffield United's Leeds-born striker Brian Deane for £2.9m, then the second-highest English transfer fee, and David O'Leary, the 35-year-old Arsenal centre-half, signed on a free. The first signing hinted at a new approach, the second at a weakness for older players whom he hoped would repeat the Strachan alchemy by educating the youngsters while enjoying an Indian Summer on the field. Later he did the same with Nigel Worthington, 33, Ian Rush, 34, Mark Hateley, 35, and even brought back Chapman on loan at the age of 36. By that time he was deep in the bunker, trying to buy time for his youth players to emerge. He signed them for their character but most turned out to be derelict physical shells of once formidable footballers, costing Leeds a fortune in wages. O'Leary managed 10 games during his three-year contract after rupturing his Achilles in a 4-0 defeat by Norwich. His months in the physio room gave him a decent understanding of the club and its employees, its myths and ambitions, which would serve him in good stead a couple of years down the road.

Deane scored 11 goals in his first season, four fewer than he had scored for the Blades the year before. He lacked the attributes of an orthodox centre-forward – aerial power, adhesive technique to hold the ball up and dependable finishing. He was at his best running the channels, using his pace to gallop on to balls hit over the top and subsequently came into his own wide on the left but that was not what Leeds had sought and rectifying it presented Wilkinson with another expensive headache which dogged him until the end. The players, too, were often exasperated, playing perfect balls up the middle for the ghost of Lee Chapman and seeming bewildered when they bounced off Deane. They began the season shakily before a 14-match unbeaten run helped them climb to second by mid-December, a commendable if deceptive recovery given that Manchester United were 14 points ahead of them. Midway through their upsurge the board accepted Blackburn's £2.75m bid for Batty who was happy to leave. It is always foolish to conflate players with supporters. Batty was well-loved, a local lad with a nonchalant air who put himself about without fear or favour. His courage and short, rhythmic distribution was of the first rank but he was not sentimental about the club or the game. When Liverpool tapped him up in 1991, he indicated his positive interest and did the same when Kenny Dalglish rang him before making a formal Blackburn bid. He felt his career was stagnating at Leeds, did not like the training and fancied the salary hike. Leeds needed cash for payments on the stand and took the money. Cue more outrage. Having sold the fans' favourite Cantona who helped Manchester United to the title in his first season there, they now sold their second-favourite player who won the Premiership the following year at Ewood Park. Leeds would try to shift the blame, pointing out with justification that he wanted to go. It's a disingenuous argument – most players will leave for wealthier clubs if offered the chance after a bid has been accepted. Income dried up every autumn after the initial gush of TV and season-ticket receipts and cashflow demanded either Silver dug deep again or sold an asset. They chose the latter.

If centre-forward was a problem deferred, Wilkinson emphatically solved the right-back issue with a brilliant hunch. Gary Kelly, a perennially homesick Irish forward who had made four substitute appearances in the title-winning campaign, had thought he was about to be bombed out. "The year after winning the First Division, I was playing at Oakwell in the reserves, out on the right wing," Kelly says. "I didn't get a run at all that year in the first team, didn't even make a couple of squads. Howard came in at half-time and went through me. He said: 'Do you want to go home? I'll have a ticket for you first thing in the morning.' Thing is, I did want to go home. I always did. Second half if anything, not on purpose, I played sort of worse but he came in after and said, 'that's better'. I remember thinking: 'Jeez, what do I have to do? Get me home!'

"Then the next pre-season up at Trinity and All Saints College at Yeadon, he pulled us and said: 'I'm going to try you at right-back.' And he played me every game in pre-season. He gave everyone else a rest. In training he kept putting Rod Wallace on the left to attack me all the time and at the end he said: 'You'll be all right.' It went from there to [the first game of the season] Manchester City away and I was in. I went to the World Cup the next summer with Ireland and didn't miss a Leeds game for two-and-a-half years.

"Howard is a father figure to me. He looked after us, I'll always be in his debt because he gave me a chance and stuck with us. I'll always be grateful to him. He was always focused, always on it in terms of preparation. It's changed now and a lot of teams go out on the morning of the match at 11am for a walk. Howard was on the bus at 10 o'clock on a Saturday morning, home and away. We'd get our kit and we'd go to some dogshit park and do set-pieces and keep-ball. A sharp 40 minutes of that and back on the bus. It was drummed into us and we didn't leak many goals. I was just 19, playing with Strachan, a schoolboy hero, Lukic, Speedo, Batts, Rod, Hodgey, Macca... Great days, great memories."

Kelly and Leeds ended the season in fifth. Five away wins had proved the difference between a battle against relegation and just falling short of a European place, though the boost was not enough to bridge the chasm to Manchester United who were 22 points better off, over the hill and far away. Wilkinson planned another transformation job in the summer, paying £2.6m for the midfielder Carton Palmer, a favourite of Graham Taylor's when England manager, and proposing to turn him into a centre-half. The experiment lasted 20 games, including a first victory over Manchester United for 13 years, until he was pushed back into his normal position for the remainder of his Leeds career. Geoff Sleight, the chief scout, recommended two South Africa players, Lucas Radebe and Phil Masinga, who were snapped up for £525,000, the former becoming one of the club's greatest players, the latter, a loping, whole-hearted striker, making more initial impact with his goals. Halfway through the season, Wilkinson tightened the midfield by switching to a fluid 4-5-1 when the opposition had the ball, which switched to 4-3-3 with Deane and Wallace out wide when Leeds were on the attack. The system required a more dynamic striker and reliable finisher than either Noel Whelan or Masinga.

In January 1995, thanks to Fotherby's coup, they found one and trailed it on their premium-rate Clubcall service with "Leeds sign African superstar". The superstar in question was Tony Yeboah who had fallen out with Eintracht Frankfurt's manager, Jupp Heynckes, and joined Leeds on loan until the end of the season. When Wilkinson picked him to start after a couple of substitute appearances, he scored eight times in his first nine games and his power, occasionally languid grace and exceptional dead-eyed finishing saw him fully embraced by the crowd. The loss of Cantona and Batty left a hole in Leeds fans' hearts, Yeboah plugged the gap, never more so than in the club's run to fifth again and European qualification at the end of that season. The chant "Who needs Cantona, when we've got Yeboah?" required mangling the pronunciation of Tony's name to get it to fit, but it was sung with full-throated glee as Cantona languished in France after his ban for kung-fu kicking a racist in the chest.

The following season things got even better – a stunning, dipping volley against Liverpool, the chest-knee-whirl-smash goal of the season against Wimbledon, a hat-trick away at Monaco as Leeds returned to the Uefa Cup, a blistering, 25-yard strike against Sheffield Wednesday and a barnstorming run from the halfway line and subtle chip over Peter Schmeichel in a Christmas Eve 3-1 victory over Manchester United. But it all unravelled so quickly, the humiliation at Wembley by Aston Villa in the 1996 League Cup Final proving the symbolic if not the actual end of Wilkinson's reign. It all went wrong suddenly in 1995-96, after Yeboah's spectacular autumn, yet the seeds had been sown by recruitment failures, established players' unrest and Wilkinson's constant recourse to alumni of Sheffield Wednesday and Sheffield United. After missing out on Faustino Asprilla, Rubén Sosa and Tomáš Skuhravý, Fotherby, now the highest-paid director in the Premiership on £240,000 a year, bought Tomas Brolin from Parma for £4.5m.

At his best Brolin was a slick, perfectly-balanced attacking scurrier, whose control and vision made him perfect for the tight spaces of Serie A. The player Leeds signed had a pin holding his ankle together and looked to be carrying a lot of weight. His touch remained sublime but he was ponderous and seemed to think the place was all rather beneath him. Wilkinson immediately smelt a rat yet still went ahead with it. By the League Cup Final, Leeds' first competitive trip to Wembley for 23 years, Wilkinson was sick of his attitude, stuck him on the bench and picked a strange side with five at the back and starting places for the abrasive Mark Ford and the raw Andy Gray, son of Frankie, nephew of Eddie. It was a disaster. Villa overran a confused defence, the wing-backs could not tell if they were supposed to be Arthur or Martha and McAllister could not get on the ball. At half-time they were 1-0 down and chants for Brolin intensified when they fell further behind. Wilkinson, cutting an increasingly forlorn figure, was informed that he didn't know what he was doing and then booed when he eventually sent the Sweden forward on. Brolin made no positive contribution, in common with all his colleagues bar Gray. If it vindicated Wilkinson's judgment, he reaped no benefit and, following the 3-0 defeat, became the first and so far last manager to be canned off by his own team's supporters at a Wembley final. It profoundly upset him and he should have agreed a package to step down. He was drained and grey but his sense of duty, loyalty to the 10-year plan and faith in the outstanding next crop of Paul Hart's youngsters persuaded him to stay on. They had been humiliated in Europe, losing 8-3 on aggregate against PSV and in the week building up to the League Cup Final Leeds had been humped 3-0 by Liverpool in an FA Cup quarter-final replay after losing 5-0 at Anfield in the league. Following Wembley they lost seven of their remaining nine games, sliding to 13th. To no avail Wilkinson blooded some of the youth team, including Ian Harte and Harry Kewell and must have been relieved to get it over.

Summer was far from the tranquil haven he needed. In March Silver, then 71, and his wife Sheila had been victims of a brutal burglary by three masked raiders at their home in Scarcroft. The couple were separated, manacled and threatened until they handed over jewellery and cash. It knocked him sideways and he resolved to retreat from the public eye. In April he announced that the club was up for sale, having in 1993 initiated a financial restructuring of the club that had left Fotherby, Gilman and the chairman holding 98 per cent of the 'management shares', paying £35,000 each for their stakes. There were three bids – from Caspian plc (a media company backed by corporate shareholders which had made its money in sporting rights), Conrad (which owned Le Coq Sportif and Bobby Charlton's Soccer Schools) and Resource Group International, the Norwegian fishing conglomerate whose offer was fronted by the agent, Rune Hauge, who had made payments to the Arsenal manager George Graham which resulted in his dismissal and an FA ban. Gilman opposed the choice of Caspian, backed by Fotherby and Silver, but was outvoted and the three of them eventually split £16.5m for their shares. Caspian pledged to cover the £10m overdraft and invest another £10m in players. The deal was done late in the summer break after Gilman tried to use a court injunction to stop it. Fotherby, who bought himself a green Bentley, was promoted to chairman and Wilkinson remained in place.

Speed felt he was in a rut and pushed through a transfer to his boyhood favourites, Everton, while the captain McAllister went to Coventry. Those sales plus the cash injection financed the fees and wages to recruit Ian Rush, Lee Sharpe, Lee Bowyer and Nigel Martyn. Caspian spoke of building a sporting and multimedia empire by taking over Leeds RLFC and building an arena to house new basketball and ice hockey franchises, a cinema and a concert venue. Their grand design was built on sand – nothing was added to the portfolio but the language they used, gobbets of corporate speak, reams of optimism, clashed jarringly with Wilkinson's Eeyore pronouncements. He lasted five games, two victories following an opening day draw and defeat by Sheffield Wednesday buying him time. And then Manchester United came to Elland Road, thrashed a pitiful Leeds

4-0 and the home supporters made rare common cause with the visitors by joining in with the choruses of "sacked in the morning", "Wilko for City" and 'Wilko for England" that equalled the pillorying he had endured at Wembley. Fotherby sacked him the next day, an act Wilkinson feels was merciful given the strain.

"Nobody ever says thank you," Brian Clough once remarked of the manager's predicament. It is not strictly true – they do but usually only years after the event. It took time for Wilkinson's legacy to be fully appreciated and when it was incinerated in eight short years of corporate lunacy, he received the recognition he had always deserved. Arguing that Leeds should have maintained faith with his project – they won the FA Youth Cup again in 1997 – makes sense only in hindsight. The most vocal supporters were tired of him, his methods and the kind of players he favoured. It is glib to damn them as fickle. The last nine months and parts of the preceding three seasons were a mess. Little things – not picking Rocastle, dropping Wallace, selling Whelan, buying Paul Beesley – contributed to a bigger picture of an obstinate man. It may have been different had Strachan stayed but he had left in 1995 shortly before his 38th birthday, seduced by Coventry offering him what Wilkinson called 'dopey' money. Strachan had too much respect for Wilkinson to have seen himself as the heir apparent, presuming the manager would be around for years. Had Leeds kept him, though, he would have been the perfect consigliere for the manager and ready to step up when the time came. Whether Caspian would have appointed a disciple is uncertain but it would have allowed Wilkinson to remain as director of football and provide a voice of reason to a board hell bent on joining the gold rush. "When I was in trouble as a manager, he was the first port of call," says Strachan. "He always knew exactly what was needed. If you ask him today or asked 30 years ago, he would tell you the answer was something different because he understands the game moves on. He's a pragmatist. A clever fella who has never got the credit in football he should have had. But anyone who's worked with him would know that he is a top manager." Leeds have had only one better.

One of Caspian's shareholders, the former QPR chairman Richard Thompson, was a friend and neighbour of George Graham's. As soon as his ban expired on 1 July, the first rumours of his impending move into Wilkinson's job emerged. It took Caspian just 10 weeks from the end of his suspension to complete the switch. Manchester City thought he had agreed to join them a week before a vacancy arose at Elland Road but Graham changed his mind and was conveniently available at precisely the right moment. "Leeds, like Arsenal, are a big club but when I took over at Arsenal the team had three internationals in the back four and a young Tony Adams. Even then we worked for a year until I drilled into them the method that won us big trophies." He lost seven of his first nine games as he and his assistant, O'Leary, riffled through Wilkinson's squad, discarding those who did not meet his standards. Graham's Plan A at every club he joined was to wage war on the high earners and he did so again at Leeds, turning on Palmer, Dorigo and Yeboah, sticking Rush out on the right wing and tolerating Sharpe only until he could offload him in the summer.

Graham slowly began to exert his influence and a 2-0 victory over Chelsea in December, when Lucas Radebe man-marked Gianfranco Zola out of the game, showed that his negative approach could work. It encouraged him to continue to pack midfield with centre-backs and sometimes use full-backs in front of full-backs. It saved them from spiralling further but it was a mind-numbing season of dreadful tedium in which Leeds scored merely 28 goals. Kelly, who scored two of them, witnessed the best of Graham on the training field. "So I kept Leeds up that year?" he laughs. "George was one of those tactical managers, so defensive-minded. He would always tell us: 'If you don't concede a goal, you're guaranteed to get a point. Don't concede!' He was brilliant. As someone learning the trade at right-back, being a defender, he would just drum it into you. Whoever was unfortunate enough to be sitting in front of the back four would be with the defence and everyone else would be off on the other pitches doing crossing and finishing, diving headers. He would just drill us. You'd hear the others all laughing and joking and for us it was, 'Go again… again, show him inside, now show him down the line. It was a pain in the arse but had to be done. It'd be in your head all the time. You'd find yourself at home in the kitchen, standing on the half-turn, looking across the line." No wonder there were nine 0-0 draws. They used the stifling tactics to beat Arsenal in the FA Cup fourth round but Graham could not help leaving the impression that making his old employers miserable meant more to him than bringing joy to his new club. Conservatism worked to stabilise Leeds United but was not the profile Caspian wanted. The PLC bought Elland Road back from the council with a view to establishing the Beeston sporting empire, sacked Fotherby and gave Graham the funds to buy the kind of players to change the image and style.

His first act was driving Palmer, Yeboah, Deane and Rush out. He scoffed at Brolin's shape on the forward's return from a year on loan at Parma, fined him when he persisted in missing training and eventually arranged a pay-off to terminate his contract. Graham treated his job as if he were Hercules confronted by the Augean stables and should be praised for it.

He brought in Jimmy Floyd Hasselbaink for £2m, the midfielders Alf-Inge Haaland, Bruno Ribeiro and David Hopkin for a combined £5.3m and the work he had done with Bowyer, Kelly, Radebe and the steady Eddies he had bought the previous season worked wonders. Hasselbaink, sinewy, quick, with a vicious, whip-lash, right-foot shot, scored on opening day and settled down in the autumn. His partnership with a rejuvenated Rod Wallace contributed 35 goals while Harry Kewell came in from the youth team managed by Eddie Gray and provided youthful insouciance, thrust and dazzling ball skills on the left wing. They were inconsistent but increasingly enjoyable to watch, playing a powerfully athletic attacking game and on occasions hinting at genuine cohesion and promise. They annihilated Derby 5-0, Blackburn 4-0, beat Chelsea at home and drew with them away, having played the second half with nine men, and stormed to the FA Cup quarter-final where they timidly surrendered to First Division Wolves. Graham, though, would not commit further than renting a flat in Harrogate. He returned to his London home and the beloved garden he often used as a metaphor for his managerial philosophy as frequently as he could. It saved him the anguish suffered in March 1998 by his squad returning from a 3-0 defeat at West Ham. Having taken off from Stansted in their chartered Emerald Airlines Hawker-Siddeley turbo-prop aircraft, the starboard engine exploded 12 seconds into the flight, forcing the captain, John Hackett, to abort and head straight back. "It's hard to say what's going through your mind when you hit the ground and you're sliding on the runway," said O'Leary, who forced open the emergency exit over the wing with a shoulder barge. "You're hoping you won't hit anything, that it won't explode. The plane was like a roller-coaster. There was a lot of fire and everyone just got off as fast as possible. We are all pretty shaken up but the overwhelming feeling is that we're glad to get out in one piece." Hackett and his crew were guests of honour at the next home game where their skill in averting a disaster were rewarded with gifts and the appreciation of the crowd. An understandable wariness about flying still haunts some of the survivors.

Graham took them to fifth in his only full season and departed for Tottenham after a seven-game unbeaten start to the next campaign. Having been courted by Spurs all week before Leeds' trip to White Hart Lane, he bowed in public to professional courtesy while signalling with his eyes and his measured words that he wanted to go. The travelling supporters correctly interpreted his equivocation and regaled him with advice to "fuck off", which he did after the 3-3 draw once Tottenham had agreed the compensation package. Spurs fans had also protested against his appointment and his three years there were punctuated by demonstrations and criticism of his style. His work at Elland Road is underrated but Leeds' effect on him was just as profound. United detoxified a fine but tainted manager before he ended up alienating them as he also did with Arsenal and Tottenham. Leeds' new chairman made a show of trotting down to the away section at White Hart Lane to upbraid them in case the fans' songs drove Graham into Spurs' arms. That he could not appreciate that it was far too late for that was worrying, as was his fondness for the public grand gesture. When Peter Ridsdale had succeeded Fotherby, he immediately rang Ray Fell, the veteran chairman of the Leeds United Supporters' Club. "Remember Ray, I'm one of you," he said, a phrase that could have been Leeds United's death knell.

24

DREAMTIME

There are certain people like Sir Ian Botham or Joy Division/New Order's Peter Hook whose admirable feats are for some overshadowed by their capacity to strike a discordant tone. It might be a perceived arrogance, or perhaps a certain gaucheness – in David O'Leary's case there was a fondness for flattery and excessive professions of his humility, which was interpreted as insincerity. It has contaminated his reputation. A man whose lowest-place finish was fifth in four years, who took Leeds to semi-finals in the Uefa Cup and Champions League, whose team drew the highest average attendance to Elland Road in the club's history for three successive seasons, has spent just three of the years since he was sacked in 2002 engaged in his primary trade of football manager.

Aston Villa's fans wrote his epitaph with their 2006 banner: "We're not fickle we just don't like you." Yet in his first two years after succeeding George Graham at Leeds, he proved himself a manager of rare vision, creating a vibrant, attacking side with modest signings financed by the sale of Jimmy Floyd Hasselbaink to Atlético Madrid. And he had a knack of pushing the right buttons to enhance his credibility with the fans, from executing the 'Leeds salute' to packing the side with Eddie Gray's youth-team graduates and sending them out to play a fearless style of football, full of vigour and verve. In his latter two years he became obsessed with spin and the eulogies to his "babies" soon lost their lustre as the club went on a reckless transfer market splurge that eventually brought it to its knees. Even so, to say his culpability for the meltdown has parity with Peter Ridsdale's, as the former chairman has tried to maintain, illustrates how feebly the board took its executive responsibilities. The vitriol heaped on him after the folly of publishing a book called *Leeds United on Trial* after the verdicts in the court case involving Lee Bowyer and Jonathan Woodgate was understandable. Its most telling repercussion, though, is not. It has thoroughly overwhelmed his reputation as a manager, one who coaxed players such as Bowyer, Woodgate, Alan Smith, Danny Mills, Stephen McPhail, Ian Harte and Harry Kewell to play like they had never done before and never managed subsequently. That it all fell apart in an orgy of indiscipline – fuelled at one level by Bacardi Breezers, at another by corporate hubris – reflects badly on the entire club, not just him. For a couple of years he took Howard Wilkinson's bequest, George Graham's organisation, Gray's sense of adventure and produced a team which kept advancing. It was a heady, exhilarating cocktail. It is O'Leary's tragedy that too many remember only the hangover.

Graham's assistant was not Ridsdale's first choice. Martin O'Neill, the Leicester City manager, was the one that got away three times from the Leeds chairman. On this, the first occasion, Leicester simply would not entertain the approach, pointing to a contract that gave O'Neill no wiggle room and stressing their determination to enforce its clauses. The away supporters' songs urging O'Neill to stay when Leicester beat Leeds at Elland Road in the first match after Graham's departure also played their part in his decision to stay at Filbert Street. O'Leary, in caretaker charge, stuck to his predecessor's template for that defeat but with Gray assisting him, went for the bold option against Forest and in the away leg of the Uefa Cup tie against Roma. Both games featured the apple of Gray's eye, the youth team's most incisive passer, Stephen McPhail, while Woodgate, so deceptively pale and gaunt the 'Slim Shady' analogies would write themselves, made a compelling debut in the draw at the City Ground. Leeds lost 1-0 in Rome, having played with impressive authority for a team reduced to 10 men, and one so callow, and two hours after the conclusion of a home 'Super Sunday' 0-0 draw with Chelsea, O'Leary was confirmed as the new manager on a two-and-a-half-year deal. "This is a fantastic opportunity for me," O'Leary said. "My ambition is simple here, I just want to win things with Leeds... to go out and beat George." Ridsdale had been blocked in his pursuit of O'Neill and turned down by Gordon Strachan. He had a candidate who desperately wanted the opportunity and yet the chairman made the self-styled 'rookie manager' the fifth-highest earner in the league on £700,000 a year. If Ridsdale recognised he had leverage, he bafflingly chose not to exert it. When would he ever?

O'Leary's first win came against Sheffield Wednesday and the next week they recorded only their second victory at Anfield since 1972. At 1-0 down with 14 minutes to play, Leeds threw on the young forward Alan Smith, a BMX fanatic and FA School of Excellence dropout who had just turned 18. John Arlott once described Billy Bremner as "10 stone of barbed wire". Had the great poet, writer and commentator lived long enough to see the abrasive Smith, electrified razor wire would have served. Teetotal, quiet and charming off the pitch, Smith was a Tasmanian Devil on it, a Rothwell lad with pluck and skill matched only by a ferocity he struggled to contain.

He scored the equaliser with his first kick, sweeping a shot from 16 yards into the bottom left corner. Hasselbaink added two more in the last nine minutes, a controlled left-foot shot and a scorcher with his right to earn the points and end Liverpool's experiment with co-managers. Smith was irrepressible in the late winter and spring, driving the BBC's Barry Davies into paroxysms of ecstasy with his uncanny composure in the penalty box, a bantam, effervescent David up against the Premiership's Goliaths. One by one the surviving stalwarts of the Wilkinson and Graham teams – Robert Molenaar, David Wetherall, David Hopkin, David Robertson and even relatively new signings such as Danny Granville and Clyde Wijnhard – were eased out and replaced by upgrades from the youth team. Ridsdale had pledged to find money for signings when appointing O'Leary and bought back David Batty, after five years away, in a move that fulfilled every criteria, boosting the quality, tickling the public and righting a perceived wrong. They paid £4.5m for him and in his first game back he broke a rib that led to pleurisy and pericarditis, which kept him out for four months. He returned to helm a victory over Tottenham in March when Graham received the 'Judas' treatment, an inevitable knee-jerk response given Leeds were seemingly better off without him. Around the same time the club's official magazine produced a sticker of his face to be placed for target practice in subscribers' lavatory pans. In football, spite gleefully surpasses logic. Graham countered by topping Leeds' offer for on-loan Willem Korsten. Satisfyingly, it helped O'Leary dodge a bullet because the lanky winger was barely fit thereafter. Batty, meanwhile, showed all his old tenacity and new maturity in an outstanding performance against Arsenal in the penultimate match of the season which was settled by Hasselbaink's late diving header, his 42nd and final goal for the club, a winner that ruined Arsenal's title chances and confirmed Leeds in fourth.

Hasselbaink's impact at Leeds had alerted some of Europe's elite clubs and with typical Dutch forthrightness he made it plain that he wanted either an enormous increase on his wages or to leave. Ridsdale extracted a £10m profit on him from Atlético Madrid and O'Leary invested it in Michael Bridges, Danny Mills, Michael Duberry and Eirik Bakke while pruning his squad of several names, including the former captain Wetherall. Mills, a 22-year-old prematurely bald right-back, had been bought because Gary Kelly had missed the preceding season with a mystifying complaint. On his return he witnessed O'Leary's worst side, a genial bluster, which diminished his standing. "It was such a bad injury with my shins," he says. "They'd treated me for shin splints, and it wasn't that. They drilled each shin three times and there was blood in my bones, something weird. It took ages to sort out. But I had a real go and started to get fit. Danny struggled when he came to Leeds at first. He had a good couple of games and I came on for him at Spurs away. And I remember on the bus, Dave O'Leary saying, 'You'll be starting next week. I'm delighted for you.' But we got to next week and he called a team meeting and said: 'I'm going to stick with Danny.' He brought me on at Highfield Road in the next game and he left me in. I'd been out for a year and then made the all-star team. It was a massive achievement, in my head more than anything. It goes to show: 'Never give up. Keep going.'"

It took O'Leary's team 10 games to climb to the top of the table despite early defeats by Manchester United and Liverpool. Kewell and Bowyer were inspired as unconventional wide midfielders, the former floating about the attack, often leaving left-back Harte exposed but for Batty's covering intuition. Bowyer, tucked in on the right, covered so much ground, timing his attacking runs perfectly to meet lay-offs around the 18-yard line and tracking back with such swift acceleration that he could blindside opponents who assumed they were clear. Up front, Bridges was a revelation. Having already endeared himself by rejecting Graham and Tottenham, whose £5m bid was the first to be accepted by Sunderland, the 20-year-old played with a distinct hint of Dennis Bergkamp about his poise, touch and dribbling. Bought initially as a No10, he took over the goalscoring mantle as well, bagging 19 league goals. Indeed Bridges had such assurance in control and the cheek to try the extraordinary that at times the comparison with Bergkamp did not seem sacrilegious.

An improperly diagnosed Achilles injury ruled Batty out for more than a year from November 1999. With him in the side they had won 10 successive matches in the autumn, and Leeds stayed in first place without him even after defeats at the turn of the Millennium by Arsenal and Aston Villa. They were flying in Europe, humped Manchester City 5-2 in the FA Cup fourth round and, but for Manchester United being allowed to default from the FA Cup and postpone their Premiership schedule to play in the Club World Cup, would have been about to host the champions. Instead they had two fallow weeks and the players were given time off to relax and recuperate after 31 games since mid-August.

On Tuesday 11 January 2000, several players and their entourages hit the town hard. Kewell, Bridges and reserve forward Tony Hackworth were part of one group belatedly celebrating Bowyer's birthday in the Majestyk nightclub on student night where they were eventually joined by Woodgate and a party of his childhood friends from Middlesbrough who had made their way there via bars and a lap-dancing club. When one of Woodgate's friends was thrown out of the nightclub, the footballer went with him. Over the next few minutes a fight broke out with another group of young men and, after a chase, a student from Sheffield, Sarfraz Najeib, was caught and violently assaulted. CCTV footage identified Woodgate and two of his friends, Neale Caveney and Paul Clifford in the pack chasing Najeib who was kicked and beaten unconscious and at the trial found to have Clifford's bite-marks in a wound on his cheek. A witness informed the police that Bowyer was involved and the two named players were arrested a week later along with Caveney, Clifford and subsequently Hackworth and Michael Duberry, who had arrived later and whisked Woodgate away from the scene. They were released on police bail and the story released to the press. Eyewitness accounts were published and the possibility of a racist motive explored. Ridsdale said the club had considered its options, including suspending and even sacking the players, but had wisely concluded that doing so would be prejudicial. Instead he employed a private detective to find out exactly what had happened. As Leeds' internal investigation evolved, the club found it worrying that the players admitted to details in dribs and drabs rather than coming clean from the beginning. *The Times* reported that the attack had spread "disbelief, confusion and anger" among the South Asian communities of the city and quoted one young man saying, "Bowyer and Woodgate were our heroes. How can we be sure now? Leeds means everything to us. Everything." The case was sent to Hull for trial in January 2001. It was a wound that would fester for almost two years and even when it concluded, long after it should have been, the damage was incalculable.

Defeats by Manchester United and Liverpool in February and four more in March and April destroyed their title chances but their form in Europe maintained its sheen. Woodgate, Alf-Inge Haaland and Lucas Radebe were masterly in the heart of defence against Roma in the away leg of the fourth-round tie and Nigel Martyn pulled off a string of saves. Fabio Capello, the Roma manager, said, "Leeds are a good side but they played defensively" after the 0-0 draw. They were certainly not cavalier but they did create chances on the break and in the home leg Kewell scored the only goal of the tie by shimmying past Damiano Tommasi and letting fly from 25 yards. In the closing minutes Smith irritated Antonio Zago, the two rutted with their foreheads and the Roma player was sent off for cuffing him. Smith continued to stand his ground when surrounded by irate opponents and when the substitute Darren Huckerby backed him up, Vincent Candela nutted him and was sent off, too. O'Leary embraced Kewell at the final whistle and virtually carried him off the pitch in a bear hug. They beat

Slavia Prague 4-2 in the next round, wiping the floor with them in a 3-0 win at Elland Road, and travelled to Istanbul to play Galatasaray in the first leg of the semi-final in April.

Galatasaray supporters' reputation for particularly bloodthirsty intimidation at Ataturk Airport and at their Ali Sami Yen Stadium had been indulgently glorified for years. Manchester United fans and players had been menaced in 1993 with the connivance of the police and Chelsea had withstood the usual savage rituals to win 5-0 there six months before Leeds arrived. Uefa had simply acquiesced that in Istanbul that was how it was.

"I first went there for a friendly at the age of 17 so I knew what to expect," says O'Leary. "It's strange because, in general, Turkish people are lovely and look after you so well but when you fly in or get to the ground with a football team, you can't believe how hostile it is. Our reception when we got there with Leeds was nothing different to what I'd experienced before with Arsenal and Ireland."

The four Loftus brothers, Chris, Darren, Phil and Andy, had flown in with the squad on the club's chartered flight. Kevin Speight, a 40-year-old publican from Farsley in the old cricket heartlands between Leeds and Bradford, arrived a little later but walked through the terminal chatting to the teenage striker Alan Smith. Tragically, neither Chris or Kevin would return home. Both men were among those who checked into their hotels and immediately headed to the bars of Taksim during the afternoon and early evening. Neither had any history of lairiness or troublemaking.

They drank at first at the James Joyce Irish Pub. There was singing, certainly, and no doubt a few among the 150 had too much to drink but subsequent stories cited in defence of those convicted of the killings, claiming provocation by someone showing disrespect to Turkish bank notes, the flag or the waitresses, are unfounded. Those who were there insist nothing of the kind happened. Football supporters in numbers provoke tension as much by their presence as their behaviour and, although much was made of the cultural clash between supporters and locals, this was supposedly liberal Taksim not the courtyard of the Blue Mosque.

Chris and Kevin were among a group of around 20 who peeled away to another bar. They were stalked by a spotter and at 10.30pm were attacked by a gang of 100 men, some of whom were brandishing carving knives, others machetes, bats and scaffold poles. Chris was fatally stabbed and his brother Darren beaten by his assailants and the police, who appeared during the ambush, as he tried to tend to him.

The police did not spare the good Samaritan administering mouth-to-mouth to Chris, striking him repeatedly round the head with their nightsticks. Kevin was slashed across the abdomen and the two were bundled into taxis, by their distraught friends and taken along with the wounded to Taksim Hospital. Chris was pronounced dead shortly after the Leeds chairman, Peter Ridsdale, arrived and Kevin died in the operating theatre. The blood supplies Ridsdale had been forced to source and pay for from a better-equipped hospital could not save him.

Ridsdale had raced to help after being informed at Uefa's pre-match gala dinner and earned the eternal gratitude of the families for his compassion and support. At a pre-dawn meeting he was told by the governing body that the match had to proceed, on pain of a 3-0 default, and reluctantly conceded his approval. "I was informed the night before the match that there had been incidents but it wasn't until breakfast on the morning of the game that I was told people had lost their lives," says O'Leary.

"Because the game was late in the evening, it was a long time to dwell on it and by the time of the team meeting at the hotel, I could just tell with my young team that their minds were in a different place. They were so subdued, as we all were. There were really bad vibes. I was thinking how needless the game was and because I wasn't focused on it and couldn't get them to focus, I remember thinking I'd failed them.

"Going into that stadium that night was like going into a war zone," he says, recalling the missiles thrown at the team coach, the throat-slitting gestures from men in cars and on mopeds, wearing scarves as masks, and the police's riot shields that were deployed to protect his team, while simultaneously spooking them further, as they emerged into the floodlights of 'Hell' from the underground dressing rooms. The hosts had refused Leeds' requests for a minute's silence or for their own players to wear black armbands, prompting the 300 away supporters in the stadium to turn their backs in protest. O'Leary's side lost 2-0, wilting in a cacophony of booing and unyielding aggression and could not overturn that deficit in the return leg.

"Everything fell into perspective," says O'Leary about the scarf-strewn tributes at Elland Road the following morning where he placed his bouquet after a late flight home. "No one cares about football or matches then, there was just a tremendous feeling of disappointment, such grief. The memory up here and the sadness are still unbelievably raw."

After exhausting numerous appeals procedures, the four men convicted initially in 2001 of involvement in the murders were not finally jailed until 2010, the longest sentence handed down was a mere 10 years and all have been free for a number of years. During the West Yorkshire Coroner's inquests in 2004, which returned verdicts of unlawful killing,

David Hinchcliffe severely criticised the conduct of the Turkish police. He described the force, which refused to co-operate with West Yorkshire officers, as "disorganised, uncoordinated, not in control of the situation and ill-prepared. The police seem to be out of control, and their ability was described by witnesses as being diabolical".

At Elland Road, the statue of Billy Bremner and the Elland Road gates became a shrine. There was no place more fitting than Bremner's memorial. Don Revie's captain had died cruelly early in 1997 at the age of 54 and his loss is still keenly felt. "People have said to me," he once pointed out, "you must have played hard for the manager. But the answer is yes and no. I played hard for me and for the fans. I was always very conscious of the fans." Most match-going Leeds supporters are forever conscious of the two who went to Istanbul and never made it home. The home leg was drawn 2-2 in a wildly vengeful atmosphere and the crowd turned the event into a call for justice that took a decade to be heard – and even then hardly satisfactorily.

Leeds' Premier League season had five games to run, Kewell scored an impudent chip against Sheffield Wednesday on the day he was voted Young Player of the Year and they remained unbeaten through the remaining games, finishing with a 0-0 draw at West Ham. Meanwhile, in West Yorkshire, David Wetherall – discarded by Leeds and discourteously treated by Ridsdale – headed Bradford City's winner against Liverpool that saved his new club from relegation and ultimately protected his old side's hold on third place. The goal put the 'young manager' and his 'young team' in the Champions League qualifiers.

Ridsdale had been promoted to chairman and paid chief executive of the plc by this point as well as the football club, taking over in a boardroom coup after Caspain's grand design of various sporting franchises withered in drawn out negotiations. His vice-chairman, Allan Leighton, had an enviable corporate record at Asda and, as CEO, had overseen the multi-billion-pound sale of the company. The two men, whose background was in marketing, impressed investors in the new Leeds Sporting plc and set about providing the funds for the step up to the Champions League. They chose to do this in a complex arrangement with a company called Registered European Football Finance Limited, fronted by the agent Ray Ranson, which financed the purchase of players and then leased them back to Leeds in a 'buy now, pay later' deal. It was essentially hire purchase, which was fine if the players' maintained their value in a volatile market until the instalments added up to the money paid for them. If they were sold in the interim for less than that value, the losses would begin to accrue. For obvious reasons Ridsdale did not publicise that this was the model he was using nor did the players become aware of it until much later. In all they bought eight players in this way, beginning with Olivier Dacourt for £7.2m, Mark Viduka for £6m and Dominic Matteo for £4.25m. Leeds met payments to REFF on them and paid their salaries. Each was sold at a substantial loss when Leeds collapsed and this time bomb, which the board had placed at the heart of the club's finances, exploded.

Injury kept Kewell and Batty out until December and Leeds were erratic in the league until January, an inconsistency addressed with further splurges – a loan deal for Inter's Robbie Keane which would become an £11m transfer at the end of the season and in December they stumped up £18m for West Ham's Rio Ferdinand, a record fee for a British player. He was bought because of his outrageous promise as a ball-playing centre-half, and to O'Leary's credit he helped him realise his potential, screwing the nut in terms of toughness and concentration in a manner Jack Charlton would have recognised. Nonetheless, both deals were preposterous. They had not been able to fund their summer signings in the conventional manner and were now betting even more heavily on a novel financial instrument, the disadvantages of which they had given themselves no time to test. They must have thought they had found a secret money tree. Ridsdale later claimed that there were no complaints when these deals were arranged. While there was no genuine disquiet, there was a puzzlement about how the club could afford it and an eagerness to look at the balance sheet. And it was assumed that their astounding progress in the Champions League, now rejigged into an even bigger cash machine with two group stages, must be funding the investment spree. In fact it was a punt, a huge gamble designed to bridge the gap to Europe's elite.

On the field O'Leary's side made a decent fist of it, beating 1860 Munich in the qualifier and surviving a hellishly difficult group stage after a chastening start. Barcelona beat them 4-0 on their first return to Camp Nou since Carl Shutt shook the world. Fearing the worst when O'Leary was forced to send out a makeshift centre-back partnership of Mills and Duberry against the AC Milan of Paolo Maldini, Demetrio Albertini, Andriy Shevchenko and Oliver Bierhoff, more than 35,000 turned out to witness Leeds standing their ground and stealing victory with a larcenous 30-yard Bowyer shot that Dida patted down in driving rain before freezing when it spun past his left leg and over the line. Viduka, a graceful, forceful striker with wonderful balance and touch, scored in the 6-0 victory over Besiktas and led the line in the away leg after Bridges ruptured his Achilles tendon during the draw in Istanbul. Bridges toiled resiliently through a spate of setbacks over the next four years but was never the same player again. Paired now more regularly with Smith, Viduka took the role of target man and brought to it his deft dribbling skills and bustling power. He occasionally suffered from the stereotyping afflicting broad-chested forwards, and when Leeds laboured the 'fat' and 'lazy' abuse would start in some quarters. Thankfully, he was so self-assured it did not seem to affect him.

Bowyer scored again from distance in the 1-1 home draw with Barcelona, salvaged for the visitors by Rivaldo's stoppage-time equaliser and Matteo, who had been playing on the left side of midfield in Kewell's absence, turned in a near-post header from Bowyer's corner to put Leeds 1-0 up at the San Siro. That goal, celebrated still today in song, ultimately earned Leeds a 1-1 draw and the point to put both teams through at Barcelona's expense. The travelling Leeds supporters, held in after the game to reduce the opportunities for trouble, were ecstatic to be joined by the players and staff who came back out from the dressing room. Sipping on cans of lager, they broke out the old anthems, led, inevitably, by Kelly.

"When we went on that run," he says, "We used to have sing-songs the night before the game, sing-songs on the bus going back to the hotel. Everyone would have a go. Rio, Dubes, Harry, Bow. There were no iPhones and people taking videos. It was just bonding. We'd get back and no one would just go to their room. We'd be in the lobby and playing cards, order pizzas, talking. Just like a normal pub team. Singing to the fans wasn't anything planned but so many people mention they were there and I know it meant a lot to them. It did to me, too. Afterwards Peter Ridsdale kept coming up when we'd won and say: 'C'mon sing to the fans again.' But it just doesn't happen like that. It's something that's spontaneous, it just happens. You can't plan it."

The first group was difficult enough – the second comprised Real Madrid, Lazio and Anderlecht. Leeds came through it with three victories, a draw and two defeats by Real, the first a proper hiding, 0-2 at Elland Road, the second stolen 3-2 at the Bernabéu when Raul punched one in. Smith scored a superb winner in Rome and a fine chip among two goals in Brussels when Leeds overwhelmed Anderlecht 4-1 with Batty and Kewell both back and Ferdinand, soon to replace the brilliant Radebe as captain, alongside the 'Chief' at the back. Anderlecht's manager, Aimé Anthuenis, had called Leeds an average side before the game and when he came over to shake his counterpart's hand at the end of the game, O'Leary reminded him. "We heard what you said about us," O'Leary said. "Goodbye."

Leeds qualified for the quarter-finals with two games to spare and the club's league form, once bolstered by new additions and players returning from injury, recovered the previous season's spark. After a 3-1 defeat by Newcastle in January that left them in 13th, they won 12 of their last 16 games, including victories at Anfield, at high-flying Sunderland and made it five victories out of five against George Graham's Spurs.

Leeds upsurge had taken place in the late winter and early spring while Bowyer, Woodgate, Duberry and Hackworth were on trial in Hull. Although Leeds spirited Bowyer back from his days in court to play and he performed at the peak of his abilities, Woodgate could not cope with the strain, lost weight and did not feature for the first-team after January. Duberry, Hackworth, Woodgate and his Middlesbrough friends were cleared of conspiracy to pervert the course of justice but before the jury could reach a decision over counts of affray and GBH with intent against Bowyer, Woodgate, Clifford and Caveney, the *Sunday Mirror* published an interview with Sarfraz Najeib's father on the eve of the verdicts in which he said his son had ben the victim of a racist attack. On the Monday the judge asked the jury if any of them had read the piece and when some confirmed they had, he ordered a mistrial and dismissed them. A new date was set in October for a retrial of the four remaining defendants.

The Champions League odyssey, after trips to Barcelona and Real Madrid, continued its Iberian theme when Leeds were drawn to play the Liga champions Deportivo La Coruña in the quarter-final and later Valencia in the semi. Javier Irureta, Depor's manager, and his midfielder Víctor blessed their luck at being paired with the last eight's "weakest team". "Anderlecht said much the same thing and look how that one turned out," said Ferdinand. "It simply brought the boys closer together and made us even more determined to prove them wrong." Indeed Leeds blitzed the visitors in the first leg. Harte, whose dead-ball dip, pace and accuracy masked his defensive flaws, whipped a free-kick in from 25 yards and crossed for Smith and Ferdinand to make it 3-0 in the second half. Deportivo's late rally signalled that the "miracle" Irureta demanded in the second leg might be possible but it did not dampen the fervour around Elland Road nor the delighted chants of "3-0 to the weakest links".

Leeds took a pasting in the second leg, Depor scored twice and beat out a tattoo on the woodwork framing Nigel Martyn's goal but Leeds survived the hair-raising experience and welcomed Valencia to Elland Road in the last four. They held their own at home even though Gaizka Mendieta roasted Harte down the right as Matteo's positioning and nose for danger bailed out his team-mate and Bowyer's thrusts down the other flank stopped the game tilting away from them. Smith and Bowyer both had chances, Kewell, at times, was slippery and elusive while Ferdinand was majestic. A 0-0 draw was a decent result against a team that was a gilded version of themselves, just as relentless and sharp with a greater depth of sophistication and experience. Yet Leeds had conceded nine goals and lost each match on their three visits to Spain so far and they could not buck the trend. Bowyer, retrospectively suspended by Uefa for a stamp unseen by the referee, missed the game and Bakke, drafted in on the right, could not find the same penetrating vigour. Leeds fell behind to another handball goal and Harte was tormented by Mendieta once again. Valencia won comfortably, 3-0, but not before Smith, who had been yellow-carded seven times in his first season, booked 11 times and sent off once in his second, was red-carded for the second time in his third campaign (to go with the 12 cautions) for a wild lunge at Vicente.

Leeds were out and had two games left to try to finish third and qualify once again for the Champions League. They won both but Liverpool protected their advantage and took the spot by a point. Leeds were back in the Uefa Cup but had only found their best when Batty joined Dacourt in central midfield, Kewell came back and Ferdinand settled in. They had withstood 15 medium- to long-term injuries, finished fourth and made it to the Champions League semis. There was a strange sense of anti-climax as well as confidence amongst the supporters that momentum was building. If only it had ben more widely known that the finances were staked at football's casino.

Brian Kidd, Alex Ferguson's former assistant, had joined Leeds to run the academy in 2000. O'Leary had promoted him to head coach in March 2001 on the eve of a 1-1 draw with Manchester United in a move interpreted as trolling Ferguson and a snub to his assistant, Gray. Kidd had a terrific track record as a coach at Manchester United and was loved by the players at Leeds who came to his defence in public when the fans turned on him and blamed him for tempering the frenzied style for a more measured approach in 2001-02 that did not work. While Kidd took his first pre-season and O'Leary retreated to a more supervisory role, Ridsdale completed the signing of Keane and brought in two more players his manager coveted – Liverpool's Robbie Fowler for £11m and Seth Johnson from Derby for £7m. Now Leeds had four international strikers plus Kewell, four international centre-backs, two capped right-backs, Ireland's left-back, seven international midfielders and the England and England U21 goalkeepers. In the context of 2001 and much smaller squads than today it was an attitude reminiscent of Imelda Marcos' approach to shoes.

Take Fowler, for instance. Leeds did not need him but could not resist a forward with such subtlety, skill and electric reflexes. O'Leary had the right to make the request to his board. The board had an obligation to its shareholders to think of the consequences. Instead it focused on qualifying for the Champions League in 2001-02 to complete the circle.

All seemed set fair at least in terms of their league position by December. However, there were rumblings about caution creeping into the team's game and some dreary 0-0 draws. On 14 December they were third when the jury returned with their verdicts from the retrial. Bowyer was acquitted, Woodgate and Caveney were cleared of GBH with intent but convicted of affray and sentenced to 100 hours of community service and Clifford was found guilty on both charges and sentenced to six years' imprisonment. Bowyer was ordered to pay his seven-figure costs because his statements to police had been "littered with lies", according to the judge. They were characterised as irredeemable yobs by the press, the feral rich, who trotted out previous crimes and misdemeanours to emphasise their wickedness. Leeds fined Woodgate eight weeks' wages and Bowyer four. The defender accepted the sanction. Bowyer did not, arguing, not without merit, that it was unfair given he had been acquitted of all charges. He put in a transfer request but Leeds were adamant that they were punishing him for a breach of club discipline – being out in the city centre when told to rest – nothing else. Reluctantly, he paid up and came off the transfer list. Sarfraz Najeib's leg had been broken in the assault, his cheekbone and nose shattered, an impression of a boot heel left on his face as well as Clifford's bite marks. He had suffered severe head trauma and received multiple bruises. "I got kicked on the street by total strangers," he said, "and nearly two years later I got kicked in the teeth by the courts. No justice has been done." In 2005 Bowyer settled a civil case brought by Najeib and his brother without admitting liability and paid £170,000. Ridsdale addressed the issue at a press conference following the verdicts. "Leeds United have not been on trial," he said. "Originally four and then two of our employees were on trial. If either had been found guilty of grievous bodily harm with intent they would not have played for this football club again. As it is I will be making both players available to David O'Leary for selection. There is no hint of racism within Leeds United Football Club."

Even as he spoke the *News of the World* was preparing to serialise a book written by O'Leary and another club employee, head of press David Walker. The title? *Leeds United on Trial*. They even dedicated the book "to chairman Peter Ridsdale, the board of directors and all genuine Leeds United supporters". The chairman, dumbfounded and humiliated to learn what everyone in football journalism already knew, was raging. O'Leary washed his hands of it, claiming, "I can't help the timing. I don't get any pennies or monies for what the *News of the World* took out of my book." Leeds briefed that the title was "ironic" but it smelt like a cheap cash-in. It was a gross misjudgement and Leeds and he paid a heavy price for it. His criticisms of Bowyer and Woodgate caught the headlines while a deeper reading exposed damning words for several players. They would not be forgotten or forgiven.

From top of the league on New Year's Day 2002, Leeds crashed to fifth after a 2-1 defeat by Cardiff in the FA Cup started a run of eight games without a win. Smith was sent off at Ninian Park, his sixth red card in three seasons, as his temper and aggression turned toxic for referees. The players escaped a riot in Wales when the home supporters, inflamed by Sam Hammam standing in front of them and repeatedly "doing the Ayatollah", invaded the pitch at the final whistle. Next month they were knocked out of the Uefa Cup by PSV and crawled to the end of the season with their fans denouncing Kidd as an Old Trafford plant, O'Leary constantly shuffling selection and attempting to deflect blame and certain players adamant that he had lost their trust. He signed on as BBC pundit for the 2002 World Cup where he proved as garrulous as ever on the subjects of Leeds United, interest in Ferdinand and whether, having lost millions for the second year running by missing out on Champions League qualification, they could afford to keep him. He came home at the end of June and was sacked. Typically Ridsdale tried to massage it at first as an amicable parting of the ways but O'Leary insisted he told the truth and the chairman finally came clean. Some felt O'Leary had flown too close to the sun, others that he never learnt to keep his mouth shut. All the talk of succeeding Ferguson, of interest from Lazio and Inter, was usually laughed away with 'ever so 'umble' protestations of naivety. What was refreshing at first quickly paled through constant repetition and led to the growing sense amongst some fans that it was all about him. He was right in one way: he was very naïve not to recognise that when he needed more rope, he had reached the end of the board's tether.

Ridsdale immediately turned to Martin O'Neill again and was told he would listen in 2003 at the end of his contract, not before. Steve McClaren, a boyhood Leeds fan and a year into his first job at Middlesbrough, was the favourite until either Leighton or the chairman, precisely who is unclear, proposed the former England, Barcelona and Tottenham manager, Terry Venables. Ridsdale flew to Spain to meet him and was impressed by his charisma and vision. The 59-year-old was given a two-year contract on

£2m per annum and, according to him, was given the leeway to keep Ferdinand if he let other players go – Bowyer, irked by the fine and refusing to sign a new contract, for £9m, Dacourt for £15m and Keane for £10m were mentioned. Ridsdale had negotiated with REFF that the repayments owed on eight players should be restructured to ease the outflow and now only half the purchase fee would fall due over the length of each contract with a lump sum due on his sale. Leeds had the players independently valued and carried those figures, completed during a bull market, as assets. Trouble was, after the collapse of OnDigital in 2002 and the failure of the limited Premier League pay-per-view service to draw in the kinds of revenues predicted, the market crashed. In 2001 the club had borrowed £60m in a securitisation loan to pay off its bank debt and, by its 25-year-terms, repayment would be made from a 'locked box' where season ticket and executive box revenues were gathered. In short, Leeds Sporting, with debts of £77m, needed to sell players in a dwindling market to keep trading. Venables may have wanted Ferdinand to stay but he wanted to go and the club needed Manchester United's £30m. The captain was sold and the new manager was left feeling cheated before a ball had been kicked.

Bowyer decided to run down his contract rather than move to Liverpool, Dacourt refused a transfer to Lazio and Keane told Venables he would only move to Tottenham, whose chairman, Daniel Levy – as he would do several times over the next 18 years – nailed a desperate Leeds to the floor, paying £7m for a forward bought for £11m and who had just enjoyed a stellar World Cup. Venables bought in Teddy Lucic, a Sweden defender quickly dubbed 'Stig of the Dump', Paul Okon, an Australian midfield plodder, and Nick Barmby. He employed a 4-3-3 and tried to make do. It did not work. Leeds lost their drive. Patient build-up play did not suit the players or the fans. Smith added a red card for England to another one in the league and the board's dawning realisation, when they slumped to 16th in December, that Champions League qualification would be impossible panicked them into a fire sale. In January they sold Fowler to Manchester City for a £5m loss and agreed to cover some of his salary and Bowyer for £100,000 to West Ham simply to get him off the wage bill. It barely touched the sides. Ridsdale, therefore, accepted a £9m offer from Newcastle for Woodgate and announced the deal on deadline day alongside a thunder-faced Venables who openly disagreed with his chairman and looked like his hostage. "What we have done is to ensure we're financially robust. We have taken the right decision for the long term," said Ridsdale. "Should we have spent so heavily in the past? Probably not. But we lived the dream. We enjoyed the dream. Only by making the right decisions today can we rekindle the dream once again in the future. And that is what we intend to do."

In that moment we saw that Leeds' Icarus was Ridsdale, not O'Leary, and he also had the entire club handcuffed to him. Debts were mounting, share price and book value of the players plummeting, manager and chairman were locked in dispute, the fans contemptuous of a manager and his spineless team and here was Ridsdale talking like some guru about "the dream". Instead of 'rekindling' it or, better still, waking up, he had conjured up a nightmare.

25

DOWN THE DIP

Terry Venables always understood the first maxim of football management: 'Never resign'. Even though he felt he had been misled, Leeds United were now reduced to selling their 'crown jewels' to cover the cost of the cratering of their investments, the crowd was on his back and the company he worked for had lost more than 75 per cent of its value, he hung on. "I feel like I'm jammed into an unwinnable position," he said and there was some sympathy for him from those who knew exactly what was going on. "If you didn't learn from Terry Venables on the training field,' says Gary Kelly, "you didn't want to learn. Dave O'Leary had the lucky time at Leeds, he was told: 'You go and get who you want.' And Terry had them and then they were taken from him. It was hard for him. It was the other side of what O'Leary had."

Some of Venables' decisions were culpable for the plight of the team, however. They should not have been as low as 16th and knocked out of the FA Cup by First Division Sheffield United by the time he was sacked and paid off in mid March. Missing a week of pre-season to appear on a Channel 5 holiday programme in the Seychelles was excusable given Leeds approached him only after the World Cup. But he made mistakes with his personnel: Nigel Martyn was a better goalkeeper than Venables' preference, Paul Robinson, Kelly a superior right-back to Danny Mills and a more spirited captain than Dominic Matteo. David Batty was not 'finished' and should not have been exiled while indulging Harry Kewell's desire to play as a No.10 meant wasting Alan Smith in midfield where, if possible, he was prone to making even worse challenges. Does it really matter that Venables did not arrange the furniture satisfactorily while the house burned down around him? He didn't start the fire but the deterioration of their results in the autumn and winter accelerated the conflagration. His friends in the media said he left with his record unblemished, having been sold a pup. Brian Reade in the *Daily Mirror* was markedly less generous: "He shuffles out like an embarrassed old man caught with his trousers down in a place he should have had more sense than to enter."

Ridsdale went back to O'Neill and thought he had an agreement for the Celtic manager to join in the summer, which sent him off in search of a caretaker. He rang the out-of-work Peter Reid, who had taken Sunderland to two seventh-places before being sacked five months previously. People told Reid he would be crazy to take it. He accepted, reasoning: "There are only a limited number of great clubs and if you have the opportunity to manage one you grasp it with both hands. I knew I would be in a no-lose situation. The club was in a mess but it wasn't of my making and, even more important, there was still so much quality in the ranks that I knew if I did a decent job I would keep Leeds in the Premier League." He was given eight games and an incentivised two-month deal of £5,000 a point plus a £500,000 bonus for avoiding relegation. Reid's first game was lost at Anfield, a 3-1 defeat in which only the patched-up warrior Radebe emerged with any credit. The travelling fans targeted a hare-eyed Ridsdale in the directors' box and he took it all, clasping his hands. When the Kop joined in with a sarcastic 'One Peter Ridsdale', his race was run and he resigned. One notably charitable correspondent wrote: "When football's historians come to judge him, they will focus on his actions in Istanbul." And it remains true that he deserves praise for his conduct that night. When he stepped down, however, he shook his fist at the world and not at the mirror. It was the market's fault. The managers. Even Al-Qaeda's, citing 9/11 as the reason global investment tanked and ruined his plans for a new £60m stadium near Garforth. When he wrote his memoirs, he came across as someone saying that it is pointless arguing whether it was Thelma or Louise who was driving when the car fell into the canyon. It cannot be emphasised too often. Ridsdale, as chairman and chief executive, was at the wheel. Max Clifford, who was employed by the club as a PR consultant in 2002-03, could not spin that away.

Reid reportedly found Viduka moody and distrustful but buttered him up sufficiently. He scored 10 times in the last seven games, enough to earn four victories and a draw. At Highbury, a match missed by Smith after his third red card of the season, the Australian scored a superb winner two minutes from time to inflict a 3-2 defeat on Arsenal, which would be their last for 17 months. Reid added £565,000 to his retainer for points accrued and staying up and was offered the job on a full-time basis by the new chairman, Professor John McKenzie. He had joined the board only in February, six weeks before Ridsdale's resignation, and held what was described as a significant stake in the club. He had been working as rector, then director of international development at the London Institute and as an adviser to government, cultural and academic bodies in the Far East. His appointment screamed that Leeds' search for a rescuing angel would begin in China. The Professor added Eddie Gray and Brian Kidd to the 17 redundancies announced in March and allowed the publication of details of the expenditure authorised by the board under his predecessor, revealing the infamous rented goldfish and hundreds of thousands on private jets and car leasing contracts. All came to symbolise Ridsdale's profligacy and exposed his fellow directors, especially Allan Leighton, as, at best, permissive. Because the fish were so trivial, they came to symbolise everything wrong with Leeds Sporting rather than the player lease-to-buy scheme, which principally sank them. Publicising this information could have been a sign that McKenzie would be encouragingly ruthless. Instead he swam ever more out of his depth by the day.

First Kewell, who had only a year left on his contract, told the club he would leave at the end of it for free unless they sold him to Liverpool. There was interest from Barcelona and a firm £7m bid from Manchester United, which, said McKenzie, was ultimately matched by Liverpool. When the deal was completed it turned out that it was worth just £5m, £2m of which McKenzie had agreed to pay to Kewell's agent, Bernie Mandic. McKenzie felt Leeds had been diddled when he had been strong-armed by Kewell exploiting the weakness of the club's bargaining position. It is doubtful whether any former player would earn a more hostile reception than Kewell if he showed his face at Elland Road today, especially after leaving Liverpool for Galatasaray – Leeds fans were incensed by his decision to go there before justice for the murders in 2000 had been served.

Dacourt left for Roma for £3.5m, half the fee Leeds had borrowed from REFF to buy him and, when Robinson turned down the wages offered by Aston Villa after Leeds agreed a £3.5m fee, Reid sold Martyn instead for £500,000. He had very little money to play with and used it unwisely. Over the course of a few days, Leeds brought in five France-based players on loan, all affiliated with the agent Willie McKay, and also borrowed Arsenal's teenage winger Jermaine Pennant. Pennant played well sporadically but of the others only Didier Domi in spurts and Salomon Olembe, who should have been used more, found any form. To compound his weak position, Reid also had problems with a disenchanted Viduka, whose longed-for move to AC Milan broke down late, and sent 17-year-old James Milner, who had played with skill, maturity and versatility in his debut season, out on loan. McKenzie tried to dismiss Reid but bungled it when doorstepped by the press during the meeting then sacked him at the second attempt in November after a 6-1 defeat by newly promoted Portsmouth which sent them to the bottom of the league. Reid had dropped Viduka after a bust-up at the training ground and tried to hide Roque Júnior, a World Cup-winning Brazil centre-back bought hastily in on loan, in midfield. Portsmouth's sixth goal was the 20th conceded by Leeds in Roque Júnior's fifth appearance in the starting line-up. He never played for the club again.

McKenzie lit the bat signal for a caretaker once more and Eddie Gray responded, six months after being made redundant. The chairman announced losses of £49.5m for the previous year even after selling Ferdinand and spoke, in tones that brought to mind the *Fast Show* character Swiss Toni, about his optimism. "Two years ago we were struggling to swim against the current," he said. "Now we are treading water. In a year's time I hope to have one foot on the sand, which is where we want to be as quickly as possible. And following that I would hope to be on the sand running with a beautiful blonde." Trevor Birch was not blond and he and McKenzie never made it to the beach together. He was brought in on Leighton's recommendation to become chief executive, having successfully held debt-laden Chelsea together until Roman Abramovich switched on his cash pipeline. Various saviours of various hues were sought over the next few months on the playing and business sides – the club spoke to George Graham about coming back, courted Gordon Strachan through the press and pursued Nottingham Forest's Paul Hart, all in vain – and entertained reports of interest from Leighton, who stepped down to try to form a consortium, from Bahrain, China, Uganda and Huddersfield.

In the meantime Birch held off REFF and institutional creditors with a standstill agreement, negotiated with former players and managers who were owed money, and tried to persuade the players to defer some of their wages. The latter provoked a dressing-room split when the captain, Matteo, backed Birch's proposal while Batty argued that he knew players were angling to leave during the January window and that they should be sold to raise the funds. Details of the disagreement leaked and Batty found himself scapegoated as uncaring and arrogant. He played his final game at the beginning of January, hung out to dry by a club he had served twice with such vigour.

McKenzie departed in mid-December, hinting about a Chinese saviour and was barely heard of again. Gray did his best by binning most of the loan players and a mini-run of two wins and three draws in December took them to within a point of safety. Leeds played rock-bottom Wolves in their next game, arrived at Molineux confident that victory would push them as high as 16th and only three points off 10th. They threw away a 1-0 lead, Matteo was sent off and the match was ultimately lost 3-1. Leeds were beaten four times in succession after that and the jig looked up. For all that, they were not a terrible side: Pennant and Milner were penetrative on the wings, Radebe inspirational when fit, Harte still incisive at set-plays, Kelly a driving force and Viduka and Smith high-class if volatile strikers. Too often they were like a balloon with a slow puncture, deceptively pumped up then slowly deflating as a match progressed.

On 22 March, after a sequence of one win in 12 games and back at the bottom of the league, the team ran out to play Manchester City at Elland Road under new ownership. Two days earlier a consortium called Adulant Force, led by insolvency accountant Gerald Krasner, had bought the club for £20m after Birch and the new owners had resolved a settlement with the bondholders, owed £60m, and REFF, owed £22m. They guaranteed debts held by the football creditors, former managers, players and clubs waiting for transfer instalments, put Leeds Sporting plc into administration with Leeds United FC spun off, and announced that the "club was off life support and could now move forward". Spotting that Krasner's partners included David Richmond – son of Geoffrey Richmond, who had left Bradford City on its knees financially when he left the chairmanship there – and Simon Morris, a 29-year-old property developer with an interesting reputation, prompted disquiet among supporters. One, a former club mascot, told *The Times*: "These people are to football what King Herod was to babysitting. I fear for my club."

There were 10 games left and Leeds were five points from safety. They won three and drew one of the first five with Viduka to the fore to take them level on points with the club in 16th. The Great Escape was on until Viduka, playing the Gordon Jackson role, betrayed himself with indiscipline, earned a suspension for an unnecessary booking and missed the must-win home game against Portsmouth. By that point it had become clear that of the £28m raised for purchase price and running costs by the Krasner consortium, £15m had been borrowed from the property developer Jack Petchey on a short-term, high interest basis with eye-watering penalties for missed payments. After a month they were already looking to flip the club. A day before the Portsmouth game it was revealed there was a split between the partners over a £20m offer from haulier Steve Parkin, which had eventually been rejected. It seemed they were still gambling on staying up, a hope that was smashed the next day when Portsmouth won 2-1 and confirmed a week later in Bolton when they were hammered 4-1 and Viduka got himself sent off for two lunatic fouls. There were tears in the stands and on the pitch. Fourteen years after Bournemouth, Leeds were relegated with two games to spare.

Adulant Force began to liquidate some of their assets before the season ended. Smith was chaired around Elland Road after the final home game. He played while Robinson was omitted from the starting line-up for the club's last top-flight match for 16 years, a 1-0 defeat at Chelsea, for fear of injury scuppering his £1.5m sale to Tottenham. It was not Eddie Gray's decision. He had not cried at the Reebok. His eyes were clear as he spoke about the long road back he had embarked upon in 1982 with a potless and prostrate club. Krasner sacked him and installed Reid's assistant, Kevin Blackwell, a protégé of Neil Warnock, who had been kept on as Gray's No.2 because he had the Uefa coaching badges Gray lacked. After Bolton, Smith had revealed "the board said they would move heaven and earth to keep me but then told me I wouldn't be getting a new contract. That's not my idea of moving heaven and earth". It emerged between his valedictory home game and the trip to Stamford Bridge that he had agreed to move to Manchester United for £7m, going back on his seemingly sincere if foolish pledge never to join them. That he had gone to the highest bidder and altruistically waived his rights to 10 per cent of that fee so that the new owners who had welched on their pledge could keep the club going, should have mitigated his about-turn but he remains unforgiven in some quarters. Next out of the door were Viduka and Milner, for £4.5m and £3.5m respectively, followed by seven internationals all given free transfers and settlements to rinse them off the books. The club received £7m as a parachute payment but the new owners' miracle cure, selling 2,000 20-year season tickets at £4,000 a pop, found only 100 souls who could afford it and were willing to place a bet that there would be a club left to honour them by 2024.

Blackwell used his contacts to amass a couple of dozen triallists and ultimately recruited 11 players on free transfers to start the season. If he said "in pre-season there was only me, Gary Kelly and the tea ladies here" once, he said it a thousand times to emphasise how threadbare his resources and chances were. Of course both were straitened but it was a gross exaggeration. Radebe signed a new contract, Michael Duberry, Eirik Bakke and Seth Johnson were still around, if injured, and there were four or five first-team ready young professionals such as Aaron Lennon and Matt Kilgallon who had already played in the Premiership. There was a touch of *The Wild Geese* about the teams Blackwell sent out, built around veteran 'solid professionals', such as the one-paced centre-half and captain Paul Butler, and there was nothing sophisticated about their tactics, which was pure Warnock-ball with its accompanying incessant criticism of referees. They won three of their first 10 games, the former England striker Michael Ricketts, who was leading the line, never looked like scoring and when

Blackwell teamed Butler with the rugged Sean Gregan at the back, it felt like an early Bremner team. They dropped as low as 19th in November and December but by mid January were up to 14th and still attracting respectable crowds of above 25,000.

It was sometimes hideous to watch, if increasingly reliable, a caveat that could not be applied to Adulant Force's ownership. Over the autumn and winter Krasner and his fellow directors sold parcels of land around the ground, then the freehold of Howard Wilkinson's talent factory at Thorp Arch and took out a 25-year lease. Next, to discharge Petchey's loan, they also sold Elland Road itself to the new owner of Thorp Arch, Jacob Adler. He was a 35-year-old 'property investor', who was said to be "fiercely protective of his privacy", denied any relationship to the current owners and described himself as someone who was only trying to help. It was reported that he paid £8m for the freehold, granted Leeds a 25-year lease at an annual rent of £1.15m plus buy-back options. The deal was done by Shaun Harvey, the Leeds United chief executive brought in by the Richmonds. Harvey had worked with Geoffrey Richmond at Scarborough and had been managing director of Bradford when they ran up unsustainable debts during their Premiership years. He took over day-to-day operations while the owners looked for a way out.

A takeover bid fronted by Sebastian Sainsbury and backed by Nova Financial Partners was discussed in May 2004 and again in the autumn as both sides briefed the press. Lawyers and accountants had a field day scrutinising all kinds of arrangements tying the Adulant Force partners together, details of the offer and funding. Months of purgatory ensued, a rival emerged led by Norman Stubbs and was entertained until Sainsbury met the former Chelsea chairman, Kenneth William Bates, at the Dorchester and asked him to join his bid. Bates said he told Sainsbury he had £10m to invest but would want control and since Sainsbury could not tell him the source of his funding, he would not be part of it. On 21 January 2005, Leeds United and Bates announced that 50 per cent of the club had been sold to the Geneva-based Forward Sports Fund and that Bates would be the chairman. The other half, because of contractual liabilities to the bondholders, would be bought in 2007. Was he Leeds United's new owner? No and yes, as he told the *Telegraph*'s Mihir Bose, seeming to relish having it both ways: "'It is a fund which I advise,' he said before adding with a smile, 'says he with dilated nostrils.' I persisted: 'Technically you are not an owner of Leeds, merely an adviser?' Bates replied: 'Well, let's not get into that. We shall leave it, for that is clearly Machiavellian.' And with that he burst into loud laughter."

Bates was 73, some 10 months into retirement in Monaco having sold Chelsea to Roman Abramovich in the summer of 2003. He had made £17m from the sale of Chelsea, the club he had bought for £1 in 1982. Chelsea Village had been built, complete with hotel and restaurants, funded by debts of £80m secured against the value of the complex. Bates first became involved in football in 1965 when he used profits from his quarrying and concrete companies to buy Oldham Athletic. In a policy common to all his football businesses, he proposed making Boundary Park a 365-day-a-year venue with talk of discos and catering. As he would also do at Chelsea and Leeds, he waged war on supporters' groups and the local paper. Nationally, football clubs gave him the public platform he craved. His other business interests, notably his deal to buy large tracts of two British Virgin Islands in the late Sixties after he sold Oldham, brilliantly exposed by *The Square Ball*, were often completed offshore and away from the glare of scrutiny. He left a vapour trail wherever he went. The UK government paid £1.5m to buy him out of his Caribbean deal to prevent civil disorder. The collapse of the Irish Trust Bank in 1976, which he set up at the start of the decade, cost the Irish taxpayer millions to reimburse savers and prompted his relocation to Australia before he turned up in London with his pound note to buy Chelsea. The press lamely called him 'Blaster' Bates because of his abrasive nature rather than his tone. Indeed he doesn't shout at all, but talks in an urgent Cockney whisper, like a Strepsil-dependent chimney sweep. When he arrived at Leeds he had enjoyed 23 years of prominence in the game, guaranteed a back-page lead for his latest feud, intemperate outburst or sacking. Some supporters were relieved that someone – anyone – had turned up who would end the turmoil and took comfort from knowing "he may be a bastard but now he's our bastard", trusting his spikiness would be at the service of the club. No one, it was said, would dare to take advantage of Leeds United again.

The club, Bates reported, had £17m of debt but no cash. He immediately settled the £1.2m owed to HMRC, a proportion of a total of £4.8m outstanding to the taxman, which was due in seven days. Missing the payment could have put the club in receivership. The rest could be paid off over 30 months. He also made settlement of a loan put in by David Richmond, persuaded the other shareholders to leave their loans of £4.5m in for four years and began to negotiate with Messrs O'Leary, Venables and Reid on the sums outstanding from their contracts and compensation. He retained Harvey as chief executive and Peter Lorimer, put on the board by Adulant Force, as a director. Photographs were taken of the new chairman with the East Stand façade behind him. The collar of his overcoat was turned up and the camera captured only his incisors as he flashed a smile beneath leaden January skies. For the next 10 years it was the default picture used for any piece about Leeds and their chairman, an image that could serve as the video Joy Division never made for *Day of the Lords*.

Bates brought some order if not the "lorra, lorra laughs" he promised at his inaugural press conference. The team was stabilised with the signings of Shaun Derry, Rob Hulse and David Healy to bolster the players bought during Blackwell's July trolley dash and they ultimately finished 14th. Bates went on the record to say that he had never thought goalkeepers, Blackwell's former trade, made good managers but he was willing to give the man he inherited time and used part of the last tranche of parachute payments in the summer of 2005 to strengthen the squad. He also put season ticket prices up by 25 per cent and addressed the losses that were bleeding the club dry. Mentioning that half the wage bill was going on four players, over his first 18 months he agreed settlements to get rid of O'Leary holdovers Johnson, Bakke and Duberry and sold Lennon, a sprite of a right-winger and recipient of a boom-era contract, to Tottenham for a bargain £1m. Lennon would become the third graduate of the 2002 youth team, following Scott Carson and James Milner, sold by Leeds as teenagers during the meltdown who would go on to play for England. What Wilkinson had envisaged as the lifeblood of the club, a pathway for players from their pre-teens to the first team and international honours, now became its financial lifeline.

Patchy form at the start of the new season did not harm Blackwell's side and they were bunched in a pack pursuing the early bolters Reading and Sheffield United by the end of September when they came from 3-0 down with 19 minutes to play at Southampton to win 4-3. Thrilling results were not the product of equally exciting play – Gregan and Butler sat deep, defensive-minded wide midfielders protected the full-backs, Derry won the ball and they shifted it up quickly to the strikers. They won the next three games and, after two defeats on the road, the next four in succession, too. The points pushed them up to third and kept them comfortably in the play-off positions when they stumbled in the run-in. With 10 games to play they were six points behind Sheffield United in second with a game in hand but when they turned up at Bramall Lane for a kicking contest between the feuding Blackwell and Warnock, five draws and two defeats had killed any prospect of automatic promotion. They limped to fifth but were inspired in the play-off semi-finals by Preston's manager Billy Davies, a smile-phobic Scotsman, who proclaimed himself delighted after his side secured a 1-1 draw at Elland Road in the first leg. Leeds. "We can ask for no more, we've come here, done the job and it now swings towards us." The floodlights failed at Deepdale but Leeds didn't, winning 2-1 in a foul and card-strewn match by virtue of Hulse's header from a corner and Frazer Richardson turning in the striker's cross-shot. The travelling supporters reminded Davies of his "job done" cockiness and some of the players paid him back by leaving the very same message written in bold letters on the away dressing room chalkboard. "In 16 months, Leeds have hot-wired the hearse," wrote Rick Broadbent in the aftermath.

They had to wait 13 days for the final against Watford at the Millennium Stadium. The Coca-Cola promotions team had pulled out all the usual stops in their quest to make an 'occasion' out of an already tense and exciting fixture. Forty thousand Leeds fans sat through a wearying two-hour pre-match hoopla from the on-pitch PA announcer, only to recognise as soon as the teams walked out and several players were spooked by one of the sponsor's pyrotechnic blasts, that Leeds would ultimately crumble before Watford's bombardment. Not one Leeds player emerged with any credit as – on a bog of a pitch – Ashley Young ran riot on the wing and Neil Sullivan and the Leeds centre-backs were beasted in the air to the tune of a 3-0 defeat, a scoreline that should have been doubled. It was difficult for anyone who was there to discern whether they even tried to give Watford a game. "It hurt like hell," said Blackwell. More pain for him was imminent. While under a long-standing convention the losing team were awarded the gate receipts, but now the parachute payments had dried up he was forced to sell players, including his prize centre-forward Hulse to Sheffield United for £2.2m.

Wild optimism installed Leeds as pre-season favourites for promotion, a bet taken only by the loyal and those blind to form or reason. The slow centre-backs were a season older and slower, the best forward had been sold, Blackwell kept playing central strikers out wide, Kevin Nicholls, his No.1 transfer target bought in shambolic circumstances, was injured in pre-season and the manager's sour remarks and Warnock-esque tendency to shirk responsibility for set-backs alienated most of the players. Leeds scored only four goals in the first eight games and lost five of them. "I've turned this club around from nothing so I can turn it around from here," said Blackwell after the fourth loss. "I think the fans are fed up with what's happened at Leeds." They were, and also fed up with him and his negative tactics, obtuse selections and deflection of blame on to referees. It was hardly wise, either, to take the credit for the turnaround on his shoulders and not mention Bates once. Nor would raising the spectre of fan unrest have gone down well. Bates sacked him and, after four more defeats under the caretaker John Carver, the last a 5-1 trouncing by Luton Town, appointed the former Chelsea captain Dennis Wise as the full-time replacement.

Wise and Bates had got on well at Stamford Bridge over the 11 years they were there together, forging such a close relationship that Wise called his chairman 'Batesy' in public and Bates stood as godfather to his son. He had been linked with replacing Blackwell when he resigned as Millwall manager in 2005 and eventually moved to Leeds in October 2006 after five months managing League Two Swindon Town. He brought his Swindon assistant and former Chelsea team-mate, Gustavo Poyet, with him once compensation had ben agreed. They left Swindon in third place to join United who were 28 places higher in the pyramid, 23rd in the Championship. "I've told them I want them to be like the Leeds of before, who were horrible," he said. "I've explained I want a bit of nastiness." It was horrible, all right. Terrible mostly, too. He exiled Gary Kelly, a first-team regular since 1993, now in the last year of his contract. Wise made him train with the kids and refused to allow the players to attend a tribute evening held to raise funds for the cancer treatment centre he had set up in his home town in memory of his late sister. Wise appointed Nicholls as captain, which lasted a few weeks until he told his manager he was homesick for Luton, and scapegoated Derry.

Results and performances were unremittingly awful throughout December and they ended the year with only six wins and a goal difference of -23. Gregan, Butler and Sullivan were shipped out and 15 players were brought in on loan by the new technical director, Gwyn Williams, who had worked with Bates for years at Chelsea. The players referred to the new regime, without fondness, as "The London Crew". The supporters simply chanted: "Get the Chelsea out of Leeds." There was no honeymoon because there was no relief from miserable results and antagonising words and gestures. Leeds managed seven victories in the second half of the season as Bates and Wise sidelined players whose faces did not fit and questioned the loyalty of fans who would not turn up to watch such dross especially after the summer price hike. More may have stomached it if results had been better but the clubs spent 10 games at the bottom of the table in midwinter until three wins and two draws starting in March conjured up false hope. They returned to their old ways of shipping late goals, going down at Colchester and Southampton before conceding with 100 seconds to go when ahead against Ipswich in the penultimate game. Needing three points to stay alive, some members of the crowd invaded the pitch. It did not work at the Hawthorns in 1982 and did not save the situation now.

Postponement was never an option. The game was completed and Leeds were relegated to the third tier for the first time. They still had one game to play and Bates used that week to place the club in administration. To add injury to insult, Leeds United were bust as well as relegated. They had been broke before but never broken. Mockery was rife. Yet that was easier to bear than condescending sympathy. Dignity is overrated. The only salient question was whether a football club could be salvaged from the wreckage.

26

MASTERS OF WAR

Rumours of impending insolvency had dogged Leeds United for two months before their relegation was confirmed. On the Monday morning after they went down employees of KPMG were already at Elland Road, announced the club was £35m in debt and required an immediate cash injection of £10m to stay afloat. The catalyst was missing two scheduled monthly payments of £200,000 due to HMRC as part of the arrangement to pay down their liabilities. Default on the agreement had provoked HRMC into issuing a winding up order for the entire arrears of £8m and with that Damoclean sword above them, it took KPMG just five days to declare Leeds United Association Football Club Ltd insolvent. The Football League duly applied its rules and docked the club 10 points, a meaningless punishment for an already-relegated club, like shooting a corpse.

If Leeds thought they were in the clear, KPMG's second announcement, that it had authorised the sale of LUAFC Ltd to Leeds United Football Club Ltd, whose directors numbered Ken Bates, Shaun Harvey and the club's solicitor, Mark Taylor, exposed an unguarded flank.

"The important thing to note is not to view this as the end but the beginning of a new era," said Bates while KPMG issued redundancy notices to many long-serving members of staff.

The offer made by LUFC Ltd of 1p in the pound to the unsecured creditors would have to be accepted by 75 per cent of them for the company to be placed into a Company Voluntary Arrangement. The CVA would transfer the assets and Leeds United, having written off 99 per cent of its debts to non-football creditors, would rise like a phoenix out of the ashes.

Five other offers with proof of funds to buy the club out of administration were lodged with the accountants but it emerged that the biggest single creditor, Astor Investor Holdings Ltd registered in the British Virgin Islands, which, according to the account books, was owed more than £12,700,000, told KPMG that it would vote down all bids other than Bates'. Bates and Taylor provided sworn letters stating that they had no relationship with Astor and the offshore company gave a similar assurance. Bates could also count on the support of the votes of the Krato Trust, registered in Nevis, which was owed almost £2.5m, and, of course, Forward Sports Fund, the Cayman Islands-registered owners he advised, who were owed £2.4m.

When the vote was held and Bates, in emollient mood, upped the offer to 8p in the pound, 75.2 per cent of eligible creditors backed his vehicle's bid. One of those giving its assent and added to the list at the 11th hour, it was later revealed, was Yorkshire Radio, which was owed £480,000 and thus had 1.3 per cent of the votes. Bates and Taylor were directors of that company whose principal asset was the rights to Leeds United's home games. While it would be normal for a broadcaster to pay substantially for those rights, it seemed Leeds had given the digital station a financial undertaking that had to be honoured. HMRC disputed that debt and Astor's. Also, as a general principle, it was determined to test in court the Football League's rules, which protected only football creditors as preferential and left everyone else unsecured.

A hearing was set for early September, after the start of the season, which meant Leeds could not exit administration by the Football League's prescribed route with a CVA. Bates, therefore, withdrew the bid and KPMG put the club back up for sale. A new Bates offer of 11p in the pound was submitted by Leeds United 2007 Ltd as part of an otherwise undisclosed bid, KPMG accepted it under the threat of a deadline and the shares in the club were made over to Forward Sports Fund. To square the offshore circle Elland Road was now also owned by a British Virgin Islands company and the ultimate owners shielded by its banking secrecy code. It was all so convoluted that keeping track was like knitting fog. Bates liked to portray himself as a straight talker, except when it came to explaining why the ownership had to be so impenetrable.

Having at last resolved the ownership of the club, Bates argued that the Football League should hand over Leeds United's 'golden share', which the club had relinquished on going into administration and which was required to compete. Playing the exceptional circumstances card because HMRC's wider quarrel with the league had blocked the CVA path, he expected sympathy and understanding from the 71 clubs. After a week of deliberations the Football League board agreed to restore their membership at a cost of a 15-point deduction. Leeds appealed it and two days before the season started the governing body and its chairman, Lord Mawhinney, were backed by 54 clubs, Leeds United by 16. There would be no solidarity between competitors. Of the 23 other clubs in League One, only two backed United, and Cardiff City's chairman, a certain Peter Ridsdale who had left Leeds Sporting massively in debt, cast his vote in favour of the

League. Bates sought counsel and eventually served the League with a High Court writ citing unfairness and malpractice. Dennis Wise, meanwhile, having 'Rag-Arse Rovered' through pre-season in old kit and unable to sign anyone, prepared for the season's opener at Tranmere Rovers knowing he would need five wins just to reach ground zero. "They've not only taken my arms and legs off, they've cut my balls off as well," he said.

We do not know whether Wise went the full Henry V St Crispin's Day in his motivational speech at half-time and 1-0 down against Tranmere at Prenton Park, but he had assembled a squad, a happy few, who were willing to scrap for the cause and he united them to right the wrong he said had been done to the club. After the bollocking, Matt Heath headed the equaliser from a clever free-kick routine, keeper Casper Ankergren kept Leeds in it and Trésor Kandol, a hard-working if limited striker, scored the late winner. He scored five more and his strike partner Jermaine Beckford, a quick, raw and rangy forward, eight in the first 13 games to get Leeds off to a blistering start. The 15 points were knocked off in five straight victories and, with David Prutton and Andy Hughes blending in midfield, Rui Marques brawnily thwarting forwards with his positioning and interceptions, Leeds were up to sixth after the 13th game, a 4-2 home win over Millwall watched by a crowd of 30,319. It marked a year's anniversary for Wise and Gus Poyet, 12 months, he told the press using the words of his coach Joe Allon, in which he'd gone from "Bin Laden to Elvis". Leeds had won 11 and drawn two and, save for the deduction, would have been 11 points clear at the top. Then again, who can say that they would have managed such defiant advancement without a sense of injustice?

Just as everything was on a roll and mission impossible seemed achievable, Tottenham, so often the vulture club during Leeds' demise, paid £565,000 compensation to take Poyet as assistant manager to Juande Ramos. Bates and Wise thought he might stay and fought to keep him. The lure of his old club was too magnetic and Bates has never forgiven him (for the record, Wise is no longer in his good books either). After Poyet's departure the manager employed Dave Bassett, his old boss at Wimbledon, as his assistant and the balance between fight and fluency tilted in the former's favour. They lost the following game and four more over the next three months. Wise, working extremely long hours away from his family, lost his bounce once he swapped his friend for his mentor and, with Leeds in fifth at the end of January, accepted an offer from Mike Ashley to become Newcastle United's executive director. Bates took Newcastle's £1m but was personally wounded by Wise's determination to go. Wise, who tripled his salary to £1.5m at St James' Park and was allowed to base himself in the south, has scarcely spoken about Leeds and his name has been barely heard at Elland Road in the 12 years since.

Bates turned to the former United captain Gary McAllister as caretaker until the end of the season and the Scot, who once told this author that he "would crawl over broken glass" if the Leeds job ever came up, was a popular choice. McAllister had been widowed in 2006 when his wife Denise died of breast cancer, an illness that had ended his only previous managerial job at Coventry City. He had spent the last couple of years taking care of his children and was warmly welcomed by the supporters. It was a canny appointment by Bates and over four months, after a stuttering start, McAllister acted with the style and intelligence he had shown as a player. Moreover his presence gave the fans a Leeds United they could recognise again. "I'm joining a winning club," he said. "Quite simply, the job brief is to get promoted. We've got 17 games to go, I'm here until June and my job is to kick-start things again." He was sensible enough not to make too many changes, although upgrading the target man from Kandol to the veteran Scotland striker Dougie Freedman paid dividends as his superior hold-up play, vision and calmness were vital in the run-in. The job brief would have been fulfilled by a margin of nine points had the arbitration panel upheld Leeds' appeal against the 15-point penalty in late April. Six wins in their last seven games secured fifth and an escape route through the play-offs.

As in 1987 and 2006, they had to come from behind to win the semi-final, Jonny Howson's two goals at Carlisle, the last in stoppage time like Keith Edwards' 21 years previously, putting them through to Wembley to play Doncaster Rovers.

The final sparked a scramble for tickets and Leeds supporters, having snapped up their allocation, the Club Wembley sections and some Doncaster seats, comfortably outnumbered Rovers' by a ratio of about 4:1. Kaiser Chiefs played their grand homecoming gig at Elland Road the night before, but Leeds wilted on the bigger stage. Doncaster passed them to death, once again the players in white seemed overwhelmed by the occasion. Leeds were unable to muster their usual drive up the wings and midfield control to release Beckford. McAllister's preference for more agile midfielders deprived him of the inspirational Andy Hughes, who was left too long on the bench and robbed Leeds of any dog in the fight. For the second time in two years, more than 40,000 Leeds supporters had paid fortunes for tickets, travel and accommodation to watch a play-off final yet left bitterly disappointed. From where they were in August, being there was a kind of triumph but no consolation.

Gwyn Williams and McAllister made some astute summer signings, picking up Robert Snodgrass, a ball-playing winger, and Luciano Becchio, a bright, industrious forward, for peanuts, signalling that the manager envisaged the team evolving into a passing side. The emergence of Fabian Delph, as bright a prospect as Leeds had had since a teenage Harry Kewell, and decent early results glossed over some nervous defending, anodyne tippy-tap keep-ball in midfield and an inability to score when dominating possession. Ultimately, McAllister's blueprint, which appeared to be to turn Leeds into the Arsenal of League One, was wrecked by a lack of pace out wide, an inability to defend set-pieces, indecision over selection and the loss of Beckford to injury in November when sixth in the league. The embarrassment of defeat at non-League Histon in a televised FA Cup-tie that should have been postponed was compounded by cries of 'You don't know what you're doing' and followed by three defeats in the league, two of them from winning positions. McAllister had his philosophy but what he didn't have was the players to put it into effect. When he tried to meld some kind of compromise between ambition and resources, it fell apart. Bates, coincidentally nicknamed 'Bad Santa' for a while by Leeds fans, sacked him four days before Christmas but without rancour. McAllister, freed from a job that had palpably eaten his soul, spoke only of his regret at letting the club he loved down.

Gus Poyet rang Bates to ask for the job, an initiative the chairman rejected with gleeful scorn. Instead he turned to another former player, the seventh time the club had turned to 'one of our own', the Blackpool manager Simon Grayson. A youth team contemporary of David Batty, Grayson had been given two first-team run-outs by Billy Bremner and was sold by Howard Wilkinson during the title-winning season to Leicester, where he prospered. He had taken Blackpool up from League One via the play-offs and finished safely in 19th in his first Championship season. Grayson's side was sitting in 16th place in the league above when he agreed to drop 17 places to return to his boyhood club after a brief wrangle over compensation. A good start tapered off with back-to-back defeats by Huddersfield and Hereford. Two thousand Leeds fans were at Edgar Street and booed the players off after spending most of the second-half singing, "We're shit and we're sick of it". Grayson said he told Bates that month that he had outlasted Brian Clough and Jock Stein to make it through 44 days. "You nearly didn't after the Hereford defeat," the chairman replied with more twinkle than menace. It proved the turning point and Grayson demonstrated his spikier side by comparison with the more urbane McAllister when he tore into players who were accustomed to Wise's fire. He brought in the Leeds-born Ipswich centre-back Richard Naylor at the base of a spine now featuring Delph and the fit-again Beckford. Naylor's organisation addressed the dumb defensive lapses, Beckford and Becchio clicked and they won 11 and drew three of their 15 remaining matches to qualify in fourth for the play-offs again. "The [Hereford] night served a purpose but when your own fans are saying that about you, it hurts people," said Grayson. "You have to be a special type of person to play for this football club, to perform to the standards that are required."

Beckford and Becchio, who had scored 41 goals between them, failed to find the net at Millwall in the first leg of the semi-final. There were only 13,228 people in the New Den but they created a racket of hostile intensity that spilt over into a pitch invasion when Millwall's old warhorse Neil Harris scored the winner on 70 minutes and they ran on again at the end. Almost three times that crowd were at Elland Road for the second leg, producing a cracking atmosphere and a match that teetered on a knife-edge. Beckford had an iffy penalty saved, as was Delph's opportunity to ram in the rebound before Becchio poked in a left-wing cross to level the tie. Leeds poured forward in naïve desperation for the winner. Beckford was thwarted by a brilliant covering tackle but when they committed even more bodies into attack Millwall sucker-punched them on the break and went 2-1 up on aggregate through Jimmy Abdou. It was enough to knock Leeds out. At least they would be spared Wembley disappointment in 2009, not so Millwall, who were beaten by Scunthorpe in the final.

"We'll get over it, start again and give it a real good go for automatic promotion next season," said Grayson. "The players gave it all for the club. The fans gave it all for the club. It was an absolutely electric atmosphere. We have to stick together. This group will come back stronger. It's a very young group. The average age of our midfield was 22. We've got young talented players – Fabian Delph, Ben Parker, Robert Snodgrass and Jonny Howson – and they want to be here next year. There's a lot of hype over selling, but we don't have to sell. If we get ridiculous offers, we'll consider them, but I expect them to be here next season."

Delph was the first of the four to leave, sold to Aston Villa before the start of the 2009-10 season for a little less than the £8m they were originally quoted. Beckford had been transfer listed during the season when he refused to sign a new contract but when Leeds turned down bids he came off the list and opted for a game of brinkmanship, saying he would stay for the last year of his deal and then walk for free. Leeds would not bend and he was up front with Becchio as United started the season in sensational form, winning their first six games and losing only once in the league, inevitably at Millwall, until the middle of January.

They also gave Liverpool a fright in a home League Cup third-round tie, which they lost 1-0 after being robbed of a goal by a mistaken offside ruling. Their performance in that match, the rugged Australia centre-back Patrick Kisnorbo outstanding at the back in front of a gate of 38,000, stood them in great stead when they were drawn away at Manchester United in the third round of the FA Cup. It was coming up for 28 years since their last victory at Old Trafford and yet the League One side beat the Premier League champions. The goal satisfyingly caught England veterans Wes Brown and Gary Neville napping, Howson chipping a 60-yard pass and Beckford's speed compensating for his heavy touch to create the angle for him to roll a left-foot shot past the advancing keeper. Manchester United were poor throughout, and when Naylor and Kisnorbo were not hounding Wayne Rooney and Dimitar Berbatov into errors, Leeds' slick passing earned the 'Olé!' treatment. Leeds took Tottenham to a replay in the fourth round after Beckford equalised twice in the 2-2 draw at White Hart Lane and Grayson's men did themselves justice in another televised tie despite going down 3-1 at home.

When Delph had been sold, the money, according to Bates, was placed in "Simon's fighting fund" yet only free transfers had joined for the start of the campaign. Given that Leeds were flying at the top of League One, it was understandable that it was deemed unnecessary to invest but two unplanned for sell-out cup ties at home and visits to Spurs and Manchester United created an expectation that Grayson's 'pot' would be brimful in the summer.

The FA Cup run also brought fatigue and a blip. Beckford's new national fame following his showings at Old Trafford and White Hart Lane triggered rumours that he had signed a pre-contract to move to Everton and part of the crowd turned on him. Up front Max Gradel – a slippery winger with a temper, bought from Leicester after a loan spell – added unpredictability and flair yet could not, at first, arrest the slide. They were overtaken by Norwich after two defeats sandwiched by the cup run and dropped to fourth after five losses and five draws in the 12 games leading up to Easter. Kisnorbo ruptured his Achilles tendon when Millwall completed the double over Leeds and anxiety infected the crowd and players equally. It took the captain Naylor to settle the jitters, scoring twice in a gale at Yeovil on Easter Monday then, after three further wins and a loss that helped them back to second place, Naylor transformed the butterflies into tap-dancing rhinos with an 87th-minute own goal in the 1-0 defeat at Charlton in the penultimate game. Only victory in the final match against Bristol Rovers at Elland Road would guarantee promotion and salvation from play-off purgatory. Grayson had dropped Beckford to the bench for the previous four games. Now he made him captain.

The man in the armband calmly put the ball in Rovers' net after 34 minutes from an offside position and when play was stopped for the free-kick, Gradel sought out Daniel Jones, who had fouled him 90 seconds earlier in the first phase of the move, and stamped on his toes. Jones hit the deck clutching his face and out came the handbags as players squared up to one another, egged on by a baying Kop. Beckford, as if born to the role, walked into the fray and spirited Gradel away into the Leeds ranks. The referee had already made up his mind and sent Gradel off, a decision that prompted the winger to go spare. First he fought off Beckford's restraining hold and motioned as if to lamp his captain, then Michael Doyle pulled him away with the help of Bradley Johnson, and Andy Hughes tried to talk him down from the edge. In the end two tunnel stewards had to come on to the pitch to escort him off.

Gradel's explosion left Leeds 55 minutes to win the game with 10 men. At half-time Grayson found himself walking down the tunnel with Jones and could not resist giving him something to prey on his mind for the second half. "When that final whistle goes, if we've not got promoted, all the best getting off this fucking pitch," he said. In the dressing room he stopped the players' heated criticism of Gradel and told them to focus. He kept his head, too, when Rovers scored after his defenders failed to cut out both a deep left-wing cross and the square lay-off back into the box. Switching to three at the back, he sent on Howson, who was perfectly placed five minutes later. Johnson, now playing as a wing-back, slipped as he whipped in a cross from the left, Becchio, stunned the ball and laid it off to Howson 20 yards out to the right of the D and the substitute wrapped his instep around a shot that arced past a defender and dipped in at the near post. Because Charlton and Millwall were winning, a draw would not be enough, but the Leeds faithful had to wait merely four minutes for Johnson to latch on to a fluffed clearance, steam down the left of the box and torpedo over a cross that hit a defender. It sat up invitingly to hit on the volley. Beckford was not close enough, however, and had to take it on the bounce as it spun away from him. For all his goals – 84 in 151 Leeds appearances without the captaincy – he was not a gold standard finisher. He hit this one awkwardly with the side of his heel, still guiding it into the net. Words were not formed for the next minute. A wild, mass, full-throated roar was sustained for longer than seemed possible. The rest of the match, 27 long minutes, was played out to "Leeds are going up" and "Marching on Together" until the final whistle provoked an encore of ecstatic screaming and a jubilant pitch invasion. It was not 'like' an exorcism. It was one. The Championship was not the supporters' preferred destination but it was better than where they had been.

Promotion presented Grayson with a dilemma. "We are not in the Championship to make up the numbers," he said. "But the sensible aim would be to make sure that we don't waste a lot of seriously hard work by going straight back down." Consequently he used his pot to bolster the defence, signing a couple of centre-backs, two full-backs and the goalkeeper Kasper Schmeichel on a free. It made sense. Naylor was now 33, Kisnorbo injured and he had lost faith with Ankergren for the run-in. Beckford completed his move to Everton and Williams used his scouting network to bring in Billy Paynter to play off Becchio alongside Davide Somma, who had joined the club in September 2009 and spent much of the previous season on loan at Lincoln to gain first-team experience. Somma was a sharp finisher whose all-round play was improving until injury destroyed his career. The only thing that need detain us about Paynter, a busy centre-forward, is that he was not called 'Barndoor Bill' for nothing. He managed three goals in two seasons.

It took Grayson's side a while to get going in the second tier and they lost six of their first 13 matches, three of them exposing a defence that had been creaking since the Manchester United game. Barnsley thrashed them 5-2, they threw away a 4-1 lead at home against Preston to lose 6-4 and Cardiff's Craig Bellamy showed them what a Premier League player could do to a limited side by shredding them in a 4-0 hiding. The problem was obvious: Leeds had a good range of passing midfielders but no one to put a foot in. Amdy Faye had been signed for the defensive midfield role and had the right pedigree. Sadly, his legs had gone and no one else effectively shielded the suspect back four. Even so Becchio was a shining light, and when the Ireland centre-half Andy O'Brien joined on loan after the Cardiff debacle Leeds began to get a grip on the division. Snodgrass and Johnson worked well out wide, Gradel moved into the middle and Howson sat a little deeper. They went on a 12-match unbeaten run, climbing as high as second after beating Neil Warnock's Championship leaders QPR the week before Christmas and Grayson was named manager of the month for December.

It was at this moment that Bates chose to pick a fight with two of his first-team regulars. It is a rule of thumb in football that no club thrives for very long when its chairman is its most newsworthy source. Bates had been using his programme notes for five years to settle scores with people, uninhibited by £50,000 damages awarded against him in 2009 when a campaign he mounted against a former Adulant Force director, in which he called him a "shyster" and accused him of blackmailing the club, were found by the High Court to constitute "grave libels". Costs estimated at £1.5m were also awarded against the club. Nonetheless Bates continued to use the platform to denounce those with whom he disagreed with scattergun venom.

"Let us leave the EEC, abolish the Human Rights Laws, take the TV sets, pool tables and telephones out of prisons," he wrote in one sample. "A 10-year prison sentence should mean 10 years. Bring back both corporal and capital punishment, slash benefits and put single-mothers into hostels instead of giving them council flats. Finally if we chucked out all the illegal immigrants and asylum seekers there would be enough jobs for everybody, even if it's sweeping the streets or emptying the dustbins."

He also took to the airwaves of Yorkshire Radio once a week in an interview conducted by the host from a kneeling position and Bates used both outlets to take umbrage with anyone who complained about the club's once opaque ownership structure or asked for further investment in its principal asset, the football operation. He dismissed them as "idiots", "dissidents", "sickpots" and "morons".

Further down the line the chairman of the Leeds United Supporters Trust would find wholly irrelevant details about a family member splashed in *The Daily Mail* by a former *News of the World* journalist whose byline also appeared on an exclusive interview with the chairman. This time, however, it was Johnson and Neil Kilkenny who got it in the neck for asking for pay rises to sign new contracts that Bates did not wish to meet. He ridiculed them, called them greedy and they left at the end of the season on free transfers, Grayson's admiration and need for them notwithstanding.

Without January reinforcements, Leeds' promotion chances blew up when they gleaned only five points from seven games in April and they finished three points off the play-offs in seventh. Two months before the Premier League had intimated that should United go up, it would require far more transparency about the club's owners than a court case, a parliamentary inquiry and the Football League had made Bates divulge. Having maintained all along that he did not know the identity of the owners, his solicitor in court said that Bates was the co-owner of Forward Sports Fund along with Patrick Murrin. Within five months he had sworn that the assertion had been made in error and was untrue. Confused? Most parties were as they tried to plait the sawdust of all these companies in far-flung jurisdictions. The Premier League, though, was not to be trifled with and in May 2011 Bates announced he had bought the club himself via a company registered in Nevis for an undisclosed sum.

In the summer Schmeichel, after a promising first season, was sold against his wishes to Leicester for £1m and Gradel returned to France for £2.5m. It was hard to reconcile the low-key signings of inferior goalkeepers with Bates' talk of "Simon's pot" and the club's rude financial health until it emerged in dribs over the next 18 months that future season ticket sales had been mortgaged, as had executive catering contracts, and advance payments sought from sponsors. Grayson lasted seven months of the 2011-12 season, cutting an increasingly beleaguered figure. Leeds' transfer dealings during January 2012 – a month they began in eighth, the excellent form of Becchio, Snodgrass and Ross McCormack unable to fully undo the harm done by keepers chucking them in and distracted defenders – were dispiriting enough. They sold the club captain Howson for £2m to Norwich and signed a handful of players on loan, the last of them, Tottenham full-back Adam Smith, who became, remarkably, Grayson's 33rd loan signing in 37 months at Elland Road. The volume of loan signings was a microcosm of the way the club had been run, taking one season at a time with no obvious long-term strategy in place.

Meanwhile, the East Stand of a ground the club did not own nor claim to know who did, underwent a significant £5m redevelopment funded by them, creating function rooms and 24 corporate hospitality boxes, all part of Bates' long-stated intention to turn Elland Road into a 365-day-a-year revenue-generating operation. Bates saw this, as well as plans for a hotel and restaurants, as his sustainability project, "rebuilding Leeds brick-by-brick". Because so much revenue had been diverted into construction, Grayson was unable to afford the players he wanted to stay or buy replacements. But he was not without blame for the team's struggles. The defence was increasingly shambolic, he dithered over substitutions and some of his signings, especially Alex Bruce, Leigh Bromby and Paul Connolly, were given lengthy runs, bombed out of the side amidst whispers that he would like them to leave and then recalled. Charging top-six Premier League prices to watch all the best players leave and the remaining ones toil in mid-table pushed supporters away. By bringing in someone new, the chairman would have hoped for a bounce to split the progressively more militant 'Bates Out' demonstrators. His choice was the out-of-work Warnock, who had taken QPR up in 2011 and was sacked a month before Grayson in January 2012. He was given a 15-month contract.

Warnock had turned down the Chelsea job in the early Nineties and Bates had always respected his caustic style. There were those who thought his habit of prefixing sentences with "If I'm honest" was telling, others knew it was a Sheffield tic. It would be unfair to characterise him as an old school manager loved most by old school players because he had coaxed capricious talents such as Adel Taarabt to deliver consistently in the past. The style when he did not have players around him he fancied was always functional. He often harangued referees and feuded with opponents. But he took teams up. "I feel I have one big challenge left in me and believe Leeds is a club that should be in the Premier League," he said. "I want to be the man who is able to deliver this for a set of fans who never cease to amaze me with their numbers and their loyalty." He was supposed to be only observing the home match against Doncaster Rovers on 18 February 2012, but went down at half-time to make some suggestions that, it was boasted, turned defeat into a 3-2 win. However, Leeds won only three of 13 until the end of the season with him in the dugout. Bates had charged him with making the play-offs – a 14th-placed finish was not what he had in mind. "I think we are miles away from where we should be," Warnock said after defeat by Watford. "I couldn't see us scoring in a brothel today. We will have to invest. It needs major surgery. This is as big a job as I have ever had."

The surgical instruments were not forthcoming. In May, Leeds United announced that the board was in talks with an investor without disclosing any details. During the hiatus, while speculation mounted, Snodgrass asked to leave and was the third member of the League One promotion side to join Norwich. Leeds received £3m for their captain and gave some of it to Warnock to sign 11 players on contract plus four on loan, taking four from cash-strapped Portsmouth and, most notable of all, El-Hadji Diouf, a player he had once called a "sewer rat". Six of the recruits were in their thirties, a clear signal that this was to be an all-or-nothing gamble from Warnock. Other deals were lined up and several turned into sagas until they broke down because Leeds could not come up with the fees. For all that, the two best players during a stilted campaign were products of Thorp Arch, Sam Byram and Tom Lees.

Negotiations dragged during the anonymous bidder's period of exclusivity and Leeds fans responded wryly by posting scores of pens to Bates' home in Monaco to encourage him to hurry up and sign over the shares. In November, when Leeds fell to 17th after a 6-1 home defeat by Watford, protests in the Elland Road car park and during games gathered force. These fans were "idiots", said Bates, "an ignorant, illiterate minority". Gulf Financial House Capital had been outed as the bidders in September and on 20 November the private equity firm, licenced in Dubai and a subsidiary of the Bahrain-based Gulf Financial House, announced that it had agreed to buy the club from Bates for £17m plus add-ons if they were promoted before 2017. Bates would stay on as chairman until the end of the season and then ascend to the title of 'club president'.

"There have been a number of reasons why it hasn't succeeded before," said Bates, conveying his delight at the takeover. "One of them being there are so many liars, chancers and conmen attracted to football and it's been a very slow, steady, careful process in weeding out those people and not letting them anywhere near Elland Road." After eight years of unbroken turmoil and discord, of talent being flipped to sustain the losses, of soaring legal fees and ticket prices, all-pervasive secrecy, denouncements and insults, relegation, play-off misery and pointless conflict, Bates had sold Leeds in the same position in the Championship at which he had bought them. As he entered his final months as chairman his supporters, his 'silent majority', must have taken solace that he had saved the club from "liars, chancers and conmen".

27

BALL OF CONFUSION

A period of silence after eight years of noise from Ken Bates would have been welcome to many Leeds fans. A few months of peace while the new owner put down roots, assessed priorities and diverted focus back towards the pitch. Those who delighted in having "our Leeds United back" missed out two words: "football club". Gulf Finance House Capital themselves pledged that this was a reset moment. The days of blood on the carpet were over and it was time to get the ball out again, to build a vibrant team that would earn promotion. It did not matter that GFHC's motive involved selling a Premier League Leeds. What else would a private equity firm want with a business investment other than to profit from it? Its own publicly available documents outlined the opportunities its "bargain purchase" afforded. The least Leeds could expect, then, were professional standards, well-informed decisions, competent corporate governance and, because they had a long-term goal, an end to short-termism. Instead the club went from frying pan to fire, another rescue act that drove Leeds from purgatory into the Inferno.

At first nothing much changed. Bates was still chairman, Neil Warnock remained as manager and there was little cash for January transfers. Luciano Becchio had scored 19 goals so far that season but was disillusioned by the terms offered in a new contract and by playing for a struggling side. Warnock had said he would build his team around him, but the manager's tactics meant more long balls up to him than crosses from the flanks. Anyhow, Warnock said, his head "had been turned" by speculation. Warnock accepted Norwich's offer of £200,000 plus Steve Morison, a burly Wales centre-forward who thrived as a goalscorer at Millwall and nowhere else. "For me, he is a player who has everything," said Warnock. "He'll be a legend here." The manager began to switch to 4-5-1 to accommodate the new signing, which upset Ross McCormack, who made a show of screaming "fuck off" at Warnock when brought off the bench to score against Derby. A crowd of 21,384 watched that defeat in April, the third in a row, and most of them shared McCormack's frustration, throwing Warnock's "Can't fault the effort, they're a great bunch of lads" default soundbite back at him as he rubbed his face on the touchline. Most of his clubs warm to him. This one never did and he was sacked a week later.

If all GFHC had done was sack holdovers from the Bates era, respect for them would have lasted longer. Yorkshire Radio was shut down and broadcast rights were sold to the BBC, Shaun Harvey and Gwyn Williams were given their P45s and Bates himself was eventually ousted on the grounds that he had committed the club to a three-year private jet contract for his weekly commute from Monaco. The club modernised its digital presence and outlined its commitment to openness and 'customer focus' yet David Haigh, Salem Patel and Hisham Alrayes, garrulous when praise was being showered upon them, clammed up when the veracity of some of their claims was tested. How, for example, could Haigh claim to be a Beeston-born lifelong fan of the club when all public evidence suggested he had been born over the Pennines and brought up in Penzance where his principal enthusiasm had been owls? They had not expected the scrutiny buying a football club brings. The kind of things many people would blurt out in job interviews or use to burnish CVs are not serious offences yet it provoked unease that someone could be unwise enough to utter untruths or exaggerations that would be checked. What did they think people were doing on the internet all day?

Fans welcomed the positive engagement at first and the appointment of Brian McDermott with five games to go. McDermott, a gracious, thoughtful coach, had been Premier League manager of the month for January 2013 with Reading, the club he had taken up in the summer. He was dismissed in March and agreed to come to Leeds barely a month later. His side won three of the remaining five games, moving up from 16th to 13th and it was clear that players were not so quick to hoof it long, promising something better to watch might be in the offing the following season. Scott Wootton and Luke Murphy were bought in the summer, both for £1m, the club happy to trumpet the latter while not publicising the fee for Wootton, a versatile Manchester United trainee who gave his all but was undermined by concentration lapses and a lack of speed. Murphy would rise to the captaincy without imposing himself on matches. Bought as a playmaker, he played as the kind of tidy, vanilla midfielder safely marked six out of 10 by journalists before a ball had been kicked.

McCormack and the new signing Matt Smith eventually formed a complementary partnership up front during the 2013-14 season, but the failure of some of McDermott's other picks, especially Noel Hunt, caused disquiet among the directors. One of them resorted to canvassing the advice of a select group of fans with social media followings, posted questions under a pseudonym on the most popular forums and consulted ratings used in computer games to assess the merits of the manager's targets. Journalists who had any dealings with the GFHC regime were bombarded by people who had been engaged to work on the principals' profiles. There were plenty willing to do their bidding for free on Twitter, too.

McDermott could not resolve the defensive frailties that had been naked since 2010. To his credit he got a better tune out of Warnock's players than the man who recruited them and coaxed them to fifth before Christmas. By that point the club was for sale and had entered a period of exclusivity with Sport Capital, a vehicle put together by Haigh which included the shirt sponsor, Enterprise Insurance. Andrew Flowers, the managing director of the company, and Haigh agreed to fund the club before completion and loaned it £1.7m. Doubts had been raised prior to GFHC's takeover about the viability of their ownership. Its parent company had losses of $250m in June 2012 and only $6m in cash. Bates had mortgaged the season ticket revenue and catering receipts. How would they meet the monthly liabilities only on individual match ticket sales, merchandising and paltry Championship TV income? By November Leeds were losing £1m a month and Bates indicated that before he had been sacked he had arranged a loan of £1m from a company that had once held preference shares in Leeds United but which he maintained was unconnected to him. Bates contradicted himself in interviews making the logic difficult to follow but was adamant GFHC had needed an injection as early as March. Haigh spoke of his grand plans and deep feeling for the club but his bid collapsed in January and an orgy of leaking, briefing, claim and counterclaim began as the directors fought like rats in a bag.

One source revealed that Alrayes, GFH's chief executive, had demanded that Haigh and Patel sack McDermott at half-time of the 6-0 defeat by Sheffield Wednesday in January. Others published transcripts of some dopey WhatsApp conversations between Bahrain and Leeds. Someone then provided the memo sent by Alrayes to McDermott after the Hillsborough game, saying United had been "humiliated live on television against a local rival" and "for each game now onward, you will be required to submit a report on strategy to be undertaken, list of players and squad formation a (minimum) of 24 hours prior to the game for group CEO and chairman's approval". Alrayes was based in Bahrain, had no football experience and expected team approval. No wonder their form had evaporated yet McDermott stoically carried on. He was sacked on 31 January but not by GFHC. Massimo Cellino, the owner of Cagliari, did the deed a couple of hours after agreeing to buy United.

Cellino had been president of the Sardinian club since 1992. His father, Ercole, had founded a European grain conglomerate and his son rose up the family business. He was renowned for his volatility as an employer of coaches, making 36 changes at Cagliari, disputes with local government which he addressed by relocating home fixtures 500 miles from the Mediterranean to the Adriatic, and had two convictions for fraud. His desire to get out of Cagliari was well-known. There had been petulant walkouts in the past and he had recently pursued bids for West Ham and Crystal Palace. Haigh courted him as an investor and for a while he was part of his consortium. In January 2014 he launched a solo bid and GFHC accepted an offer said to be worth £30m for 75 per cent of the equity and responsibility for the £24m debt. He brought his compatriot, the former Boro defender Gianluca Festa, over with him, had him watch training and announced from Elland Road that McDermott was out on the eve of a home match against Huddersfield. Fans raced down to the ground in support of the manager and chased Cellino's taxi around the car park in an attempt to blockade his exit and make him change his mind. McCormack rang Sky Sports News in his capacity as captain to protest and the following morning Haigh intervened, pointing out that Cellino was not authorised to act before the takeover had been completed. He reinstated McDermott, who stayed away from the game, but his assistant Nigel Gibbs overruled Festa's selections and Leeds won 5-1.

Cellino began his whisky, beer and fags charm offensive, ligging and jamming with bands, talking to supporters and spouting off about Haigh. An uneasy truce was established with McDermott who saw out a season in which McCormack scored 28 goals. The Football League initially blocked the Italian for failing its Owners & Directors Test in March, the first person to do so, not for earlier convictions but for being fined €600,000 for import tax evasion on a yacht. Cellino successfully appealed pending a written report from the judge in the case, took executive control in April and sacked McDermott in May. Haigh also left the club and told the police, when Cellino discovered surveillance equipment in the boardroom, that it had been installed at his direction because of rumours of drug use. Haigh flew to Dubai to meet his former GFH colleagues where he was arrested, held in custody for a year without charge and convicted on a 'breach of trust' indictment. When he was released in 2016, he maintained he had endured acute psychological suffering, rape and torture while in prison. In 2020 England's High Court upheld a UAE ruling that GFHC could pursue Haigh for a sum of more than £3m he had been convicted of embezzling via more than 100 false invoices.

Whether Cellino had undertaken due diligence is unclear. Little good it did to dissuade Bates in 2005 or GFHC in 2012 in any case. What he found in terms of the club's finances in the spring and summer of 2014 surprised him. Immediately he set about slashing budgets by temporarily shutting down Thorp Arch, emptying the pool and closing the canteen. Security staff were laid off, cleaners axed and their duties given to the first and second-year professionals. McDermott's dismissal provided further scope for cost-cutting and he employed Dave Hockaday, a former Swindon full-back, well-regarded youth coach and one-time manager of non-League Forest Green Rovers, on a salary of £80,000, about a tenth of the going rate. Hockaday was the most unusual Leeds appointment since Bill Lambton and universally ridiculed. He was unlikely to prosper in the best of circumstances. Cellino's explosive mood swings gave him no chance. Benito Carbone lasted four months in a role with the longest job title in the game – Special Consultant to the Board of Directors for Sport Matters including Facilities & Academy – Hockaday merely 70 days. Nineteen players left during the summer and the money accrued – £11m for McCormack, fees in the hundreds of thousands for Tom Lees and Matt Smith, vindictively sold, it seems, since both were young, had done well and would have been happy to stay – was spent on 11 mostly Serie B players from Italy, a couple from South America and three Hockaday picks, Liam Cooper, Billy Sharp and Nicky Ajose. One win and three defeats did for Hockaday by the end of August, academy head coach Neil Redfearn acted up as caretaker for four games, earning 10 points, until Cellino appointed Sturm Graz's Darko Milanic as the club's first non-British or Irish manager. Milanic was said to speak five languages, not that he used any of them to say anything memorable. "He does not talk much and is very pragmatic," said Cellino. "I like him. He is a very cool guy." Milanic can put on his CV that he broke a record held by two greats of the trade, Brian Clough and Jock Stein. He was out in 32 days following three defeats and three draws. Cellino then reverted to Redfearn, giving a 12-month rolling contract to a boyhood supporter who had watched the Revie team from a West Stand paddock seat with his dad.

Redfearn's lifelong connection with the club and knowledge of the fans' customs and practices turned Cellino's eyes green. Without much help he stabilised the team. There was only one person to do analysis, his assistant was hired late and then put on gardening leave. Andrea Lore, a furniture salesman who had impressed Cellino in Miami, was always around monitoring training and the Italian players spoke directly to the self-styled 'President'. In December the Football League received the judge's report from the tax evasion case and disqualified him from acting as a director for three months and, after Cellino erupted, extended it until the end of the season. He put Andrew Umbers, a banker who had brokered Bates' sale to GFHC, in charge but left only in person, not in spirit.

Redfearn's youth team graduates – Lewis Cook, Alex Mowatt, Sam Byram and Charlie Taylor – were picked alongside a better blend of the imports and Warnock veterans. It took a while to work but by January the gap between the clusters of defeats lengthened. The curve was heading upwards when Cellino intimated he wanted the bearded Italian forward Mirco Antenucci dropped in case he scored the goals that would trigger a new contract. Redfearn refused, his assistant was suspended on spurious grounds and the team promptly lost four games. They were due to play Charlton next and in the 36 hours before the Serie B 'Sicknote Six', Antenucci, showing no gratitude, Giuseppe Bellusci, Dario Del Fabro, Marco Silvestri, Souleymane Doukara and Edgar Cani declared themselves unfit to travel. None were picked again by Redfearn, none sanctioned by Cellino. That Gaetano Berardi boarded the bus even though he was genuinely injured earned him the undying respect of the supporters while 'The Six' are forever held in contempt.

Cellino returned to Elland Road at the end of May in a foul temper and railed about Redfearn not attending his homecoming party. The manager's position had been in jeopardy for months and the owner's social media allies, the ones who called Cellino 'The President' and befriended his children on Instagram, began to heap abuse on him. At a press conference at the end of May, Cellino spoke with such rage, condemning Redfearn for excessive passion, that one was relieved he went off for a smoke in the hope it would temper his incoherence. He returned, if anything, even more wound-up and continued where he left off. Adam Pearson, the new executive director, once a Ridsdale ally as commercial director until he left in 2001, did the deed and Leeds welched on the agreement that Redfearn could resume his old job as academy director, a safety net he had insisted upon knowing Cellino's reputation. Shamefully and, it proved, illegally, Leeds United then also sacked Redfearn's partner, Lucy Ward, welfare officer at the academy, a woman who had helped the development of hundreds of players including Aaron Lennon, Fabian Delph and James Milner, and cooked for the kids because she felt a duty of care when Cellino closed the canteen. She took Leeds to an employment tribunal and was awarded £290,000 for unfair dismissal and sexual discrimination.

Uwe Rösler had been studying Leeds United for six months before he was appointed as Cellino's fifth full-time manager in a year. He was a coach with a distinct style of patient, probing build-up play with a long-term strategy. He would have been better off studying Cellino, who sacked him after only two victories, neither of them at home, in 11 league games. "I wanted them to play heavy rock football but instead it was like country music," Cellino said. "We were just trying not to lose. We were not trying to win." Next man up was Steve Evans, like Cellino a convicted tax evader. He signed a contract taking him until the end of the season. Throughout the fanbase the question 'Why?' was on most lips. "Someone has got to get it right here," said Evans, the former Boston United, Crawley Town and Rotherham manager. "Why not me? I have won a lot of football matches." Not so many in the Championship, though. He seemed pumped at his first match in charge, a disconcerting look as he appeared to be wearing eyeliner. Leeds drew 1-1 with Fulham and lost his first home game 2-0 against Blackburn Rovers when the South Stand ended the song 'Time to go, Massimo' with a roof-raising "Fuck off!" Cellino punished them by raising ticket prices by £5 to include a mandatory pie, telling a journalist that he had done it out of spite but denying that was his motive when confronted with his words. The good he did – critically in excising GFHC's influence from the club – was overshadowed by his torrid manner. His advocates advised everyone to "buckle up and enjoy the ride". But the rollercoaster made plenty of the supporters nauseous, including, it seems Cellino himself who wearily agreed to sell a majority stake to Leeds Fans Utd Community Benefit Society for £30m. When the fans group started to raise the funds in earnest, Cellino changed his mind.

Elsewhere, Byram was sold in January to West Ham for £3.7m, the 'Celliebers' launched a cyber attack on him for desertion and they would do the same again when Cook left for Premier League Bournemouth in the summer. Evans hung on in the perhaps sincere belief that he had done enough by finishing another spiritually crushing season in 13th. He never bit when Cellino baited him in public and spoke of the job as being as exciting as "weddings, babies born, your first date rolled into one". But he could not command any affection, the football was dire and Cellino judged the mood perfectly for once.

In March 2016, Kenny Dalglish met Andrea Radrizzani, who had built up his sports media rights company into a major player, securing contracts with Fifa, Uefa, the Premier League and F1. Radrizzani was in the process of selling the agency for £1bn and was intrigued when Dalglish spoke warmly of Leeds United as the last true sleeping giant of English football. He began to analyse the club and approached Cellino to talk about a 50 per cent stake and eventual sale for a total of £45m. Before the negotiations began Cellino settled on Garry Monk, who had taken Swansea City to eighth in the Premier League in 2015, as his new manager after being turned down by Bristol Rovers' Darrell Clarke. Monk had to sell Cook but snapped up Kemar Roofe, Luke Ayling and loaned two players he had worked with at Swansea, Pablo Hernández and Kyle Bartley. Leeds started the 2016-17 campaign slowly, losing four of their first six games, and rumours that Cellino's trigger finger was itchy abounded. It was unclear whether Radrizzani acted as a brake on his partner's impulsiveness because of decorum or whether he recognised that the midfield was improving and Chris Wood was looking sharper under the tutelage of the coach and former England forward James Beattie. Whatever the reasons, fortuitously they stuck with Monk, gave him time for his young players to understand how he wanted them to play and bed in the signings. Hernández was a revelation, a Spanish playmaker with more skill and vision than Leeds had enjoyed from a floating winger than any since Harry Kewell. To address the problems at the back, the Sweden centre-back Pontus Jansson joined on loan from Torino and had an immediate galvanising effect alongside the tall, strong defensive leader Bartley. His competence, confidence and volubility transformed the side but, more importantly, his willingness to get stuck in, thunderous swearing and tremendous heading power acted like a defibrillator on the crowd. The sense of team spirit and positivity was palpable when they went on a run of 12 wins in 15 games that lifted them up to third just as the January transfer window closed. Eighteen-year-old Ronaldo Vieira was unflappable in front of the back four and Wood punched his weight with 27 goals. Sky Sports virtually had a channel dedicated to them, rescheduling 18 games to be shown live on television, inciting the 'Sky TV is fucking shit' song to be given an airing at almost half the games for the next four seasons by those sick of the constant disruption to their weekend rhythm.

The atmosphere at Elland Road was electric for the first time since the last season in League One and there was a belief that something special and sustainable was happening. It seemed strange, then, that two wingers were brought in on loan in January rather than the striker Ashley Fletcher from West Ham, a deal Cellino said was oven-ready but blocked by Monk. The manager maintained his faith in his core group, stuck dogmatically to 4-2-3-1 and their challenge petered out. One win in their last eight games sank their play-off chances and they completed their most exciting season for six years in seventh. Cellino's last season was his best. It could not have been a coincidence that it was also his quietest season. Radrizzani completed the purchase, Cellino retreated to Miami but could not stay away from old habits for long. Within the month he bought Serie B Brescia and got through nine managers in his first three seasons.

Radrizzani was true to his word and shortly after buying the remaining 50 per cent of the shares, one of his companies completed the purchase of Elland Road from its Cayman Island owners 14 years after its initial sale. It was not in the club's ownership but it was manifestly in the owner's ownership – and that was a welcome change. Leeds United were granted a lease on it, initially rent free, and signs of transformation and renewal were quickly evident. Towering banners swooping down from the top of the stands featuring heroes of the past and the squad's leading lights may be only superficial adornments but they reveal a willingness to acknowledge that this is a place that thousands of people treasure, rather than merely a once-a-fortnight revenue generator. Slogans that may seem trite to others – Billy Bremner's "side before self", "the only place for us" and "marching on together" from the song *Leeds, Leeds, Leeds* – were writ large on everything from seats to façades and shirt collars, homilies and commandments that have nourished the club's identity across decades. The Leeds United Superstore was well-stocked and staffed. Just a few years ago, when neglect was hard to differentiate from contempt, the range was so meagre the club filled some shelves with scores of discount packs of Ainsley Harriott Savoury Rice.

Monk's one-year deal had an automatic extension clause that Radrizzani wanted to exercise but the manager resigned and left for Middlesbrough. The vacancy at the Riverside had arisen when Boro had dismissed Aitor Karanka and his director of football, Victor Orta, who was hired for the same role at Leeds as Radrizzani established a professional structure. A partnership was struck with San Francisco 49ers, a former Real Madrid director joined the board and Radrizzani recruited Angus Kinnear from West Ham as chief executive. It was assumed that Orta would recommend Karanka as Monk's replacement and he soon became the bookies' favourite. The club sprang a surprise, however, when it was announced that the choice was Thomas Christiansen, a disciple of Johan Cruyff from La Masia, who had won two caps for Spain. He had just won the double in Cyprus with APOEL, which had never been much of a recommendation before. Leeds were not looking for a manager. The point of creating and filling departments throughout the club to take care of scouting, sports science, analysis and recruitment was to establish continuity and prevent mass hirings and firings whenever the manager changed. From now on the head coach would be the equivalent of the government on the playing side working alongside a permanent civil service. Christiansen fitted the bill and

Orta provided him and the Under-23 coach with the players in a complete revamp of the junior sides.

Twenty-four players were brought in during the summer window and eight in the winter funded by the sale of Chris Wood for £15m and Charlie Taylor for £6m, both to Burnley. The players wanted to go but left significant holes that were never adequately filled. Nonetheless Christiansen's side started at a dash. New signings such as the stumpy attacking midfielder Samu Sáiz played with pep and imagination, the ageless Hernández prompted and teleported himself into dangerous positions and Jansson was a tower of strength in defence. Leeds were unbeaten in their first seven games, winning five, which was enough to claim top spot and they stayed there for a fortnight. They played attractive, passing football, using geometry and a sure touch in possession to manoeuvre defences out of position. They were not as clinical as they had been with Wood nor as physical at the back now Bartley had been reclaimed by Swansea. The new goalkeeper, Felix Wiedwald, also looked nervy. They were ripe for a bullying which is precisely what Millwall did to them and once that template had been set, other teams lined up to destroy their confidence with bosh and the steamroller treatment. They lost eight of 11 matches after reaching first place and plummeted to 10th. Lightweight players' determination to stand up for themselves often took the form of petulance and snide retaliation, leading to a rapidly escalating card count. Despite a rally in December that launched United back into play-off contention, January was wild and bleak. Saiz was sent off for spitting in the FA Cup defeat at League Two Newport and banned for six matches, they played 53 minutes with 10 men in defeats by Ipswich and Millwall after red cards, and Berardi was sent off before half-time, the fifth dismissal of his Leeds career, during a 4-1 defeat by Warnock's Cardiff at Elland Road. Christiansen was sacked the following day.

It came at the end of a week of ridicule for the club. They had attempted to rebrand the club with a new badge, which had happened many times before. Don Revie banished the owl, the cursive LUFC monogram was ditched in favour of Paul Trevillion's vivid 'egg yolk' smiley badge and successive eras had footballs, peacocks, white roses and the 'Continental shield'. The new constructivist design featured a white-shirted and seemingly decapitated man beating his heart with his fist in the traditional Leeds salute. It was widely derided and represented the first significant misstep off the field under Radrizzani. There would be others – the post-season trip to Myanmar brought protests from many fans, five Leeds MPs, the Foreign and Commonwealth Office and Amnesty International.

Paul Heckingbottom was head coach for the Myanmar games. He had been recruited from Barnsley in February when they had been 11 places below United. He was a decent man even if his coalfield accent made him sound like 'Our Jud' from *Kes*. When his ancient quips about his childhood hatred of Leeds came to light, it was too tempting, if unfair, to echo Billy Casper and call him "a big bleedin' bastard" who "wants puttin' in t'bin". Salvation, as he outlined it, lay in grim toil on the long road back and the recruitment of established Championship scufflers. He had been brought in and instructed to aim for the play-offs yet presided over an improvement in neither form nor discipline. He evidently did not rate many of the players he had inherited. Out went the pass-pass-pass, in came a jumbled hybrid and they lost eight of his 16 games, winning only four. He spoke of his admiration for Swansea's raw-boned centre-forward Oli McBurnie and said: "I want to make big changes to the dynamic of the squad, a better balance in terms of having players who can affect the game when we've not got the ball and affect the game through physicality." Having paid £500,000 to release him from his Barnsley contract, Leeds sacked him when he flew back from Yangon.

"Who would be your ideal coach?" Radrizzani asked Orta after they had interviewed Claudio Ranieri for the position. Orta, thinking they were playing fantasy manager, replied: "Marcelo Bielsa. His ideas would fit us at this moment. But obviously I am not nominating him because I think it is impossible."

"Why don't you at least try?" asked Radrizzani.

28

HELP OF THE HELPLESS

Marcelo Bielsa took the call. The 62-year-old Argentinian was regarded as the most influential philosopher-coach in football, looked up to and obsessed over by the great innovators of the gilded super clubs such as Diego Simeone, Pep Guardiola and Mauricio Pochettino. He was feted by the sages and evangelists of the tactical bibles. But like the film director Michael Powell, who was venerated as a genius in the Seventies and Eighties by Martin Scorsese and Francis Ford Coppola yet could not get his own films made, Bielsa would have preferred working to being idolised. Since leaving the Chile job in 2011, he had spent two years with Athletic Bilbao, a season with Marseille, two days with Lazio and a handful of games with Lille. Bielsa's successes with his presiding passion, hometown club Newell's Old Boys, as head coach of his own national team and their neighbours across the southern Andes, had been based on humility, a fierce work ethic, positional rotation and whirling movement. He demanded intensity and commitment but had no airs. He spoke with precision, using simple language, and stuck to his principles. Bielsa was stubborn rather than intolerant, certain only that he did not know it all. He was as hungry to learn as he was to teach. Evidence from his last three jobs could be twisted to portray him as difficult and prickly yet he had a profound sense of honour, his loyalty to his ideas and the supporters he hoped to serve. If he felt it was being betrayed he went back to Rosario, where coaching pilgrims beat a path to his door.

Leeds United needed a head coach with vision and integrity, someone who could shape a generation and the culture of the club just as Don Revie and Howard Wilkinson once had. He invited Andrea Radrizzani, Angus Kinnear and Victor Orta to fly to Argentina to discuss the offer, and in the meantime studied every one of their matches from the previous season. He also assessed Leeds players and the opposition in exhaustive detail and somehow managed to get hold of plans of Thorp Arch. The project had piqued his interest. What he wanted to know was whether they understood what hiring him would entail and whether he could trust their resolve. He asked for modifications to be made to the training pitches and the old accommodation block, agreed a £6m-a-year salary for him and his brigade of staff and, when granted the work permits, flew to Leeds. His first press conference lasted 90 minutes, not unusual by his standards, and he behaved with uncommon civility even through the prophylactic of an interpreter. When asked a question he would continue until he felt he had explained himself properly, recognising nuance and treating every inquiry as valid. There was none of the defensiveness or exasperation normally on display at these events.

The players were put through the most demanding pre-season of their careers. Thorp Arch was brought back to life, becoming what Howard Wilkinson had envisaged all along. Players were in for 12 hours a day, taking naps there in newly constructed bedrooms between fitness work and tactical seminars. Diets were changed, strength and conditioning programmes tailored and when they emerged for friendly matches it was evident how leaner many were. Flexibility became the norm for midfielders and wide players who took up new roles to broaden their outlook. When the two most obvious flaws of the previous season – lack of goals and a hole at left-back – were addressed with the signings of Patrick Bamford and Barry Douglas, Ronaldo Vieira was sold to Sampdoria to help fund the deals. Radrizzani emphasised repeatedly that he was not a sugar daddy and would not take speculative risks in a competition grossly distorted by parachute payments, creative accountancy and those willing to gamble on going up before they would have to pay the fine for breaking profit and sustainability regulations. It did not make him more popular but it did not make him wrong. Leeds were trying to do it a different way, hence the arrival of Bielsa who had bought into the new approach in Argentina in May.

Bielsa's reputation as 'El Loco' preceded him and many feared the worst when he sent out nine players who had finished 13th the previous season, plus Mateusz Klich, discounted and exiled by Thomas Christiansen, and Douglas for their first match against Stoke City. Leeds United dizzied a side that had only just come down from the Premier League with a tornado of movement, passing, pressing and overloading. They were even better against Derby County and Norwich City – the fervent but impetuous Gaetano Berardi brought the ball out from the back with genuine poise, Kalvin Phillips, a gifted but previously inconsistent midfielder, sat deep and augmented the centre-backs to allow rapid switches of formation and the endlessly inventive Pablo Hernández probed away, squaring up defenders and dribbling past them. Up front the elusive Klich surprised defences with the timing of his clever runs and Kemar Roofe, a square peg in a round hole out wide or off the main striker in the previous two seasons, became a tireless pest of a centre-forward, running the channels, turning and spinning, holding his own up tight against centre-backs.

Despite a spate of injuries – to Adam Forshaw, Berardi, Hernández, Bamford, Douglas, Phillips and Roofe – Leeds lost only three of 24 games by Boxing Day, clocking up seven victories in a row in resounding fashion by coming back from 2-0 down against Aston Villa to win 3-2 in the 95th minute on December 23 and from 2-1 behind against Blackburn Rovers after 90 minutes on Boxing Day itself to take the three points with another 3-2 victory. All three stoppage-time goals were scored by Roofe, who ran ecstatically into the corners, stopped only by the confines of the stadiums. The players spoke of their hunger, literally owing to the weight loss and Spartan meals, and figuratively because of the euphoria they had roused in the crowd and wider city. If this was the buzz of being top at Christmas, they did not need to imagine how intense it would be if they were the engineers of Leeds' deliverance come May. It made all the bland food, torture on the running track, marathon video analysis tutorials and Murderball sessions worthwhile.

Back-to-back defeats immediately after beating Blackburn meant their lead at the top was squeezed to three points for the visit of Derby County in January. On the eve of the game Derbyshire police sent out a cryptic tweet about a 'suspicious male' who was 'spying' on Derby's training ground. When confronted over the allegations not only did Bielsa not deny them, he coughed to them before the match in public, having already telephoned the Derby manager Frank Lampard to explain that he had been sending scouts to watch opponents train for 20 years. Lampard was angered, more so when his team lost 2-0 and the press was split between those fond of Lampard, the darling of the mixed zone, who echoed his condemnation of non-British practices while others lampooned the hysterical, borderline xenophobic reaction by some in the game. The next year Lampard, by now manager of Chelsea, chastised Liverpool's Jürgen Klopp for his exuberance after winning the title, confirming his self-appointment as the game's moral majority. The priggish code of the British 'Football Man' at last has its chief constable.

Five days later Bielsa convened a press conference at Thorp Arch. There were fears he would resign, feeling that his honour had been maligned. Instead he outlined his approach. There was no cover-up, no lies, no contesting the thrust of Derby's complaint, although the Derbyshire police's clarifications about the details contrasted sharply with the version County had originally made public. Bielsa spoke for 70 minutes and gave a PowerPoint presentation on Derby's players and their statistics, plus clips of the essential moments of each game from two seasons. He demonstrated the breadth of his research on each match, the significant events within them and any players who feature in them, all to explain that sending a Leeds intern to watch the opposition train was a tiny component of his team's work, not crucial but important because having the most comprehensive audit possible saved him from the angst of thinking the picture was incomplete. "I do not need to go to a training session to find out an opponent," he said. "Why do I go? Because it is not against the rules and I didn't know it would cause such an issue. You have around 20 people who create a volume of information. Not all of which is necessary. So why? Because we feel guilty if we don't work enough and in my case because I'm stupid enough to allow myself this behaviour." Leeds were formally reprimanded when 11 Championship clubs called on the Football League to act and fined £200,000 for a breach of "good faith" rather than for breaking any existing regulation. They did not appeal it and Bielsa insisted on paying it himself.

In early February they were outplayed by Norwich at Elland Road and lost 3-1, dropping behind the visitors into second place. Defeat by Queens Park Rangers at the end of February added to a dismal record in the capital and conspired to leave Bielsa's side in third behind Sheffield United as injures continued to mount and goals dried up at the crucial time. They went back above the Blades, even after losing a tight match against them with nine to play, but blew their opportunity to cement their position when beaten by 10-man Wigan and losing at Brentford over Easter. A terrible conversion rate blighted their prospects more than the injury epidemic. They led the charts for chances created but were fifth in the table of goals scored. In March it slipped to 2.5 per cent and some of the chances missed almost beggared belief, Bamford in particular guilty of snatching at right-foot shots and fluffing several sitters with his head. It consigned Leeds to the play-offs, a road to promotion on which their conversion rate – 0 out of 4 – was even worse.

As the third-placed team United were drawn against Derby who had finished sixth and their comfortable 1-0 victory at Pride Park reflected the ease with which they had done the double over them during the season proper. Sticking to the theme of the campaign Leeds should have scored more but it did not seem to matter when they went 2-0 up on aggregate on 24 minutes of the home leg. The club had handed out free scarfs to every member of the crowd that night and those caught in the rapture twirled them above their heads to celebrate Stuart Dallas' goal. The taunting of Lampard escalated to a dangerously hubristic peak. Yet Roofe, the goalscorer in the first game, had succumbed to injury and Bamford, back after a two-match ban for simulation, was unable to hold the ball up as proficiently. It was not his fault that Kiko Casilla, the former Real Madrid goalkeeper recruited in January and the club's highest earner, impulsively raced out of his goal – as he had done at Ipswich the week before – and panicked Liam Cooper, resulting in a collision that left both men stranded and put Derby's Jack Marriott clean through to bring the scores level on the night. Leeds, clearly rattled, lost the poise and precision on which Bielsa's pattern of play relies. In 13 second-half minutes Derby twice exploited a Casilla flap and a gratuitous Cooper foul to take a 3-2 aggregate lead and, though Dallas levelled, Leeds looked dazed in the headlights of an oncoming train, unable even to brace themselves for impact. Berardi's rashness returned at the least opportune moment, he was sent off for two daft fouls in nine minutes, and Derby scored the winner five minutes from time. On the final whistle Lampard, mocked for 130 minutes by Leeds fans, gambolled across the pitch like David Pleat, minus the tan slip-ons, at Maine Road. Naturally, he goaded them back. Bielsa waited patiently to congratulate him. And waited. And waited. Lampard did not come. It was not in his code.

After every match Bielsa had a word of consolation or encouragement for his opponent and always a statement of commendation. Not once did he demand a flashy signing or whinge and sulk at injuries or the grisly standard of refereeing in the Championship. In April the manager had ordered his players to allow Aston Villa to equalise after they had breached an unwritten and arbitrarily applied 'rule' to kick the ball out if a player goes down with a seemingly serious injury, a goal which killed off their vanishing chances of automatic promotion, but when Fifa awarded him and Leeds a fair play award for his gesture, he was ridiculed by the football phone-in establishment, who greeted it with the contempt Gore Vidal reserved for Henry Kissinger receiving the Nobel Peace Prize. Bielsa, as ever, demanded the blame for their failure against Derby and incited alarm when suggesting that walking away would be the most noble and rational course of action. "The fact that we couldn't reach something that was reachable always places doubt around the head coach," he said. "If you have the resources to win something and you don't, you have to assume responsibility."

At Elland Road distress was absolute and the players, on their haunches or prostrate, hid their heads and cried. There was no shame in it. Bielsa had introduced a Rolls-Royce system without Rolls-Royce parts. Even so he had inspired every man jack of them to play at the very extremities of their impressively enhanced stamina and capabilities to reach this far. It was not heart that they lacked, but at times the side's collective and individual composure and concentration were found wanting. Leeds had come third in a season which contrived to be both a triumph and a disappointment simultaneously. Had this story finished there, it would have been a fitting if unwelcome epitaph for a century of Leeds United's history.

29

VAMOS, LEEDS! CARAJO!

Happy endings camouflage fraught beginnings. *Take Me Home,* Amazon's fly-on-the wall documentary series on the 2018-19 season concluded with a daring grab at an upbeat finale. It was delivered via Angus Kinnear's rallying cry – "the goal for next season is automatic, we're not dicking around with the play-offs anymore" – but such phrases, however pithily expressed, are football's version of whistling in the dark. Courage could not be nurtured by mere words and in mid-May 2019, in the immediate aftermath of defeat by Derby in the play-offs, Leeds were in a more precarious position than they let on. Marcelo Bielsa had not unequivocally committed to a second season and allowing him to return to Rosario for a short break before public confirmation he was staying seemed like a strategic error. Andrea Radrizzani had always been candid about the financial consequences of another season in the Championship and there were genuine fears that the easiest way to fund the new campaign would be to sell Kalvin Phillips to Aston Villa and bank the £25m downpayment they were flaunting. It is what every previous chairman would have done save, perhaps, for Harry Reynolds. But this Leeds board recognised that easy did not mean painless. Cashing in on Phillips would risk provoking Bielsa and the support, compounding both pre-season problems. For all their bluster, though, Championship clubs had long since surrendered their capacity to resist players being seduced by Premier League offers, haggling only about price. Phillips, the only Leeds-born regular, solved it for them by his uncertainty. When Victor Orta asked him whether he wanted to go, he said he was conflicted. "If you don't know, then I'm not selling you," said the sporting director. They would do it the hard way.

At the end of May Leeds announced that Bielsa had agreed to stay and triggered the second year of his rolling contract. He had laid down several conditions, typically split between architecture and personnel, requesting further enhancement of the facilities at Thorp Arch, targeted investment to secure Category One status for the academy, the retention of Phillips and the recruitment of Hélder Costa, the Portugal winger, from

Wolves. To pay for it United began with the low-hanging fruit, harvesting £6.5m for four players who had been out on loan. They went on to sell Jack Clarke to Tottenham, a club that had been second only to Leeds in benefiting from the Thorp Arch academy since 2004, for £11m, Kemar Roofe to Anderlecht for £7m and Bailey Peacock-Farrell to Burnley for £3.5m. Clarke had been a terrier of a winger before Christmas but was muzzled after falling ill during the draw with Middlesbrough in February. His later brief appearances off the bench were uncomfortable to watch. Not only had he lost his zip and confidence, he appeared to have misplaced his balance. Roofe had been a more effective centre-forward than Patrick Bamford yet the club had balked too long at offering him parity with his team-mate's wages, leaving themselves at his mercy as he approached the final year of his contract. As for Peacock-Farrell, the goalkeeper had made a useful contribution at the start of the season, but having committed to paying £30,000-a-week to Kiko Casilla, a player with as many strengths and flaws, the Northern Ireland international was a handily realisable asset. Promising young keepers were a cheap commodity throughout Europe. None of the three deals were celebrated – they were accepted as pragmatic. The fourth, Pontus Jansson, was jolting, even more so when his demeanour during an interview after joining Brentford for £5.5m was that of a hostage.

Jansson had embodied the rise of Leeds United under Radrizzani's ownership. He was an extrovert, boisterous, loud and a terrific Championship defender. As a fervent Malmo supporter he understood viscerally the emotions of fandom. His personality had been instrumental in reconnecting the team to the crowd. Jansson had been the first player to have his own bespoke song for years, signalling that the era of bulk, short-term signings and homegrown talent sold before its prime was drawing to a close. If he hogged the spotlight – conducting the singing, his half-endearing, solo protest in trying to stop Aston Villa scoring the walk-in goal Bielsa had instructed them to concede and picking the most picturesque spot, slumped against a hoarding, the heels of his hands burrowing into his eye sockets, half a pitch away from his team-mates to bare his despair after the play-off defeat – he would be forgiven. He was brash, tough and canny but he was also headstrong and wholly incapable of masking his annoyance. Perfecting a poker face may have served him better in the long run. Where Jansson acted as if he was exceptional – no one could be seen to 'care' quite as much as him – Bielsa saw him as expendable. Graciously the manager was classy as well as firm, telling the press that Jansson was his best player and sold only to comply with Profit and Sustainability regulations.

Only 18 players had started 10 or more league games in 2018-19 and now Bielsa was preparing for a season with a slimmer core of senior players. There is a distinct streak of purism rather than perfectionism to his approach. It is a misconception that he his intolerant of mistakes on the field – he expects them and always rationalises them so long as the players' motives are right. Intention is just as important as execution.

To replace the departed, Leeds used some of the £33m raised to boost the academy ranks but the first-team squad made do with six loan signings: Jack Harrison, back for a second season from Manchester City; Costa, with a clause to buy him for £16 million at the season's end; Clarke, making a brief return from Spurs; Illan Meslier, an agile, string-bean, teenage goalkeeper with an Inbetweeners haircut; Arsenal's much-coveted livewire striker Eddie Nketiah; and, to replace the captain of Sweden, 21-year-old Ben White from Brighton who had yet to play at a higher standard than League One.

Pre-season was split between their usual Yorkshire haunts, a money-spinning tour Down Under to take on Manchester United in Perth and Western Suburbs in Sydney, a home friendly against Al-Ittihad and a trip to Sardinia to make common cause with Cagliari as survivors of Massimo Cellino. Results were not encouraging since Bielsa had split the squad into two, fulfilling his promotional duties in Australia while leaving most of the new signings to be drilled in their new assignments in triple daily sessions at home. Losses inflamed the West Stand 'Mona Lotts' to announce apocalypse now with the usual grim relish. Nevertheless, weight of money behind them installed Leeds as favourites to win the Championship.

It took barely 10 minutes of the opening fixture against Bristol City to acknowledge that White could help the lamenters shake off Jansson's exit. He glided smoothly upfield, was confident on the ball, timed his tackles sweetly, adapted to the compact lines that kept the space compressed between him and the centre-forward, Patrick Bamford, and looked assured in the attacking triangular and parallelogram passing patterns that manipulate the opposition's defence out of position. It was obvious that he was a natural and destined to play for England. He was a year behind the 10 most regular starters in playing the Bielsa way but betrayed no sign of his novice status. Leeds' oldest and best player, Pablo Hernández, had looked 'right sloughened', in that old Yorkshire phrase, after losing in the play-off. His moist eyes had taken on the kind of glaze actors would reach for when cast as Vietnam vets pickling themselves in Rust Belt bars in the first batch of films about the war. At Ashton Gate he was rejuvenated. Twice Hernández nutmegged Callum O'Dowda and left him staring, his mouth gaping, as he jittered past. He kept demanding the ball, taking responsibility and continually probing, sometimes unsuccessfully but going again, facing up defenders and dribbling past them. His positivity was infectious. He also opened the scoring in the 3-1 victory, taking the ball in the D with his back to goal, employing two touches to turn and use a flummoxed defender as a screen before buckling a left foot shot around him and the diving keeper from 20 yards. It would become the defining motif of the season. Whenever Leeds needed an injection of belief, Hernández stood up to provide it. In 1990 signing Vinnie Jones and co had been a catalyst for promotion. Thirty years later it would be Pablo and his cojones.

White's composure enabled Bielsa to employ his 3-1-3-3/3-3-3-1 formations more regularly. During the season before he switched to the system that made his reputation for innovation sporadically by dropping Kalvin Phillips from the defensive midfield role into the heart of the defence and pushing the full-backs on. Leeds enjoyed greater security now because White had the range and vision to thrive in the middle with Luke Ayling to the right, Liam Cooper to the left and Phillips just in front. With Leeds' wing-backs funnelling attackers inside, the strategy became suffocation, reducing the time for accuracy, hence a dearth of opponents' shots on target. Yet the way Leeds played made them vulnerable to being mugged for the points in games they had superficially bossed. They climbed to the top of the league after a handful of matches but slapdash finishing left them vulnerable. Games they should have won against Forest and Derby were thrown away to late equalisers while Swansea, Charlton and Millwall all beat them by allowing them to monopolise the ball but retained their own defensive shape and battered Leeds at set-pieces. The Millwall victory also owed something to an unmerited red card shown to Gaetano Berardi after 14 minutes. It was overturned on appeal and the kind of refereeing farce rife in the Championship that had Leeds fans yearning for the fool's paradise of VAR.

During the defeat by Charlton, Jonathan Leko reported that Kiko Casilla had called him a "fucking n-----". The Leeds goalkeeper denied the accusation and was backed by the club but when his case was heard by an independent FA regulatory commission five months later, he was found guilty, fined £60,000 and banned for eight matches. Regrettably, there have been no words or signs of remorse.

Exasperation intensified over Marcelo Bielsa's miserly use of the on-loan Nketiah, and the support's constant frustration with the sparseness of signings glowed with molten irritation when leads and points were blown. Injuries to Cooper, Ayling and Hernández disrupted the team's flow. They only truly scaled the heights of the previous season's fluency during the victories over Stoke and Middlesbrough but kept winning, progressing on the field without the typical melodrama, hugging the wall in the promotion race. Above all it was down to a new consistency of concentration, absent at crucial junctures the year before, leading to them making far fewer errors at the back.

In November and December they won seven successive matches, the last of which sent them top above West Brom. Stuart Dallas, a bright player without a settled role or place for four years, made a virtue of his versatility, becoming as valuable to Bielsa as Paul Madeley was to Don Revie. He played at right-back, left-back, sweeper, central midfield and on either wing, sometimes all six at various points of the same game. It was never a case of simply 'filling in'. From utility player he became an automatic pick with an appetite for leadership shown when he took the fight to Derby singlehandedly as his colleagues tottered in the second leg of the play-off semi-final. He was the first to fathom the flexibility Bielsa required and rise to it. As someone crying out for direction, Dallas, recalling the words of Johnny Giles, treated his manager's method as 'manna from heaven'.

The run came to a screeching halt at 3-0 up with half an hour left to play against Cardiff at Elland Road. In the first half they had been as slick as they had been at Stoke but the defence started to lose aerial challenges, Casilla began to flap about and Bielsa sewed further confusion with his substitutions. They were not defeated but a 3-3 draw from that position felt like it. A week later they lost 2-1 at Fulham whose manager Scott Parker, an England contemporary and team-mate of Frank Lampard's, could barely disguise his contempt for the hype around Bielsa's 'genius', calling Leeds predictable and their moves "scripted". Manuel Pellegrini got off worse when confronted by Alan Pardew in his most idiotically rude manner but this streak of parochial chippiness was becoming more frequent from a handful of rivals, particularly men from London, as Bielsa's second season progressed. It was unfair because he would be the last to make any smart alec claims for himself. He behaved at all times with unpretentious charm and courtesy, whether disturbed numerous times each day while pottering about in Wetherby or listening intently to every question and framing answers respectfully, even if he sometimes directed them at his shoes as he avoided eye contact. By not saying much he profits from the Chauncey Gardner effect – having a kind of righteousness projected upon him, which he protests he does not warrant but is powerless to prevent. It got up critics noses but then so have Leeds United for 55 years.

Losing at Fulham was the first of five defeats over nine games, only two of which were won, both chaotically. They had to regain the lead twice against Birmingham to win 5-4 in the 95th minute and came back from 2-0 down at home against Millwall to win 3-2. Patrick Bamford, the object of the crowd's frustration for the number of chances he missed, scored twice in the latter game and cupped his ear after a tap-in to labour a point. He would be a divisive presence among supporters and those who carped about his finishing and languid style sacrificed him on the altar of cod science and xG. But it was always foolish to berate Bamford without realising it also meant knocking Bielsa, who kept picking him. The manager continued to stress that the centre-forward's movement and ability to occupy defenders with his runs into the inside-forward channels and out to the flanks was crucial to his attacking philosophy. Without them the team could not overload defenders and worm into space so readily. It was why he preferred him to Nketiah and led to the loan striker's return to Arsenal.

Of more legitimate concern was the form of Casilla after missing that punch and making a gift of a goal that sparked Cardiff's recovery in the 3-3 draw. Against Sheffield Wednesday at home he let in an 87th-minute shot at the near post which initiated the run of four defeats in five games that defeathered their plump, 11-point cushion to third place. Next, he air-punched on the line at a corner and let the ball dip under the bar against Wigan, let Sammy Ameobi's shot sneak in at the near post at Nottingham Forest and slipped, having miscontrolled a horizontal pass across his six-yard box at Griffin Park, to leave Said Benrahma with an open goal to give Brentford the lead. The team seemed to have lost their resilience in midwinter, their wiry frames bouncing off the more robust physiques of opponents at QPR and Forest. Indeed after losing at the City Ground, which left them on the same number of points as third-placed Fulham, Ayling was close to inconsolable, reflecting a rising tide of panic among the normally, beerily bullish, travelling support. United's form over the preceding 10 games left them ranking 24th in the Championship for errors leading to goals, 24th equal for clean sheets, 23rd for save percentage and 22nd equal for goals conceded. No wonder the right-back sounded forlorn. "The first goal killed us," he said. "We played some nice football again but no cutting edge, so same old story."

"Leeds are falling apart again" had rung out gleefully from the Trent End in the same shit-eating tone familiar from visits to the Den, Craven Cottage and Loftus Road. Bielsa, however, was not fazed. He did not abandon Bamford or Casilla as he was urged to do and throw in the new on-loan striker Jean-Kévin Augustin. He showed his players the Forest match, highlighting the positive features of their play, came as close as he could bear to throwing an arm around their shoulders, at least in words, brought back Phillips from suspension and sent them out against Brentford. "I am 100 per cent sure that they fear us going into this game," said the Bees' manager, Thomas Frank, 48 hours before the match. It was at best an incautious stimulant for defiance. The way Leeds played after Casilla's howler, stroking the ball across the pitch and up the wings, shutting Brentford's midfield out of the game, their sureness of control in narrow pockets, was the turning point of the season. That they only managed to draw after Cooper's equaliser was inconsequential. Leeds had heard the wail of last season's ghosts and howled them away. "Leeds are the best team in the division," said Frank afterwards.

United kept five clean sheets in their next five matches, winning all five, scoring nine, one of them a Van Basten-lite, balletic back-post volley from Ayling against Huddersfield the week after they put four past Hull. They were top of the league once more, seven points clear of Fulham in third place, at the moment that Arsenal's Mikel Arteta tested positive for Covid-19 and football beat the country into lockdown.

Leeds went through a more sombre lockdown than most clubs. While the deaths of Norman Hunter and Trevor Cherry, two of the city's favourite adopted sons, were mourned, grief would continue to linger until their lives could be commemorated en masse and with appropriate ceremony. Throughout those 14 weeks, the community work of the club and players was exemplary, bringing tangible benefits to scores of vulnerable people, and even the tokens, such as the videos released on Thursday evenings before the weekly applause for key workers, were executed with panache and perception. Tracking down the reclusive David Batty to join in may not seem all that significant but because he always symbolised the spirit of the supporter, his presence after all these years was a genuine tonic. Bielsa, whose humility and workaholism resuscitated the club, spent the early part of lockdown studying every goal scored from a set-piece in Europe's top five leagues and instructed his coaches to devise ways of exploiting their findings. Months deprived of working with players must have felt like purgatory for him and to see him back at the training ground towards the end of May, observing the drills and gruelling 'murderball' sessions, was to witness a man in his element.

It was no surprise that when they did return behind closed doors, theirs was the last fixture of the Championship round as they were picked by Sky Sports for live broadcast. They lost 2-0 at Cardiff after an insipid performance, both goals coming from shoddy passes, by Phillips and

Cooper. A scene from a 30-year-old drama became ubiquitous once more. The meme came from *Twin Peaks* and featured 'The Giant' whispering chillingly to Special Agent Dale Cooper: "It is happening again." Six days later they played Fulham, took a rare early lead against the run of play by virtue of a neat Bamford shot, were battered for 35 minutes until Bielsa made a tactical switch at half-time, introducing Hernández, who had a tight hamstring and was being cossetted for those moments when they could not cope without him. He popped up everywhere, soaking up possession, holding on to the ball, drawing defenders and set up the third in the 3-0 victory with a wonderful first-time, 40-yard, round-the-corner pass. Parker, dressing up as an extra from *Quadrophenia*, said nothing about scripts this time.

The games were coming every three days and the hypothesis was that Brentford and West Brom, playing the day before Leeds, would crank up the pressure, especially Brentford who were in irrepressible form. That was the notion, anyway, after Leeds had to scramble a home draw with bottom-placed Luton when both Costa and Bamford missed good late chances. But from then on, Leeds were like a poker player who kept raising every time their pursuers raised on them, counteracting victory with victory to maintain the gap Brentford's Frank kept telling them to mind, until everyone else folded.

Bamford's early goal against Blackburn, another excellent left-foot shot set up by Mateusz Klich's blindside tackle, gave them the ballast to withstand a few first-half scares. Had Bamford's right foot and head been the equal of his left, he would have been challenging Dixie Dean. But had he been so blessed, he would not have been available for £7m. First-half goals, even in behind-closed-doors games without a skittish crowd, acted like tranquillisers. They compelled teams to push their midfielders forward and gave Leeds' wingers the room to exploit the superior, relentless running power of their own full-backs and Klich. Phillips even scored their first goal direct from a free-kick for nearly three years. They would end the season against Charlton almost teasing their supporters by scoring with a header from a corner in a season when they had not managed it in 353 other attempts.

Stoke were hammered 5-0 to restore Leeds' lead over West Brom to a point and six over Brentford with four to play. The latter side won and Albion lost before Leeds took on Swansea at the Liberty Stadium two days after Jack Charlton died aged 85 from lymphoma. Now Don Revie's whole half-back line – Bremner, Charlton and Hunter – were gone but the passing of 'Big Jack', who had been suffering from dementia for a number of years, aroused a cheering celebration of his life. Hunter, nine years Jack's junior, who had died from Covid-19, had been a constant presence at Elland Road ever since leaving the coaching staff in 1988. A club ambassador before the concept had been invented, he took time for everyone as the age of the autograph book gave way first to the staged, corporate jolly and then to the selfie. A crocodile of supporters would good-naturedly stalk his every move in the West Stand until the moment when he would find sanctuary by climbing the stairs to the commentary gantry where he would instinctively flinch, nod and jerk, like a puppy enjoying a good dream, still besotted by the game and his club. The No.5 was loved but had been gone for almost 50 years. The No.6 came back home. The lockdown made the prospect of promotion a uniquely intimate and simple act of deliverance not at all commensurate with the scale of bliss and relief. But above all it was suitably poignant, thinking of Norman and many others who would not have wanted to miss it for the world.

Seven points from their remaining four games would do it. They took all 12, beating Swansea 1-0 with Hernández's 89th-minute goal. Ayling, the man who had encapsulated the adapted Newell's cry 'Vamos, Leeds! Carajo!' ('Fucking come on, Leeds!') since pulling himself up off the floor after the Forest defeat, galloped down the right and picked out Hernández by the penalty spot. Hernández swept his shot in at the right post with such nonchalance that he hit it like a conceded three-foot putt that you take anyway, as if there was no pressure at all, as if the final whistle had already gone. He wheeled away before the ball had hit the back of the net. The screams of delight from the Leeds United TV crew, directors and staff were disconcertingly high-pitched without a home crowd to baffle them or visiting fans to augment them. The tone matched the hysteria. They nicked the next game, too, beating Barnsley 1-0 without Phillips, whose knee had been strapped up to allow him to continue against Swansea but had been ruled out for the remaining three matches. They missed him, allowing Mads Andersen, Conor Chaplin and Cauley Woodrow fine chances. Meslier, playing his eighth game in goal since Casilla's ban, kept them in it and Bielsa riffled through so many formations some of the players seemed as bewildered as the audience. Michael Sollbauer settled it by turning Bamford's stabbed cross past his own keeper though Leeds owed a debt to Berardi who played in three different positions, thwarting attacks in each. It was Berardi, Leeds' most demonstrative player, who had almost throttled Bamford and chinned Ayling after Hernández's goal at Swansea in the intensity of his emotional release. He may come from the rich Alpine pasture bordering the north of Italy but he got Leeds and Leeds got him.

Now they needed a point from their last two games if West Brom and Brentford did not slip up. The day after defeating Barnsley, the players assembled at Elland Road to watch on TV as Huddersfield took on Albion and beat them. Four minutes from time Emile Smith Rowe scored Town's winner and 100 years after Huddersfield saved themselves from becoming Leeds United, they did them a favour. In the end Leeds did not fall apart. They were promoted when someone else did. Immediately people began to flock to the ground and Bielsa's flat. In Wetherby the manager bumped elbows with everyone who wanted to embrace and tolerantly wagged his finger at a giddy supporter who told him he was 'God'. "No, no, no!" he said, smiling sheepishly. Later he would join his squad, reserving the warmest bearhugs for Phillips, Hernández and Bamford. For once he seemed relaxed about carbs and players who might have been hiding their bottles behind their backs when he entered began to be more brazen. The squad was still alight the following morning as they waited outside the main building at Thorp Arch to give him a raucous reception as he arrived for training. Brentford's defeat later that day made them champions. Was winning promotion and the title not on the field an anti-climax? After 16 years, everyone should be so lucky.

The fixture list rather than instant karma sent Leeds to Derby the next day. The club that had hurt them 14 months before treated them with good grace, a guard of honour and a bottle of vintage Dom Pérignon. Leeds won 3-1 and finished the season with a final champagne performance in a 4-0 victory over Charlton. After all that fretfulness in February, they won the title by 10 points, the biggest margin for 10 seasons. Supporters assembled in their thousands on the Friday after Huddersfield's victory, in Millennium Square on Sunday for Derby, and again on Lowfields Road during the Charlton game. Understandably, they were chided for their irresponsibility and disregard for social distancing but what did people expect after 16 years? One journalist decided to greet their promotion with a memory lane trawl of every cliché, surmising: "Leeds remind all of club's flaws with disgraceful behaviour of fans." Anyone who lived through 1990 was accustomed to the routine.

Bielsa was more considerate, speaking of how success, its style and the pursuit of happiness are entwined. "The joy we give to supporters is important too, but they are linked," he said. "I don't want to put the focus on me, I want to put it on to the players and supporters. I'm really enjoying the joy we created but defeat produces a lot of sadness. It's very hard to lose when you know you are making supporters feel sad. Everybody knows that the money we earn is too big but it's fair when you take into account how hard it is when you lose and know you are making a lot of people sad. It's like the club pay you for this. For example, Phillips suffered last season and now he is so happy for the joy he has given to the people. He is one of them."

And so is Bielsa, though he would not claim it. His heart is forever Newell's red and black but his time in West Yorkshire, healing a disjointed club, will leave an enduring legacy. Howard Wilkinson grasped that a club cannot live on its heritage and that nostalgia is corrosive to current generations. The burden of the past is only tolerable when there is hope. Leeds United have a duty to honour Don Revie, Billy Bremner, John Charles, Gary Sprake, Paul Madeley, Norman Hunter, Jack Charlton, Trevor Cherry, Gary Speed et al but the players cannot and should not have to live up to their achievements. Their only obligation is to strive, as Bielsa says, to bring joy. The Promised Land is not the Premier League or any destination, what Bielsa called "the tyranny of trophies". It is a state of mind. Too often Leeds have forgotten that. It has been vital to their revival and pivotal to the future. Persevere with it and 101 years' experience tells us only then will Leeds go marching on, on, on.

ABOUT THE AUTHOR

Rob Bagchi worked for Sportspages for 10 years, joined the sports desk of the *Guardian* as a writer and editor in 2002 and left for a similar role at *The Telegraph* in 2013 where he remains. A lifelong Leeds fan, this is his first solo book, his second about United after 2002's *The Unforgiven* and his fifth overall.